Schindler's Ark

Schindler's Ark

Thomas Keneally

BOOK CLUB ASSOCIATES LONDON

This edition published 1983 by
Book Club Associates
by arrangement with Hodder & Stoughton Ltd.

*To the memory of Oskar Schindler, and to Leopold Pfefferberg
who by zeal and persistence caused this book to be written.*

Printed in Great Britain by
Richard Clay (The Chaucer Press) Ltd
Bungay, Suffolk

GLOSSARY

SS Ranks and their Army Equivalents

COMMISSIONED RANKS

Oberstgruppenführer	general
Obergruppenführer	lieutenant general
Gruppenführer	major general
Brigadeführer	brigadier general
Oberführer	(no army equivalent)
Standartenführer	colonel
Obersturmbannführer	lieutenant colonel
Sturmbannführer	major
Hauptsturmführer	captain
Obersturmführer	first lieutenant
Untersturmführer	second lieutenant

NON-COMMISSIONED RANKS

Oberscharführer	a senior non-commissioned rank
Unterscharführer	equivalent to sergeant
Rottenführer	equivalent to corporal

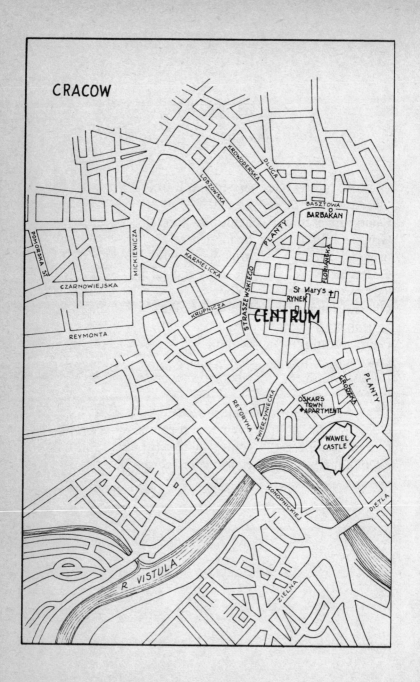

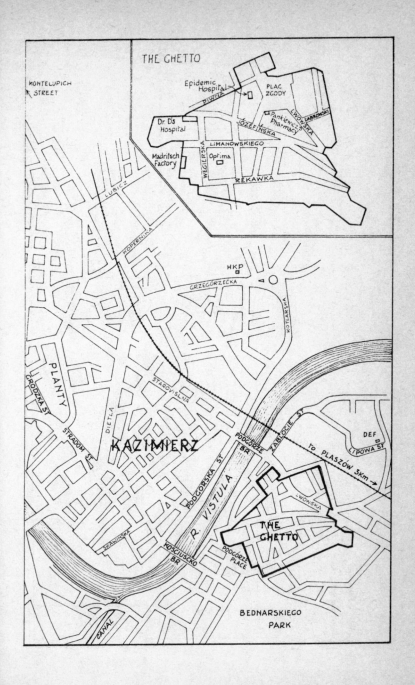

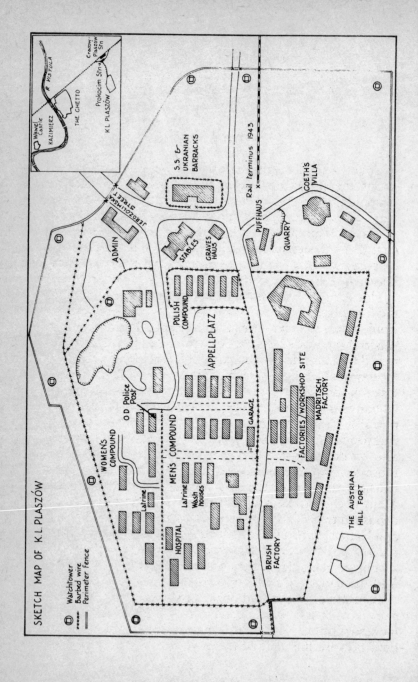

SKETCH MAP OF K.L. PLASZÓW

Watchtower
Barbed wire
Perimeter Fence

THE GHETTO
Wawel Castle
KAZIMIERZ
R. VISTULA
Cracow–Plaszów Stn
Prokocim Stn
K.L. PLASZÓW

S.S. & UKRANIAN BARRACKS
Rail Terminus 1943
PUFFHAUS
GOETH'S VILLA
QUARRY
JEROZOLIMSKA STREET
ADMIN
STABLES
GRAVES HAUS
POLISH COMPOUND
APPELLPLATZ
O D Police Post
WOMENS COMPOUND
Latrine
MENS COMPOUND
GARAGE
Latrine
Wash houses
HOSPITAL
FACTORIES / WORKSHOP SITE
MADRITSCH FACTORY
BRUSH FACTORY
THE AUSTRIAN HILL FORT

Author's Note

In 1980 I visited a luggage store in Beverly Hills and asked about the prices of briefcases. The store belonged to Leopold Pfefferberg, a Schindler survivor. Beneath Pfefferberg's shelves of imported Italian leather goods, I first heard of Oskar Schindler, the German *bon vivant*, speculator, charmer, and sign of contradiction, and of his salvage of a cross-section of a condemned race during those years now known by the generic name, Holocaust.

This account of Oskar's astonishing history is based in the first place on interviews with fifty Schindler survivors from seven nations – Australia, Israel, West Germany, Austria, the United States, Argentina and Brazil. It is enriched by a visit, in the company of Leopold Pfefferberg, to locations which figure prominently in the book – Cracow, Oskar's adopted city; Plaszów, the scene of Amon Goeth's labour camp; Lipowa Street, Zablocie, where Oskar's factory still stands; Auschwitz–Birkenau, from which Oskar extracted his women prisoners. But the narrative depends also on documentary and other information supplied by those few wartime associates of Oskar's who can still be reached, as well as by the large body of his postwar friends. Many of the hundreds of testimonies regarding Oskar and deposited by Schindler Jews at Yad Vashem, The Martyrs' and Heroes' Remembrance Authority, further enriched the record, as did written testimonies from private sources and a body of Schindler papers and letters, some supplied by Yad Vashem, some by Oskar's friends.

To use the texture and devices of a novel to tell a true story is a course which has frequently been followed in modern writing. It is the one I have chosen to follow here; both because the craft of the novelist is the only craft to

9

which I can lay claim, and because the novel's techniques seem suited for a character of such ambiguity and magnitude as Oskar. I have attempted to avoid all fiction, though, since fiction would debase the record, and to distinguish between reality and the myths which are likely to attach themselves to a man of Oskar's stature. Sometimes it has been necessary to attempt to reconstruct conversations of which Oskar and others have left only the briefest record. But most exchanges and conversations, and all events, are based on the detailed recollections of the *Schindlerjuden* (Schindler Jews), of Schindler himself, and of other witnesses to Oskar's acts of outrageous rescue.

I would like to thank first three Schindler survivors – Leopold Pfefferberg, Justice Moshe Bejski of the Israeli Supreme Court, and Mieczyslaw Pemper, who not only passed on their memories of Oskar to the author and gave him certain documents which have contributed to the accuracy of the narrative, but also read the early draft of the book and suggested corrections. Many others, whether Schindler survivors or Oskar's postwar associates, gave interviews and generously contributed information through letters and documents. These include Frau Emilie Schindler, Mrs. Ludmila Pfefferberg, Dr. Sophia Stern, Mrs. Helen Horowitz, Dr. Jonas Dresner, Mr. & Mrs. Henry and Mariana Rosner, Leopold Rosner, Dr. Alex Rosner, Dr. Idek Schindel, Dr. Danuta Schindel, Mrs. Regina Horowitz, Mrs. Bronislawa Karakulska, Mr. Richard Horowitz, Mr. Shmuel Springmann, the late Mr. Jakob Sternberg, Mr. Jerzy Sternberg, Mr. & Mrs. Lewis Fagen, Mr. Henry Kinstlinger, Mrs. Rebecca Bau, Mr. Edward Heuberger, Mr. & Mrs. M. Hirschfeld, Mr. & Mrs. Irving Glovin and many others. In my home city, Mr. & Mrs. E. Korn not only gave of their memories of Oskar but were a constant support. At Yad Vashem, Dr. Josef Kermisz, Dr. Shmuel Krakowski, Vera Prausnitz, Chana Abells and Hadassah Mödlinger provided generous access to the testimonies of Schindler survivors and to video and photographic material.

Last, I would like to honour the efforts which the late Mr.

Martin Gosch expended on bringing the name of Oskar Schindler to the world's notice, and to signify my thanks to his widow, Mrs. Lucille Gaynes, for her cooperation with this project.

Tom Keneally

Prologue *Autumn 1943*

In Poland's deepest autumn, a tall young man in an expensive overcoat, double-breasted dinner jacket beneath it and – in the lapel of the dinner jacket – a large ornamental gold-on-black enamel swastika, emerged from a fashionable apartment block in Straszewskiego Street on the edge of the ancient centre of Cracow, and saw his chauffeur waiting with fuming breath by the open door of an enormous and, even in this blackened world, lustrous Adler limousine.

"Watch the pavement, Herr Schindler," said the chauffeur. "It's icy like a widow's heart."

In observing this small winter scene, we are on safe ground. The tall young man would to the end of his days wear double-breasted suits, would, being something of an engineer, always be gratified by large dazzling vehicles, would, though a German and at this point in history a German of some influence, always be the sort of man with whom a Polish chauffeur could safely crack a lame, comradely joke.

But it will not be possible to see the whole story under such easy character headings. For this is the story of the pragmatic triumph of good over evil, a triumph in eminently measurable, statistical, unsubtle terms. When you work from the other end of the beast, when you chronicle the predictable and measurable success evil generally achieves, it is easy to be wise, wry, piercing, to avoid bathos. It is easy to show the inevitability by which evil acquires all of what you could call the *real estate* of the story, even though good might finish up with a few imponderables like dignity and self-knowledge. Fatal human malice is the staple of narrators, original sin the mother-fluid of historians. But it is a risky enterprise to have to write of virtue.

In fact *virtue* is such a dangerous word that we have to rush to explain; Herr Oskar Schindler, chancing his glimmering shoes on the icy pavement in this old and elegant quarter of Cracow, was not a virtuous young man in the customary sense. In this city he kept house with his German mistress and maintained a long affair with his Polish secretary. His wife Emilie chose to live most of the time at home in Moravia, though she sometimes came to Poland to visit him. There's this to be said for him, that to all his women he was a well-mannered and generous lover. But under the normal interpretation of *virtue* that's no excuse.

Likewise he was a drinker. Some of the time he drank for the pure glow of it, at other times with associates, bureaucrats, SS men for more palpable results. Like few others, he was capable of staying canny while drinking, of keeping his head. That again, though, under the narrow interpretation of morality, has never been an excuse for carousing. And although Herr Schindler's merit is well documented, it is a feature of his ambiguity that he worked within or, at least, on the strength of, a corrupt and savage scheme; one which filled Europe with camps of varying but consistent inhumanity and created a submerged, unspoken-of nation of prisoners. The best thing, therefore, may be to begin with a tentative instance of Herr Schindler's strange virtue and of the places and associates to which it brought him.

At the end of Straszewskiego Street, the car moved beneath the black bulk of Wawel Castle, from which the National Socialist Party's darling lawyer Hans Frank ruled the Government General of Poland. As from the palace of any evil giant, no light showed. Neither Herr Schindler nor the driver glanced up at the ramparts as the car turned south-east towards the river. At the Podgórze Bridge, the guards, placed above the freezing Vistula to prevent the transit of partisans and other curfew-breakers between Podgórze and Cracow, were used to the vehicle, to Herr Schindler's face, to the Passierschein presented by the chauffeur. Herr Schindler passed this check-point frequently, travelling either from his factory (where he also had an apartment) to the city on business, or else from his Straszewskiego Street apartment to his works in the suburb of Zablocie. They were used to seeing him after dark, too, attired formally or semi-formally, passing one way or another to a dinner, a party, a bedroom; perhaps, as was the case tonight, on his way ten kilometres out of town to the forced labour camp at Plaszów, to dine there with SS Hauptsturmführer Amon Goeth, that highly placed sensualist. Herr Schindler had a reputation for being generous with gifts of drink at Christmas, and so the car was permitted to pass over into the suburb of Podgórze without much delay.

It is certain that by this stage of his history, in spite of his liking for good food and wine, Herr Schindler approached tonight's dinner at Commandant Goeth's more with loathing than with anticipation. There had in fact never been a time when to sit and drink with Amon had not been a repellent business. Yet the revulsion Herr Schindler felt was of a piquant kind, an ancient exultant sense of abomination such as, in a medieval painting, the just show for the damned. An emotion, that is, which stung Oskar rather than unmanned him.

In the black leather interior of the Adler as it raced along the tramtracks in what was until recently the Jewish ghetto, Herr Schindler chain smoked, as ever. But it was composed chain smoking. There was never tension in the hands; he was stylish. His manner implied that he knew where the next cigarette was coming from and the next bottle of cognac. Only he could have told us whether he had to succour himself from a flask as he passed by the mute, black village of Prokocim and saw, on the railway line to Lwów, a string of stalled cattle wagons, which might hold infantry or prisoners or even – though the odds on this were long – cattle.

Out in the countryside, perhaps ten kilometres from the centre of town, the Adler turned right at a street named – by an irony – Jerozolimska. This night of sharp frosty outlines,

15

Herr Schindler saw beneath the hill first a ruined synagogue, and then the bare shapes of what passed these days as the city of Jerusalem, Forced Labour Camp Plaszów, barrack town of twenty thousand unquiet Jews, Polacks and Gypsies. The Ukrainian and Waffen SS men on the gate greeted Herr Schindler courteously, for he was known at least as well here as on the Podgórze Bridge.

When level with the Administration Block, the Adler moved on to a prison road paved with Jewish gravestones. The camp site had been till two years before a Jewish cemetery. Commandant Amon Goeth, who claimed to be a poet, had used in the construction of his camp whatever metaphors were to hand. This metaphor of shattered gravestones ran the length of the camp, splitting it in two, but did not extend eastwards to the villa occupied by Commandant Goeth himself.

On the right, past the guard barracks, stood a former Jewish mortuary building. It seemed to declare that here all death was natural and by attrition, that all the dead were laid out. In fact the place was now used as the commandant's stables. Though Herr Schindler was used to the sight, it is possible that he still reacted with an ironic little cough. Admittedly if you reacted to every little irony of the new Europe you took it into you, it became part of your luggage. But Herr Schindler possessed an immense capacity for carrying that sort of secret drollery.

A prisoner called Poldek Pfefferberg was also on his way to the commandant's villa that evening. Lisiek, the commandant's nineteen-year-old orderly, had come to Pfefferberg's barracks with passes signed by an SS NCO. The youngster's problem was that the commandant's bath had a stubborn ring around it, and Lisiek feared that he would be beaten up for it when Commandant Goeth came to take his morning bath. Pfefferberg, who had been Lisiek's teacher in high school in Podgórze, worked in the camp garage and had access to solvents. So, in company with Lisiek, he went to the garage and fetched a long stick with a swab on the end and a can of solvent. To approach the commandant's villa was always a dubious business, but involved the chance that you would be given food by Helen Hirsch, Goeth's misused Jewish maid, a generous girl who had also been a student of Pfefferberg's.

When Herr Schindler's Adler was still a hundred metres from Goeth's villa, it set the dogs barking, the Great Dane, the Wolfhound, and all the others the commandant kept in the kennels beyond the house. The villa itself, a square building with an attic, had a balcony along the upper floor. All around the walls was a terraced patio with a balustrade. Amon Goeth liked sitting out of doors in the summer. Since he'd come here, he'd put on weight. Next summer he'd make a fat sun-worshipper. But in this particular version of Jerusalem he'd be safe from mockery.

An SS unterscharführer with white gloves had been put on the door tonight. Saluting, the sergeant admitted Herr Schindler to the house. In the hallway the Ukrainian orderly, Ivan, took Herr Schindler's coat and homberg. Schindler patted the breast pocket of his suit to be sure he had the gift for his host, a gold plated cigarette case, black market. Amon was doing so well on the side, especially out of confiscated jewellery, that he would be offended by anything less than the best gold plate. Yet even the best gold plate was to Amon nothing but a pleasant token.

At the double doors giving on to the dining room, the Rosner brothers were playing, Henry on violin, Leo on accordion. On Hauptsturmführer Goeth's command they had taken off the tattered clothing of the camp paint shop where they worked in the daytime and adopted the evening suits they kept in their barracks for such events. Oskar Schindler knew that although the commandant admired their music the Rosners never played at ease in the villa. They had seen too much of Amon. They knew he was erratic and given to *ex tempore* executions. They played studiously and hoped that their music would not suddenly give offence.

At Goeth's table that night there would be seven men. Apart from Schindler himself, the guests included Oberführer* Julian Scherner, head of the SS for the Cracow

* An SS rank, higher than colonel, lower than brigadier, for which there is no army equivalent.

17

region, and Obersturmbannführer Rolf Czurda, the lieutenant colonel who was chief of the Cracow branch of the SD, the late Reinhard Heydrich's security service. They were the guests of highest honour, for this camp was run by their authority. They were some ten years older than Goeth, and SS police chief Scherner looked definitely middle-aged with his glasses and bald head and slight obesity. Even so, in view of his protégé's profligate living habits, the age difference between himself and Amon didn't seem so great.

The oldest of the company was Herr Franz Bosch, a veteran of the first war, manager of various workshops, legal and illegal, inside Plaszów. He was also an 'economic adviser' to Julian Scherner and had business interests in the city.

Oskar despised Bosch and the two police chiefs, Scherner and Czurda. However, their cooperation was essential to the existence of his own peculiar plant in Zablocie, and so he regularly sent them gifts. The only guests with whom Oskar shared any fellow feeling were Julius Madritsch, owner of the Madritsch uniform factory inside this camp of Plaszów, and Madritsch's manager, Raimund Titsch. Madritsch was a year or so younger than Oskar and Goeth. He was an enterprising but humane man, and if asked to justify the existence of his profitable factory inside the camp, would have argued that it kept nearly four thousand prisoners employed and therefore safe from the death mills. Raimund Titsch, a man in his early forties, slight and private and likely to leave the party early, ran the Madritsch works on a daily basis, smuggled in truckloads of food for his prisoners (an enterprise which could have earned him a fatal stay in Montelupich prison, the SS jail, or else Auschwitz) and agreed with Madritsch.

Such was the regular bag of dinner companions at Herr Commandant Goeth's villa.

The four women guests, their hair formally done up and their gowns expensive, were younger than any of the men. They were better-class whores, German and Polish, from Cracow. Some of them were regular dinner guests here. Their number permitted a range of gentlemanly choice for the two senior officers. Goeth's German mistress, Majola, generally stayed at her apartment in the city during these feasts. She looked on Goeth's dinners as exclusively male and therefore offensive to her sensibilities.

There is no doubt that in their way the police chiefs and the commandant liked Oskar. There was, however, something odd about him. They might have been willing to write it off in part to his origins. He was Sudeten German, Arkansas to their Manhattan, Liverpool to their Cambridge. There were signs that he wasn't *right thinking*, though he paid well, was a good source of scarce commodities, could hold his drink and had a slow and sometimes rowdy sense of humour. He was the sort of man you smiled and nodded at across the room, but it was not necessary or even wise to jump up and make a fuss of him.

It is most likely that the SS men noticed Oskar Schindler's entrance because of a frisson among the four girls. Those who knew Oskar in those years speak of his easy magnetic charm, exercised particularly over women, with whom he was unremittingly and improperly successful. The two police chiefs, Czurda and Scherner, now probably paid attention to Herr Schindler as a means of keeping the attention of the women. Goeth also came forward to take his hand. The commandant was as tall as Schindler, and the impression that he was abnormally fat for a man in his early thirties was aided by this height, an athletic height on to which the obesity seemed unnaturally grafted. The face seemed scarcely flawed at all, except that there was a vinous light in the eyes. The commandant drank indecent quantities of the local brandy.

He was not, however, as far gone as Herr Bosch, Plaszów's and the SS's economic wizard. Herr Bosch was purple nosed; the oxygen which by rights belonged to the veins of his face had for years gone to feed the sharp blue flame of all that liquor. Schindler, nodding to the man, knew that tonight Bosch would, as always, put in an order for goods.

"A welcome to our industrialist," intoned Goeth, and then he made a formal introduction to the girls around the room. The Rosner brothers would have played through this,

Henry's eyes wandering only between his strings and the emptiest corner of the room, Leo smiling down at his accordion keys. And from it all arising the notes which Strauss put on paper for the titillation of gentlefolk.

Herr Schindler was now introduced to the women. He felt some small pity for these Cracow working girls, since he knew that later, when the slap and tickle began, the slap might leave welts and the tickle gouge the flesh. But for the present Hauptsturmführer Amon Goeth, a mad satrap when drunk, was an exemplary Viennese gentleman.

The pre-dinner conversation was unexceptional. There was talk of the war, and while SD chief Czurda took it upon himself to assure a tall German girl that the Crimea was securely held, SS chief Scherner informed one of the other women that a boy he knew from Hamburg days, a decent chap, an Oberscharführer in the SS, had had his legs blown off when the partisans bombed a restaurant in Czestochowa. Schindler talked factory talk with Madritsch and his manager Titsch. There was a genuine friendship between these three entrepreneurs. Herr Schindler knew that little Titsch procured illegal quantities of black-market bread for the prisoners of the Madritsch uniform factory, and that much of the money for the purpose was put up by Madritsch. This was the merest humanity; since the profits in Poland were large enough, in Herr Schindler's opinion, to satisfy the most inveterate capitalist and justify some illegal outlay on extra bread. In Herr Schindler's case itself the contracts of the Rustungsinspektion, the Armaments Inspectorate – a body that solicited bids and awarded contracts for the manufacture of every commodity the German forces needed – had been so rich that he had exceeded his desire to be successful in the eyes of his father. Unhappily, Madritsch and Titsch and he, Oskar Schindler, were the only ones he knew who regularly spent money on black-market bread.

Towards the time when Goeth would call them to the dinner table, Herr Bosch approached Schindler, took him by the elbow and led him over by the door where the musicians played, as if he expected the Rosners' impeccable melodies to cover the conversation.

"Business good, I see," said Bosch.

Schindler smiled at the man. "You *see* that, do you, Herr Bosch?"

"I do," said Bosch. And of course Bosch would have read the official bulletins of the Main Armaments Board, announcing contracts awarded – on the basis of successful bids – to the Schindler factory.

"I was wondering," said Bosch inclining his head, "if in view of the present boom, founded, after all, on our general successes on a series of fronts . . . I was wondering if you might feel like a generous gesture. Nothing big. Just a gesture."

"Of course," said Schindler. He felt the nausea that goes with being used, and at the same time a sensation close to joy. The office of police chief Scherner had twice used its influence to get Oskar Schindler out of jail. They were willing now to build up the obligation of having to do it again.

"My aunt in Bremen's been bombed out, poor old dear," said Bosch. "Everything! The marriage bed. The sideboards, all her Meissen and crockery. I wondered could you spare some kitchenware for her. And perhaps a pot or two – those big tureen things turned out at DEF."

Deutsche Emailwaren Fabrik, the German Enamel Works, was the name of Herr Schindler's booming business. Germans called it DEF for short, but the Poles and the Jews had a different sort of shorthand, calling it Emalia.

Herr Schindler said, "I think that can be managed. Do you want the goods consigned direct to her or through you?"

Bosch did not even smile. "Through me, Oskar. I'd like to enclose a little card."

"Of course."

"So it's settled. We'll say half a gross of everything – soup bowls, plates, coffee mugs. And half a dozen of those stew pots."

Herr Schindler, raising his jaw, laughed frankly. There

was also some weariness in the laugh. But when he spoke he sounded complaisant. As indeed he was. He was always reckless with gifts. It was simply that Bosch regularly seemed to suffer from bombed-out kinsfolk.

Oskar murmured, "Does your aunt run an orphanage?"

Bosch looked him in the eye again, nothing furtive about this drunk. "She's an old woman with no resources. She can barter what she doesn't need."

"I'll tell my secretary to see to it."

"That Polish girl?" said Bosch. "The looker?"

"The looker," Schindler agreed.

Bosch tried to whistle, but the tension of his lips had been destroyed by the overproof brandy which was his tipple, and the sound emerged as a low raspberry. "Your wife," he said, man to man, "must be a saint."

"She is," Herr Schindler admitted with disquiet. Bosch was welcome to his kitchenware, but he didn't want him talking about his wife.

"Tell me," said Bosch. "How do you keep her off your back? She must know . . . Yet you seem to be able to control her very well."

All the humour left Schindler's face now. Anyone could have seen frank distaste there. But the small, potent growl which arose from him was not unlike his normal voice.

"I never talk about intimacies like that," he said.

Bosch rushed in. "Forgive me. I didn't . . ." He went on incoherently begging pardon. Herr Oskar Schindler did not like sodden Herr Bosch enough to explain to him at this advanced night of his life that it wasn't a matter of controlling anyone, that the Schindler marital disaster was instead a case of an ascetic temperament, Frau Emilie Schindler's, and a hedonistic temperament, Herr Oskar Schindler's, willingly and against good advice binding themselves together. But Oskar's anger at Herr Bosch was more profound than even he would have admitted. Emilie was very like his late mother, Frau Louisa Schindler, whom Herr Schindler senior had left in 1935. So Oskar had a visceral feeling that in explaining away the Emilie-Oskar

22

marriage, Bosch was also demeaning the marriage of the senior Schindlers.

The man was still rushing out apologies. This grape-faced speculator, a hand in every till in Cracow, was now in a sweating fright at the chance of losing six dozen sets of kitchenware.

The guests were summoned to the table. Onion soup was carried in and served by the maid. While the guests supped and chatted, the Rosner brothers continued to play, moving in closer to the diners, but not so close as to impede the movements of the maid or of Ivan and Petr, Goeth's two Ukrainian orderlies. Herr Schindler, sitting between the tall girl whom Scherner had appropriated and a sweet-faced, small-boned Pole who spoke German, saw that both girls watched this maid. She wore the traditional domestic uniform, black dress and white apron. She bore no Jewish star on her arm, no stripe of yellow paint on her back, yet she was Jewish just the same. What drew the attention of the other women was the condition of her face. There was bruising along the line of the jaw, and you would have thought that Goeth had too much shame to display a servant in that condition in front of the guests from Cracow. Both the women and Herr Schindler could see, as well as the injury to her face, a more alarming purple, not always covered by her collar, at the junction where her thin neck joined her shoulder.

Not only did Amon Goeth neglect to leave the girl unexplained in the background, but he turned his chair towards her, gesturing at her with a hand, displaying her to the assembled company. Herr Schindler had not been at this house for six weeks now, but his informants told him the relationship between Goeth and the girl had developed this way. When with friends he used her as a conversational device. He only hid her away when senior officers from beyond the Cracow region were visiting.

"Ladies and gentlemen," he called, mimicking the tones of a fake-drunken master of cabaret, "may I introduce Lena? After five months she is now doing well in cuisine and deportment."

"I can see from her face," said the tall girl, Scherner's, "that she's had a collision with the kitchen furniture."

"And the bitch can have another," said Goeth with a genial liquid gurgle. "Yes. Another. Couldn't you, Lena?"

"He's hard on women," the SS chief boasted, winking at his tall consort. Scherner's intention might not have been unkind, since he did not refer to *Jewish* women but to women in general. It was when Goeth was reminded of Lena's Jewishness that she took more punishment, either publicly, in front of dinner guests, or later, when the commandant's friends had gone home. Scherner, being Goeth's superior, could have ordered the commandant to stop beating the girl. But that would have been bad form, would have soured the friendly parties at Amon's villa. Scherner came here not as a superior, but as a friend, an associate, a carouser, a savourer of women. Amon was a strange fellow, but no one could turn on parties the way he could.

Next there was herring in sauce, then pork knuckles, superbly cooked and garnished by Lena. They were drinking a heavy Hungarian red wine with the meat; the Rosner brothers moved in with torrid Hungarian music, and the air in the dining room thickened, all the officers removing their uniform jackets. There was more gossip about war contracts. Madritsch, the uniform manufacturer, was asked about his Tarnow factory. Was it doing as well with Armaments Inspectorate contracts as was his factory inside Plaszów? Madritsch referred to Titsch, his lean, ascetic manager. Goeth seemed suddenly preoccupied, like a man who has remembered in the middle of dinner some urgent business detail he should have cleared up that afternoon and which now calls out to him from the darkness of his office.

The girls from Cracow were bored, the small-boned Pole, glossy-lipped, perhaps twenty, likely eighteen, placing a hand on Herr Schindler's right sleeve. "You're not a soldier?" she murmured. "You'd look very chic in uniform." Everyone began to chuckle, Madritsch too. He'd spent a while in uniform in 1940 until released because his managerial talents were so essential to the war effort. But Herr Schindler was so influential that he had never been threatened with the Wehrmacht. Madritsch laughed knowingly.

"Did you hear that?" Oberführer Scherner asked the table at large. "The little lady's got a picture of our industrialist as a soldier. Private Schindler, eh? Eating out of one of his own mess kits with a blanket round his shoulders. Over in Karkov."

In view of Herr Schindler's well-tailored elegance it *did* make a strange picture, and Schindler himself laughed at it.

"Happened to . . ." said Bosch, trying to snap his fingers, "happened to, what's his name up in Warsaw?"

"Toebbens," said Goeth, reviving without warning. "Happened to Toebbens. Almost."

The SD chief Czurda said, "Oh yes. Close thing for Toebbens." Toebbens was a Warsaw industrialist. Bigger than Schindler, bigger than Madritsch. Quite a success. "Heini," said Czurda (Heini being Himmler), "went to Warsaw and told the armaments man up there, Get the fucking Jews out of Toebbens's factory and put Toebbens in the army *and* . . . and send him to the front. I mean, the *front*! And then Heini told my associate up there, he said, Go over his books with a microscope!"

Toebbens, however, was a darling of the Armaments Inspectorate, which had favoured him with war contracts and which in return he had favoured with gifts. The Armaments Inspectorate's protests had succeeded in saving Toebbens, Scherner told the table solemnly, and then leaned out across his plate to wink broadly at Schindler. "Never happen in Cracow, Oskar. We all love you too much."

All at once, perhaps to indicate the warmth the whole table felt for Herr Schindler the industrialist, Amon Goeth climbed to his feet and sang a wordless tune in unison with the main theme from *Madam Butterfly* on which the dapper brothers Rosner were working as industriously as any artisan in any threatened factory in any threatened ghetto.

*

By now Pfefferberg and Lisiek the orderly were upstairs in Goeth's bathroom, scrubbing away at the heavy bath ring with a swab of solvent. They could hear the Rosners' music and the bursts of laughter and conversation. It was coffee time down there, and the bruised girl Lena had brought the tray in to the dinner guests and retreated unmolested back to the kitchen.

Madritsch and Titsch drank their coffee quickly and excused themselves. Schindler prepared to do the same. The little Polish girl had put a hand on his shirt sleeve, but this was the wrong house for him. Anything was permitted at the Goethhaus, but Oskar found that his inside knowledge of the limits of SS behaviour in Poland threw sickening light on every word you spoke here, every glass you drank, let alone over any proposed sexual exchange. Even if you took a girl upstairs, you could not forget that Bosch and Scherner and Goeth were your brothers in joy, were – on the stairs or in a bathroom or bedroom – going through the same movements. Herr Schindler, no monk, would rather be a monk than have a woman at *chez* Goeth.

He spoke across the girl to Scherner, talking about war news, Polish bandits, the likelihood of a bad winter. Letting the girl know that Scherner was a brother and that he would never take a girl from a brother. Saying good night, though, he kissed her on the hand. He saw that Goeth, in his shirt sleeves, was disappearing out of the dining-room door, making for the stairwell supported by one of the girls who had flanked him at dinner. Oskar excused himself and caught up with the commandant. He reached out and laid a hand on Goeth's shoulder. The eyes the commandant turned on him struggled to focus. "Oh," said Goeth in a liquid way. "Going, Oskar?"

"I have to be home," said Oskar. At home was Ingrid, his German mistress.

"You're a bloody stallion," said Goeth.

"Not in your class," said Schindler.

"No, you're right. I'm a frigging Olympian. We're going, where're we going. . . ?" He turned his head to the girl but answered the question himself. "We're going to the kitchen to see that Lena's clearing away properly."

"No," said the girl, laughing. "We aren't doing that."

She steered him to the stairs. It was decent of her, the sisterhood in operation, to protect the thin, wounded girl in the kitchen.

Herr Oskar Schindler watched the uneven animal, the hulking officer, the slight, supporting girl, struggling crookedly up the staircase. Goeth looked like a man who would have to sleep at least till lunchtime, but Oskar knew the commandant's amazing constitution and the clock that ran in him. By 3 a.m. Goeth might even decide to rise and write a letter to his father in Vienna. By seven, after only an hour's sleep, he'd be on the balcony, infantry rifle in hand, ready to shoot any dilatory prisoners.

When the girl and Goeth reached the first landing, Schindler sidled down the hallway towards the back of the house.

Pfefferberg and Lisiek heard the commandant, earlier than they had expected him, entering the bedroom and mumbling at the girl he'd brought upstairs. In silence they picked up the swab and the solvent can, crept through into the bedroom and tried to slide out by a side door. Still standing and able to see them on their line of escape, Goeth blanched and recoiled at the sight of the cleaning stick, suspecting that the two men might be assassins. When Lisiek stepped forward, however, and began a tremulous report, the commandant understood that they were merely prisoners.

"Herr Commandant," said Lisiek, panting with justified fear, "I wish to report that there has been a ring around your bath. . ."

"Oh," said Amon. "So you called in an expert?" He beckoned to the boy. "Come here, darling."

Lisiek edged forward and was struck so savagely that he went sprawling, skidding halfway under the bed. Amon again uttered his invitation, as if it might amuse the girl to see him speaking endearments to prisoners. Young Lisiek rose and tottered towards the commandant again, to receive another assault. As the boy picked himself up the second time, Pfefferberg, an experienced prisoner, prepared himself for anything – that they'd be marched down to the garden and shot by Ivan. Instead the commandant simply raged at them to leave, which they did at once.

When Pfefferberg heard a few days later that Lisiek was dead, shot by Amon, he presumed it was over the bathroom incident. In fact it was for a different matter altogether – Lisiek had harnessed a horse and buggy for Herr Bosch without first asking the commandant's permission.

In the kitchen of the villa, the maid, Helen Hirsch (Goeth called her Lena out of laziness she would always say) looked up to see one of the dinner guests in the doorway. She put down the dish of meat scraps she'd been holding and stood to attention with a jerky suddenness. "*Herr* . . ." She looked at his dinner jacket and sought the word for him. "Herr Direktor, I was just putting aside the leftovers for the Herr Commandant's dogs."

"Please, please," said Herr Schindler. "You don't have to report to me, Fräulein Hirsch."

He moved around the table. He did not seem to be stalking her, but she feared his intentions. Even though Amon enjoyed beating her, her Jewishness always saved her from overt sexual attack. But there were Germans who were not as fastidious on racial matters as Amon.

This one's tone of voice, however, was that of ordinary social exchange. It was a tone to which she was not accustomed, even from the SS officers and NCOs who came to the kitchen to complain about Amon.

"Don't you know me?" he asked, just like a man, a soccer star or actor, whose sense of his own celebrity has been hurt by a stranger's failure to recognise him. "I'm Schindler."

She bowed her head. "Herr Direktor," she said. "Of course, I've heard . . . And you've been here before. I remember . . ."

He put his arm around her. He could surely feel the clenching of her body as he touched her cheek with his lips.

He murmured, "It's not that sort of kiss. I'm kissing you out of pity, if you want to know."

She couldn't avoid starting to weep. Herr Direktor Schindler bussed her hard now in the middle of the forehead, in the manner of Polish farewells at railway stations, a resounding Eastern European smack of the lips. She saw that he had begun to weep too. "That kiss is something I bring you from . . ." He waved his hand, indicating some honest tribe of men out in the dark, sleeping in tiered bunks or hiding in forests, people for whom by absorbing punishment from Hauptsturmführer Goeth she was in part a buffer.

Herr Schindler released her and reached into the side pocket of his jacket, bringing out a large confectionery bar. In its substance it too seemed pre-war.

"Keep that somewhere," he advised her.

"I get extra food here," she told him, as if it were a matter of pride that he wouldn't presume she was starving. Food, in fact, was the least of her worries. She knew she would not survive Amon's house, but it wouldn't be for lack of food.

"If you don't want to eat it, trade it," Herr Schindler told her. "Or why not build yourself up?" He stood back and surveyed her. "Itzhak Stern told me about you."

"Herr Schindler," murmured the girl. She put her head down and wept neatly, economically, for a few seconds. "Herr Schindler, he likes to beat me in front of *those* women. On my first day here, he beat me because I threw out the bones from dinner. He came down to the basement at midnight and asked me where they were. For his dogs, you understand. That was the first beating . . . I said to him . . . I don't know why I said it, I'd never say it now . . . Why are you beating me? He said, The reason I'm beating you now is you asked me why I'm beating you."

She shook her head and shrugged, as if reproving herself for talking so much. She didn't want to say any more, she couldn't convey the history of her punishments, her repeated experience of the Hauptsturmführer's knuckles.

Herr Schindler bent his head to her and became even

more confidential. "Your circumstances are appalling, Helen," he told her.

"It doesn't matter," she said. "I've accepted it."

"Accepted it?"

"One day he'll shoot me."

Schindler shook his head and she thought it was too glib an encouragement to her to hope. Suddenly, the good cloth and the cosseted flesh of Herr Schindler were a provocation. "For God's sake, Herr Schindler, I see things. We were up on the roof on Monday, chipping off the ice, me and young Lisiek. And we saw the Herr Commandant come out of the front door and down the steps by the patio, right below us. And, there on the steps, he drew his gun and shot a woman who was passing. A woman carrying a bundle. Through the throat. Just a woman on her way somewhere. You know. She didn't seem fatter or thinner or slower or faster than anyone else. I couldn't guess what she'd done. The more you see of the Herr Commandant, the more you see that there's no set of rules you can keep to. You can't say to yourself, If I keep these rules, I'll be safe . . ."

Schindler took her hand and wrung it for emphasis. "Listen, my dear Fräulein Helen Hirsch, for all that, it's still better than Majdanek or Auschwitz. If you can keep your health . . ."

She said, "I thought it would be easy to keep my health in the commandant's kitchen. When I was sent here, from the camp kitchen, the other girls were jealous."

A pitiful smile spread on her lips.

Schindler raised his voice now. He was like a man enunciating a principle of physics. "He won't kill you, because he enjoys you too much, my dear Helen. He enjoys you so much he won't even let you wear the Star. He doesn't want anyone to know it's a Jew he's enjoying. He shot the woman from the steps because she meant nothing to him; she was one of a series, she neither offended nor pleased him. You understand that. But you . . . it's not decent, Helen. But it's life."

Someone else had said that to her. Untersturmführer Leo John, a second lieutenant, the commandant's deputy. John had said, "He won't kill you till the end, Lena, because he gets too much of a kick out of you." But coming from John it hadn't had the same effect. Herr Schindler had just condemned her to a painful survival.

He seemed to understand that she was stunned. He murmured encouragement. He'd see her again. He'd try to get her out. Out? she asked. Out of the villa, he explained, into my factory. Surely you have heard of my factory. I have an enamelware factory.

"Oh yes," she said like a slum child speaking of the Riviera. "Schindler's Emalia. I've heard of it."

"Keep your health," he repeated. He seemed to know it would be the key. He seemed to draw on a knowledge of future intentions – Himmler's, Frank's – when he said it.

"All right," she conceded.

She turned her back on him and went to a dresser, levering it forward from the wall, an exercise of strength which in such a diminished girl amazed Herr Schindler. She removed a brick from the section of wall the dresser had previously covered. She brought out a wad of money, occupation zloty.

"I have a sister in the camp kitchen," she said. "She's younger than me. I want you to spend this buying her back if ever she's put on the cattle wagons. I believe you often find out about these things beforehand."

"I'll make it my business," Schindler told her, but with ease, not like a solemn promise. "How much is it?"

"Four thousand zloty."

He took it negligently, her nest egg, and shoved it in a side pocket. It was still safer with him than in a niche behind Amon Goeth's dresser.

So the story of Oskar Schindler is begun perilously, with Gothic Nazis, with SS hedonism, with the thin and brutalised girl, and with a figure of the imagination somehow as popular as the golden-hearted whore: the good German.

On the one hand, Oskar has made it his business to know the full face of the system, the rabid face behind the veil of bureaucratic decency. He knows, that is, earlier than most would dare know it, what Sonderbehandlung means, that though it says *Special Treatment* it means pyramids of cyanosed corpses in Belzec, Sobibor, Treblinka, and in that complex west of Cracow known to the Poles as Oświecim–Brzezinka but which will be known to the West by its German name, Auschwitz–Birkenau.

On the other hand he is a businessman, a dealer by temperament, and he does not openly spit in the system's eye. He has already reduced the pyramids and, though he does not know how this year and the next they will grow in size and number and overtop the Matterhorn, he knows the mountain is coming. Though he cannot predict what bureaucratic shifts will occur in its construction, he still presumes there will always be room and need for Jewish labour. Therefore, during his charitable visit to Helen Hirsch, he insists, "Keep your health." He is sure, and out in the darkened Arbeitslager of Plaszów wakeful Jews stir and promise themselves that no régime, the tide set against it, can afford to do away with a plentiful source of free labour. It's the ones who break down, spit blood, fall to dysentery who are put on the Auschwitz transports. Herr Schindler himself has heard prisoners, out on the Appellplatz – parade ground – of Plaszów labour camp, murmur, "At least I still have my health," in a tone which in normal life only the aged use.

So, this winter night, it is both early days and late days for Herr Schindler's practical engagement in the salvage of certain human lives. He is in deep, he has broken Reich laws to an extent that would earn him a multiplicity of hangings, beheadings, consignments to the draughty huts of Auschwitz or Gröss-Rosen. But he does not know yet how much it will really cost. Though he has spent a fortune already, he does not know the extent of payments still to be made.

Not to stretch belief so early, the story begins with a quotidian act of kindness, a kiss, a soft voice, a sugared bar.

Helen Hirsch would never see her four thousand zloty again – not in a form in which they could be counted and held in the hand. But to this day she considers it a matter of small importance that Oskar was so inexact with sums of money.

I

General Sigmund List's armoured divisions, driving north from the Sudetenland, had taken the sweet south Polish jewel of Cracow from both flanks on September 6th, 1939. And it was in their wake that Oskar Schindler entered the city which, for the next five years, would be his oyster. Though within the month he would show that he was disaffected with National Socialism, he could still see that Cracow, with its railway junction and its as yet modest industries, would be a boom town of the new dispensation. He wasn't going to be a salesman any more. Now he was going to be his own tycoon.

It is not immediately easy to find in Oskar's family's history the origins of his impulse towards rescue. He was born on April 28th, 1908, into the Austrian Empire of Franz Josef, into the hilly Moravian province of that ancient Austrian realm. His home town was the industrial city of Zwittau, to which some commercial opening had brought the Schindler ancestors from Vienna at the beginning of the sixteenth century.

Herr Hans Schindler, Oskar's father, approved of the imperial arrangement, considered himself culturally an Austrian, and spoke German at table, on the telephone, in business, in moments of tenderness. Yet when in 1918 Herr Schindler and the members of his family found themselves citizens of the Czechoslovak republic of Masaryk and Beneš, it did not seem to cause any fundamental distress to the father, and still less to his ten-year-old son. The child Hitler, according to the man Hitler, was tormented even as a boy by the gulf between the mystical unity of Austria and Germany and their political separation. No such neurosis of disinheritance soured Oskar Schindler's childhood. Czechoslovakia was such a bosky, unravished little dumpling of a republic that the German-speakers took their minority stature with some grace, even if the Depression and some minor governmental follies would later put a certain strain on the relationship.

Zwittau, Oskar's native town, was a small, coal-dusted city in the southern reaches of the mountain range known as the Jeseniks. Its surrounding hills stood partly ravaged by industry and partly forested with larch and spruce and fir. Because of its community of German-speaking Sudetendeutschen it maintained a German grammar school which Oskar attended. There he took the Realgymnasium Course, which was meant to produce engineers – mining, mechanical, civil – to suit the industrial landscape of the area. Herr Schindler himself owned a farm machinery plant, and Oskar's education was a preparation for this inheritance.

The family Schindler was Catholic. So too was the family of young Amon Goeth, by this time also completing the Science Course and sitting for the Matura examinations in Vienna.

Oskar's mother, Louisa, practised her faith with energy, her clothes redolent all Sunday of the incense burned in clouds at High Mass in the church of St. Maurice. Hans Schindler was the sort of husband who drives a woman to religion. He liked cognac, he liked coffee houses. A redolence of brandy-warm breath, good tobacco, and confirmed earthiness came from the direction of that good monarchist, Herr Hans Schindler.

The family lived in a modern villa, set in its own gardens, across the city from the industrial section. There were two children, Oskar and his sister, Elfriede. But there are no witnesses left to the dynamics of that household, except in the most general terms. We know, for example, that it distressed Frau Schindler that her son, like his father, was a negligent Catholic.

But it cannot have been too internecine a household. From the little that Oskar would say of his childhood, there was no darkness there. Sunlight shines among the fir trees in the garden. There are ripe plums in the corner of those early summers. If he spends a part of some summer morning at Mass, he does not bring back to the villa much of a sense of sin. He runs his father's car out into the sun in front of the garage and begins ferreting inside its engine. Or else he sits on a side step of the house, filing away at the carburettor of the motorbike he is building.

Oskar had a few middle-class Jewish friends, whose parents also sent them to the German grammar school. These children were not village Ashkenazim – quirky, Yiddish-speaking, orthodox – but multilingual and not-so-ritual sons of Jewish businessmen. Across the Hana Plain and in the Beskidy Hills, Sigmund Freud had been born of just such a Jewish family, and that not so long before Hans Schindler himself was born to solid German stock in Zwittau.

Oskar's later history seems to call out for some set piece in his childhood. The young Oskar should defend some bullied Jewish boy on the way home from school. It is a safe bet it didn't happen, and we are happier not knowing, since the event would seem too pat. Besides, one Jewish child saved from a bloody nose proves nothing. For Himmler himself would complain, in a speech to one of his Einsatzgruppen, that every German had a Jewish friend. "This is one of those things that are easily said. 'The Jewish people are going to be annihilated,' says every Party member. 'Sure it's in our programme, elimination of the Jews, annihilation – we'll take care of it.' And then they all come trudging, eighty million worthy Germans and each one has his one decent Jew. Sure, the others are swine, but this one is an A-1 Jew."

Trying still to find, in the shadow of Himmler, some hint of Oskar's later enthusiasms, we encounter the Schindlers' next door neighbour, a liberal rabbi called Dr. Felix Kantor. Rabbi Kantor was a good disciple of Abraham Geiger, the German liberaliser of Judaism who claimed that it was no crime, in fact was praiseworthy to be a German as well as a Jew. Rabbi Kantor was no rigid village scholar. He dressed in the modern mode and spoke German in the house. He called his place of worship by the pluralist term, *Temple*, and not by that older name, *Synagogue*. His *Temple* was attended by Jewish doctors, engineers and proprietors of textile mills in Zwittau. When they travelled, they told other businessmen, "Our rabbi is Doctor Kantor – he writes articles not only for the Jewish journals in Prague and Brno, but for the dailies as well."

Rabbi Kantor's two sons went to the same school as the son of his German neighbour, Schindler. Perhaps both boys were bright enough to become two of the rare Jewish professors at the German University of Prague in later life. These close-cropped German-speaking prodigies raced in knee-length shorts around the summer garden of either house. Chasing the Schindler children and being chased. And Kantor, watching them flash in and out among the yew hedges, might have thought it was working as Geiger and Graetz and Lazarus and all those other nineteenth century German Jewish liberals had predicted. We lead enlightened lives, we are greeted by German neighbours – Herr Schindler will even make snide remarks about Czech statesmen in our hearing. We are secular scholars as well as sensible interpreters of the Talmud. We belong both to the twentieth century *and* to an ancient tribal race. We are neither offensive nor offended against.

Later, in the mid thirties, the rabbi would revise this happy estimation and make up his mind in the end that his sons could never buy off the National Socialists with a German language Ph.D., that there was no outcrop of twentieth century technology or secular scholarship behind which a Jew could find sanctuary, any more than there could ever be a species of rabbi acceptable to the new German legislators. In 1936 all the Kantors moved to Belgium. The Schindlers never heard of them again.

Race, blood and soil meant little to the adolescent Oskar. He was one of those boys for whom a motorbike is the most compelling model of the universe. And his father – a mechanic by temperament – seems to have encouraged the boy's zeal for red-hot machinery. In the last year of high school, Oskar was riding around Zwittau in a red 500cc Italian Galloni. A school friend, Erwin Tragatsch, watched with unspeakable desire as the red Galloni farted its way down the streets of the town and arrested the attention of promenaders on the square. Like the Kantor boys it too was a prodigy, not only the sole Galloni in Zwittau, not only the only 500cc Galloni in Moravia, but probably a unique machine in the whole of Czechoslovakia.

In the spring of 1928, the last months of Oskar's adolescence and prelude to a summer in which he would fall in love and decide to marry, he appeared in the town square on a 250cc Moto-Guzzi, of which there were only four others on the continent outside Italy, and those four owned by international racers – Giessler, Winkler, the Hungarian Joo and the Pole Kolaczkowski. There must have been townspeople who shook their heads and said that Herr Schindler was spoiling the boy.

But it would be Oskar's sweetest and most innocent summer. An apolitical boy in a skull-fitting leather helmet revving the engine of the Moto-Guzzi, racing against the works teams in the mountains of Moravia, son of a family for whom the height of political sophistication was to burn a candle for Franz Josef. Just around the pine-clad curve, an ambiguous marriage, an economic slump, seventeen years of fatal politics. But on the rider's face no knowledge, just the wind-pressed grimace of a high speed mover who – because he is new, because he is no pro, because all his records are as yet unset – can afford the price better than the older ones, the pros, the racers with times to beat.

His first contest was in May, the mountain race between Brno and Sobeslav. It was high-class competition, so that at least the expensive toy which prosperous Herr Hans Schindler had given his son was not rusting in a garage. He came third on his red Moto-Guzzi behind two Terrots which had been souped up with English Blackburne engines.

For his next challenge he moved farther from home to the Altwater circuit in the hills on the Saxon border. The German 250cc champion Walfried Winkler was there for the race and his veteran rival Kurt Henkelmann on a water-cooled DKW. All the Saxon hotshots – Horowitz, Kocher and Kliwar – had entered, the Terrot-Blackburnes were back and some Coventry Eagles. There were three Moto-Guzzis, including Oskar Schindler's, as well as the big guns from the 350cc class and a BMW 500cc team.

It was nearly Oskar's best and most unalloyed day. He kept within touch of the leaders during the first laps and watched to see what might happen. After an hour Winkler, Henkelmann and Oskar had left the Saxons behind, and the other Moto-Guzzis fell away with some mechanical flaw. In what Oskar believed was the second last lap he passed Winkler and must have felt, as palpably as the tar itself and the blur of pines, his imminent career as a works rider, and the travelling obsessed life it would permit him to lead.

In what then he assumed was the last lap, Oskar passed Henkelmann and both the DKWs, crossed the line and slowed. There must have been some deceptive sign from officials because the crowd also believed the race was over. By the time Oskar knew it wasn't, that he had made some amateur mistake, Walfried Winkler and Mita Vychodil had passed him, and even the exhausted Henkelmann was able to nudge him out of third place.

He was fêted home. But for a technicality, he'd beaten Europe's best.

Tragatsch surmised that the reasons Oskar's career as a motorbike racer ended there were economic. It was a fair guess. For that summer, after a courtship of only six weeks, he hurried into marriage with a farmer's daughter, and so fell out of favour with his father, who happened also to be his employer.

The girl he married was from a village to the east of Zwittau in the Hana Plain. She was convent-schooled and had the sort of reserve he admired in his mother. Her widowed father was no peasant, but a gentleman farmer. In the Thirty Years War, her Austrian ancestors had survived the recurrent campaigns and famines which had swept that fecund plain. Three centuries later, in a new era of risk, their daughter entered an ill-advised marriage with an unformed boy from Zwittau. Her father disapproved of it as much as Oskar's had.

Hans didn't like it because he could see that Oskar had married in the pattern of his, Hans's, own uneasy marriage. A sensual husband, a boy with a wild streak, looking too early in his life for some sort of peace from a nunlike, gracious, unsophisticated girl.

Oskar had met the girl at a party in Zwittau. Her name was Emilie and she was visiting friends from her village of Alt-Molstein. Oskar knew the place, having sold tractors in the area.

When the banns were announced in the parish churches of Zwittau, some people thought the couple so ill-matched that they began to look for motives other than love. It is possible that even that summer the Schindler machinery works were in trouble, for they were geared to the manufacture of steam-driven tractors of the type already going out of style with farmers. Oskar was pouring a large part of his wages back into the business, and now, with Emilie, came a dowry of half a million Reichsmarks, an honest and alleviating lump of capital in anyone's language. The suspicion of the gossips was unfounded, though, for that summer Oskar was infatuated. And since Emilie's father would never find grounds to believe the boy would settle down and be a good husband, only a fraction of the half million was ever paid.

Emilie herself was delighted to escape torpid Alt-Molstein by marrying handsome Oskar Schindler. Her father's closest friend had always been the dull parish priest, and Emilie had grown up serving the two of them tea and listening to their naïve opinions on politics and theology. If we are still seeking significant Jewish connections, there had been some in Emilie's girlhood – the village doctor who treated her grandmother; and Rita, granddaughter of the storekeeper Reif. During one of his visits to the farmhouse, the parish priest told Emilie's father that it was not good on principle for a Catholic child to have a particular friendship with a Jew. Out of the almost glandular stubbornness of girlhood, Emilie resisted the priest's edict. The friendship with Rita Reif would survive till the day in 1942 when local Nazi officials executed Rita in front of the store.

*

After the marriage, Oskar and Emilie settled in an apartment in Zwittau. For Oskar, the thirties must have seemed a mere epilogue to his glorious mistake on the Altwater circuit in the summer of 1928. He did his military service in the Czechoslovak army and, although it gave him the chance to drive a truck, found that he abhorred the military life – not on pacifist grounds but on grounds of discomfort. Home again in Zwittau, he neglected Emilie in the evenings, staying in cafés like a single man, talking to girls neither nunlike nor gracious. The family business went bankrupt in 1935, and that same year his father left Frau Louisa Schindler and took an apartment of his own. Oskar detested him for that and went and drank tea with his aunts and denounced Hans to them, and, even in cafés, made speeches about his father's treachery to a good woman. He seems to have been blind to the resemblance between his own faltering marriage and his parents' broken one.

Because of his good business contacts, his conviviality, his gifts of salesmanship, his ability to hold drink, he had got a job even in the midst of the Depression as sales manager of Moravian Electrotechnic. Its head office was located in the grim provincial capital of Brno and Oskar commuted between Brno and Zwittau. He liked the travelling life of course. It was half the destiny he'd promised himself when he'd passed Winkler on the Altwater circuit.

When his mother died he rushed back to Zwittau and stood beside his aunts, his sister Elfriede and his wife Emilie on one side of the grave, while treacherous Hans stood solitary – except, of course, for an unctuous parish priest – at the head of the coffin. Louisa's death had consecrated the enmity between Oskar and Hans. Oskar couldn't see – only the women could – that Hans and Oskar were in fact two brothers separated by the accident of paternity.

By the time of that funeral, Oskar was wearing the Hakenkreuz, the swastika emblem of Konrad Henlein's Sudeten German Party. Neither Emilie nor the aunts approved, but they did not take it too hard; it was something young Czech Germans were wearing that season. Only the Social Democrats and the Communists did not sport the badge or subscribe to Henlein's party, and, God knew, Oskar was neither a Communist nor a Social Democrat. Oskar was a salesman. All things being equal, when you went in to a German company manager wearing the badge, you got the order.

Yet, even with his order book wide open and his pencil flying, Oskar – in the months in 1938 before the German divisions entered the Sudeten – also felt a sense of a grand shift in history, and was seduced by the itch to be party to it.

Whatever his motives for running with Henlein, it seems that as soon as the divisions entered Moravia he suffered an instant disillusionment with National Socialism, as thorough and as quick as the disillusionment that had set in after marriage. He seems to have expected that the invading power would allow some brotherly Sudeten Republic to be founded. In a later statement he said he was appalled by the new régime's bullying of the Czech population, by the seizure of Czech property. His first documented acts of rebellion would occur very early in the coming world conflict, and there is no need to doubt that the Protectorate of Bohemia and Moravia, proclaimed by Hitler from Hradschin Castle in March 1939, surprised him with its early showing of tyranny.

Besides that, the two people whose opinions he most respected – Emilie, and his estranged father – were not taken in by the grand Teutonic hour and both claimed to know Hitler could not succeed. Their opinions were not sophisticated, but neither were Oskar's. Emilie believed, with a straightforward country fixity, that the man would be punished for making himself God. Herr Schindler senior, as his position was relayed to Oskar by an aunt, fell back on basic historical principles. Just outside Brno was the stretch of river where Napoleon had won the battle of Austerlitz. And what had befallen this triumphant Napoleon? He'd become a nobody, growing potatoes on an island in the mid-Atlantic. The same would happen to this fellow. Destiny, said Herr Schindler senior, was not a limitless rope. It was a piece of elastic. The harder you went forward, the more fiercely you were jerked back to your starting point. That was what life, marriage, and the economic slump had taught Herr Hans Schindler, failed husband and gentle worldling.

But perhaps his son Oskar was not yet a clear enemy of the new system. One evening that autumn, young Herr Schindler attended a party at a sanatorium in the hills outside Ostrava, up near the Polish border. The hostess was the sanatorium manager, a client and friend Oskar had acquired on the road. She introduced him to a thin and personable German, Eberhard Gebauer. They talked about business and what jumps France and Britain and Russia might make. Then they went off with a bottle to a spare room so that, as Gebauer suggested, they could talk more frankly. There Gebauer identified himself as an officer of Admiral Canaris's Abwehr intelligence and offered his new drinking companion the chance to work for the Foreign Section of the Abwehr. Oskar had accounts over the border in Poland, throughout its south and Upper Silesia. Would he undertake to supply the Abwehr with military intelligence from that region? Gebauer said he knew from his friend the hostess that Oskar was intelligent and convivial. With these gifts, he could make use not only of his own observations of industrial and military installations in the area but of those of any German Poles he might happen to recruit in restaurants, bars, or during business meetings.

Again, apologists for the young Oskar would say that he agreed to work for Canaris because, as an Abwehr agent, he was exempt from army service. That was a large part of the proposal's charm. But he must also have believed that a German advance into Poland would be appropriate. Like the slim officer sitting on the bed with him and plying the bottle, he must still have approved of the national business though he did not like the management. For Oskar, Gebauer may have possessed a moral allure, for he and his colleagues of the Abwehr considered themselves a decent Christian élite. Though it did not prevent their planning for a military intrusion into Poland, it gave them a contempt for Himmler and the SS, with whom, they believed high-

44

handedly, they were in competition for the control of Germany's soul.

Later, a very different intelligence-gathering body would find Oskar's reports to be full and praiseworthy. On his Polish journeys for the Abwehr, he showed a gift for charming news out of people, especially in a social context, at the dinner table, over cocktails. We do not know the exact nature or importance of what he found out for Gebauer and Canaris, but he came to like the city of Cracow very well, however, and to discover that though it was no grand industrial metropolis, it was an exquisite medieval town with a fringe of metal, textile and chemical plants.

As for the unmotorised Polish army, its secrets were rather too apparent.

2

In late October 1939 two German NCOs of a grenadier regiment entered the showroom of J. C. Buchheister & Company in Stradom Street, Cracow, and insisted on buying some expensive bolts of cloth to send home. The Jewish employee behind the counter, a yellow star sown to his breast, explained that Buchheister's did not sell direct to the public but supplied garment factories and retail outlets. The boys could not be dissuaded from taking the fabric. When it was time to settle their bill, they did it whimsically with a Bavarian banknote of 1858 and a piece of German army occupation scrip dated 1914. "Perfectly good currency," one of them told the Jewish book-keeper they were dealing with. They were healthy looking young men who had spent all spring and summer on manoeuvres, the early autumn yielding them an easy triumph and then all the latitude of conquerors in a sweet city. The book-keeper agreed to the transaction and got them out of the shop before ringing up a sale on the cash register.

Later in the day the young German accounts manager, an official appointed by the deftly named East Trust Agency to take over and run Jewish businesses, visited the showroom. He was one of two German officials assigned to Buchheister. The first was Sepp Aue, the supervisor, a middle-aged unambitious man, and the second this young world beater. The young man inspected the books and the till. He took out the valueless currency. What did it mean, this comic opera money?

When the Jewish book-keeper told his story, the accounts manager accused him of substituting the antique notes for hard zloty. Later in the day, in Buchheister's warehouse upstairs, the world beater reported to Sepp Aue and said they should call in the Schutzpolizei.

Herr Aue and the young accountant both knew that such an act would lead to the imprisonment of the book-keeper in the jail in Montelupich Street. The accountant thought that this would set an excellent example for Buchheister's remaining Jewish staff. But the idea distressed Aue, who had a secret liability of his own, his grandmother having been Jewish, though no one had yet found out.

Aue sent an office boy with a message to the company's original accountant, a Polish Jew called Itzhak Stern who was at home with influenza. Aue was something of a political appointment and had little accounting experience. Now he wanted Stern to come into the office and look into the impasse over the bolts of linen. He had just sent the message off to Stern's house in Podgórze when his secretary came into the office and announced that a Herr Oskar Schindler was waiting outside, claiming to have an appointment. Aue went into the outer room and saw a tall young man, placid as a large dog, tranquilly smoking. The two had met at a party the night before. Oskar had been there with a Sudeten German girl, Ingrid, Treuhänder – supervisor – of a Jewish hardware company called Cs', just as Aue was Treuhänder of Buchheister's. They were a glamorous couple, Oskar and this Ingrid, frankly in love, stylish, with lots of friends in the Abwehr.

Herr Schindler was looking for a career in Cracow. Textiles? Aue had suggested. It isn't just uniforms. The Polish domestic market itself is large enough and inflated enough to support us all. You're welcome to look Buchheister's over, he'd urged big Oskar, not knowing how he might regret this tipsy camaraderie at 2 p.m. the next day.

Schindler could see that Herr Aue had possible second thoughts about his invitation. If it's not convenient, Herr Treuhänder, Oskar suggested.

Herr Aue said not at all and took Schindler through the warehouse and across the yard to the spinning division, where great rolls of golden fabric were running off the machines. Schindler asked if the Treuhänder had had trouble with the Poles. No, said Sepp, they're cooperative.

47

Stunned if anything. After all, it's not exactly a munitions factory.

Herr Oskar Schindler had so much the air of a man with good connections that Aue could not resist the temptation to test the point. Did Oskar know the people at the Main Armaments Board? Did he know General Julius Schindler, for example. Perhaps General Schindler was a relative?

That makes no difference, said Herr Schindler disarmingly. (In fact General Schindler was no relative of his.) The General wasn't such a bad fellow, compared to some, said Oskar.

Aue agreed. But he himself would never dine with General Schindler or meet him for drinks, that was the difference.

They returned to the office, encountering on the way Itzhak Stern, Buchheister's Jewish accountant, waiting on a chair provided by Aue's secretary, plying a handkerchief and coughing cruelly. He stood up, joined his hands one on top of the other in front of his chest and with immense eyes watched both conquerors approach, pass him and enter the office. There Aue offered Schindler a drink and then, excusing himself, left Oskar by the fire and went out to interview Stern.

He was so thin, with a scholarly dryness to him; he had the manners of a Talmudic scholar but also of a European intellectual. Aue told him the story of the book-keeper and the NCOs and the assumptions the young German accountant had made. He produced from the safe the currency, the 1858 Bavarian, the 1914 occupation. "I thought you might have instituted an accounting procedure to deal with just this situation," said Aue. "It must be happening a great deal in Cracow just now."

Itzhak Stern took the notes and studied them. He had developed a procedure, he told the Herr Treuhänder. Without a smile or a wink, he moved to the open fire at the end of the room and dropped both notes into it, then coughed and worked at the coals with a poker.

"I write these transactions off to profit and loss, under *free samples*," he said. There had been a lot of free samples since September.

Aue liked Stern's dry, effective style with the legal evidence. He began to laugh, seeing in the accountant's lean features the complexities of Cracow itself, the parochial canniness of a small city. Only a local knew the ropes. In the inner office Herr Schindler sat in need of local information.

Aue led Stern through into the manager's office to meet Herr Schindler. The tall, heavy German was standing staring at the fire, an unstoppered hip flask held absently in one hand. The first thing Itzhak Stern thought was, This isn't a manageable German. Aue wore the badge of his Führer, a miniature Hakenkreuz, as negligently as a man might wear the badge of a cycling club. But big Schindler's coin-sized emblem took the light from the fire in its black enamel. It, and the young man's general affluence, were all the more the symbols of Stern's autumn griefs as a Polish Jew with a cold.

Aue made the introductions. According to the edict already issued by Governor Frank, Stern made his statement, "I have to tell you, sir, that I am a Jew."

"Well," Herr Schindler growled at him, "I'm a German. So there we are!"

All very well, Stern almost intoned privately behind his sodden handkerchief. In that case, lift the edict.

For, even now, in only the seventh week of the new order in Poland, Itzhak Stern was a man under not one edict but already under many. Hans Frank, Governor General of Poland, had already initiated and signed six restrictive edicts, leaving others to his district governor, SS Gruppenführer (Major General) Dr. Wächter, to implement. Stern, besides declaring his origins, had also to carry a distinctive registration card marked by a yellow stripe. The Orders-in-Council forbidding kosher preparation of meats and commanding forced labour for Jews were three weeks old when Stern stood coughing in Schindler's presence. And Stern's official ration as an Untermensch (subhuman) was little more than half that of a non-Jewish Pole, the latter being tainted by Untermenschen-ship himself.

Finally, by an edict of November 8th, a general registration of all Cracovian Jews was required to be completed by November 24th.

Stern with his calm and abstract cast of thought knew that the edicts would continue, would circumscribe his living and breathing further still. Most Cracow Jews expected such a rash of edicts. There would be some disruption of life — Jews from the shtetls (villages inhabited almost exclusively by Jews) being brought to town to shovel coal, intellectuals being sent into the countryside to hoe beet. There would also be sporadic slaughters for a time, like the one over at Tursk where an SS artillery unit had kept people working on a bridge all day and then herded them into the village synagogue in the evening and shot them. There would always be such intermittent instances. But the situations would settle, the race would survive by petitioning, by buying off the authorities — it was the old method, it had been working since the Roman Empire, it would work again. In the end the civil authorities needed Jews, especially in a nation where they were one in every eleven.

Stern, however, wasn't one of the sanguine ones. He didn't presume the legislation would soon achieve a plateau of negotiable severity. For these were the worst of times. So, though he did not know that the coming fire would be different in substance as well as degree, he was already resentful enough for the future to think, All very well for you, Herr Schindler, to make generous little gestures of equality.

This man, said Aue, introducing Stern, was Buchheister's righthand man. He had good connections in the business community here in Cracow.

It was not Stern's place to argue with Aue about that. Even so, he wondered if the Treuhänder wasn't gilding the lily for the distinguished visitor.

Aue excused himself.

Left alone with Stern, Schindler murmured that he'd be grateful if the accountant could tell him what he knew about some of the local businesses. Testing Oskar, Stern suggested that perhaps Herr Schindler should speak to the officials of the Trust Agency.

"They're thieves," said Herr Schindler genially. "They're bureaucrats too. I would like some latitude." He shrugged.

"I am a capitalist by temperament and I don't like being regulated."

So Stern and the self-declared capitalist began to talk. And Stern was quite a source, he seemed to have friends or relatives in every factory in Cracow – textiles, garments, confectionery, joinery, metalwork. Herr Schindler was impressed and took an envelope from the breast pocket of his suit. "Do you know a company called Rekord?" he asked.

Itzhak Stern did. It was a bankrupt estate, he said. It had made enamelware. Since it had gone bankrupt some of the metal press machinery had been confiscated and now it was largely a shell, producing – under the management of one of the former owners' relatives – a fraction of its capacity. His own brother, said Stern, represented a Swiss company who were major creditors of Rekord. Stern knew that it was permitted to reveal a small degree of fraternal pride and then to make a noise of mild disgust. "The place was very badly managed," said Stern.

Oskar Schindler dropped the envelope on to Stern's lap. "This is their balance sheet. Tell me what you think."

Itzhak said that Herr Schindler should of course ask others as well as himself. Of course, Oskar told him. But I would value your opinion.

Stern read the balance sheets quickly, then, after some three minutes of study, felt all at once the strange silence of the office and looked up, finding Herr Oskar Schindler's eyes full on him.

There was, of course, in men like Stern an ancestral gift for sniffing out the just Goy, who could be used as a buffer or a partial refuge against the savageries of the others. It was a sense for where a safe house might be, a zone of potential shelter. And from now on the possibility of Herr Schindler as sanctuary would colour the conversation as might a half glimpsed, intangible sexual promise colour the talk between a man and a woman at a party. It was a suggestion of which Stern was more aware than Schindler, and nothing explicit would be said for fear of damaging the tender connection.

"It's a perfectly good business," said Stern. "You could

speak to my brother. And, of course, now there's the possibility of military contracts . . ."

"Exactly," murmured Herr Schindler.

For almost instantly after the fall of Cracow, even before Warsaw's siege ended, an Armaments Inspectorate had been set up in the Government General of Poland, its mandate being to enter into contracts with suitable manufacturers for the supply of army equipment. In a place like Rekord, mess-kits and field-kitchenware could be turned out. The Armaments Inspectorate was headed, Stern knew, by a Major General Julius Schindler of the Wehrmacht. Was the General a relative of Herr Oskar Schindler's? Stern asked. No, I'm afraid not, said Schindler, but as if he wanted Stern to keep his non-relationship a secret.

In any case, said Stern, even the skeleton production at Rekord was grossing more than half a million zloty a year, and new metal pressing plant and furnaces could be acquired relatively easily. It depended on Herr Schindler's access to credit.

Enamelware, said Herr Schindler, was closer to his line than textiles. His background was in farm machinery and he understood steam presses and so forth.

It did not any longer occur to Stern to ask why an elegant German entrepreneur wished to talk to him about business options. Meetings like this one had occurred throughout the history of his tribe, and the normal exchanges of business did not quite explain them. He talked on at some length, explaining how the Commercial Court would set the fee for the leasing of the bankrupt estate. Leasing with an option to buy – it was better than being a Treuhänder. As a Treuhänder, you were completely under the control of the Economics Ministry.

Stern lowered his voice then and risked saying it. "You will find you are restricted in the people you'll be allowed to employ . . ."

Schindler was amused. "How do you know all this? About ultimate intentions?"

"I read it in a copy of the *Berliner Tagblatt*. A Jew is still permitted to read German newspapers."

Schindler continued to laugh, reached out a hand and let it fall on Stern's shoulder. "Is that so?" he asked.

In fact, Stern knew these things because Aue had received a long directive from Reich Secretary of State Eberhard von Jagwitz of the Economics Ministry, outlining the policies to be adopted in Aryanising businesses. Aue had left it to Stern to make a digest of the document. Von Jagwitz had indicated more in sadness than in anger that there would be pressure from other government and party agencies, such as Heydrich's RHSA, the Reich Security Main Office, to Aryanise not just the ownership of companies, but also the management and workforce. The sooner Treuhänders filtered out the skilled Jewish employees the better – always, of course, bearing in mind the maintenance of production at an acceptable level.

At last Herr Schindler put the accounts of Rekord back in his breast pocket, stood up and led Itzhak Stern out into the main office. They stood there for a time, among the typists and clerks, growing philosophical, as Oskar liked to do. It was here that Oskar brought up the matter of Christianity having its base in Judaism, a subject which for some reason, perhaps even because of his boyhood friendship with the Kantors in Zwittau, exercised his mind. Stern spoke softly, at length, learnedly. He had published articles in journals of comparative religion. Oskar, who wrongly fancied himself a philosopher, had found an expert. The scholar, Stern, whom some thought a pedant, found Oskar's understanding shallow, a mind genial by nature but without much conceptual deftness. Not that Itzhak Stern was about to complain. An ill-assorted friendship was firmly established. So that Stern found himself drawing an analogy, as Oskar's own father had, from previous empires and giving his reasons why Adolf Hitler could not succeed.

The opinion slipped out before Stern could withdraw it. The other Jews in the office bowed their heads and burrowed their eyes into worksheets. Herr Schindler did not seem to be disturbed.

Towards the end of their talk, Oskar did say something that had novelty. In times like these, he said, it must be hard for the churches to go on telling people that their Heavenly Father cared about the death of even a single sparrow. He'd hate to be a priest, Herr Schindler said, in an era like this, when life did not have the value of a packet of cigarettes. Stern agreed but suggested, in the spirit of the discussion, that the Biblical reference Herr Schindler had made could be summed up by a Talmudic verse which said that he who saves the life of one man, saves the entire world.

"Of course, of course," said Oskar Schindler. Rightly or wrongly, Itzhak always believed that it was then that he had dropped the right stone in the well, that the crucial dictum had been deposited.

3

There is another Cracow Jew who gives an account of meeting Schindler that autumn of 1939 as well as coming close to killing him. This man's name was Leopold (Poldek) Pfefferberg. He had been a lieutenant, a company commander in the Polish army during the recent tragic campaign. After suffering a leg wound during the battle for the river San, he'd limped around the Polish hospital in Przemysl, helping with the other casualties. He was no doctor but had graduated from the Jagiellonian University of Cracow with a degree in physical education and so had some knowledge of anatomy. He was resilient, he was self-confident, twenty-seven years old and built like a wedge.

With some hundreds of other captured Polish officers from Przemysl, Pfefferberg was on his way to Germany when his train drew into his home city of Cracow and the prisoners were herded into the first-class waiting room until new transport could be provided. His home was ten blocks away. To a practical young man, it seemed outrageous that he could not go out into Pawia Street and catch a Number 1 tram home. The bucolic looking Wehrmacht guard at the door seemed a provocation.

Pfefferberg had in his breast pocket a document signed by the German hospital authority of Przemysl indicating that he was free to move about the city with ambulance details tending to the wounded of both armies. It was spectacularly formal, stamped and signed. He took it out now and, going up to the guard, thrust it at him.

"Can you read German?" Pfefferberg demanded.

This sort of ploy had to be done right of course. You had to be young, you had to be persuasive, you had to have retained, undiminished by summary defeat, a confident bearing of a particularly Polish nature, something disseminated by its plentiful aristocrats to the Polish officer corps, even to those rare members of it who were Jewish.

The man had blinked. Of course I can read German, he said. But after he'd taken the document he held it like a man who couldn't read at all – held it like a slice of bread. Pfefferberg explained in German how the document declared his right to go out and attend to the ill. All the guard could see was a proliferation of official stamps. It looked like quite a document to him. With a wave of the head, he indicated the door.

Pfefferberg was the only passenger on the Number 1 tram that morning. It was not even six o'clock yet. The conductor took his fare without concern, for in the city there were still many Polish troops not yet processed by the Wehrmacht. The officers had to register, that was all.

The tram swung round the Barbakan, through the gate in the ancient wall, down Floriańska to the church of St. Mary, across the central square and so within five minutes into Grodzka Street. Near his parents' apartment at Number 48, repeating a childish trick, he jumped from the moving vehicle before the air brakes went on, letting the momentum of the jump, combined with that of the tram, bring him up with a soft thud against the door jamb of his parents' building.

After his escape, he had lived not too uncomfortably in the apartments of friends, visiting Grodzka 48 now and then. The Jewish schools opened briefly – they would be closed again within six weeks – and he even returned to his job. He was sure the Gestapo would take some time to come looking for him, and so he applied for ration papers. He began to dispose of jewellery – as an agent and in his own right – on the black market which operated in Cracow's central square, in the arcades of the Sukiennice and beneath the two unequal spires of St. Mary's church. Trade was brisk, even among the Poles themselves but more so for the Polish Jews. Their ration books, full of precancelled coupons, entitled them to only two-thirds of the meat and half of the butter allowance that went to Aryan citizens, while *all* the cocoa and rice coupons were cancelled. And so the black market which had operated through centuries of occupation and the few decades of Polish autonomy became the food and income source and the readiest means of resistance for respectable bourgeois citizens, especially those who like Professor Leopold Pfefferberg were streetwise.

He presumed that he would, in the near future, travel over the ski routes around Zakopane in the Tatras, across Slovakia's slender neck into Hungary or Rumania. He was equipped for the journey; he had been a member of the Polish national ski squad. On one of the high shelves of the porcelain stove in his mother's apartment he kept an elegant little .22 pistol, armoury both for the proposed escape and in case he was ever trapped inside the apartment by the Gestapo.

It was with this pearlhandled semi-toy, that Pfefferberg would come close to killing Herr Schindler one day in November. Schindler, double-breasted suit, party badge at the lapel, had decided to call on Mrs. Mina Pfefferberg, Poldek's mother, to offer her a commission. He had been given a fine modern apartment in Straszewskiego Street by the Reich housing authorities. It had previously been the property of a Jewish family by the name of Nussbaum. These allocations of apartments were carried out without any compensation to the previous occupier. On the day Oskar came calling, Mrs. Mina Pfefferberg was worried that it would happen to her apartment in Grodzka.

A number of Schindler's friends would claim later – though it is not possible to prove it – that Oskar had gone looking for the dispossessed family at their lodgings in Podgórze and had given them a sum close to fifty thousand zloty in compensation. With this sum, it is said, the Nussbaums bought themselves an escape to Yugoslavia. And however good a light this rumoured action places Oskar in, it has to be said that it is probable. Fifty thousand zloty signified substantial dissent, but there would be other similar acts of dissent by Oskar before Christmas. Some friends would in fact come to say that generosity was a disease in

Oskar, a frantic thing, one of his passions. He would tip taxi drivers twice the fare on the meter. This has to be said, too – that he thought the Reich housing authorities were unjust and told Stern so, not when the régime got in trouble, but even in that, its sweetest autumn.

In any case, Mrs. Pfefferberg had no idea what the tall, well tailored German was doing at her door. He could have been there to ask after her son, who happened to be in the kitchen just then. He could have been there to commandeer her apartment, and her decorating business, and her antiques, and her French tapestry.

In fact by the December feast of *Hanukkah* the German police would, on the orders of the housing office, get around to the Pfefferbergs, arriving at their door and then ordering them, shivering in the cold, downstairs on to the pavement of Grodzka. When Mrs. Pfefferberg asked to go back for a coat she would be refused, when Mr. Pfefferberg made for a bureau to fetch an ancestral gold watch he would be punched on the jaw. "I have witnessed terrible things in the past," Hermann Göring had said, "little chauffeurs and Gauleiters have profited so much from these transactions that they now have about half a million." The effect of such easy pickings as Mr. Pfefferberg's gold watch on the moral fibre of the Party might distress Göring. But in Poland that year, it was the style of the Gestapo to be unaccountable for the contents of apartments.

When Herr Schindler first came to the Pfefferbergs' second-floor apartment, however, the family were still in tenuous occupation.

Mrs. Pfefferberg and her more or less on-the-run son were talking among the samples and bolts of fabric and wall-paper when Herr Schindler knocked. Leopold was not too alarmed. There were two front entrances to the flat – the business door and the kitchen door faced each other across a landing. Leopold retreated to the kitchen and looked through the crack in the door at the visitor. He saw the formidable size of the man, the fashionable cut of his suit. He returned to his mother in the living room. He had the feeling, he said, that the man was Gestapo. When you let

58

him in at the office door, I can always slip out through the back.

Mrs. Mina Pfefferberg was trembling. She opened the office door. She was of course listening for sounds along the corridor.

Pfefferberg had in fact picked up the pistol and put it in his belt and intended to wed the sound of his exit to the sound of Herr Schindler's entry. But it seemed folly to go without knowing what the German official wanted. There was a chance that the man would have to be killed, and then there would need to be some concerted family flight into Rumania.

If the magnetic drift to the event had drawn Pfefferberg to fire, the death, the flight, the reprisals would have been considered unexceptional and appropriate to the history of the month. Herr Schindler would have been briefly mourned and summarily avenged. And this would have been, of course, the brisk ending to all Oskar's potentialities. And back in Zwittau they would have said, "Was it someone's husband?"

The voice surprised the Pfefferbergs. It was calmly modulated, suited to the doing of business, even to the asking of favours. In six weeks they had got used to the tone of decree and summary expropriation. This man sounded fraternal. That was somehow worse. But it intrigued you, too.

Pfefferberg had slipped through from the kitchen and concealed himself behind the double doors of the dining room. He could see a sliver of the German. You're Mrs. Pfefferberg? the German asked. You were recommended to me by Herr Nussbaum. I have just taken over an apartment in Straszewskiego Street and I would like to have it redecorated.

Mina Pfefferberg kept the man at the door. She spoke so incoherently that the son took pity on her and appeared in the doorway, his jacket buttoned up over the weapon. He asked the visitor in and at the same time whispered reassurances in Polish to his mother.

Now Oskar Schindler gave his name. There was some measuring up, for Schindler could tell that the young man had appeared to perform an act of primal protection. Pfefferberg was a Slavic blockhouse of a figure. Schindler showed his respect by talking now through the son as through an interpreter.

"My wife is coming up from Czechoslovakia," he said, "and I'd like the place redone closer to the sort of thing she goes for." He said the Nussbaums had maintained the place excellently, but they went in for rather heavy drapes and sombre colours. Frau Schindler's tastes were more lively — a little French, a little Swedish.

Mrs. Pfefferberg had recovered enough to say that she didn't know — it was a busy time with Christmas coming up. Leopold could feel an instinctive resistance in her to developing a German clientele, but the Germans might be the only race this season with enough confidence in the future to go in for interior design. And Mrs. Pfefferberg needed a fat contract — her husband had been removed from his job and worked now for a pittance in the housing office of the Gemeinde, the Jewish self-help and welfare bureau.

Within two minutes the men were chatting like friends. The pistol in Pfefferberg's belt had now been relegated to the status of armament for some future remote emergency. There was no doubt that Mrs. Pfefferberg was going to do the Schindler apartment, no expense spared, and when that was settled, Schindler mentioned that Leopold Pfefferberg might like to come around to the apartment to discuss other business. "There is the possibility that you can advise me on acquiring local merchandise," Herr Schindler said. "For example, your very elegant blue shirt. I don't know where to begin to look for that kind of thing myself." His ingenuousness was a ploy, but Pfefferberg appreciated it. "The stores, as you know, are empty," murmured Oskar like a hint.

Leopold Pfefferberg was the sort of young man who survived by raising the stakes. "Herr Schindler, these shirts are extremely expensive, I hope you understand. They cost twenty-five zloty each."

He had multiplied the price by five. There was all at once an amused knowingness in Herr Schindler — not enough though to imperil the tenuous friendship or remind Pfefferberg that he was armed.

"I could probably get you some," said Leopold Pfefferberg, "if you give me your size. But I'm afraid my contacts will require money in advance."

Herr Schindler, still wearing that knowingness in the corners of the mouth and the eyes, took out his wallet and handed Pfefferberg two hundred Reichsmarks. The sum was flamboyantly too much and, even at Pfefferberg's inflated price, would have bought shirts for a dozen tycoons. But Pfefferberg knew the game and did not blink. "You must give me your measurements," he said.

A week later, Pfefferberg brought a dozen silk shirts to Schindler's apartment on Straszewskiego Street. There was a pretty German woman in the apartment who was introduced to Pfefferberg as Treuhänder of a Cracow hardware business. Then, one evening, Pfefferberg saw Oskar in the company of a blonde and large-eyed Polish beauty. If there was a Frau Schindler, she did not appear, even after Mrs. Pfefferberg had transformed the place. Pfefferberg himself became one of Schindler's most regular connections to that market in luxuries – silk, furnishings, jewellery – which flourished in the ancient town of Cracow.

4

The next time Itzhak Stern met Oskar Schindler was on a morning in early December. Schindler's application to the Polish Commercial Court of Cracow had already been filed, yet Oskar had the leisure to visit the offices of Buchheister and, after conferring with Aue, to stand near Stern's desk in the outer office, clap his hands, and announce in a voice which sounded already tipsy, "Tomorrow, it's going to start. Józefa and Izaaka Streets are going to know all about it!"

There *were* in Kazimierz a Józefa Street and an Izaaka Street. There were in every ghetto, and Kazimierz was the site of the old ghetto of Cracow, once an island ceded to the Jewish community by Kazimier the Great, now a neat suburb nestled in an elbow of the Vistula River.

Herr Schindler bent over Stern, and Stern felt his brandy-warm breath and considered this question: Did Herr Schindler know something would happen in Józefa Street and Izaaka Street, Kazimierz? Or was he just brandishing the names?

In any case, Stern suffered a nauseating sense of disappointment. Herr Schindler was whistling up a pogrom, boasting inexactly about it, as if to put Stern in his place.

It was December 3rd. When Oskar said 'tomorrow', Stern presumed he was using the term not in the sense of December 4th, but in the terms in which drunks and prophets always used it, as something that either would, or damn well should, happen soon. Only a few of those who heard, or heard about, Herr Schindler's half-boozed warning took it literally. Some packed an overnight bag and moved their families across the river to Podgórze.

As for Oskar, he felt he had passed on hard news at some risk. He had got it from at least two sources, new friends of his. One, a police officer attached to SS Oberführer Scherner's staff, was a sergeant, Wachtmeister Herman Toffel. The other, Dieter Reeder, belonged to the staff of SD chief Czurda. Both these contacts were characteristic of the sympathetic officers Oskar always managed to sniff out.

He was never good though at explaining his motives for speaking to Stern that December. He would say later that in the period of the German occupation of Bohemia and Moravia he had seen enough seizure of Jewish and Czech property, and forcible removal of Jews and Czechs from those Sudeten areas considered German, to cure him of any zeal for the new order. His leaking of the news to Stern, far more than the unconfirmed Nussbaum story, goes some way towards proving his case.

He must have hoped also, as did the Jews of Cracow, that after its initial fury the régime would relax and let people breathe. If the SS raids and incursions of the next few months could be mitigated by the leaking of advance information, then perhaps sanity would reassert itself in the spring. After all, both Oskar and the Jews told themselves, the Germans were a civilised nation.

The SS invasion of Kazimierz would, however, arouse in Oskar a fundamental disgust; not yet one which would impinge too visibly on the level at which he made his money, entertained women or dined with friends, but one that would, the clearer the intentions of the reigning power became, lead, obsess, imperil and exalt him. The operation was meant in part to be a raid for jewellery and furs. There'd be some evictions from houses and apartments in the better off borderland between Cracow and Kazimierz. But apart from these practical results, that first Aktion was also meant to serve a form of notice to the dismayed people of the old Jewish quarter. For that purpose, Reeder told Oskar, a small detachment of Einsatzgruppe men would drive down

Stradom and into Kazimierz in the same trucks as the boys of the local SS and the Field Police.

Six Einsatzgruppen had come to Poland with the invading army. Their name had subtle meanings. 'Special duty groups' is a close translation. But the amorphous word 'Einsatz' had another shade of meaning, to do with challenge, with picking up a gauntlet, with knightliness. These squads were recruited from Heydrich's Sicherheitsdienst (hence, SD). They already knew their mandate was broad. Their supreme leader had six weeks ago told General Keitel that "in the Government General of Poland there will have to be a tough struggle for national existence which will permit of no legal restraints." In the lofty rhetoric of their leaders, as the Einsatz soldiers knew, a struggle for national existence meant racial warfare, just as Einsatz itself, Special Chivalrous Duty, meant the hot barrel of a gun.

The Einsatz squad destined for action in Kazimierz that evening were an élite. They would leave to the piece-workers of the Cracow SS the task of searching the tenements for diamond rings and fur-trimmed coats. They themselves would take part in some more radically symbolic activity to do with the very instruments of Jewish culture, that is with the ancient synagogues of Cracow.

They had for some weeks been waiting to exercise Einsatz, as had the local SS Sonderkommandos (or Special Squads) and the Security Police of SD chief Czurda, also assigned to this first Cracow Aktion. The army had negotiated with Heydrich and the higher police chiefs a stay of operations until Poland passed from military to civil rule. This passage of authority had now taken place, and throughout the country the Knights of Einsatz and the Sonderkommandos were unleashed to advance with an appropriate sense of racial history and professional detachment into the old Judaic ghettos.

At the end of the street in which stood Oskar's apartment rose the fortified rock outcrop of Wawel from which Hans Frank ruled. And if Oskar's Polish future is to be understood, there is a need to look at the linkage between Frank and the young field operatives of the SS and SD, and then between Frank and the Jews of Cracow.

In the first place, Hans Frank had no direct kingship over these boys moving into Kazimierz. Heinrich Himmler's police forces, wherever they worked, would always be their own lawmakers. As well as resenting their independent power, Frank also disagreed with them on practical grounds. He had as refined an abomination of the Jewish population as anyone in the Party and found the sweet city of Cracow intolerable because of its manifold Jews. In past weeks he'd complained when the authorities tried to use the Government General, and especially Cracow with its railway junction, as a dumping ground for Jews from the cities of the Wartheland, from Lódź and Poznan. But he did not believe the Einsatzgruppen or the Sonderkommandos could really make a dent in the problem using current methods. It was Frank's belief, shared with Himmler in some stages of Heini's mental vagaries, that there should be a single vast concentration camp for Jews, that it should at least be the city of Lublin and the surrounding countryside, or even more desirably, the island of Madagascar. The Poles themselves had always believed in Madagascar. In 1937 the Polish government had sent a commission to study that high-spined island so far from the coasts of their European sensibilities. The French Colonial Office, to which Madagascar belonged, was willing to make a deal, government to government, on such a resettlement; for a Madagascar crowded with Europe's Jews would make a grand export market. The South African Defence Minister, Oswald Pirow, had acted for a time as negotiator between Hitler and France in the matter of the island. Therefore Madagascar, as a solution, had an honourable pedigree. Hans Frank had his money on it and not on the Einsatzgruppen. For their sporadic raids and massacres could not cut down the sub-human population of Eastern Europe. During the time of the campaign around Warsaw, the Einsatzgruppen had strung up Jews in the synagogues of Silesia, ruptured their systems with water torture, raided their homes on Sabbath evenings or feast days, cut off their prayer locks, set their prayer shawls alight, stood them against a wall. It had barely counted. There were many indications from history, Frank proposed, that threatened races generally outbred the genocides. The phallus was faster than the gun.

What no one knew – neither the parties to the debate, the well-educated Einsatzgruppen boys in the back of one truck, the not-so-refined SS boys in the back of another, the evening worshippers in the synagogues, nor Herr Oskar Schindler on his way home to Straszewskiego Street to dress for dinner – what none of them knew and many a Party planner scarcely hoped for was that a technological answer would be found, that a disinfectant chemical compound named Zyklon B would supplant Madagascar as the solution.

There had been an incident involving Hitler's pet actress and director, Leni Riefenstahl. She had come to Łódź with a roving camera crew soon after the city fell and seen a line of Jews, visible Jews, the prayer-locked variety, executed with automatic weapons. She had gone straight to the Führer who was staying at Southern Army headquarters and made a scene. That was it – the logistics, the weight of numbers, the considerations of public relations, they made the Einsatz boys look silly. But Madagascar, too, would look ridiculous once means were discovered to make substantial inroads into the subhuman population of central Europe at fixed sites with adequate disposal facilities which no fashionable moviemaker was likely to stumble upon.

As Oskar had forewarned Stern in the front office of Buchheister's, the SS carried economic warfare from door to door in Jakoba and Izaaka and Józefa. They broke into apartments, dragged out the contents of cupboards, smashed the locks on desks and dressers. They took valuables off fingers and throats and out of watch-fobs. A girl who would not give up her fur coat had her arm broken, a boy from Ciemna Street who wanted to keep his skis was shot.

Some of those whose goods were taken – unaware that the SS were operating outside legal restraint – would complain at police stations tomorrow. Somewhere, history told them, was a senior officer with a little integrity who would be embarrassed and might even discipline some of these fellows. There would have to be an enquiry into the business of the boy in Ciemna and the wife whose nose was broken with a baton.

While the SS were working the apartment buildings, the Einsatz squad moved against the fourteenth century synagogue of Stara Bozníca. As they expected, they found at prayer there a congregation of traditional Jews with beards and sidelocks and prayer shawls. They collected a number of the less orthodox from surrounding apartments and drove them in as well, as if they wanted to measure the reaction of one group to the other.

Among those pushed across the threshold of Stara Boznica was the gangster Max Redlicht, who would not otherwise have entered an ancient temple or been invited to do so.

They stood in front of the Ark, these two poles of the same tribe who would on a normal day have found each other's company offensive. An Einsatz NCO opened the Ark and took out the parchment Torah scroll. The disparate congregation on the synagogue floor were to file past and spit at it. There was to be no faking – the spittle was to be visible on the calligraphy.

The traditional people were more rational about it than those others, the agnostics, the liberals, the self-styled Europeans. It was apparent to the Einsatz men that the modern ones baulked in front of the scroll and even tried to engage your eye as if to say, Come on, we're all too sophisticated for this nonsense. The SD men had been told in their training that the European character of liberal Jews was a tissue-thin façade, and in Stara Boznica the backsliding reluctance of the ones who wore short haircuts and contemporary clothes went to prove it.

Everyone spat in the end except Max Redlicht. The Einsatzgruppe men may have seen that this was a test worth their time, to make a man who visibly does not believe, renounce with spittle a book which he sees with his intellect to be antique tribal drivel but which his blood tells him is still sacred. Could a Jew be retrieved from the persuasions of his ridiculous blood? Could he think as clearly as Kant? That was the test.

Redlicht would not pass it. He made a little speech. "I've done a lot. But I won't do that." They shot him first, and then shot the rest anyway and set fire to the place, making a shell of the oldest of all Polish synagogues.

5

Victoria Klonowska, a Polish secretary, was the beauty of Oskar's front office, and he immediately began a long affair with her. Ingrid, his German mistress, must have known, as surely as Emilie Schindler knew about Ingrid. For Oskar would never be a surreptitious lover. He had a childlike sexual frankness. It wasn't that he boasted. It was that he never saw any need to lie, to creep into hotels by the back stairs, to knock furtively on any girl's door in the small hours. Since Oskar would not seriously try to tell his women lies, their options were reduced; traditional lovers' arguments were not possible.

Blonde hair piled up, her pretty foxy face vividly made up, Victoria Klonowska looked like one of those good-time girls to whom the inconveniences of history are a temporary intrusion into the real business of life. This autumn of simple clothes, Klonowska was luxuriant in her jacket, frilled blouse and flat-bellied skirt. Yet she was hard-headed, efficient, and adroit. She was a nationalist, too, in the robust Polish style. She would eventually negotiate with the German dignitaries for her Sudeten lover's release from SS institutions. But for the moment Oskar had a less chancy job for her.

He mentioned that he would like to find a good bar or cabaret in Cracow where he could take friends. Not *contacts*, not senior people from the Armaments Inspectorate. Genuine friends. Somewhere lively where middle-aged officials would not turn up.

Did Klonowska know of such a place?

She found an excellent jazz cellar in the narrow streets north of the Rynek, the city square. It was a place that had always been popular with the students and younger staff of the university, but Victoria herself had never been there before. The sort of middle-aged man who had pursued her in peacetime would never want to go to a place like that. If you wished to, it was possible to rent an alcove and so hold private parties behind a curtain, under cover of the Afro-pulsations of the band. For finding this music club, Oskar nicknamed Klonowska 'Columbus'. The Party line on jazz was that it not only was artistically decadent but expressed an African, a subhuman animality. The Ump-pa-pa of Viennese waltzes was the preferred beat of the SS and of Party officials, and they scrupulously avoided jazz dives.

Round about Christmas in 1939, Oskar got together a party at the club for a number of his friends. Like any instinctive cultivator of contacts, he would never have any trouble drinking with men he didn't like. But that night the guests were men he *did*. Additionally, of course, they were all useful, junior but not uninfluential members of sundry organs of the occupation; and all of them more or less double exiles – not only were they away from home but, home or abroad, they were all variously uneasy under the régime.

There was, for example, a young German surveyor from the Government General's Division of the Interior. He had marked out the boundaries of Oskar's enamel factory in Zablocie. At the back of Oskar's works, Deutsche Email Fabrik, stood a vacant area on which two other plants abutted, a box factory and a radiator works. Schindler had been delighted to find that most of the waste area belonged, according to the surveyor, to DEF. Visions of economic expansion swam before him. The surveyor had, of course, been invited because he was a decent fellow, because you could talk to him, because he might be handy to know for future building permits.

The policeman, Herman Toffel, was there too and the SD man Reeder, as well as a young officer – also a surveyor, named Steinhauser – from the Armaments Inspectorate. Oskar had met and taken to these men while seeking the permits he needed to start his plant. He had already enjoyed drinking bouts with them. He would always believe that the best way to untie bureaucracy's Gordian knot, short of straight-out bribery, was booze.

Finally there were two Abwehr men. The first was Eberhard Gebauer, the lieutenant who had recruited Oskar into the Abwehr the year before. The second one was Lieutenant Martin Plathe of Canaris's headquarters in Breslau. It had been through his friend Gebauer's recruitment, through an accidental comradeship that ran through the bed of the sanatorium supervisor, that Herr Oskar Schindler had discovered what a city of opportunity Cracow was.

There would be a by-product from the presence of Gebauer and Plathe. Oskar was still on the Abwehr's books as an agent and, in his years in Cracow, would keep the Breslau office of Canaris satisfied by passing on to them reports on the behaviour of their rivals in the SS. Gebauer and Plathe would consider his bringing along of more or less disaffected men like Toffel of the SS and Reeder of the SD as an intelligence favour, a gift quite apart from the good company and the drink.

Though it is not possible to say exactly what the members of the party talked about that night, it is possible from what Oskar said later of each of these men to make a plausible reconstruction.

It would have been Gebauer who made the toast – saying he would not give them governments, armies or potentates; instead he would give them the enamel works of their good friend Oskar Schindler. He did so because if the enamel works prospered then there would be more parties, parties in the Schindler style, the best parties you could imagine.

But after the toast had been drunk, the talk turned naturally to the subject that bemused or obsessed all levels of the civil bureaucracy. The Jews.

Toffel and Reeder had spent the day at Mogilska Station supervising the unloading of Poles and Jews from eastbound trains. These people had been shipped in from the Incorporated Territories, newly conquered regions which had been German in the past, and which now were being restored to a state of unalloyed Aryan purity. Toffel wasn't making a point about the comfort of the passengers in the rolling stock of the Ostbahn, although he confessed that the weather had been cold. The transport of populations in livestock carriages was new to everyone and the wagons were not as yet inhumanly crowded. What confused Toffel was the policy behind it all.

There is a persistent rumour, said Toffel, that we are at war. And in the midst of it the Incorporated Territories are too damn simon-pure to put up with a few Poles and a half million Jews. "The whole Ostbahn system," said Toffel, "has to be turned over to delivering them to *us*."

The Abwehr men listened, slight smiles on their faces. To the SS the enemy within might be the Jew, but to the Canaris the enemy within was the SS.

The SS, Toffel said, had reserved the entire rail system from November 15th on. Across his desk in Pomorska Street, he said, had crossed copies of angry SS memoranda addressed to army officials and complaining that the army was welching on its arrangement, had gone two weeks over schedule in its use of the Ostbahn. For Christ's sake, Toffel asked, shouldn't the army have first use, for as long as it liked, of the railway system? How else is it to deploy east and west? Toffel asked, drinking excitedly. On bicycles?

Oskar was half amused to see that the Abwehr men did not comment. They suspected Toffel might be a plant instead of simply being drunk.

The surveyor and the man from the Armaments Inspectorate asked Toffel some questions about these remarkable trains that were arriving at Mogilska. Soon such shipments wouldn't be worth talking about: transports of humans would become a cliché of resettlement policy. But on the evening of Oskar's Christmas party, they were still a novelty.

"They call it," said Toffel, "*concentration*. That's the word you find in the documents. *Concentration*. I call it bloody obsession."

The owner of the music club brought in plates of herring and sauce. The fish went down well with the fiery liquor, and as they wolfed it Gebauer spoke about the Judenrats, the Jewish councils set up in each Jewish community on the

72

order of Governor Frank. In cities like Warsaw and Cracow the Judenrat had twenty-four elected members personally responsible for the fulfilment of the orders of the régime. The Judenrat of Cracow had been in existence for less than a month; Marek Biberstein, a respected municipal authority, had been appointed its president. But, Gebauer remarked, he had heard that it had already approached Wawel Castle with a plan for a roster of Jewish labour. The Judenrat would supply the labour details for digging ditches and latrines and clearing snow. Didn't everyone find that excessively cooperative of them?

Not at all, said engineer Steinhauser of the Armaments Inspectorate. They thought that if they supplied the labour squads it would stop random pressganging. Pressganging led to beatings and the occasional bullet in the head.

Martin Plathe agreed. They'll be cooperative for the sake of avoiding something worse, he said. It's their method, you have to understand that. They'd always bought the civil authorities off by cooperating with them, and then negotiating.

Gebauer seemed to be out to mislead Toffel and Reeder by pushing the point, by seeming more passionately analytic about Jews than he really was. "I'll tell you what I mean by cooperation," he said. "Frank passes an edict demanding that every Jew in the Government General wears a star. That edict's only a few weeks old. In Warsaw you've got a Jewish manufacturer churning them out in washable bakelite, at three zloty each. It's as if they've got no idea what sort of law it is. It's as if the thing were an insignia of a bicycle club."

It was suggested then that since Schindler was in the enamel business, it might be possible to press a deluxe enamel badge at the Schindler works and retail it through the hardware outlet which his girlfriend Ingrid supervised. Someone remarked that the star was *their* national insignia, the insignia of a state which had been destroyed by the Romans and which existed now only in the minds of Zionists. Perhaps people were proud to wear the star.

"The thing is," said Gebauer, "they don't have any

73

organisation for saving themselves. They've got weathering-the-storm sorts of organisations. But this one's going to be different. This storm will be managed by the SS." Gebauer, again, sounded as if, without being too florid about it, he approved of the professional thoroughness of the SS.

"Come on," said Plathe, "the worst that can happen to them is that they'll get sent to Madagascar, where the weather is better than it is in Cracow."

"I don't believe they'll ever see Madagascar," said Gebauer.

Oskar demanded a change of subject. Wasn't it *his* party?

In the bar of the Hotel Cracovia, in fact, Oskar had already seen Gebauer hand over forged papers to a Jewish businessman for a flight to Hungary. Maybe Gebauer was taking a fee, though he seemed too morally sensitive to deal in papers, to sell a signature, a rubber stamp. But it was certain, in spite of his act in front of Toffel, that he was no abominator of the tribe. Nor were any of them. At Christmas 1939 Oskar found them simply a relief from the orotund official line. Later they would have more positive uses.

6

The Aktion of the night of December 4th had convinced Stern that Oskar Schindler was, that rarity, the just Goy. There is the Talmudic legend of the *Hasidei Ummot Ha-olam*, the Righteous of the Nations, of whom there are said to be – at any point in the earth's history – thirty-six. Stern did not believe literally in the mystical number, but the legend was psychologically true for him and he believed it a decent and wise course to try to make of the German a living and breathing sanctuary.

Schindler, after all, needed capital – the Rekord plant had been partially stripped of machinery, except for one small gallery of metal presses, enamel bins, furnaces, lathes. While Stern might be a substantial spiritual influence on Oskar, the man who could put him in touch with capital on good terms was Abraham Bankier, the office manager of Rekord, whom Oskar had won over.

The two of them – big sensual Oskar and the squat Bankier – went visiting possible investors. By a decree of November 23rd, the bank and safe deposits of all Jews were held by the German administration in fixed trust, without allowing the owner any right of access or interest. Some of the wealthier Jewish businessmen, those who knew anything about history, kept secret funds in hard currencies. But they could tell that for a few years under Governor Hans Frank currencies would be risky; portable wealth – diamonds, gold, trade goods – would be desirable.

Around Cracow there were a number of men Bankier knew who were willing to put up investment money in return for a guaranteed quantity of product. The deal might be an investment of fifty thousand zloty in return for so many kilos of pots and pans a month, delivery to begin July, 1940, and to continue for a year. For a Cracow Jew, given Hans Frank in the Wawel, kitchenware was safer and more disposable than zloty.

The parties to these contracts, Oskar, the investor, Bankier as middleman, brought away from these arrangements nothing, not even minutes of agreement. Full-fledged contracts were of no use and could not be enforced anyhow. Nothing could be enforced. It all depended on Bankier's accurate judgment of this Sudeten manufacturer of enamelware.

The meetings would take place, perhaps, in the investor's apartment in the Centrum of Cracow, the old inner city. The Polish landscapes which the investor's wife adored, the French novels his bright and fragile daughters savoured, would glow in the light of the transaction. Or else the investing gentleman had already been thrown out of his apartment and lived in poorer quarters in Podgórze. And he would be a man already in shock, his apartment gone and himself now an employee in his own business, and all this in a few months, the year not over yet.

At first sight it seems a heroic embellishment of the story to say that Oskar was never accused of welching on these informal contracts. He would in the new year have a fight with one Jewish retailer over the quantity of product the man was entitled to take from Deutsche Email Fabrik's loading dock in Lipowa Street. And the gentleman would be accusatory of Oskar on those grounds to the end of his life. But that Oskar did not fulfil deals – that was never said.

For Oskar was by nature a payer, a man who somehow gave the impression he could make limitless payments out of limitless resources. In any case, Oskar and other German opportunists would make so much in the next four years that only a man consumed by the profit motive would have failed to repay what Oskar's father would have called a debt of honour.

Emilie Schindler came up to Cracow, to visit her husband

there for the first time, in the new year. She thought the city was the most delightful she had ever been in, so much more gracious and pleasant and old-fashioned than Moravia's big city, Brno, with its clouds of industrial smoke.

She was impressed with her husband's new apartment. The front windows looked across at the Planty, an elegant ring of parkland that ran right around the city following the route of the ancient walls long since knocked down. At the bottom of the street the great fortress of Wawel rose and amidst all this antiquity was Oskar's modern apartment. She looked around at Mrs. Pfefferberg's fabrics and wall hangings. His new success was palpable in them.

"You've done very well in Poland," she said.

Oskar knew that she was really talking about the matter of the dowry, the one her father had refused to pay a dozen years back when travellers from Zwittau had rushed into the village of Alt-Molstein with news that his son-in-law was living and drinking like an unmarried man. His daughter's marriage had become exactly the marriage he had feared it would and he was damned if he'd pay.

And though the non-arrival of the four hundred thousand Reichsmarks had altered Oskar's prospects a little, the farmer of Alt-Molstein did not know how the non-payment would pain his daughter, make her even more defensive, nor that twelve years later when it no longer counted for Oskar it would be still at the front of Emilie's mind.

"My dear," Oskar was always growling, "I never needed the damn money."

Emilie's intermittent relations with Oskar seem to have been those of a woman who knows her husband is not and will not be faithful, but who nonetheless doesn't want evidence of his affairs shoved under her nose. She must have moved warily in Cracow, going to parties where Oskar's friends would surely know the truth, would know the names of the other women, the names she did not really want to hear.

One day a young Pole — it was Poldek Pfefferberg who had nearly shot her husband, but she could not know that — arrived at the door of the apartment with a rolled-up

77

rug over his shoulder. It was a black-market rug from Istanbul via Hungary, and Pfefferberg had been given the job of finding it by Ingrid, who had moved out for the duration of Emilie's visit.

"Is Frau Schindler in?" asked Pfefferberg. He always referred to Ingrid as Frau Schindler because he thought it was less offensive.

"*I* am Frau Schindler," said Emilie, knowing what the question meant.

Pfefferberg showed some sensitivity in covering up. Actually he did not need to see Frau Schindler, though he'd heard so much about her from Herr Schindler. He had to see Herr Schindler about some business matter.

Herr Schindler wasn't in, said Emilie. She offered young Pfefferberg a drink but he hastily refused. Emilie knew what that meant too. That he was just a little shocked by Oskar's personal life and thought it indecent to sit and drink with the victim.

The factory Oskar had leased was across the river in Zablocie at Number 4 Lipowa Street. The offices which faced the street were modern in design and Oskar thought it might be possible and convenient for him to move in at some time, to have an apartment on the third floor, even though the surroundings were industrial and not as exhilarating as Straszewskiego Street.

When Oskar took over the Rekord works, renaming it Deutsche Email Fabrik, there were forty-five employees involved in a modest output of kitchenware. Early in the new year he received his first army contracts. They were no surprise. He had cultivated various influential Wehrmacht engineers who sat on the Main Armaments Board of General Schindler's Armaments Inspectorate. He had gone to the same parties and taken them to dinner at the Cracovia Hotel. There are photographs of Oskar sitting with them at expensive tables, everyone smiling urbanely at the camera, everyone well-fed, generously liquored, and the officers elegantly uniformed. Some of them put the right stamps on his bids and wrote the crucial letters of recommendation to General Schindler merely out of friendship and because they believed Oskar had the plant and would deliver. Others were influenced by gifts, the sort of gifts Oskar would always proffer to officials, cognac and carpets, jewellery and furniture and hampers of luxury food. As well as that, it became known that General Schindler was acquainted with and liked very much his enamelware-producing namesake.

Now, with the authority of his lucrative Armaments Inspectorate contracts, Oskar was permitted to expand his plant. There was room. Beyond the entryway and offices of DEF stood two large industrial hangars. Some of the floor space in the building on the left as you emerged from the DEF entryway into the interior of the factory was occupied by present production. The other building was totally empty.

He bought new machinery, some locally, some from the homeland. Apart from the military demand, there was the all-devouring black market to serve. Oskar knew now that he could be a magnate. By the mid-summer of 1940 he would be employing two hundred and fifty Poles and would be faced with instituting a nightshift. Herr Hans Schindler's agricultural machinery plant in Zwittau had at the best of times employed fifty. It is a sweet thing to outstrip a father whom you haven't forgiven.

At times throughout the year, Stern would call on Schindler to arrange employment for some young Jew – a special case, an orphan from Lódź, the daughter of a clerk in one of the departments of the Judenrat. Within a few months Oskar was employing one hundred and fifty Jewish workers and his factory had a minor reputation as a haven.

It was a year when, like each succeeding year for the rest of the war, Jews would be looking for some employment considered essential to the war effort. In April, Governor General Frank had decreed an evacuation of Jews from his capital Cracow. It was a curious decision, since the Reich authorities were still moving Jews and Poles back into Frank's Government General at the rate of nearly ten thousand a day. Yet conditions in Cracow, Frank told his cabinet, were scandalous. He knew of German divisional commanders who had to live in apartment buildings that contained Jewish tenants. Higher officials were also subjected to the same quite scandalous indignity. Over the next six months, he promised, he would make Cracow *judenfrei*. There would be a permitted remnant of five to six thousand skilled Jewish workers. All the rest were to be moved into other cities in the Government General, into Warsaw or Radom, Lublin or Czestochowa. Jews could emigrate voluntarily to the city of their choice as long as they did it before August 15th. Those still left in the city after that date would be trucked out with a small amount of luggage to whatever place suited the administration. From November 1st, said Hans Frank, it would be possible for the Germans of Cracow to breathe 'good German air', to walk abroad without seeing the streets and lanes 'crawling with Jews'.

That year Frank would not manage to reduce the Jewish population of the city to quite so low a level. But when his plans were first announced, there was a rush among the Jewish population of Cracow, especially among the young, to acquire skilled qualifications. Men like lean Itzhak Stern, official and unofficial agents of the Judenrat, had already developed a list of sympathisers, Germans to whom they could appeal. Schindler was on that list, so was the Viennese Julius Madritsch, who had recently managed to get himself released from the Wehrmacht and taken up the post of Treuhänder of the Optima Uniform Works. Madritsch could see the benefits of Armaments Inspectorate's contracts and now intended to open a uniform factory of his own in the suburb of Podgórze. In the end he would make an even larger fortune than Schindler, but in the *annus mirabilis* of 1940 he was still on a salary. He was known to be humane, that was all.

By November 1st, 1940, Frank had managed to move twenty-three thousand Jewish volunteers out of Cracow. Some of them went to the new ghettos in Warsaw and Lódź. The gaps at table, the grieving on railway stations can be imagined, but people took it meekly, thinking, We'll do this, and that will be the brunt of what they ask. Oskar knew it was happening, but, like the Jews themselves, hoped it was a temporary excess.

That year would very likely be the most industrious of Oskar's life – a year of building the place up from a bankrupt manufactory to a company government agencies could take seriously. As the first snows fell, Schindler noticed and was irritated when, on any given day, sixty or more of his Jewish employees would be absentees. They would have been detained by SS squads on the way to work and employed in clearing snow. Schindler visited his friend Toffel at SS headquarters in Pomorska to complain. On one day, he told Toffel, he had a hundred and twenty-five absentees.

Toffel confided in him. "You've got to understand that some of these fellows here don't give a damn about production. To them it's a matter of national priority that Jews be made to shovel snow. I don't understand it myself . . . it's got a ritual significance for them, Jews shovelling snow. And it's not just you, it's happening to everyone."

Oskar asked if all the others were complaining too. Yes, said Toffel. However, he said, an economic big shot from the SS Budget and Construction Office had come for lunch in Pomorska and said that to believe the Jewish skilled worker had a place in Reich economics was treasonable. "I think you're going to have to put up with a lot of snow shovelling yet, Oskar."

Oskar, for the moment, assumed the stance of the outraged patriot, or perhaps of the outraged profiteer. "If they want to win the war," said Oskar, "they'd have to get rid of SS men like that."

"Get rid of them?" asked Toffel. "For Christ's sake, they're the bastards who're on top."

As a result of such conversations, Oskar became an advocate of the principle that a factory owner should have unimpeded access to his own workers, that these workers should have access to the plant, that they should not be detained or tyrannised on their way to and from the factory.

It was, in Oskar's eyes, a moral axiom as much as an industrial one. In the end, he would apply it to its limit at Deutsche Email Fabrik.

7

Some people from the big cities – from Warsaw and Lódź with their ghettos and Cracow with Frank's *judenfrei* ambitions – went to the countryside to lose themselves among the peasants. The Rosner brothers settled in the old village of Tyniec on a pretty bend of the Vistula with an old Benedictine abbey on a limestone cliff above. It was anonymous enough for the Rosners. It had a few Jewish storekeepers and orthodox artisans with whom nightclub musicians had little to converse about. But the peasants, busy with the tedium of the harvest, were as genial as the Rosners could have hoped, finding musicians in their midst.

They'd come to Tyniec not from Cracow, not from that great marshalling point outside the botanical gardens in Mogilska Street where young SS men pushed people on trucks and called out bland and lying promises about the later delivery of all adequately labelled baggage. They had come in fact from Warsaw, where they had been enjoying an engagement at the Basilisk. They had left the day before the Germans sealed up the Warsaw ghetto. Henry and Leopold and Henry's wife Manci and five-year-old son Olek.

The idea of a south Polish village like Tyniec, not far from their native Cracow, appealed to the Rosner brothers. It offered the option, should conditions improve, of catching a bus into Cracow and finding work. Manci Rosner, an Austrian girl, had brought with her her sewing machine and the Rosners set up a little clothing business in Tyniec. In the evenings they played in the taverns and became a sensation in a town like that. Villages welcome and support occasional wonders, even Jewish ones. And the fiddle was, of all instruments, most venerated in Poland.

One evening a travelling Volksdeutscher, a German-speaking Pole, from Poznan, heard the brothers Rosner playing outside the inn. The Volksdeutscher was a municipal official from Cracow, one of those Polish Germans in whose name Hitler had taken Poland in the first place. The Volksdeutscher told Henry that the Mayor of Cracow, Obersturmbannführer Pavlu, and his deputy, the renowned skier Sepp Röhrl, would be visiting the countryside at harvest time, and he would like to arrange for them to hear such an accomplished pair as the Rosners.

On an afternoon when the bound sheaves lay drowsing in fields as quiet and as abandoned as on Sunday, a convoy of limousines ground through Tyniec and up a rise to the villa of an absentee Polish aristocrat. The Rosner brothers waited on the terrace, and when all the ladies and gentlemen had been seated in a room which might once have been used for balls, they were invited to perform. Henry and Leopold felt both exaltation and fear at the seriousness with which Obersturmbannführer Pavlu's party had geared themselves for their playing. The women wore white dresses and gloves, the military officials full dress, the bureaucrats their winged collars. When people went to such trouble, it was easier to disappoint them. For a Jew, even to impose a cultural disappointment on the régime was a serious crime.

But the audience loved them. They were a characteristic *gemütlich* crowd, they loved Strauss, the confections of Offenbach and Lehár, André Messager and Leo Fall. At request time they grew mawkish.

And as Henry and Leopold performed, the ladies and gentlemen drank champagne from long-stemmed glasses brought in by hamper.

Once the official recital had finished, the brothers were taken down the hill to where the peasants and the soldiers of the escort had been gathered. If there was to be some crude racial demonstration, it would take place here. But, again, once the brothers had climbed on to a wagon and looked the crowd in the eye, Henry knew they would be safe. The pride of the peasants, partly a national thing, the Rosners being for the night a credit to Polish culture – all that protected them. It was so like old times that Henry found himself smiling down at Olek and Manci, playing to her, capable of ignoring the rest. It did seem for those seconds that the earth had at last been pacified by music.

When it was finished, a middle-aged SS NCO – a Rottenführer perhaps, Henry not being as familiar as he might become with the gradations of SS rank – approached the two men as they stood by the wagon receiving congratulations. He nodded to them and barely smiled. "I hope you have a nice harvest holiday," he said, bowed, and left.

The brothers stared at each other. As soon as the SS man was out of hearing, they gave in to the temptation to discuss the meaning of his statement. Leopold was convinced. "It's a threat," he said. It went to prove what they had feared in their marrow when the Volksdeutsch official first spoke to them – that these days it didn't do to stand out, to acquire a distinctive face.

But the harvest holiday came and went and the Rosners were left alone in Tyniec.

That was life in the country in 1940. The curtailment of a career, the rustic tedium, the scratching out of a trade, the occasional terror, the pull of that bright core called Cracow. To that, the Rosners knew, they would eventually return.

Emilie had returned home in the autumn, and when Stern next came to Schindler's apartment on business it was Ingrid who brought in the coffee. Oskar made no secret of his weaknesses, and never seemed to think that ascetic Itzhak Stern needed any apologia for the presence of Ingrid in the apartment in Straszewskiego. Similarly, when the coffee was finished, Oskar went to the drink cupboard and brought back a fresh bottle of brandy, plumping it down on the table between his seat and Stern's, as if Stern were really likely to help him drink it.

Stern had come that evening to tell Oskar that a family whom we shall call the Cs were spreading stories about him. Old David and young Leon C. Saying even on the streets in Kazimierz, let alone in parlours, that Oskar was a German gangster, a thug. When Stern passed on these accusations to

Oskar, he didn't use terms that were quite as vivid as that.

Oskar knew Stern wasn't looking for a response, that he was just passing on intelligence. But he would have felt he had to answer anyway.

"I could spread stories about them," said Oskar. "They're robbing me blind. Ask Ingrid if you like?"

Ingrid worked at the Cs' hardware outlet in Stradom Street. She was a benign Treuhänder and, being only in her twenties, commercially inexperienced. The rumour was that Schindler himself had got the girl appointed so that he would have an assured outlet for his kitchenware. The Cs, however, still did pretty well what they wanted with their company. If they resented the idea that it was held in trust by the occupying power, no one could blame them for that.

Stern waved his hand. Who was he to want to grill Ingrid? It wasn't much use to compare notes with the girl anyhow.

"They run rings around Ingrid," said Oskar. They turned up at Lipowa Street to take delivery of their orders and altered the invoices on the spot and took away more than they had paid for. "*She* says it's all right," they'd tell Schindler employees. "*He*'s arranged it with Ingrid."

The son had in fact been gathering crowds and telling them that Schindler had had the SS beat him up. But this story varied – the beating was supposed to have occurred at Schindler's factory, in a storeroom from which young C emerged with a swollen head and broken teeth. Then it was supposed to have occurred on Limanowskiego, in front of witnesses. A man called H, an employee of Oskar's and a friend of the Cs, had said he'd heard Oskar stamping up and down in his office in Lipowa Street and threatening to kill old David C. Then Oskar was said to have driven round to Stradom and raided the C cash register, and to have stuffed his pockets with currency and told them that there was a new order in Europe, and then to have beaten up old David in his office.

It was no defence for Oskar to explain that he paid the Cs a monthly executive salary of seven hundred and fifty zloty. In both Oskar's eyes and Stern's, the business belonged to the Cs anyhow.

Was it possible that Oskar could let fly at old David C and land him in bed with bruises? Was it likely he would call on friends in the police to assault Leon? On one level Oskar and the Cs were gangsters, selling tons of kitchenware illegally, without sending records of sales to the Transferstelle, without use of the required merchandising coupons called the Bezugschein. On the black market, the dialogue was primitive and tempers were short. Oskar admitted he'd raged into the Cs' showroom and called father and son thieves and indemnified himself out of the till for the kitchenware the Cs had taken without authorisation. Oskar admitted he'd punched young Leon. But that was the limit of his admissions.

And the Cs whom Stern had known since childhood – they had one of those reputations. Not exactly criminal but sharp in dealing. And, significant in this case, a name for squealing when caught.

Stern knew Leon C's bruises *did* exist. Leon wore them down the street and was willing to elaborate on them. The SS beating *did* take place somewhere or other, but it could have had a dozen causes. Stern not only did not believe but also had the feeling that to believe or disbelieve what was said to have happened in this case was irrelevant to his own wider purposes. It would become relevant only when and if Schindler established a brutal pattern. For Stern's purposes, occasional lapses did not count. Had Oskar been without sin, this apartment would not exist in its present form, and neither would Ingrid be waiting in the bedroom.

And it is yet again one of those things which must be said, that Oskar would save all of them – Mr. and Mrs. C, Leon C, Mr. H, Miss M, old C's secretary – and that they would always admit that, but that they would also and always stick to their story of the bruises.

That evening Itzhak Stern also brought news of Marek Biberstein's jail sentence. He had got two years in the prison in Montelupich Street, this Marek Biberstein who was the president of the Judenrat – or who had been until his arrest. In other cities the Judenrat was already cursed by the general Jewish population, for its main work had become the drawing up of lists for forced labour, for transfers to camps. The Judenrats were regarded by the German administration as organs of its will, but in Cracow Marek Biberstein and his cabinet still saw themselves as buffers between the offices of Frank and Wächter and Pavlu and police chiefs Scherner and Czurda on one hand, and the Jewish inhabitants of the city on the other. In the Cracow German newspaper *Cracower Zeitung* of March 13th, 1940, a Dr. Dietrich Redecker said that on a visit to the Judenrat office he was struck by the contrast between its carpet and plush chairs and the poverty and squalor of the Jewish quarters in Kazimierz. But Jewish survivors do not remember the early members of Cracow Judenrat as men who insulated themselves from the people. Hungry for revenue, however, they had made the mistake the Judenrats of Łódź and Warsaw had made before them, permitting the affluent to buy their way off forced labour lists, compelling the poor on to the roster in return for soup and bread. But even later, in 1941, Biberstein and his council still had the respect of the Jews of Cracow.

That first membership of the Judenrat was made up of twenty-four men, most of them intellectuals. Each day, on his way to Zablocie, Oskar passed their corner office in Podgórze into which were crowded a number of secretariats. In the manner of a cabinet each member of the council took care of a different aspect of government. Mr. Schenker had charge of taxes, Mr. Steinberg of buildings, an essential job in a society where people drifted in and out, this week trying the option of refuge in some small village, next week walking back to town surfeited with the narrowness of the peasants. Leon Salpeter, a pharmacist by profession, had care of one of the social welfare portfolios. There were secretariats for food, cemeteries, health, travel documentation, economic affairs, administrative services, culture, even – in the face of the ban on schooling – of education.

Biberstein and his council believed on principle that the Jews who were expelled from Cracow would end up in worse places and so they decided to fall back on an ancient stratagem: bribery. The hard-up Judenrat treasury allocated two hundred thousand zloty for the purpose. Biberstein and the Housing Secretary, Chaim Goldfluss, had sought out an intermediary, in this case a Volksdeutsch called Reichert, a man who had contacts in the SS and on the Wawel. Reichert's task was to pass on the money to a series of officials beginning with Obersturmführer – first lieutenant – Seibert, the liaison officer between the Judenrat and the Government General. In return for the money, the administration was to permit another ten thousand Jews of the Cracow community to remain at home despite Frank's orders. Whether Reichert had insulted officials by retaining too large a margin for himself and making too low an offer, or whether the gentlemen involved felt that Governor Frank's most cherished ambition to render his city *judenfrei* made the taking of bribes too perilous, no one could tell from the court proceedings. But Biberstein had got two years in Montelupich, Goldfluss six months in Auschwitz. Reichert himself had got eight years. Yet everyone knew he would have a softer time of it than the other two.

Herr Schindler shook his head at the idea of putting two hundred thousand zloty on such a fragile hope. "Reichert is a crook," he murmured. Just ten minutes earlier they had been discussing whether he and the Cs were crooks and had let the question stand. But there was no doubt about Reichert. "I could have told them Reichert was a crook," he kept insisting.

Stern commented – as a philosophic principle – that there were times when the only people left to do business with were crooks.

Schindler laughed at that. A wide, toothy, almost rustic laugh. "Thank you very much, my friend," he told Stern.

8

It wasn't such a bad Christmas that year. But there was a wistfulness and snow lay like a question in the parkland across from Schindler's apartment, like something posed, watchful and eternal on the roof of the Wawel up the road and under the ancient façades of Kanonicza Street. No one believed any more in a quick resolution, neither the soldiery nor the Poles nor the Jews on either side of the river.

Schindler bought a poodle, a ridiculous Parisienne thing acquired by Pfefferberg for his Polish secretary, Klonowska, that Christmas. For Ingrid he bought jewellery and sent some also to gentle Emilie down in Zwittau. Poodles were hard to find, Leopold Pfefferberg reported. But jewellery was no trouble. Because of the times, gems were in a high state of movement.

Oskar seems to have pursued his simultaneous attachments to three women and sundry casual friendships with others, all without suffering the normal penalties which beset the womaniser. Visitors to his apartment cannot remember ever finding Ingrid sulking. She seems to have been a generous and complaisant girl. Emilie, with even more grounds for complaint, had too much dignity to make the scenes Oskar richly deserved. If Klonowska had any resentment, it does not seem to have affected her manner in the front office of DEF nor her loyalty to the Herr Direktor. One could expect that in a life like Oskar's, public confrontations between angry women would be common events. But no one among Oskar's friends and workers — witnesses willing enough to admit and even in some cases chuckle over Oskar's sins of the flesh — remembers such painful confrontations, so often the fate of much more restrained philanderers than Oskar.

To suggest as some have that any woman would be pleased with partial possession of Oskar is to demean the women involved. The problem was, perhaps, that if you wanted to talk to Oskar about fidelity, a look of childlike and authentic bewilderment entered his eyes, as if you were proposing some concept like relativity which could be understood only if the listener had five hours to sit still and concentrate. Oskar never had five hours and never understood.

Except in his mother's case. That Christmas morning, for his dead mother's sake, Oskar went to Mass at St Mary's. There was a space above the high altar where Wit Stwosz's wooden triptych had until weeks ago diverted worshippers with its crowd of jostling divinities. The vacancy, the pallor of the stone where the triptych's fixings had been, distracted and abashed Herr Schindler. Someone had stolen the triptych. It had been shipped to Nuremberg. What an improbable world it had become!

Business was wonderful that winter just the same. In the new year his friends in the Rustungsinspektion began to talk to Oskar about the possibility of opening an armaments division to manufacture anti-tank shells. Oskar was not as interested in shells as in pots and pans. Pots and pans were easy engineering. You cut out and pressed the metal, dipped it in the tubs, fired it at the right temperature. You didn't have to calibrate instruments: the work was nowhere near as exacting as it would be for arms. Also, there was no under-the-counter trade in shell casings, and Oskar liked under-the-counter, liked the sport of it, the disrepute, the fast returns, the lack of paperwork.

But, because it was good politics, he established a munitions section, installing in one gallery of his Number Two workshop a few immense Hilo machines, for the precision pressing and tooling of shell casings. The munitions section was so far developmental; it would take some months of planning, measuring and test production before any shells appeared. The big Hilos however gave the Schindler works, as a hedge against the questionable future, at least the appearance of essential industry.

Before the Hilos had even been properly calibrated, Oskar began to get hints from his SS contacts at Pomorska Street that there was to be a ghetto for Jews. He mentioned the rumour to Stern, not wanting to create alarm. Oh yes, said Stern, the word was around. Some people were even looking forward to it. We'll be inside, the enemy will be outside. We can run our own affairs. No one will envy us, no one stone us in the streets. The walls of the ghetto will be fixed. The walls would be the final, fixed form of the catastrophe.

The edict, named Gen. Gub. 44/91, posted on March 3rd, 1941, was published in the Cracow dailies and blared forth from loudspeakers on trucks in Kazimierz. Walking through his munitions department, Oskar heard one of his German technicians comment on the news. "Won't they be better off in there?" asked the technician. "The Poles hate them, you know."

The edict used the same excuse. As a means of reducing racial conflict in the Government General a closed Jewish quarter would be set up. Enclosure in the ghetto would be compulsory for all Jews, but those with the proper labour card could travel from the ghetto to work, returning in the evening. The ghetto would be located in the suburb of Podgórze just over the river. The deadline for entering it would be March 20th. Once in, you would be allocated housing by the Judenrat, but Poles presently living in the area of the ghetto and who therefore had to shift were to apply to their own housing office for apartments in other parts of town.

A map of the new ghetto was appended to the edict. The north side would be bounded by the river, the east end by the railway line to Lwów, the south side by the hills beyond Rekawka, the west by Podgórze Place. It would be crowded in there.

But there was hope that repression would take definite form now and provide people with a basis on which to plan their restricted futures. For a man such as Juda Dresner, a textile wholesaler of Stradom Street who would come to know Oskar, the past year and a half had brought a bewildering succession of decrees, intrusions and confiscations. The Trust Agency had taken his business, he had lost his car, his apartment. His bank account had been frozen. His children's schools had been closed, or else they had been expelled from them. The family's jewellery had been seized, and their family radio. He and his family were forbidden entry to the centre of Cracow, denied any travel by train. They could use only segregated trolley cars. His wife and daughter and sons were subject to intermittent round-ups for snow shovelling or other compulsory labour. You never knew, when you were forced into the back of a truck, if the absence would be a short or long one, or what sort of hair-trigger madman might be supervising the work you would be forced to. Under this sort of regimen you felt that life offered no footholds, that you were slithering into a pit which had no bottom. But perhaps the ghetto was the bottom, the point at which it was possible to take organised thought.

Besides, the Jews of Cracow were accustomed – in a way that could best be described as congenital – to the idea of a ghetto. And now that it had been decided, the very word had a soothing and ancestral ring. Their grandfathers had not been permitted to emerge from the ghetto of Kazimierz until 1867, when Franz Josef signed a decree permitting them to live wherever they wished in the city. Cynics said that the Austrians had needed to open up Kazimierz, socketed as it was in the elbow of the river so close to Cracow, so that Polish labourers could find accommodation close to their places of work. But Franz Josef was nonetheless revered by the older people from Kazimierz as energetically as he was in the childhood household of Oskar Schindler.

Although their liberty had come so late, there was at the same time among the older Cracow Jews a nostalgia for the old ghetto of Kazimierz. A ghetto implied certain squalors, a crowding in tenements, a sharing of taps and water closets, disputes over drying space on clothes lines. Yet it also consecrated the Jews to their own specialness, to a richness of shared scholarship, to songs and Zionist talk, elbow to elbow, in coffee houses rich in ideas if not in cream. Evil rumours emanated from the ghettos of Lódź and Warsaw, but the Podgórze ghetto as planned was more generous with space, for if you superimposed it on a map of the Centrum, you found that the ghetto was in an area about half the size of the Old City – by no means enough space, but not quite strangulation.

There was as well in the edict a sedative clause that promised to protect the Jews from their Polish countrymen. Since the early thirties, a wilfully orchestrated racial contest had prevailed in Poland. When the Depression began and farm prices fell, the Polish government had sanctioned a range of anti-Semitic political groups of the kind who saw the Jews as the base of all their economic troubles. Sanacja, Marshal Pilsudski's Moral Cleansing Party, made an alliance after his death with the Camp of National Unity, a right wing Jew-baiting group. Prime Minister Skladkowski, on the floor of Parliament in Warsaw, declared, "Economic war on the Jews? All right!" Rather than give the peasants land reform, Sanacja encouraged them to look at the Jewish stalls on market day as the symbol and total explanation of Polish rural poverty. There were pogroms against the Jewish population in a roster of towns, beginning in Grodno in 1935. The Polish legislators also entered the struggle and Jewish industries were starved under new laws on bank credit. Craft guilds closed their lists to Jewish artisans, and the universities introduced a quota, or what they themselves, strong in classics, called *numerus clausus aut nullus* (a closed number or nil) on the entry of Jewish students. Faculties gave way to National Unity insistence that Jews be appointed special benches in the quadrangle and be exiled to the left side of the lecture halls. Commonly enough in Polish universities, the pretty and brilliant daughters of city Jewry emerged from lecture halls to have their faces savaged by a quick razor stroke delivered by a lean, serious youth from the Camp of National Unity.

In the first days of the German occupation, the conquerors had been astounded by the willingness of Poles to point out Jewish households, to hold a prayer-locked Jew still while a German docked the orthodox beard with scissors – or, pinking the face flesh also, with an infantry bayonet. In March, 1941, therefore, the promise to protect the ghetto dwellers from the Polish national excess fell on the ear almost credibly.

Although there was no great spontaneous joy among the Jews of Cracow as they packed for the shift to Podgórze, there were strange elements of homecoming to it, as well as that sense of arriving at a limit beyond which, with any luck, you wouldn't be further uprooted or tyrannised. Enough so that even some people from the villages around Cracow, from Wieliczka, from Niepolomice, from Lipnica Murowana and Tyniec hurried to town lest they be locked out on March 20th and find themselves in a comfortless landscape. For the ghetto was, by its nature, almost by definition, habitable even if subject to intermittent attack. The ghetto represented *stasis* instead of flux.

The ghetto would introduce a minor inconvenience in Oskar Schindler's life. It was usual for him to leave his stylish apartment in Straszewskiego, pass the limestone lump of the Wawel stuck in the mouth of the city like a cork in a bottle, and so roll down through Kazimierz, over the Kosciuszko Bridge and left towards his factory in Zablocie. Now that route would be blocked by the ghetto walls. It was a minor problem, but it made the idea of maintaining an apartment on the top floor of his office block in Lipowa Street more reasonable. It wasn't such a bad place, built in the style of Walter Gropius. Lots of glass and light, fashionable cubic bricks in the entranceway.

Whenever he did travel between the city and Zablocie in those March days before the deadline, he would see the Jews of Kazimierz packing; and on Stradom Street would pass, early in the period of grace, families pushing barrows piled high with chairs, mattresses and clocks towards the ghetto. Their families had lived in Kazimierz since the time it was an island separated from the Centrum by a stream called Stara Wisla. In fact, since the time Kazimier the Great had invited them to Cracow when, elsewhere, they were footing the blame for the Black Death. Oskar surmised that their ancestors would have turned up in Cracow like that, pushing a barrowful of bedding, over five hundred years ago. Now they were leaving, it seemed, with the same barrowful. Kazimier's invitation had been cancelled.

During those morning journeys across town, Oskar noticed that the plan was for the city trams to go on rolling down Lwówska Street, through the middle of the ghetto. All walls facing the tramline were being bricked up by Polish workmen, and where there had been open spaces, cement walls were raised. As well, the trams would have their doors closed as they entered the ghetto and would not stop until they emerged again in the Umwelt, the Aryan world, at the corner of Lwówska and ś.w. Kingi Street. Oskar knew people would catch that tram, anyhow. Doors closed, no stops, machine guns on walls – it wouldn't matter. Humans were incurable about these things. People would try to get off it, someone's loyal Polish maid with a parcel of sausage. And people would try to get on, a fast-moving athletic young man such as Leopold Pfefferberg with a pocketful of diamonds or occupation zloty or a message in code for the partisans. People responded to any slim chance, even if it was an outside one, moving at speed between mute walls, its doors locked shut.

From March 20th, Oskar's Jewish workers would not receive any wages and were meant to live entirely on their rations. Instead he would pay a fee to SS headquarters in Cracow. Both Oskar and Madritsch were uneasy about that, for they knew the war would end eventually and the slaveholders, just as in America, would be shamed and stripped naked. The dues he would pay to the police chiefs were the standard SS Main Administrative and Economic Office fees – seven and a half Reichsmarks per day for a skilled worker, five Reichsmarks for unskilled and women. They were, by a margin, cheaper rates than those which operated in the open labour market. But for Oskar and Julius Madritsch both, the moral discomfort outweighed the economic advantage. The meeting of his wage bill was the least of Oskar's worries that year. Besides, he was never an ideal capitalist. His father had accused him often in his youth of being reckless with money. While he was a mere sales manager, he'd maintained two cars, hoping that Hans would get to hear of it and be shocked. Now, in Cracow, he could afford to keep a stableful – a Belgian Minerva, a Maybach, an Adler cabriolet, a BMW.

To be a prodigal and still be wealthier than your more careful father, that was one of the triumphs Schindler wanted from life. In boom times the cost of labour was beside the point.

It was that way for Madritsch, too. Julius Madritsch's uniform mill stood on the western side of the ghetto, a mile or so from Oskar's enamelworks. He was doing so well that he was negotiating to open a similar plant in Tarnow. He too was a darling of the Armaments Inspectorate, and his credit was so good that he had received a loan of a million zloty from the Bank Emisyjny (Issue Bank)

Whatever ethical queasiness they felt, it is not likely that either entrepreneur, Oskar or Julius, felt a moral obligation to avoid employing any more Jews. That was a stance, and since they were pragmatists, stances weren't their style. In any case Itzhak Stern as well as Roman Ginter, a business-man and representative of the Relief Office of the Judenrat, called on Oskar and Julius both and begged them to employ more Jews, as many as could be fitted in. The objective was to give the ghetto an economic permanence. It was almost axiomatic, Stern and Ginter considered at that stage, that a Jew who had an economic value in a precocious empire hungry for skilled workers was safe from worse things. And Oskar and Madritsch agreed.

For two weeks they trundled their barrows through Kazimierz and over the bridge into Podgórze, middle-class families whose Polish servants had come with them to help push the cart. At the bottom of the barrows lay the remain-ing brooches, the fur coats; under mattresses and kettles and skillets. Crowds of Poles on Stradom and Starovislna Streets jeered and hurled mud. "The Jews are going, the Jews are going. Goodbye Jews."

Beyond the bridge, a fancy wooden gate greeted the new citizens of the ghetto. White with scalloped ramparts which gave it an Arabesque look, it had two wide arches for the trams going from and coming to Cracow, and at the side was a white sentry box. Above the arches, a title in Hebrew sought to reassure. *Jewish Town*, it proclaimed. High barbed-wire fences had been strung along the front of the ghetto, facing the river, and open spaces were sealed with round-topped cement slabs nine-feet-tall, resembling strings of gravestones for the anonymous.

At the ghetto gate the trundling Jew was met by a representative of the Judenrat Housing Office. If he had a wife and large family, a man might be assigned two rooms and have the use of a kitchen. Even so, after the good living of the twenties and thirties, it was painful to have to share your private life with families of different rituals and habits, of another, distasteful musk. Mothers screamed and fathers said things could be worse and sucked on hollow teeth and shook their heads. In the one room, the orthodox found the liberals an abomination.

On March 20th the movement was complete. Everyone outside the ghetto was forfeit and at risk. Inside, for the moment, the ghetto dwellers were at rest.

Twenty-three year old Edith Liebgold was assigned a first-floor room to share with her mother and her baby. The fall of Cracow eighteen months back had put her husband into a mood verging on despair. He'd wandered away from home as if he wanted to look into the courses open to him. He had ideas about the forests, about finding a safe clearing. He had never returned.

From her end window Edith Liebgold could see the Vistula through the barbed-wire barricade, but her path to other parts of the ghetto, especially to the hospital in Wegierska Street, took her through Plac Zgody, the Place of Peace, the ghetto's only square. Here on the second day of her life inside the walls she missed by twenty seconds being hustled into an SS truck and taken to shovel coal or snow in the city. It was not just that work details often, according to rumour, returned to the ghetto with one or more fewer members than when they left. More than these sort of odds, Edith feared being forced into a truck when, half a minute earlier, you thought you were going to Pankiewicz's pharmacy, and your baby was due to be fed in twenty minutes.

Therefore she went with friends to the Jewish Employment Office. If she could get shiftwork, her mother would mind the baby at night.

The office in those first days was crowded. The Judenrat had its own police force now, the Ordnungdienst expanded and regularised to keep order in the ghetto, and a boy with a cap and an armband organised queues in front of the office.

Edith Liebgold's group were just inside the door, making lots of noise to pass the time, when a small middle-aged man wearing a brown suit and a tie approached her. They could tell that they'd attracted him with their racket, their brightness. At first they thought he intended to pick Edith up.

"Look," he said, "rather than wait, there is an enamel factory over in Zablocie."

He let the address have its effect. Zablocie is outside the ghetto, he was telling them. You can barter with the Polish workers there. He needed ten healthy women for the nightshift.

The girls pulled faces, as if they could afford to choose work and might even turn him down. Not heavy, he assured them. And they'll teach you on the job. His name, he said, was Mr. Abraham Bankier. He was the manager. There was a German owner, of course. What sort of German? they asked. Bankier grinned as if he suddenly wanted to fulfil all their hopes. Not a bad sort, he told them.

That night Edith Liebgold met the other members of the enamel works nightshift and marched across the ghetto towards Zablocie under the guard of a Jewish OD, a policeman of the ghetto Order Service. In the column she asked questions about this Deutsche Email Fabrik. They serve a soup with plenty of body, she was told. Beatings? she asked. It's not that sort of place, they said. It's not like Beckmann's razor-blade factory, more like Madritsch's. Madritsch's is all right and Schindler's too.

At the entrance to the factory, the new nightshift workers were called out of the column by Bankier and taken upstairs and past vacant desks to a door marked *Herr Direktor*. Edith Liebgold heard a deep voice tell them all to come in. They found the Herr Direktor seated on the corner of his desk, smoking a cigarette. His hair, somewhere between blond and light brown, looked freshly brushed; he wore a double-breasted suit and a silk tie. He looked exactly like a man who had a dinner to go to but had waited especially to have a word with them. He was immense, he was still young. From such a Hitlerite dream, Edith expected a lecture on the war effort and production norms.

"I wanted to welcome you," he told them in Polish. "You're part of the expansion of these works." He looked away, it was even possible he was thinking, Don't tell them that, they've got no stake in the place.

Then, without blinking, without any introduction, any qualifying lift of the shoulders, he told them, "You'll be safe working here. If you work here, then you'll live through the war." Then he said good night and left the office with them, allowing Bankier to hold them back at the head of the stairs so that the Herr Direktor could go down first and get behind the wheel of his car.

The promise had dazed them all. It was a godlike promise. How could a man make a promise like that? But Edith Liebgold found herself believing it instantly. Not so much because she wanted to, not because it was a sop, a reckless incentive. It was because in the second Herr Schindler uttered the promise it left no option but belief.

The new women of Deutsche Email Fabrik took their job instruction in a pleasant daze. It was as if some mad old gypsy with nothing to gain had told them they would marry a count. The promise had forever altered Edith Liebgold's expectation of life. If ever they did shoot her, she would probably stand there protesting, "But the Herr Direktor said this couldn't happen."

The work made no mental demands. Edith carried the enamel-dipped pots, hanging by hooks from a long stick, to the furnaces. And all the time she pondered Herr Schindler's promise. Only madmen made promises as absolute as that. Without blinking. Yet he wasn't mad. For he was a businessman with a dinner to go to. Therefore, he must *know*. But that meant some second sight, some profound contact with god or devil or the pattern of things. But again, his appearance, his hand with the gold signet ring, wasn't the hand of a visionary. It was a hand that reached for the wine, it was a hand in which you could somehow sense the latent caresses. And so she came back to the idea of his madness again, to drunkenness, to mystical explanations, to the technique by which the Herr Direktor had infected her with certainty.

Similar loops of reasoning would be traced this year and in years to come by all those to whom Oskar Schindler made his heady promises. Some would become aware of the unstated corollary. If the man was wrong, if he lightly used his powers of passing on conviction, then there was no God and no humanity, no bread, no succour. There were of course only odds, and the odds weren't good.

9

That spring Schindler left his factory in Cracow and drove west in a BMW over the border and through the awakening spring forests to Zwittau. He had Emilie to see, and his aunts and sister. They had all been his allies against his father, they were all tenders of the flame of his mother's martyrdom. If there was a parallel between his late mother's misery and his wife's, Oskar Schindler – in his coat with the fur lapels, guiding the custom-made wheel with kid gloved hands, reaching for another Turkish cigarette on the straight stretches of thawing road in the Jeseniks – did not see it. It was not a child's business to see these things. His father was a god and subject to tougher laws.

He liked visiting the aunts – the way they raised their hands palm upwards in admiration of the cut of his suit. His younger sister had married a railway official and lived in a pleasant apartment provided by the rail authorities. Her husband was an important man in Zwittau, for it was a railway junction and had large freight yards. Oskar drank tea with his sister and her husband, and then some schnaps. There was a faint sense of mutual congratulation in the room – the Schindler children hadn't turned out so badly.

It was, of course, Oskar's sister who had nursed Frau Schindler in her last illness and who had now been visiting and speaking to their father in secret. She could do no more than make certain hints in the direction of a reconciliation. She did that over the tea and was answered by growls.

Later, Oskar dined at home with Emilie. She was excited to have him there for the holiday. They could attend the Easter ceremonies together like an old-fashioned couple. Ceremonies was right, for they danced around each other ceremoniously all evening, attending to each other at table like polite strangers. And, in their hearts and minds, both Emilie and Oskar were amazed by this strange marriage disability – that he could offer and deliver more to strangers, to workers on his factory floor, than he could to her.

The question that lay between them was whether Emilie should join him in Cracow. If she gave up the apartment in Zwittau and put in other tenants, she would have no escape at all from Cracow. She believed it her duty to be with Oskar – in the language of Catholic moral theology, his absence from her house was a "proximate occasion of sin". Yet life with him in a foreign city would be tolerable only if he was careful and guarded and sensitive to her feelings. The trouble with Oskar was that you could not depend on him to keep his lapses to himself. Careless, half tipsy, half smiling, he seemed sometimes to think that if he really liked some girl, you had to like her too.

The unresolved question about her going to Cracow lay so oppressively between them that when dinner was finished he excused himself and went to a café in the main square. It was a place frequented by mining engineers, small business-men, the occasional salesman turned army officer. Grate-fully he saw some of his motorbike friends there, most of them wearing Wehrmacht uniforms. He began drinking cognac with them. Some expressed surprise that a hulking chap such as he was not in uniform.

"Essential industry," he growled. "Essential industry."

They reminisced about their motorbike days. There were jokes about the one he'd put together out of spare parts when he was in high school. Its explosive effects. The explosive effects of his big 500cc Galloni. The noise level in the café mounted, more cognac was being shouted for. From the dining annexe old school friends appeared, that look on their face as if they had recognised a forgotten laugh, as in fact they had.

Then one of them got serious. "Oskar, listen. Your father's having dinner in there, all by himself." Oskar Schindler looked into his cognac. His face burned but he shrugged.

"You ought to talk to him," said someone. "He's a shadow, the poor old bastard."

Oskar said that he had better go home. He began to stand but their hands were on his shoulders, forcing him down again. He knows you're here, they said. Two of them had already gone through to the annexe and were persuading old Hans Schindler over the remnants of his dinner. Oskar, in a panic, was already standing, hunting through his pocket for his cloakroom disc, when Herr Hans Schindler, his face in agony, appeared from the dining room propelled gently along by two young men. Oskar was halted by the sight. In spite of his hauteur towards his father, he'd always imagined that if any ground was covered between himself and Hans, he'd be the one who'd have to cover it. The old man was so proud. Yet here he was letting himself be dragged to his son.

As the two of them were pushed towards each other, the old man's first gesture was an apologetic half grin and a sort of shrug of the eyebrows. The gesture, by its familiarity, took Oskar by storm. I couldn't help it, Hans was saying. The marriage and everything, your mother and me, it all went according to laws of its own. The idea behind the gesture might have been an ordinary one, but Oskar had seen an identical expression on someone's face already that evening. On his own, as, facing the mirror in the hallway of Emilie's apartment, he put on his coat for his outing. *The marriage and everything, it's all going according to laws of its own*. He had shared that look with himself, and here — three cognacs later — his father was sharing it with him.

"How are you, Oskar?" asked Hans Schindler. There was a dangerous wheeze along the edge of the words. His father's health was worse than he remembered it.

So Oskar decided that even Herr Hans Schindler was human, a proposition he had not been able to swallow at teatime at his sister's; and he embraced the old man, kissing him on the cheek three times, feeling the impact of his father's bristles, and beginning to weep as the corps of engineers and soldiers and past motorbikers applauded the gratifying scene.

10

The council of new chairman Artur Rosenzweig's Judenrat, who still saw themselves as guardians of the breath and health and bread ration of the internees of the ghetto, impressed upon the Jewish ghetto police, the Ordnungdienst, that they were also public servants. They tended to sign up young men of compassion and some education. Though at SS headquarters the OD was regarded as just another auxiliary police force which would take orders like any police force, *that* was not the picture most OD men lived by in the summer of 1941.

It cannot be denied that as the ghettos grew older the OD man became increasingly a figure of suspicion, a supposed collaborator. Some OD men fed information to the underground and challenged the system, but perhaps a majority of them found their existence and that of their families depended increasingly on the cooperation they gave the SS. To honest men, the OD would become a corrupter. To crooks it was an opportunity.

But in its early months in Cracow, it seemed a benign force. Leopold Pfefferberg could stand as a token of the ambiguity of being a member. When all education for Jews, even that organised by the Judenrat, was abolished in December 1940, Poldek had been offered a job managing the queues and keeping the appointment book in the Judenrat housing office. It was a part-time job, but gave him a cover under which he could travel around Cracow with some freedom. In March 1941, the OD itself was founded with the stated purpose of protecting the Jews entering the Podgórze ghetto from other parts of the city. Poldek accepted the invitation to put on the cap of the OD. He believed he understood its purpose, that it was not only to ensure rational behaviour inside the walls but also to achieve that correct degree of grudging tribal obedience which, in the history of European Jewry, has tended to ensure that the oppressors will go away more quickly, will become forgetful so that, in the interstices of their forgetfulness, life may again become feasible.

At the same time as Pfefferberg wore his OD cap, he ran illegal goods – leatherwork, jewellery, furs, currency – in and out of the ghetto gate. He knew the Wachtmeister at the gate, Oswald Bosko, a policeman who had become so rebellious against the régime that he let raw materials into the ghetto to be made up into goods – garments, wine, hardware – and then let the goods out again to be sold in Cracow, all without even asking for a bribe.

On leaving the ghetto, the officials at the gate, the lounging Schmalzownicks (or informers), Pfefferberg would take off the Judaic armband in some quiet alley, before moving on to business in Kazimierz or the Centrum.

On the city walls, above fellow passengers' heads in the trams, he would read the posters of the day, the razorblade advertisements, the latest Wawel edicts on the harbouring of Polish bandits, the slogan "Jews – Lice – Typhus", the billboard depicting a virginal Polish girl handing food to a hook-nosed Jew whose shadow was the shadow of the Devil. "Whoever helps a Jew helps Satan." Outside grocers' shops hung pictures of Jews mincing rats into pies, watering milk, pouring lice into pastry, kneading dough with filthy feet. The fact of the ghetto was being validated in the streets of Cracow by poster art, by copywriters from the Propaganda Ministry. And Pfefferberg, with his Aryan looks, would move calmly beneath the artwork, carrying a suitcase full of garments or jewellery or currency.

Pfefferberg's greatest coup had been last year, when Governor Frank had withdrawn hundred and five-hundred zloty notes from circulation and demanded that existing notes of those denominations be deposited with the Reich Credit Fund. Since a Jew could exchange only two thousand zloty, it meant that all notes held secretly – in excess of two thousand and against the regulations – would no longer have any value, unless you could find someone with Aryan looks and no armband who was willing on your behalf to join the long lines of Poles in front of the Reich Credit Bank. Pfefferberg and a young Zionist friend gathered some hundreds of thousands of zloty in the proscribed denominations from friends, went off with a suitcase full of notes, and came back with the approved occupation currency, minus only the bribes they'd had to pay to the Polish Blue Police at the gate.

That was the sort of policeman Pfefferberg was. Excellent by the standards of Chairman Artur Rosenzweig, deplorable by the standards of Pomorska.

Oskar visited the ghetto in April – both from curiosity and to speak to a jeweller he had commissioned to make two rings. He found it crammed beyond what he had imagined – two families to a room unless you were lucky enough to know someone in the Judenrat. There was a smell of clogged watercloset, but the women held off typhus by arduous scrubbing and by boiling clothes in courtyards. "Things are changing," the jeweller confided in Oskar. "The OD have been issued with truncheons." As the administration of the ghetto, like that of all ghettos in Poland, had passed from the control of Governor Frank to that of the Gestapo Section 4B, the final authority for all Jewish matters in Cracow was now SS Oberführer Julian Scherner, a hearty man of somewhere between forty-five and fifty, who in civilian clothes and with his baldness and thick lenses looked like a fairly nondescript bureaucrat. Oskar had met him at cocktail parties among the German community. Scherner talked a great deal – not about the war but about business and investment. He was the sort of functionary who abounded in the middle ranks of the SS, a sport, interested in booze, women and confiscated goods. He could sometimes be discovered wearing the smirk of his unexpected power like a childish jam-stain in the corner of the mouth. He was always convivial and dependably heartless. Oskar could tell that Scherner favoured working the Jews rather than killing them, that he would bend rules for the sake of profit but that he would fulfil the general drift of SS policy, however that might develop.

Oskar had remembered the police chief last Christmas, and sent him half a dozen bottles of cognac. Now that the man's power had expanded, he would rate more this year.

It was because of this shift of power, the SS becoming not simply the arm of policy but the makers of it as well, that beneath the strengthening April sun the OD was taking on a new nature. Oskar, merely by driving past the ghetto, became familiar with a new figure, a former glazier called Symche Spira, the new force in the OD. Spira was of orthodox background and by personal history as well as temperament despised the Europeanised Jewish liberals who were still found on the Judenrat council. He took his orders not from Artur Rosenzweig but from Untersturm-führer Brandt and SS headquarters across the river. From his conferences with Brandt, he returned to the ghetto with increased knowingness and power. Brandt had asked him to set up and lead a Political Section OD and he recruited various of his friends for it. Their uniform ceased to be the cap and armband of the street OD and became instead grey shirt, cavalry britches, Sam Browne belt and shiny SS boots.

Spira's Political Section would go beyond the demands of grudging cooperation and would be full of venal men, men with complexes, with puerile grudges about the social and intellectual slights they'd received in earlier days from respectable middle-class Jewry. Apart from Symche, there were Szymon Spitz and Marcel Zellinger, Ignacy Diamond, David Gutter the salesman, Forster and Grüner and Landau. They settled in to a career of extortion and of making out for the SS lists of unsatisfactory or seditious ghetto dwellers.

Poldek Pfefferberg now wanted to escape the force. There was a rumour that the Gestapo would make all OD men swear an oath to the Führer, after which they would have no grounds for disobedience. Poldek did not want to share a profession with grey-shirted Spira or with Spitz and Zellinger, the makers of lists. He went down the street to the hospital at the corner of Wegierska to speak to the official physician to the Judenrat, a gentle, slightly buck-toothed man called Alexander Biberstein, whose brother, Marek, the first president of the council, was still doing time in mournful Montelupich prison for currency violations and attempting to bribe officials.

Pfefferberg begged Biberstein to give him a medical certificate so that he could leave the OD. It was difficult, Biberstein said. Pfefferberg did not even look sick. It would be impossible for him to feign high blood pressure. Dr. Biberstein instructed him in the symptoms of a bad back. Pfefferberg took to reporting for duty severely stooped and supporting himself with a cane.

Spira was outraged. When Pfefferberg had first asked him about leaving the OD, the police chief had pronounced – like a commander of some palace guard – that the only way out was on your shield. Inside the ghetto, Spira and his infantile friends were playing a game of élite corps. They were the Foreign Legion, they were the praetorians. "We'll send you to the Gestapo doctor," screamed Spira.

Biberstein, who had been aware of the shame in young Pfefferberg, had tutored him well. Poldek survived the Gestapo doctor's inspection and was invalided out of the OD suffering from an ailment likely to inhibit his good performance in matters of crowd control. Spira, saying goodbye to officer Pfefferberg, expressed a contemptuous enmity.

The next day Germany invaded Russia. Oskar heard the news illicitly on the BBC and knew that the Madagascar plan was finished now. It would be years before there were ships for a solution like that. Oskar sensed that the event changed the essence of SS planning, for everywhere now the economists, the engineers, the planners of movements of people, the policemen of every stripe put on the mental habits appropriate not only to a long war, but to a systematic pursuit of a racially impeccable empire.

In an alley off Lipowa, its rear pointing towards the work-shop of Schindler's enamel plant, stood the German Box Factory. Oskar Schindler, always restless and hungry for company, used to stroll over there sometimes and chat with the Treuhänder, Ernst Kuhnpast, or to the former owner and unofficial manager, Mr. Szymon Jereth. Jereth's Box Factory had become the German Box Factory two years back according to the usual arrangement – no fees being paid, no documents to which he was signatory having been drawn up. The injustice of that did not particularly worry Jereth any more. It had happened to most of the people he knew. What worried him was the ghetto. The fights in the kitchens, the pitiless communality of life there, the stench of bodies, the lice that jumped on to your suit from the greasy jacket of the man whose shoulder you brushed on the stairs. Mrs. Jereth, he told Oskar, was very low. She'd always been used to nice things, she'd come from a good family in Kleparz, north of Cracow. And when you think, he told Oskar, that with all the pineboard I could build myself a place *there*. He pointed to the waste land behind his factory. Workers played football there, vast, hard-running games in plentiful space. Most of it belonged to Oskar's factory, the rest to a Polish couple called Bielski. But Oskar did not point that out to poor Jereth or say that he too had been preoccupied by that vacant space. Oskar was more interested in the implied offer of lumber. You can 'alienate' as much pine-board as that? You know, said Jereth, it's only a matter of paperwork.

They stood together at Jereth's office window, considering the waste land. From the workshop came the sound of hammering and incessant power saws. I would hate to lose contact with this place, Jereth told Oskar. I would hate just to vanish into some labour camp and have to wonder from a distance what the damn fools were doing here. You can understand that, surely, Herr Schindler?

A man like Jereth could not foresee any deliverance. The German armies seemed to be enjoying limitless success in Russia, and even the BBC was having trouble believing that they were advancing into a fatal salient. The Armament Inspectorate orders for field kitchenware kept turning up on Oskar's desk, sent on with the compliments of General Julius Schindler scribbled at the bottom of the covering letters, accompanied by the telephoned best wishes of sundry junior officers. Oskar accepted the orders and the congratulations in their own right but took a contradictory joy from the rash letters his father was writing to him to celebrate their reconciliation. It won't last, said Schindler senior. The man – Hitler – isn't meant to last. America will come down on him in the end. And the Russians? My God, did anyone ever take the trouble to point out to the dictator just how many godless barbarians there are over there? Oskar, smiling over the letters, was not too fussed by the conflicting pleasures – the commercial exhilaration of the Armaments Inspectorate contracts and the more intimate delight of his father's subversive letters. Oskar sent Hans a monthly bank draft of a thousand Reichsmarks in honour of filial love and sedition, and for the joy of largesse.

It was a fast and, still, almost a painless year. Longer hours than Herr Oskar Schindler had ever worked, parties at the Cracovia, boozing sessions at the jazz club, visits to the gorgeous Klonowska's apartment. When the leaves began to fall, he wondered where the year had gone. The impression of vanished time was augmented by the late summer and now by autumn rains earlier than usual. The asymmetric seasons would, by favouring the Soviets, affect the lives of all Europeans. But to Herr Oskar Schindler in Lipowa Street, weather was still simply weather.

Then, in the butt-end of 1941, Oskar found himself under arrest. Someone – one of the Polish shipping clerks, one of the German technicians in the munitions hall, you couldn't tell – had denounced him, had gone to Pomorska Street and given information. Two plainclothes Gestapo men drove up Lipowa Street one morning and blocked the entrance with their Mercedes as if they intended to bring all commerce at Emalia to an end. Upstairs, facing Oskar, they produced warrants entitling them to take all his business records with them. But they did not seem to have any commercial training. "Exactly what books do you want?" Schindler asked them.

"Cash books," said one.

"Your main ledgers," said the other.

It was a relaxed arrest: they chatted to Klonowska while Oskar himself went to get his cash journal and accounts ledger. Oskar was permitted time to scribble down a few names on a pad, supposedly the names of associates with whom Oskar had appointments which must now be cancelled. Klonowska understood, though, that they were a list of people to be approached for help in bailing Oskar out.

The first name on the list was that of Oberführer Julian Scherner, the second that of Martin Plathe of the Abwehr in Breslau. That would be a long-distance trunk call. The third name belonged to the supervisor of the Ostfaser works, the drunken army veteran Franz Bosch on whom Schindler had settled some quantities of illicit kitchenware. Leaning over Klonowska's shoulder, over her piled-up flaxen hair, his finger emphasised Bosch's name. A man of influence: Bosch knew and advised every high official who played the black market in Cracow. And Oskar knew that this arrest had to do with the black market, whose danger was that you could always find officials ready to be bribed but you could never predict the jealousy of one of your employees.

The fourth name on the list was that of the German chairman of Ferrum AG of Sosnowiec, the company from which Herr Schindler bought his steel. These names were a comfort to him as the Gestapo Mercedes carried him to Pomorska Street, a kilometre or so west of the Centrum. They were a guarantee that he would not vanish into the system without trace. He was not therefore as defenceless as the thousand ghetto dwellers who had been rounded up according to Symche Spira's lists and marched beneath the frosty stars of Advent to the cattle wagons at Prokocim station. Oskar knew some heavy guns.

The SS complex in Cracow was an immense modern building, humourless but not as portentous as the Montelupich prison. Yet, even if you disbelieved the rumours of torture attached to the place, the building confused the arrestee as soon as he entered by its size, its Kafka-esque corridors, by the numb threat of the departmental names painted on the doors. Here you could find the SS Main Office, the headquarters of the Order Police, of Kripo, Sipo and Gestapo, of SS Economy and Administration, of Personnel, of Jewish Affairs, of Race and Resettlement, of the SS Court, of Operations, of SS Service, of the Reichskommissariat for the Strengthening of Germandom, of the Welfare Office for Ethnic Germans.

Somewhere in that hive a middle-aged Gestapo man, who seemed to have a more exact knowledge of accountancy than the two policemen who made the arrest, began interviewing Oskar. The man's manner was half amused, like that of a Customs official who finds that a passenger suspected of currency smuggling is really smuggling house plants for an aunt. He told Oskar that all the enterprises involved in war production were under scrutiny. Oskar did not believe it but said nothing. Herr Schindler could understand, the Gestapo man told him, that businesses supplying the war effort had a moral duty to devote all their product to that great enterprise. And to desist from undermining the economy of the Government General by irregular dealings.

Oskar murmured away in that peculiar rumble of his which could at the one time contain threat and bonhomie. Do you imply, Herr Wachtmeister, that there are reports that my factory does not fulfil its quotas?

"You live very well," said the man, but with a concessive smile, as if that was all right, it was acceptable for important industrialists to live well. And anyone who lives well, he pointed out . . . well, we have to be sure that his standard of living derives entirely from legitimate contracts.

Oskar beamed at the Gestapo man. "Whoever gave you

my name," he said, "is a fool and is wasting your time."

"Who's the plant manager of Deutsche Email Fabrik?" asked the Gestapo man, ignoring this.

"Abraham Bankier."

"A Jew?"

"Of course. The business used to belong to relatives of his."

These records might be adequate, said the Gestapo man. But if they wanted more, he presumed Herr Bankier could supply it.

"You mean you're going to detain me?" asked Oskar. He began to laugh. "I want to tell you now," he said, "when Oberführer Scherner and I are laughing about all this over a drink, I'll tell him that you treated me with the utmost courtesy."

The two who had made the arrest took him to the second floor where he was searched and permitted to keep cigarettes and a hundred zloty to buy small luxuries. Then he was locked in a bedroom, one of the best places they had, Oskar surmised. Equipped with a washbasin and water closet and dusty drapes at the barred window. The sort of room they kept dignitaries in while interrogating them. If the dignitary was released, he could not complain about a room like this, any more than he could enthuse over it. And if he were found to be treacherous, seditious or an economic criminal, then, as if the floor of this room opened like a trapdoor, he'd find himself waiting in an interrogation cell in the basement, sitting motionless and bleeding in one of the series of stalls they called tramways, looking forward to Montelupich where they hanged people in their cells. Oskar considered the door. Whoever lays a hand on me, he promised it, I'll have him sent to Russia.

He was bad at waiting. After an hour he knocked at the door from the inside and gave the Waffen SS man who answered fifty zloty to buy him a bottle of vodka. It was of course three times the price of the drink but that was Oskar's method. Later in the day, by arrangement between Klonowska and Ingrid, a bag of toiletries, books and pyjamas arrived. An excellent meal was brought to him with a half bottle of Hungarian wine, and no one came to disturb him or ask him a question. He presumed that the accountant was still slaving at the Emalia books. He would have enjoyed a radio on which to listen to the BBC news from Russia, the Far East and the newlycombatant United States, and he had the feeling that if he asked his jailers they might bring him one.

He hoped the Gestapo had not moved into his apartment on Straszewskiego, to value the furnishings and Ingrid's jewellery. But by the time he fell asleep, he'd got to the stage where he was looking forward to facing interrogators.

In the morning he was brought a good breakfast – herring, cheese, eggs, rolls, coffee – and still no one bothered him. And then, the middle-aged SS auditor, holding both the cash journal and the accounts ledger, came to visit him.

The auditor wished him good morning. He hoped he had had a comfortable night. There had not been time to conduct more than a cursory examination of Herr Schindler's records, but it had been decided that a gentleman who stands so high in the opinion of so many people influential in the war effort need not be too closely looked at for the moment. We have, said the SS man, received certain telephone calls. Oskar was convinced, as he thanked the man, that the acquittal was temporary. He received the ledgers and got his money handed back in full at the reception desk.

Downstairs Klonowska was waiting for him, radiant. Her liaison work had yielded this result – Schindler coming forth from the death house in his double-breasted suit and without a scratch. She led him to the Adler, which they had let her park inside the gate. Her ridiculous poodle sat on the back seat.

12

The child arrived at the Dresners' on the eastern side of the ghetto late in the afternoon. She had been returned to Cracow by the Polish couple who had been minding her in the country. They had been able to talk the Polish Blue Police at the ghetto gate into allowing them entry on business, and the child passed as theirs.

They were decent people, and shamefaced at having brought her up to Cracow and the ghetto from the countryside. She was a dear girl, they were attached to her. But you couldn't keep a Jewish child in the countryside any more. The municipal authorities – let alone the SS – were offering sums of five hundred zloty and upwards for every Jew betrayed. It was one's neighbours. You couldn't trust your neighbours. And then not orly would the child be in trouble, we'd all be. My God, there were areas where the peasants went out hunting Jews with scythes and sickles.

The child didn't seem to suffer too much from whatever squalors the ghetto now imposed on her. She sat at a little table among screens of damp clothing and fastidiously ate the heel of bread Mrs. Dresner gave her. She accepted whatever endearments the women sharing the kitchen happened to utter. Mrs. Dresner noticed how strangely guarded the child was in all her answers. She had her vanities, though, and – like most three year olds – a passionately preferred colour. Red. She sat there in red cap, red coat, small red boots. The peasants had indulged her passion.

Mrs. Dresner made conversation by talking about the child's real parents. They too had been living, in fact hiding in the countryside. But, said Mrs. Dresner, they were going to come and join everyone here in Cracow soon. The child nodded but it didn't seem to be shyness that kept her quiet.

In January her parents had been rounded up according to a list supplied to the SS by Spira, and while being marched to Prokocim station had passed a crowd of jeering Poles – "Bye-bye Jews." They had dodged out from the column just like two decent Polish citizens crossing the street to watch the deportation of social enemies, and had joined the crowd, jeered a little themselves, and then strolled off into the countryside around that outer suburb.

Now they too were finding life no safer out there and intended to sneak back into Cracow during the summer. The mother of Redcap, as the Dresner boys named her as soon as they got home with the work details from the city, was a first cousin of Mrs. Dresner.

Soon Mrs. Dresner's daughter, young Danka, also got home from her work as a cleaning woman and servant at the Luftwaffe Air Base. Danka was going on fourteen, tall enough to have the Kennkarte (labour card) enabling her to work outside the ghetto. She enthused over the non-committal child. "Genia, I know your mother, Eva. She and I used to go shopping for dresses together and she'd buy me cakes at the patisserie in Bracka Street."

The child kept to her seat, did not smile, looked ahead. "Madam, you're mistaken. My mother's name is not Eva. It's Jasha." She went on naming the names in the fictional Polish genealogy in which her parents and the peasants had schooled her in case the Blue Police or the SS ever questioned her. The family frowned at each other, brought to a standstill by the untoward cunning of the child, finding it obscene but not wanting to undermine it, since it might, before the week was out, be essential survival equipment.

At suppertime, Idek Schindel, the child's uncle, a young doctor at the ghetto hospital in Wegierska Street, arrived. He was the sort of whimsical, half teasing and infatuated uncle a child needs. At the sight of him, Genia became a child, getting down off her chair to rush at him. If he were here, calling these people cousins, then they *were* cousins. You could admit now that you had a mother named Eva and that your grandparents weren't really called Ludwik and Sophia.

Then Mr. Juda Dresner, purchasing officer of the Bosch plant, arrived home and the company was complete.

April 28th was Herr Schindler's birthday, and in 1942 he celebrated it like a child of the spring, loudly, profligately. It was a big day at Deutsche Email Fabrik. The Herr Direktor brought in rare white bread, regardless of expense, to be served with the noonday soup. The festivity spread into the outer office and to the workshops out at the back. Oskar Schindler, industrialist, was celebrating the general succulence of life.

This, his thirty-fourth birthday, began early at Emalia – Schindler signalled it by walking through the outer office carrying three bottles of cognac under his arm to share with the engineers, the accountants, the draughtsmen. Office workers in accounts and personnel had handfuls of cigarettes pushed at them, and by mid-morning the handouts had spread to the factory floor. A cake was brought in from a patisserie and he cut it up on Klonowska's desk. Delegations of Jewish and Polish workers began to enter the office to congratulate him and he heartily kissed a girl called Kucharska, whose father had figured in the Polish parliament before the war. And then the Jewish girls came up, and the men shaking hands, even Stern getting there somehow from the Progress Works where he was now employed to take Oskar's hand formally and find himself wrapped up in a rib-cracking embrace.

That afternoon someone, perhaps the same malcontent as before, contacted Pomorska and denounced Schindler for his racial improprieties. His ledgers might stand up to scrutiny, but no one could deny he was a Jew-kisser.

The manner of his arrest seemed more professional than the first time. On the morning of April 29th, a Mercedes blocked the factory entrance and two Gestapo men, seeming somehow surer of their ground than the last two, met him crossing the factory yard. He was charged, they told him, with breaking the provisions of the Race and Resettlement Act. They wanted him to come with them. And, no, there was no need for him to visit his office first.

"Do you have a warrant?" he asked them.

"We don't need one," they told him.

He began to grin at them. The gentlemen should understand that if they took him away without a warrant they
would come to regret it.

He said it lightly, but he could tell by their demeanour
that the level of threat in them had firmed and focused since
last year's half-comic detention. Last time the conversation
at Pomorska had been about economic laws and whether
they had been breached. This time you were dealing with
grotesque law, the law of the lower guts, edicts from the
black side of the brain. Serious stuff.

"We will have to risk regret," one of the two told him.

He assessed their assurance, their perilous indifference to
him, a man of assets, newly turned thirty-four. "On a spring
morning," he told them, "I can spare a few hours for
driving."

He comforted himself that he would again be put into one
of those urbane cells at Pomorska. But when they turned
right up Kolejowa he knew that this time it would be
Montelupich prison.

"I shall wish to speak to a lawyer," he told them.

"In time," said the driver.

Oskar had it on the reasonable word of one of his
drinking friends that the Jagiellonian Institute of Anatomy
received corpses from Montelupich.

The wall of the place stretched a long block and the
ominous sameness of the windows of the third and fourth
floors could be seen from the back seat of the Gestapo
Mercedes. Inside the front gate and through the archway,
they came to an office where the SS clerk spoke in whispers,
as if raised voices would set up head-splitting echoes in the
narrow corridors. They took his cash but told him it would
be given to him during his imprisonment at a rate of fifty
zloty a day. No, the arresting officers told him, it was not yet
time for him to call a lawyer.

Then they left and in the corridor, under guard, he
listened for the traces of screams which might, in this
convent hush, spill out through the cracks of the Judas

windows in the walls.

He was led down a flight of stairs into a claustrophobic tunnel and past a string of locked cells, one with an open grille. Some half dozen prisoners in shirt sleeves sat there, each in a separate stall, facing the rear wall so that their features could not be seen. Oskar noticed a torn ear. And someone was sniffling but knew better than to wipe his nose. Klonowska, Klonowska, are you making your telephone calls, my love?

They opened a cell for him and he went in. He had felt a minor anxiety that the place might be crowded. But there was only one other prisoner in the cell, a soldier wearing his greatcoat up around his ears for warmth and seated on one of the two low wooden bed frames, each with its pallet. There were no washbasins of course. A water bucket and a waste bucket. And what proved to be a Waffen SS Standartenführer wearing a slight stubble, a stale unbuttoned shirt under the overcoat, and muddy boots.

"Welcome, sir," said the officer with a crooked grin, raising one hand to Oskar. He was a handsome fellow, a few years older than Oskar. The odds were in favour of his being a plant. But one wondered why they had put him in uniform and provided him with such exalted rank.

Oskar looked at his watch, sat, stood, looked up at the high windows. A little light from the exercise yards filtered in but it was not the sort of window you could lean against and relieve the intimacy of the two close bunks, of sitting hands on knees facing each other.

In the end they began to talk. Oskar was very wary, but the Standartenführer chattered wildly. What was his name? Philip was his name. He didn't think gentlemen should give their second names in prison. Besides, it was time people got down to first names. If we'd all got down to first names earlier, we'd be a happier race now.

Oskar concluded that if the man was not a plant, then he had had some sort of breakdown, was perhaps suffering from shellshock. He'd been campaigning in southern Russia, and his battalion had helped hang on to Novgorod all winter. Then he had got leave to visit a Polish girlfriend in

Cracow and they had, in his words, "lost themselves in each other," and he had been arrested in her apartment three days after his leave expired.

"I suppose I decided," said Philip, "not to be too damn exact about dates when I saw the way the other bastards" — he waved a hand at the roof, indicating the structure around him, the SS planners, the accountants, the bureau-crats — "when I saw the way *they* lived. It wasn't as if I deliberately decided to go absent. But I just felt I was owed a certain damn latitude."

Oskar asked him would he rather be in Pomorska Street. No, said Philip, I'd rather be here. Pomorska looked more like a hotel. But the bastards had a death cell there, full of shining chromium bars. But, that aside, what had Herr Oskar done?

"I kissed a Jewish girl," said Oskar. "An employee of mine. So it's alleged."

Philip began to hoot at this. "Oh, oh! Did your prick drop off?"

All afternoon Standartenführer Philip continued to con-demn the SS. Thieves and orgiasts, he said. He couldn't believe it. The money some of the bastards made. They started so sea-green incorruptible, too. They would kill some poor bloody Pole for smuggling a kilo of bacon while they lived like goddam Hanseatic barons.

Oskar behaved as if it were all news to him, as if the idea of venality among the Reichsführers was a painful assault on his commercial innocence, on the provincial Sudeten-deutsch innocence which had caused him to forget himself and caress a Jewish girl. At last Philip, worn out by his outrage, took a nap.

Oskar wanted a drink. A certain measure of alcohol would help speed time, make the Standartenführer better company if he were not a plant and more fallible if he were. Oskar took out a ten zloty note and wrote down names on it and telephone numbers, more names than last time, a dozen. He took out another four notes, crumpled them in his hands and went to the door and knocked at the Judas window. An SS NCO turned up — a grave middle-aged face staring in at him. He didn't look like a man who exercised Poles to death or ruptured kidneys with his boots, but of course, that was one of the strengths of torture, you didn't expect it from a man whose features were those of someone's country uncle.

Was it possible to order five bottles of vodka? Oskar asked. Five bottles, sir? said the NCO. He might have been advising a young callow drinker uncertain of quantities. He was also pensive, however, as if he were considering reporting Oskar to his superiors. The colonel and I, said Oskar, would appreciate a bottle apiece to stimulate conversation. You and your colleagues please accept the rest with my compliments. I presume also, said Oskar, that a man of your authority has power to make routine telephone calls on behalf of a prisoner. You'll see the telephone numbers there ... yes, on the notes. You don't have to call them all yourself. But give them to my secretary, eh? Yes, she's the first on the list.

These are very influential people, murmured the SS NCO.

You're a damn fool, Philip told Oskar. They'll shoot you for trying to corrupt their guards.

Oskar slumped, apparently casual. It's as stupid as kissing a Jewess, said Philip. We'll see, said Oskar. But he was frightened.

At last the NCO came back and brought, together with the two bottles, a parcel of clean shirts and underwear, some books and a bottle of wine, packed at the apartment in Straszewskiego Street by Ingrid and delivered to the Montelupich gate. Philip and Oskar had a pleasant evening together, although at one time a guard pounded on the steel door and demanded that they stop singing. And even then, as the drink added spaciousness to the cell and an unexpected cogency to the Standartenführer's ravings, Schindler was listening for remote screams from upstairs or for the button-clicking morse of some hopeless prisoner in the next cell. Only once did the true nature of the place dilute the effectiveness of the vodka. By his cot, partially obscured by the pallet, Philip discovered a minute statement in red pencil. He spent some idle moments deciphering it, not well, his Polish much slower than Oskar's.

"*My God*," he translated, "*how they beat me!* Well, it's a wonderful world, my friend Oskar. Isn't it?"

In the morning Schindler woke clear-headed. Hangovers had never plagued him and he wondered why other people made such a fuss about them. But Philip was liverish and depressed. During the morning he was taken away and came back to collect his belongings. He was to face a court martial that afternoon but had been given a new posting at a training school in Stutthof, so he presumed they didn't intend to shoot him. He picked up his greatcoat from his cot and went off to explain his Polish dalliance. Alone, Oskar spent the day reading a book by Karl May that Ingrid had sent and, in the afternoon, speaking to his lawyer, a Sudetendeutscher who'd set up a practice in civil law in Cracow two years ago. Oskar was comforted by the interview. The cause of the arrest was certainly as stated; they weren't using his trans-racial caresses as a pretext to hold him while they investigated his affairs. "But it will probably come to the SS court and you'll be asked why you aren't in the army."

"The reason is obvious," said Oskar. "I'm an essential war producer. You can get General Schindler to say so."

Oskar was a slow reader and savoured the Karl May story, the hunter and the Indian sage in the American wilderness – a relationship of decency. He did not rush the reading, in any case. It could be a week before he came to court. The lawyer expected that there would be a speech by the president of the court about conduct unbecoming to a member of the German race and then there would be a substantial fine. So be it. He'd leave court a more cautious man.

On the fifth morning he had already drunk the half litre of black ersatz coffee they'd given him for breakfast when an NCO and two guards came for him. Past the mute doors he was taken upstairs to one of the front offices. He found there a man he'd met at cocktail parties, Obersturmbannführer Rolf Czurda, head of the Cracow SD. Czurda looked rather like a businessman in his good suit.

"Oskar, Oskar," said Czurda like an old friend reproving. We give you those Jewish girls at five Marks a day. You should kiss us, not them.

Oskar explained that it had been his birthday. He'd been impetuous. He'd been drinking.

Czurda shook his head. I never knew you were such a big timer, Oskar, he said. Calls from as far away as Breslau, from our friends in the Abwehr. Of course it would be ridiculous to keep you from your work just because you touched up some Jewess.

You're very understanding, Herr Obersturmbannführer, said Oskar, feeling the request for some sort of gratuity building up in Czurda. If ever I'm in a position to return your liberal gesture.

As a matter of fact, said Czurda, I have an old aunt whose flat has been bombed out.

Yet another old aunt. Schindler made a compassionate click with his tongue and said that a representative of Chief Czurda would be welcome any time in Lipowa Street to make a selection from the range of products turned out there.

But it did not do to let men like Czurda think of his release as an absolute favour, and of the kitchenware as the least that the luckily released prisoner could offer. When Czurda said he could go, Oskar objected. I can't very well just call my car, Herr Obersturmbannführer. After all, my fuel resources are limited.

Czurda asked if Herr Schindler expected the SD to take him home.

Oskar shrugged. He *did* live on the far side of the city, he said. It was a long way to walk.

Czurda laughed. Oskar, I'll have one of my own drivers take you back.

But when the limousine was ready, engine running, at the bottom of the main steps, Herr Schindler glancing at the blank windows above him, wanting a sign from that other republic, the realm of torture, of unconditional imprisonment, the hell beyond bars for those who had no pots and pans to barter, Rolf Czurda detained him by the elbow.

"Jokes aside, Oskar, my dear fellow, you'd be a fool if you got a real taste for some little Jewish skirt. They don't have a future, Oskar. That's not just old-fashioned Jew-hate talking, I assure you. It's policy."

13

Even that summer, people inside the walls were clinging to the idea of the ghetto as a small but permanent realm. The idea had been easy enough to credit during 1941. There had been a post office, there had even been ghetto postage stamps. There had been a ghetto newspaper, even though it contained little other than edicts from the Wawel and Pomorska Street. A restaurant had been permitted in Lwówska Street, Foerster's Restaurant where the Rosner brothers, back from the perils of the countryside and the changeable passions of the peasants, played the violin and the accordion. It had seemed for a brief time that schooling would proceed here in formal classrooms, that orchestras would gather and regularly perform, that Jewish life would be communicated like a benign organism along the streets, from artisan to artisan, from scholar to scholar. It had not yet been demonstrated finally by the SS bureaucrats of Pomorska Street that the idea of that sort of ghetto was to be considered not simply a whimsy but an insult to the rational direction of history.

So when Untersturmführer Brandt had Judenrat president, Artur Rosenzweig, round to Pomorska for a beating with the handle of a riding crop, he was trying to correct the man's incurable vision of the ghetto as a region of permanent residence. The ghetto was a depot, a siding, a walled bus station. Anything that would have encouraged the opposite view had, by 1942, been abolished.

So it was different here from the ghettos old people remembered, even affectionately. Music was no profession here. There *were* no professions. Henry Rosner went to work in the Luftwaffe mess at the airbase. There he met a young German chef-manager called Richard, a laughing boy hiding, as a chef can, from the history of the twentieth century among the elements of cuisine and bar management. He and dapper Henry Rosner got on so well that Richard would send the violinist across town to take receipt of the Luftwaffe Catering Corps pay – You couldn't trust a German, said Richard; the last one had run off to Hungary with the proceeds.

Richard, like any barman worthy of his station, heard things and attracted the affection of officials. On the first day of June, he came to the ghetto with his girlfriend, a Volksdeutsche girl wearing a sweeping cape which, on account of the June showers, didn't seem too excessive a garment. Through his profession, Richard knew a number of policemen including Wachtmeister Oswald Bosko and had no trouble in being admitted to the ghetto, even though it was officially out-of-bounds to him. Once inside the gate, Richard crossed Plac Zgody and found Henry Rosner's address. Henry was surprised to see them. He had left Richard at the Luftwaffe mess only a few hours before, yet here he was with his girl, both of them dressed as for a formal visit. It reinforced for Henry the strangeness of the season. For the past two days, ghetto people had been queueing at the old Polish Savings Bank building in Józefińska Street for the new identity cards. To your yellow Kennkarte with its sepia passport photograph and its large blue J, the German clerks now attached – if you were lucky – a blue sticker. People could be seen to leave the Bank waving their cards with the Blauschein attached as if it proved their right to breathe, their permanent validity. Workers at the Luftwaffe mess, the Wehrmacht garage, at the Madritsch works, at Oskar Schindler's Emalia, at the Progress factory, all had no trouble getting the Blauschein. But those who were refused it felt that their citizenship of even the ghetto was under question.

Richard said that Henry's son, Olek, should come and stay with his girlfriend at her apartment. You could tell that he'd heard something in the mess. He can't just walk out of the gate, said Henry. It's fixed with Bosko, said Richard.

Henry and Manci were hesitant and consulted with each

other as the girl in the cape promised to feed Olek up on chocolate. An Aktion? Henry Rosner asked in a murmur. Is there going to be an Aktion?

Richard answered with a question. You've got your Blauschein? he asked. Of course, said Henry. And Manci? Manci too. But Olek hasn't, said Richard. In the drizzling dusk, Olek Rosner, only child, newly six years old, walked out of the ghetto under the cape of Richard the chef's girlfriend. Had some policeman bothered to lift the cape, both Richard and the girl could have been shot for their friendly subterfuge. Olek would vanish too. In the childless corner of their room, the Rosners hoped they'd been wise.

Poldek Pfefferberg, runner for Oskar Schindler, had earlier in the year been ordered to begin tutoring the children of Symche Spira, exalted glazier, chief of the OD.

It was a contemptuous summons, as if Spira were saying, "Yes, we know you're not fit for man's work, but at least you can pass on to my kids some of the benefits of your education."

Pfefferberg amused Schindler with stories of the tutorial sessions at Symche's house. The police chief was one of the few Jews to have an entire floor to himself. There, amidst two-dimensional paintings of nineteenth century rabbis, Symche paced, listening to the instruction Pfefferberg gave, seeming to want to see knowledge, like petunias, sprout from his children's ears. A man of destiny with his hand hooked inside his jacket, he believed that this Napoleonic mannerism was a gesture universal to men of influence.

Symche's wife was a shadowy woman, a little bemused by her husband's unexpected power, perhaps a little excluded by old friends. The children, a boy of about twelve and a girl of fourteen, were biddable but no great scholars.

When Pfefferberg went to the Polish Savings Bank he expected to be given the Blauschein without any trouble. He was sure his labour with the Spira children would be counted as essential work. His yellow card identified him as a *High School Professor*, and in a rational world as yet only partly turned upside down it was an honourable label.

The clerks refused to give him the sticker. He argued with them and wondered if he should appeal to Oskar or to Herr Szepessi, the Austrian bureaucrat who ran the German Labour Office down the street. Oskar had been asking him for a year to come to Emalia, but Pfefferberg had always thought it would be too constricting to have such full-time work.

As he emerged from the Bank building, details of German Security Police, the Polish Blue Police, and the political detail of the OD were at work on the pavements, inspecting everyone's card and arresting those who did not have the sticker. A line of rejects, hangdog men and women, already stood in the middle of Józefińska Street. Pfefferberg affected his Polish military bearing and explained that of course he had a number of trades. But the policeman, he spoke to shook his head, saying, Don't argue with me. No Blauschein? You join that line. Understand, Jew?

Pfefferberg went and joined the line. The delicate, pretty wife he'd married eighteen months earlier worked for Madritsch and already had her Blauschein. So there was that.

When the line had grown to more than a hundred, it was marched around the corner, past the hospital and into the yard of the old Optima confectionery works. Hundreds were already waiting. The early comers had taken the shady areas of what used to be the stables, where the Optima horses had once been harnessed between the shafts of drays laden with crèmes and liqueur chocolates. It was not a rowdy group. There were professional men, bankers, pharmacists and dentists. They stood in clusters, talking calmly. The young pharmacist Bachner stood speaking to an old couple called Wohl. There were many old people in here. The old and poor who depended on the Judenrat ration. This summer the Judenrat itself, the distributor of food and even of space, had been less equitable than it had been last.

Nurses from the ghetto hospital moved among these detainees with buckets of water, which was said to be good for stress and disorientation. It was, in any case, just about the only specific medicine, other than some black-market cyanide, that the hospital had to give. The old, the poor families from the Shtetls, took the water in restive silence.

Throughout the day, police of three varieties would enter the yard with lists, and lines of people would be formed to be met at the gate of the yard by SS details and moved out to Prokocim railway station. In some people the urge rose to evade this next movement by keeping to the far corners of the yard. But it was Pfefferberg's style to hang around the gate, looking for some official to whom he could make a claim. Perhaps Spira would be there, dressed up like a movie actor and willing – with a little leaden irony – to release him. In fact there stood by the gatekeeper's hut a sad-faced boy in an OD hat studying a list, holding the corner of the page in delicate fingers. Not only had Pfefferberg served briefly with the boy in the OD but in the first year of his teaching career at Kosciuszko high school in Podgórze he had taught his sister.

The boy looked up. Professor Pfefferberg, he murmured with a respect from those vanished days at the high school just over there by the park. As if the yard were full of practised criminals, he asked what Professor Pfefferberg was doing here.

It's nonsense, said Pfefferberg, but I haven't got a Blauschein yet.

The boy shook his head. Follow me, he said. He walked Pfefferberg to a senior uniformed Schupo at the gate and gave a salute. He did not look heroic in his funny cap and with his skinny vulnerable neck. Later, Pfefferberg supposed that that had given him greater credibility. He saluted the Schupo. "This is Herr Pfefferberg from the Judenrat," he lied with a deft combination of respect and authority. "He has been visiting some relatives." The Schupo seemed bored by the mass of police work proceeding in the yard. Negligently he waved Pfefferberg out of the gate. Pfefferberg had no leisure to thank the boy or to reflect on the mystery of why a child with a skinny neck will lie for you even unto death just because you taught his sister how to use the vaulting horse.

Pfefferberg rushed straight to the Labour Office and jumped the queues. Behind the desk were Fraüleins Skoda and Knosalla, the two hearty Sudeten German girls. Liebchen, Liebchen, he told Skoda, they want to take me away because I don't have the sticker. Look at me, I ask you. Aren't I exactly the sort of fellow you'd like to keep around here?

In spite of the crowds who'd given her no rest all day, Skoda raised her eyebrows and failed to suppress a smile. She took his Kennkarte. I can't help you, Herr Pfefferberg, she told him. They didn't give it to you, so I can't. A pity . . .

But you *can* give it to me, Liebchen, he insisted in a loud, syrupy, soap-opera voice. I have trades, Liebchen, I have trades.

Skoda said that only Herr Szepessi could help him and it was impossible to get Pfefferberg in to see Szepessi. It would take days. But you will get me in, Liebchen, Pfefferberg insisted. And she did. That is where her reputation as a decent girl came from, because she abstracted from the massive drift of policy and could, even on a crowded day, respond to the individual face. A warty old man might not have done so well with her however.

Herr Szepessi, who also had a humane reputation even though he serviced the monstrous machine, looked quickly at Pfefferberg's permit, murmuring, "But we don't need gym teachers."

Pfefferberg had always refused Oskar's offers of employment because he saw himself as an operator, an individualist. He didn't want to work long shifts for meagre pay over in dreary Zablocie. But he could see now that the era of individuality was vanishing. People needed, as a staple of life, a trade. I'm a metal polisher, he told Szepessi. He had worked for short periods with a Podgórze uncle of his who ran a small metalworks in Rekawka.

Herr Szepessi eyed Pfefferberg from behind spectacles. Now, he said, that's a profession. He took a pen, thoroughly crossing out *High School Professor*, and in the process the Jagiellonian education of which Pfefferberg was so proud, and over the top he wrote *Metal Polisher*. He reached for a rubber stamp and a pot of paste and took from his desk a blue sticker. Now, he said, handing the document back to Pfefferberg, now should you meet a Schupo, you can assure him that you're a useful member of society.

Later in the year they would send poor Szepessi to Auschwitz for being so persuadable.

14

From diverse sources – from the policeman Toffel as well as drunken Bosch of Ostfaser (the SS textile company) – Oskar Schindler heard rumours that 'procedures in the ghetto' were growing more intense. The SS were moving into Cracow some tough Sonderkommando units from Lublin, where they had already done sterling work in matters of racial purification. Toffel had suggested that unless Oskar wanted a break in production, he ought to set up some campbeds for his nightshift until after the first Sabbath in June.

So Oskar set up dormitories in the offices and upstairs in the munitions hall. Some of the nightshift were happy to bed down there. Others had wives, children, parents waiting in the ghetto. Besides, they had the Blauschein, the holy blue sticker, on their Kennkartes.

On June 3rd, Abraham Bankier, Oskar's office manager, didn't turn up at Lipowa Street. Schindler was still at home, drinking coffee in Straszewskiego Street, when he got a call from one of his office girls. She'd seen Bankier marched out of the ghetto, not even stopping at Optima, straight to Prokocim depot. There'd been other Emalia workers in the group, too. There'd been Reich, Leser ... as many as a dozen.

Oskar called for his car to be brought to him from the garage. He drove over the river and down Lwówska towards Prokocim. There he showed his pass to the guards at the gate. The depot yard itself was full of strings of livestock wagons, the station crowded with the ghetto's dispensable citizens standing in orderly lines, convinced still – and perhaps they were right – of the value of passive and orderly response. It was the first time Oskar had seen this juxtaposition of humans and livestock wagons, and it was a greater shock than hearing of it; it made him pause on the edge of the platform. Then he saw a jeweller he knew. Seen Bankier? he asked. He's already in one of the wagons, Herr Schindler, said the jeweller. Where are they taking you? Oskar asked the man. We're going to a labour camp, they say. Near Lublin. Probably no worse than . . . The man waved a hand towards Cracow.

Schindler took a packet of cigarettes from his pocket, found some ten zloty notes and handed the packet and the money to the jeweller, who thanked him. They had made them leave home without anything this time. They said they'd be sending on the baggage.

Late the previous year, Schindler had seen in the SS Bulletin of Budget and Construction an invitation for bids for the construction of some crematoria in a camp south east of Lublin. Belzec. Schindler considered the jeweller. Sixty-three or four. A little thin, had probably had pneumonia last winter. Worn pinstriped suit, too warm for the day. And in the clear knowing eyes a capacity to bear finite suffering. Even in the summer of 1942 it was impossible to guess at the connections between such a man as this and those ovens of extraordinary cubic capacity. Did they intend to start epidemics among the prisoners? Was that to be the method?

Beginning from the locomotive, Schindler moved along the line of more than twenty cattle wagons, calling Bankier's name to the faces peering down at him from the open grillework high above the slats of the cars. It was fortunate for Abraham that Oskar did not ask himself why it was Bankier's name he called, that he did not pause and consider that Bankier's had only equal value to all the other names loaded aboard the Ostbahn rolling stock. An existentialist might have been defeated by the numbers at Prokocim, stunned by the equal appeal of all the names and voices. But Herr Schindler was a philosophic innocent. He knew the people he knew. He knew the name of Bankier. *Bankier, Bankier*, he continued to call.

He was intercepted by a young SS man, an Oberscharführer, an expert railway shipper from Lublin. He asked for Schindler's pass. Oskar could see in the man's left hand an enormous list, pages of names.

My workers, said Schindler. Essential industrial workers. My office manager. It's idiocy. I have Armaments Inspectorate contracts, and here you are taking the workers I need to fulfil them.

You can't have them back, said the young man. They're on the list. The SS NCO knew from experience that the list conferred an equal destination on all its members.

Oskar dropped his voice to that hard murmur, the growl of a reasonable man, well connected, who wasn't going to bring up all his cannon yet. Did the Herr Oberscharführer know how long it would take to train experts to replace those on the list? At my works, Deutsche Email Fabrik, I have a munitions section under the special protection of General Schindler, my namesake. Not only would the Oberscharführer's comrades on the Russian front be affected by the disruption of production, but the office of the Armaments Inspectorate would demand explanations as well.

The young man shook his head – he was just a harassed transit official, he was trying to say. "I've heard that sort of story before, sir," he said. But he was worried. Oskar could tell it and kept leaning over him and speaking softly with an edge of menace. "It's not my place to argue with the list," said Oskar. "Where is your superior officer?"

The boy nodded towards an SS officer, a man in his thirties carrying a frown above his spectacles. "May I have your name, Herr Untersturmführer?" Oskar asked him, already pulling a notebook from his suit pocket.

The officer also made a statement about the holiness of the list. For this man it was the secure, rational and sole basis for all this milling of Jews and movement of locomotives. But Schindler got crisper now. He'd heard about the list, he said. What he had asked was what the Untersturmführer's name was. He intended to appeal directly to Oberführer Scherner and to General Schindler of the Armaments Inspectorate.

"Schindler?" asked the officer. For the first time he took a careful look at Oskar. The man was dressed like a tycoon, wore the right badge, had Generals in the family. "I believe I can guarantee you, Herr Untersturmführer," said Schindler in his benign grumble, "that you'll be in southern Russia within a week."

The NCO going ahead, Herr Schindler and the officer marched side by side between the ranks of prisoners and the loaded wagons. The locomotive was already steaming and the engine driver leaning from his cab, looking down the length of the train, waiting to be despatched. The officer called to Ostbahn officials they passed on the platform to hold things. At last they reached one of the rear wagons. There were a dozen workers in there with Bankier; they had all boarded together as if expecting a joint deliverance. The door was unlocked and they jumped down – Bankier and Frankel from the office, Reich, Leser and the others from the factory. They were restrained, not wanting to permit anyone to detect their pleasure in being saved the journey. Those left inside began chattering merrily as if they were fortunate to be travelling with so much extra room. While, with emphasis in his pen strokes, the officer removed the Emalia workers one at a time from the list and required Oskar to initial the page.

As Schindler thanked the officer and turned to follow his workers away, the man detained him by the elbow of his suit coat. "Sir," he said, "it makes no difference to us, you understand. We don't care whether it's this dozen or that."

The officer had been frowning when Oskar first saw him, but now seemed calm as if he had discovered the theorem behind the situation. You think your thirteen little tinsmiths are important? We'll replace them with another thirteen little tinsmiths and all your sentimentality for these will be defeated. "It's the inconvenience to the list, that's all," the officer explained in the end.

Plump little Bankier admitted that the group had neglected to pick up Blauscheins from the old Polish Savings Bank. Schindler, suddenly testy, said to attend to it. But what his curtness covered was a dismay at those crowds at

Prokocim who, for want of a blue tab, stood waiting for the new and decisive symbol of their status, the cattle wagon, to be hauled by heavy engines across their range of vision. Now, the cattle transports told them, we are all beasts together.

15

From the faces of his own workers, Oskar could read something of the ghetto's torment. For people had no time to catch their breath there, no room to dig in, assert their habits or set up family rituals. Many took refuge and a sort of comfort in suspicion of everyone, of the people in the same room as much as of the OD man in the street. But then even the sanest were not sure whom to trust. "Each tenant," a young artist named Josef Bau wrote of a ghetto house, "has his own world of secrets and mysteries." Children suddenly stopped talking at any sound from the stairwell. Adults woke from dreams of exile and dispossession to find themselves exiled and dispossessed in a crowded room in Podgórze, the events of their dreams, the very taste of fear in dreams, finding continuity in the fears of the day. Fierce rumours beset them in their room, on the street, on the factory floor. Spira had another list and it was either twice or three times as long as the last. All children would go to Tarnow to be shot, to Stutthof to be drowned, to Breslau to be indoctrinated, deracinated, operated upon. Do you have an elderly parent? They are taking everyone over fifty to the Wieliczka salt mines. To work? No. To seal them up in disused chambers.

All this hearsay, much of which reached Oskar, was based on a human instinct to prevent the evil by voicing it; to forestall the fates by showing them that you could be as imaginative as they. But that June, all the worst of the dreams and whispers took concrete form, and the most unimaginable rumour became a fact.

South of the ghetto, beyond Rekawka Street, rose a hilly parkland. There was an intimacy, like that of medieval siege paintings, about the way you could look down over the ghetto's southern wall. As you rode along the brow of the hills the ghetto's map was revealed, and you could see, as you passed them, what was happening in the streets below.

Schindler had noticed this advantage while riding here with Ingrid in the spring. Now, shocked by the sights of Prokocim, he decided to go riding again. The morning after the rescue of Bankier, he hired horses from the stables in Bednarskiego Park. They were impeccably turned out, he and Ingrid, in long hacking jackets, riding britches and dazzling boots. Two Sudeten blonds high above the disturbed antheap of the ghetto.

They rode up through the woods and had a short gallop over open meadows. From their saddles they could now see Wegierska Street, crowds of people around the hospital corner and, closer, a squad of SS working with dogs, entering houses, families gushing forth into the street, pulling on coats in spite of the heat, anticipating a long absence. Ingrid and Oskar reined in their horses in the shade of trees and considered this sight, beginning to notice refinements of the scene. OD men armed with batons worked with the SS. Some of these Jewish police seemed enthusiastic, for in the space of a few minutes' viewing from the hill Oskar saw three reluctant women beaten over the shoulders. At first there was a naïve anger in him. The SS were using Jews to flog Jews. It would become clear during the day, however, that some of the OD bludgeoned people to save them from worse things. And there was a new rule for the OD anyhow: if you failed to deliver a family into the street, your own family was forfeit.

Schindler noticed, too, that in Wegierska Street two lines were continually forming. One was stable, but the other, as it lengthened, was regularly marched away in sections around the corner into Józefińska and out of sight. It was not hard to interpret this assembling and movement, since Schindler and Ingrid, fringed by pine trees and elevated above the ghetto, were a distance of only two or three short blocks from the action.

As families were routed out of the apartments, they were separated forcibly into two lines without regard for family considerations. Adolescent daughters with the proper papers went to the static line, from which they called out to their middle-aged mothers in the other. A nightshift worker, still sullen from disturbed sleep, was pointed to one line, his wife and child to the other. In the middle of the street, the young man argued with the OD policeman. The man was saying, Sod the Blauschein! I want to go with Eva and the kid.

An armed SS man intervened. Beside the nondescript mass of Ghettomenschen, such a being, in his freshly pressed summer uniform, looked superbly fed and fresh. And from the hill you could see the oil on the machine pistol in his hand. The SS man hit the Jew on the ear and was talking to him, loudly and harshly. Schindler, though he could not hear, was sure it was a speech he'd encountered before, at Prokocim station. It doesn't make any difference to me. If you want to go with your frigging Jewish whore, go! The man was led from one line to another. Schindler saw him edge along it to embrace his wife, and under cover of this act of conjugal loyalty, another woman crept back indoors and was not seen by the SS Sonderkommando.

Oskar and Ingrid wheeled their horses, crossed a deserted avenue and, after a few metres, rode out on to a limestone platform facing directly down Krakusa.

In its closer reaches, this street was not as hectic as Wegierska. A line of women and children, not so long, was being led away towards Piwna Street. A guard walked in front, another strolled behind. There was an imbalance in the line: far more children than the few women in it themselves could have borne. At the rear, dawdling, was a toddler, boy or girl, dressed in a small scarlet coat and cap. It compelled Schindler's interest because it made a statement, the way the argumentative shiftworker in Wegierska had. The statement had to do, of course, with a passion for red.

Schindler consulted Ingrid. It was definitely a girl, said Ingrid. Little girls got obsessed by colour, especially a bright colour like that.

As they watched, the Waffen SS man at the rear of the column would occasionally put out his hand and correct the drift of this scarlet node. He did not do it harshly – he could have been an elder brother. Had he been asked by his officers to do something to allay the sentimental concern of watching civilians, he could not have done better. So the moral anxiety of the two riders in Bednarskiego Park was, for an impulsive second, irrationally allayed. But it was brief comfort. For behind the departing column of women and children, to which the scarlet toddler placed a meandering full stop, SS teams with dogs worked north along either side of the street.

They rampaged through the fetid apartments – as a symptom of their rush, a suitcase flew from a second storey window and split open on the pavement. And, running before the dogs, the men and women and children who had hidden in attics or cupboards, inside drawerless dressers, the evaders of the first wave of search, jolted out into the pavement, yelling and gasping in terror of the Dobermanns. Everything seemed speeded-up, difficult for the viewers on the hill to keep pace with. Those who had emerged were shot where they stood on the pavement, flying out over the gutters from the impact of the bullets, gushing blood into the drains. A mother and a boy, perhaps eight, perhaps a scrawny ten, had retreated under a windowsill on the western side of Krakusa Street. Schindler felt an intolerable fear for them, a terror in his own blood which loosened his thighs from the saddle and threatened to unhorse him. He looked at Ingrid and saw her hands knotted on the reins. He could hear her exclaiming and begging beside him.

His eyes slewed up Krakusa Street to the scarlet child. They were doing it within half a block of *her*: they hadn't waited for her column to turn out of sight into Józefińska. Schindler could not have explained at first how that compounded the murders on the pavement. Yet somehow it proved, in a way no one could ignore, their serious intent. While the scarlet child stopped in her column and turned to watch, they shot the woman beneath the windowsill in the neck, and one of them, when the boy slid down the wall whimpering, jammed a boot down on his head as if to hold it still and put the barrel against the back of the neck – the recommended SS target – and fired.

Oskar looked again for the small red girl. She had stopped and turned and seen the boot descend. A gap had already widened between her and the next last in the column. Again the SS guard fraternally corrected her drift, nudged her back into line. Herr Schindler could not see why he did not bludgeon her with his rifle butt, since at the other end of Krakusa Street mercy had been cancelled.

At last Schindler slithered from his horse, tripped, and found himself on his knees hugging the trunk of a pine tree. The urge to throw up his excellent breakfast was, he sensed, to be suppressed, for he suspected it meant that all his cunning body was doing was making room to digest the horrors of Krakusa Street.

Their lack of shame, as men who had been born of women and had to write letters home (What did they put in them?), wasn't the worst aspect of what he'd seen. He *knew* they had no shame, since the guard at the base of the column had not felt any need to stop the red child from seeing things. But, worst of all, if there was no shame, it meant there was official sanction. No one could find refuge any more behind the idea of German culture, nor behind those pronouncements uttered by leaders to exempt anonymous men from stepping beyond their garden, from looking out of their office windows at the realities on the pavement. Oskar had seen in Krakusa Street a statement of his government's policy which could not be written off as a temporary aberration. The SS men in Krakusa Street were, Oskar believed, fulfilling the orders of the leader, for otherwise their colleague at the rear of the column would not have let a child watch.

Later in the day, after he had absorbed a ration of brandy, Oskar understood the proposition in its clearest terms. They permitted witnesses, such witnesses as the red toddler, because they believed all the witnesses would perish too.

In the corner of Plac Zgody stood the Apotheke run by Tadeusz Pankiewicz. It was a pharmacy in the old style. Porcelain amphorae with the Latin names of ancient remedies marked on them and a few hundred delicate and highly varnished drawers hid the complexity of the pharma-copoeia from the citizens of Podgórze. Magister Pankiewicz lived above the shop by permission of the authorities and at the request of the doctors in the ghetto clinics. He was the only Pole permitted to remain within the walls. He was a quiet man in his early forties and had intellectual interests. The Polish impressionist Abraham Neumann, the composer Mordche Gebirtig, philosophical Leon Steinberg and the scientist and philosopher Dr. Rappaport were all regular visitors at Pankiewicz's. The house was also a link, a postal drop for information and messages running between the Jewish Combat Organisation (ZOB) and the partisans of the Polish People's Army. Young Dolek Liebeskind and Shimon and Gusta Dranger, organisers of the Cracow ZOB, would sometimes call there, but discreetly. It was important not to implicate Tadeusz Pankiewicz by their projects, which, unlike the cooperative policies of the Judenrat, involved furious and unequivocal resistance.

The square in front of Pankiewicz's pharmacy became in those first days of June a marshalling yard. "It beggared belief," Pankiewicz would always say thereafter of Plac Zgody. In the parkland in the middle, people were graded again and told to leave their luggage – No, no, it will be sent on to you! Against the blank wall at the western end of the square, those who resisted or were found carrying the secret option of Aryan papers in their pockets were shot without any explanation or excuses to the people in the middle. The astounding thunder of rifles fractured conversation and hope. Yet in spite of the screams and wailing of those related to the victims, some people, shocked or focusing desperately on life, seemed almost unaware of the heap of corpses. Once the trucks rolled up, and details of Jewish males loaded the dead into the back, those left in the square would begin at once to talk of their futures again. And Pankiewicz would hear what he had been hearing all day from SS NCOs. "I assure you, madam, you Jews are going to work. Do you think we can afford to squander you?" Frantic desire to believe would show blatantly on the faces of those women. And the SS rank and file, fresh from the executions against the wall, strolled among the crowd and advised people how to label their luggage.

From Bednarskiego, Oskar Schindler had not been able to see into Plac Zgody. But Pankiewicz in the square, like Schindler on the hill, had never witnessed such dispassionate horror. Like Oskar, he was plagued by nausea and his ears were full of an unreal sibilance, as if he had been struck on the head. He was so confused by the mass of noise and savagery, he did not know that among the dead in the square were his friends Gebirtig, composer of that famed song, *Burn City, Burn*, and gentle Neumann the artist. Doctors began to tumble into the pharmacy, panting, having run the two blocks from the hospital. They wanted bandages – they had dragged the wounded in from the streets. A doctor came in and asked for emetics. For in the crowd a dozen people were gagging or comatose from swallowing cyanide. An engineer Pankiewicz knew had slipped it in his mouth when his wife was not looking.

Young Dr. Idek Schindel, working at the ghetto hospital on the corner of Wegierska, heard from a woman who came in hysterical that they were taking the children. She'd seen the children lined up in Krakusa Street, Genia with them. Schindel had left Genia that morning with neighbours: he was her guardian in the ghetto, her parents were still hiding in the country, intending to slip back into the – until today – relative safety of the ghetto. This morning Genia, in accordance with her general air of being her own woman, had wandered away from the woman who was minding her back to the house where she lived with her uncle. There she had been arrested. It was in this way that Oskar Schindler, from the park, had been drawn by her motherless presence in the column in Krakusa Street.

Taking off his surgical coat, Dr. Schindel rushed to the square and saw her almost at once, sitting on the grass, affecting composure within the wall of guards. Dr. Schindel knew how faked the performance was, having had to get up often enough to hush her night screams.

He moved around the periphery of the square and she saw him. Don't call out, he wanted to say, I'll work it out. He didn't want a scene because it could end badly for both of them. But he didn't need to be concerned, for he could see her eyes grow mute and unknowing. He stopped, transfixed by her pitiably admirable cunning. She knew well enough at the age of three years not to take the short-term comfort of calling out to uncles. She knew that there was no salvation in engaging the interest of the SS in Uncle Idek.

He was composing a speech he intended to make to the large Oberscharführer who stood by the execution wall. It was better not to approach the authorities too humbly or through anyone of lesser rank. Looking back again to the child, he saw the suspicion of a flutter of her eyes and then, with a dazzling speculator's coolness, she stepped between the two guards nearest to her and out of the cordon. She moved with an aching slowness which, of course, galvanised her uncle's vision, so that afterwards he would often see behind his closed eyes the image of her among the forest of gleaming SS knee boots. No one saw her. She maintained her part-stumbling, part-ceremonial bluffer's pace all the way to Pankiewicz's corner and round it, keeping to the blind side of the street. Dr. Schindel repressed the urge he had to applaud. Though the performance deserved an audience, it would by its nature be destroyed by one.

He felt he could not move behind her straight away without disclosing her feat by his adult clumsiness. Against all his usual impulses, he believed that the instinct which had taken her infallibly out of Plac Zgody would provide her with a hiding place. He returned to the hospital by the other way to give her time.

Genia returned to the front bedroom in Krakusa Street that she shared with her uncle. The street was deserted now, or if by cunning or false walls anyone was still there they did not declare themselves. She entered the house and hid under the bed. From the corner of the street, Idek, returning to the house, saw the SS, in a last sweep, come knocking. But Genia did not answer. She would not answer him when he arrived himself. It was just that he knew where to look, in the gap between curtain and window sash, and saw, shining in the drabness of the room, her red shoe beneath the hem.

By this time Schindler had returned his horse to the stable. He was not on the hill to see the small but significant triumph of red Genia's return to the place where the SS had first found her. He was already in his office at DEF, shut away for a time, finding the news too heavy to share with the dayshift. Much later, in terms uncharacteristic of jovial Herr Schindler, Cracow's favourite party guest, Zablocie's big spender, in terms that is which showed, behind the playboy exterior, an implacable judge, Oskar would lay special weight on this day. "Beyond this day," he would claim, "no thinking person could fail to see what would happen. I was now resolved to do everything in my power to defeat the system."

16

The SS kept at work in the ghetto until Saturday evening. They operated with that crispness which Oskar had observed in the executions in Krakusa Street. Their thrusts were hard to predict, and people who had escaped on Friday were caught on Saturday. Genia survived the week, however, through her precocious gift for maintaining silence and for being invisible in scarlet.

Over in Zablocie, Schindler did not dare believe that this red child had survived the Aktion process. He knew from talking to Toffel and other acquaintances from the police headquarters in Pomorska Street that seven thousand people had been cleared from the ghetto. A Gestapo official from the Jewish Affairs Office was delighted to confirm the clearance. Up in Pomorska Street, among the paper shufflers, the Aktion was voted a triumph.

Oskar had now become more exact about this sort of information. He knew, for example, that the Aktion had been led by large SS Obersturmführer Otto von Mallotke. Oskar kept no dossier, but he was preparing for another era when he would make a full report to either Canaris or the world. It would be made earlier than he expected. For the moment, he enquired after matters which he had in the past treated as temporary lunacies. He got his hard news from police contacts, but also from clear-headed Jews like Stern. Intelligence from other parts of Poland was piped into the ghetto, in part through Pankiewicz's pharmacy, by the partisans of the People's Army. Dolek Liebeskind, leader of the Akiva Halutz Resistance Group, also brought in information from other ghettos as a result of his official travelling job with the Jewish Communal Self-Help, an organisation which the Germans – with half an eye on the International Red Cross – permitted to exist.

It was no use bringing such tidings to the Judenrat. The Judenrat council did not consider it civilly advisable to tell the ghetto dwellers anything about the camps. People would merely be distressed, there would be disorder in the streets and it would not go unpunished. It was always better to let people hear wild rumours, decide they were exaggerated, fall back on hope. This had been the attitude of most Jewish councillors even under decent Artur Rosenzweig. But Rosenzweig was gone. The salesman David Gutter, helped by his Germanic name, would soon become president of the Judenrat. Food rations were diverted not only by certain SS officials but by Gutter and the new councillors, whose vicar in the streets was high-booted Symche Spira, chief of the OD. The Judenrat therefore had no interest any more in informing the ghetto people about their probable destinations, since they were confident that they themselves would not be made to travel.

The beginning of knowledge for the ghetto, and the clinching news for Oskar, was the return to Cracow – eight days after he'd been shipped off from Prokocim – of the young pharmacist Bachner. No one knew how he had got back inside the ghetto, or the mystery of why he returned to a place from which the SS would simply send him off on another journey. But it was, of course, the pull of the known that brought Bachner home.

All the way down Lwówska and into the streets behind Plac Zgody he carried his story. He had seen the final horror, he said. He was mad-eyed and his hair had silvered in his brief absence. All the Cracow people who had been rounded up in early June had been taken nearly to Russia, he said, to the camp of Belzec. When the trains arrived at the railway station the people were driven out by Ukrainians with clubs. There was a frightful stench about the place, but an SS man had kindly told people that that was due to the use of disinfectant. The people were lined up in front of two large warehouses, one marked 'Cloak Room' and the other 'Valuables'. The new arrivals were made to undress and a

148

small Jewish boy passed among the crowd handing out lengths of string with which to tie their shoes together. Spectacles and rings were removed. So, naked, the prisoners had their heads shaved in the hairdresser's, an SS NCO telling them that their hair was needed to make something special for U-boat crews. It would grow again, he said, maintaining the myth of their continued usefulness. At last the victims were driven down a barbed-wire corridor to bunkers which had copper Stars of David on their roofs and were labelled 'Baths and Inhalation Rooms'. SS men reassured them all the way, telling them to breathe deeply, that it was an excellent means of disinfection. Bachner saw a little girl drop a bracelet on the ground, and a boy of three picked it up and went into the bunker playing with it.

In the bunkers, said Bachner, they were all gassed. And afterwards squads were sent in to disentangle the pyramid of corpses and take the bodies away for burial. It had taken barely two days, he said, before they were all dead, except for him. While waiting in a great enclosure for his turn, he'd become alarmed by the tone of the reassurances issuing from the SS, and, somehow getting to a latrine, had lowered himself into the pit. He'd stayed there three days, the human waste up to his neck. His face, he said, had been a hive of flies. He'd slept standing, wedged in the hole for fear of drowning there. At last he'd crawled out at night.

Somehow he'd walked out of Belzec, following the railway line. Everyone understood that he had got out precisely because he was beyond reason. He'd been cleaned by someone's hand – a peasant woman's perhaps – and put into fresh clothes for his journey back to the starting point.

Even then, there were people in Cracow who thought Bachner's story was a dangerous rumour. Postcards had come to relatives from prisoners in Auschwitz. So if it was true of Belzec, it couldn't be true of Auschwitz. And was it credible? On the short emotional rations of the ghetto, one got by through sticking to the credible.

The chambers of Belzec, Herr Schindler found out from his sources, had been completed by March that year under the supervision of a Hamburg engineering firm and of SS engineers from Oranienburg. From Bachner's testimony, it seemed that three thousand killings a day were not beyond their capacity. Crematoria were under construction, lest old fashioned means of disposal of corpses should put a brake on the new killing method. The same company involved in Belzec had installed identical facilities at Sobibor, also in the Lublin district. Bids had been accepted and construction was well advanced for a similar installation at Treblinka near Warsaw. And both chambers and ovens were in operation at Auschwitz main camp and at vast Auschwitz Number Two camp a few kilometres away at Birkenau. The resistance claimed that ten thousand murders on a given day were within the capacity of Auschwitz Two. Then, for the Lódź area, there was the camp at Chelmno, also equipped according to the new technology.

To write these things now is to state the commonplaces of history. But to find them out in 1942, to have them break upon you from a June sky, was to suffer a fundamental shock, a derangement in that area of the brain in which stable ideas about humankind and its possibilities are kept. Throughout Europe that summer some millions of people, Oskar among them, and the ghetto dwellers of Cracow too, tortuously adjusted the economies of their souls to the idea of Belzec-like enclosures in the Polish forests.

That summer Schindler also wound up the bankrupt estate of Rekord and, under the provisions of the Polish Commercial Court, acquired by a species of *pro forma* auction, ownership of the property. Though the German armies were over the Don and on their way to the Caucasus oil fields, Oskar discerned by the evidence of what had happened in Krakusa Street that they could not finally succeed. Therefore it was a good season to legitimise to the limit his possession of the factory in Lipowa Street. He still hoped, in a way that was almost childlike and to which history would pay no regard, that the fall of the evil king would not bear away that legitimacy, that in the new era he would go on being Hans Schindler's successful boy from Zwittau.

Jereth of the box factory went on pressing him about

building huts, refuges, on his patch of waste land. Oska. .
the necessary approvals from the bureaucrats. A rest art
for the nightshift was his story. He had the timber for it – it
had been donated by Jereth himself.

When finished in the autumn, it seemed a slight and
comfortless structure. The planking had that crate-wood
greenness and looked as if it would shrink as it got darker
and let in the slanting snow. But during an Aktion in
October it was a haven for Mr. and Mrs. Jereth, for the
workers from the box factory and the radiator works, and
for Oskar's nightshift.

The Oskar Schindler who comes down from his office on
the frosty mornings of an Aktion to speak to the SS man, to
the Ukrainian auxiliary, to the Blue Police and to OD details
who would have marched across from Podgórze to escort
his nightshift home; the Oskar Schindler who, drinking
coffee, rings Wachtmeister Bosko's office near the ghetto
and tells some lie about why his nightshift must stay in
Lipowa Street this morning – that Oskar Schindler has
endangered himself now beyond the limit of cautious business practice. The men of influence who have twice sprung
him from prison cannot do it indefinitely even if he is
generous to them on their birthdays. This year they are
putting men of influence in Auschwitz. If they die there,
their widows get a terse and unregretful telegram from the
commandant. "Your husband has died in Konzentrationslager Auschwitz."

Bosko himself was lanky, thinner than Oskar. Gruff-
voiced and, like him, a German Czech. His family, like
Oskar's, was conservative and looked to the old Germanic
values. He had, for a brief season, felt a pan-Germanic
anticipation at the rise of Hitler, exactly the way Beethoven
had felt a grand European fervour for Napoleon. In Vienna,
where he had been studying his theology, he'd joined the SS,
partly as an alternative to conscription into the Wehrmacht,
partly from an evanescent ardour. He regretted that ardour
now and was, more fully than Oskar knew, expiating it. All
that Oskàr understood about him at the time was that he
was always pleased to undermine an Aktion. His responsi-

perimeter of the ghetto and from his office
/alls he looked inwards at the Aktion with a
or; for he, like Oskar, considered himself a
tness.

d not know that in the October Aktion Bosko
led some dozens of children out of the ghetto in
carabv̲̲̲ boxes. Oskar did not know either that the
Wachtmeister provided, ten at a time, general passes for the
underground. The Jewish Combat Organisation (ZOB) was
strong in Cracow. It was made up mainly of youth club
members, especially of members of Akiva, a club named
after the legendary Rabbi Akiva, scholar of the Mishna. The
ZOB was led by a married couple, Shimon and Gusta
Dranger – her diary would become a classic of the Resistance – and by Dolek Liebeskind. Its members needed to
pass in and out of the ghetto freely for purposes of recruitment, to carry currency, forged documents and copies of
their underground newspaper. They had contacts with the
left wing Polish People's Army, which was based in the
forests around Cracow and which also needed the documents Bosko provided. Even though Bosko's contacts with
the ZOB and the People's Army were sufficient to hang him,
he secretly despised himself and had contempt for partial
rescues. Bosko wanted to save everyone, and would soon try
to, and perish for it.

At fourteen, Danka Dresner, cousin of Red Genia, had
outgrown the sure infantile instincts which had led her small
relative safely out of the cordon in Plac Zgody. Though she
had her work as a cleaning woman over at the Luftwaffe
base, the truth was that by autumn any woman under fifteen
or over forty could be taken away, anyhow.

Therefore, on the morning an SS Sonderkommando and
squads of Security Police rolled into Lwówska Street, Mrs.
Dresner took Danka with her down to Dabrowski, to the
house of a neighbour who had a false wall. The neighbour
was a woman in her late thirties, a servant at the Gestapo
mess near the Wawel, who could expect some preferential
treatment. But she had elderly parents who were automatic

risks. So she had bricked up a sixty-centimetre cavity for her parents, a costly project, since each brick had to be smuggled into the ghetto in barrows under heaps of permitted goods – rags, firewood, disinfectant. God knew what her bricked up secret space had cost her – five thousand zloty, maybe ten thousand.

She'd mentioned it a number of times to Mrs. Dresner. If there was an Aktion, Mrs. Dresner could bring Danka and come herself. Therefore, on the morning Danka and Mrs. Dresner heard from around the corner of Dabrowski the startling noise, the bark of Dalmatians and Dobermanns, the megaphoned roaring of Oberscharführers, they hurried to their friend's place.

When the Dresners had gone up the stairs and found the right room they could see that the clamour had had an effect on their friend. "It sounds bad," said the woman. "I have my parents in there already. I can fit the girl in. But not you."

Danka stared, captivated, at the end wall, at its stained wallpaper. In there, sandwiched in brick, rats perhaps worrying at their feet, their senses stretched by darkness, were this woman's elderly mother and father.

Mrs. Dresner could tell that the woman wasn't rational. The girl, but not you, she kept saying. It was as if she thought that should the SS penetrate the wall they would be more forgiving on account of Danka's lesser poundage. Mrs. Dresner explained that she was scarcely obese, that the Aktion seemed to be concentrating on this side of Lwówska Street and that she had nowhere else to go. And that she could fit. Danka was a reliable girl, said Mrs. Dresner, but she would feel safer with her mother in there. You could see by measuring the wall with your eyes that four people could fit abreast in the cavity. But shots from two blocks distant swept away the last of the woman's reason. I can fit the girl, she screamed. I want you to go.

Mrs. Dresner turned to Danka and told her to go into the wall. Later Danka would not know why she had obeyed her mother and gone so mutely into hiding. The woman took her to the attic, lifted a rug from the floor, then a raft of floorboards. Then Danka descended into the cavity. It wasn't black in there: the parents were burning a stub of candle. Danka found herself beside the woman – someone else's mother but, beyond the unwashed smell, the same warm protective mask of motherhood. The woman smiled at her briefly. The husband stood on the far side of his wife, keeping his eyes closed, not to be distracted from signals from outside.

After a time the friend's mother motioned to her that she could sit if she wanted. So Danka crouched sideways and found a comfortable posture on the floor of the cavity. No rats troubled her. She heard no sound – not a word from her mother and the friend beyond the wall. Above everything else she felt unexpectedly safe. And with the sensation of safety came displeasure at herself for obeying her mother's order so woodenly, and then fear for her mother, who was out there in the world of Aktions.

Mrs. Dresner did not leave the house at once. The SS were in Dabrowski Street now. She thought she might as well stay on. If she was taken, it was no loss to her friend. It might, in fact, be a positive help. If they took a woman from this room, it would probably increase their satisfaction with their task, exempt them from a sharper inspection of the state of the wallpaper.

But the woman had convinced herself no one would survive the search if Mrs. Dresner stayed in the room and, Mrs. Dresner could see, no one would if the woman remained in that state. Therefore she stood up, calmly despairing of herself, and left. They would find her on the steps or in the hall. Why not on the street? she wondered. It was so much an unwritten rule that ghetto natives must stay on quivering in their rooms until discovered that anyone found moving on the stairways was somehow guilty of defiance of the system.

A figure in a cap prevented her from going out. He appeared on the front step, squinting down the dark corridor to the cold blue light of the courtyard beyond. He recognised her, as she did him. He was an acquaintance of her elder son, but you could not be sure that that counted for anything: you could not know what pressures they'd put on the OD boys. He stepped into the hall and approached her. "Mrs. Dresner," he said. He pointed at the stairwell. "They'll be gone in ten minutes. You stay under the stairs. Go on. Get under the stairs."

As numbly as her daughter had obeyed her, she now obeyed the OD youth. She crouched in under the stairs, but knew it was no good. The autumn light from the courtyard showed her up. If they wanted to look at the courtyard, or at the apartment door at the rear of the hallway, she would be seen. Since upright or cowering made no difference, she stood upright. From near the front door, the OD man urged her again to stay there. Then he went. She heard yells, orders and appeals, and it all seemed to be as close as next door.

At last, he was back with others. She heard the boots at the front door. She heard him say in German that he'd searched the ground floor and no one was at home. There were occupied rooms upstairs, though. It was such a prosaic conversation he had with the SS men that it didn't seem to her to do justice to the risk he was taking. He was staking his existence against the likelihood that having worked down Lwówska and so far down Dabrowski they might by now be incompetent enough not to search the ground floor themselves and so not find Mrs. Dresner, whom he dimly knew, beneath the stairs.

As it turned out, they proved equable enough to take the word of the OD man. She heard them on the stairs, opening and slamming doors on the first landing, their boots clattering on the floor in the room of the cavity. She heard her friend's raised, shrewish voice. *Of course I have a work permit, I work over at the Gestapo mess, I know all the gentlemen.* She heard them come down from the second floor with someone, with more than one, a couple, a family. Substitutes for me, she would later think. A middle-aged male voice with an edge of bronchitis to it said, "But surely, gentlemen, we can take some clothing." And in a tone as indifferent as that of a railway porter asked for timetable information, the SS man telling him in Polish, "There's no need for it. At these places they provide everything."

The sound receded. Mrs. Dresner waited. There was no

second sweep. They would return again and again now, culling the ghetto. What in June had been seen as a culminating horror had become by October a daily process. And grateful as she was to the OD boy, it was clear as she went upstairs to get Danka that when murder is as scheduled, habitual, industrial as it was here in Cracow you could scarcely, with tentative heroism, redirect the overriding energy of the system. The more orthodox of the ghetto had a slogan – "An hour of life is still life." The OD boy had given her that hour. She knew there was no one who could give her more.

Upstairs, the woman was a little shamefaced. "The girl can come whenever she wishes," she said. That is, I didn't exclude you out of cowardice, but as a matter of policy. And the policy stands. You can't be accepted, but the girl can.

Mrs. Dresner did not argue – she had a sense that the woman's stance was part of the equation that had saved her in the downstairs hall. She thanked the woman. Danka might need to accept her hospitality in the future.

From now on, since she looked young for her forty-two years and still had her health, Mrs. Dresner would attempt to survive on that basis – the economic one, the putative value of her strength to the Armaments Inspectorate or to some other wing of the war effort. She wasn't confident about the idea. These days anyone with half a grasp on truth could tell that the SS believed the death of the socially unappeasable Jew outbalanced any value he might have as an item of labour. And the question is, in such an era, Who saves Juda Dresner, factory purchasing officer? Who saves Janek Dresner, car mechanic at the Wehrmacht garage? Who saves Danka Dresner, Luftwaffe domestic, on the morning the SS finally choose to ignore their economic value?

While the OD man was arranging Mrs. Dresner's survival in the hallway of the house in Dabrowski, the young Zionists of the Halutz Youth and the ZOB were preparing a more visible act of resistance. They had acquired uniforms of the Waffen SS and, with them, the entitlement to visit the

SS-reserved Cyganeria Restaurant in s.w. Ducha Plac, across the square from the Slowacki Theatre. In the Cyganeria they left a bomb which blew the tables through the roof, tore seven SS men to fragments, and injured a further forty.

When Oskar heard about it, he knew he could have been there, buttering up some official.

It was the deliberate intent of Shimon and Gusta Dranger and their colleagues to run against the ancient pacifism of the ghetto, to convert it to a universal rebellion. They bombed the SS-only Bagatella Cinema in Karmelicka Street. In the dark Leni Riefenstahl flickered the promise of German womanhood to the wandering soldier frayed from performing the nation's works in the barbarous ghetto or on the increasingly risky streets of Polish Cracow, and the next second a vast yellow spear of flame extinguished the sight.

The ZOB would in a few months sink patrol boats on the Vistula, petrol-bomb sundry military garages throughout the city, arrange Passierscheine for people who were not supposed to have them, smuggle passport photographs out to centres where they could be used in the forging of Aryan papers, derail the elegant army-only train that ran between Cracow and Bochnia, and get their underground newspaper into circulation. They would also arrange for two of OD chief Spira's lieutenants, Spitz and Forster, who had drawn up lists for the imprisonment of thousands, to walk into a Gestapo ambush. It was a variation of an old undergraduate trick. One of the underground, posing as an informer, made an appointment to meet the two policemen in a village near Cracow. At the same time, a separate supposed informer told Pomorska Street that two leaders of the Jewish partisan movement could be found at a particular rendezvous point. Spitz and Forster were both mown down while running from the Gestapo.

Still the style of resistance for the ghetto dwellers remained that of Artur Rosenzweig, who when asked in June to make a list of thousands for deportation, had placed his own name, his wife's, his daughter's at the top.

Over in Zablocie, in the backyard of Emalia, Mr. Jereth and Oskar Schindler were pursuing their own species of resistance by planning a second barracks.

17

An Austrian dentist called Dr. Sedlacek had now arrived in Cracow and was making wary enquiries about Schindler. He had come by train from Budapest and carried a list of possible Cracow contacts and, in a false-bottomed suitcase, a quantity of occupation zloty which, since Governor General Frank had abolished the major denominations of Polish money, took up an unconscionable space.

Though he pretended to be travelling on business, he was a courier for a Zionist rescue organisation in Budapest.

Even in the autumn of 1942, the Zionists of Palestine, let alone the population of the world, knew nothing but rumours of what was happening in Europe. They had set up a bureau in Istanbul to glean hard intelligence. From an appartment in the Beyoglu section of the city, three agents sent out postcards addressed to every Zionist body in German Europe. The postcards read: "Please let me know how you are. Eretz is longing for you." Eretz meant 'the land' and, to any Zionist, Israel. Each of the postcards was signed by one of the three, a girl called Sarka Mandelblatt, who had a convenient Turkish citizenship.

The postcards had gone into the void. No one answered. It meant that the addressees were in prison, or in the forest, or at labour in some camp, or in a ghetto, or dead. All the Zionists of Istanbul had was the ominous evidence of silence.

In the late autumn of 1942, they at last received one reply, a postcard with a view of the Belvaros of Budapest. The message on it read, "Encouraged by your interest in my situation. Rahamin maher (urgent help) is much needed. Please keep in touch."

This reply had been composed by a Budapest jeweller

called Samu Springmann, who'd first received and then puzzled out the message on Sarka Mandelblatt's postcard. Samu was a slight man, jockey size, in the prime of his thirties. Since the age of thirteen, despite an inalienable probity, he had been oiling officials, doing favours for the diplomatic corps, bribing the heavy-handed Hungarian secret police. Now the Istanbul people let him know that they wanted to use him to pipe rescue money into the German empire and to transmit through them to the world some definite intelligence on what was happening to European Jewry.

In the German-allied Hungary of General Horthy, Samu Springmann and his Zionist colleagues were as bereft of solid news from beyond the Polish border as were the people in Istanbul. But he began to recruit couriers who, for a percentage of the bag or else out of conviction, would be willing to penetrate the German territories. One of his couriers was a diamond dealer, Erich Popescu, an agent of the Hungarian secret police. Another was an underworld carpet smuggler, Bandi Grosz, who had also assisted the secret police. A third was Rudi Schulz, an Austrian safe-cracker, an agent for the Gestapo Management Bureau in Stuttgart. Springmann had a gift for playing with double agents such as Popescu, Grosz and Schulz, by touching their sentimentality, their greed, and, if any, their principles.

Some of his couriers *were* idealists, working from firm premises. Sedlacek, who asked after Herr Schindler in Cracow towards the end of 1942, belonged to that species. He had a flourishing dental practice in Vienna and, in his mid forties, did not need to lug false-bottomed suitcases into Poland. But here he was, with a list in his pocket, the list having come from Istanbul. And the second name on the list, Oskar's.

It meant that someone – Itzhak Stern, the businessman Ginter, Dr. Alexander Biberstein – had forwarded Schindler's name to the Zionists in Palestine. Without knowing it, Herr Schindler had been nominated for the post of righteous person.

Dr. Sedlacek had a friend in the Cracow garrison, a fellow Viennese, a patient he'd got to know in his surgery. This was Major Franz von Korab of the Wehrmacht. On his first evening in Cracow, the dentist was to meet Major von Korab at the Hotel Cracovia for a drink. Sedlacek had had a miserable day, had gone to the grey Vistula and looked across at Podgórze, the cold fortress of barbed wire and lofty gravestoned walls, a cloud of a special dimness above it this mean winter's day, a sharper rain falling there beyond the fake eastern gate where even the policemen looked accursed. When it was time to go and meet von Korab he went gratefully.

In the suburbs of Vienna it had always been rumoured that von Korab had a Jewish grandmother. Patients would idly say so – in the Reich, genealogical gossip was as acceptable small talk as was the weather. People would seriously speculate over drinks whether it was true that Reinhard Heydrich's grandmother had married a Jew called Suss. Once, against all good sense but for the sake of friendship, von Korab had confessed to Sedlacek that the rumour was true in his case. This confession had been a gesture of trust which it would now be safe to return. Sedlacek therefore asked the major about some of the people on the Istanbul list. To Schindler's name, von Korab responded with an indulgent laugh. He knew Herr Schindler, had dined with him. He was physically impressive, said the major, and made money hand over fist. He was much brighter than he pretended to be. I can call him right now and make an appointment, said von Korab.

At ten the next morning they entered the Emalia office. Schindler accepted Sedlacek politely but watched Major von Korab, measuring *his* trust of the dentist. After a time Oskar warmed to the stranger and the major excused himself and would not be detained for morning coffee. "Very well," said Sedlacek, when von Korab was gone, "I'll tell you exactly where I come from."

He did not mention the money he had brought, nor the likelihood that in the future trusted contacts in Poland would be handed small fortunes in Jewish Joint Distribution

Commitee cash. What the dentist wanted to know, without any financial colouring, was what Herr Schindler knew and thought about the war against Jewry in Poland.

Once Sedlacek had the question out, Schindler hesitated. In that second, Sedlacek expected a refusal. Schindler's expanding workshop employed five hundred and fifty Jews at the SS rental rate. The Armaments Inspectorate guaranteed a man like Schindler a continuity of rich contracts, the SS promised him, for no more than seven and a half Reichsmarks a day per person, a continuity of slaves. It should not be a surprise if he sat back in his padded leather chair and claimed ignorance.

"There is one problem, Herr Sedlacek," he growled. "It's this. What they are doing to people in this country is beyond belief."

"You mean," asked Dr. Sedlacek, "that you're concerned my principals won't believe you?"

Schindler said, "Since I scarcely believe it myself."

He rose, went to the cabinet, poured two tumblers of cognac and brought one for Dr. Sedlacek. Returning to his own side of the desk with the other, he took a swallow, frowned at an invoice, picked it up, went to the door on the balls of his feet and swung it open as if to trap an eavesdropper. For a while he stood there framed. Then Sedlacek heard him talking in easy tones to his Polish secretary about the invoice. In a few minutes, closing the door, he returned to Sedlacek, took a seat behind the desk and, after another deep swallow, began to talk.

Even among Sedlacek's own small cell, his Viennese anti-Nazi club, it was not imagined that the pursuit of the Jews had grown quite so systematic. The story Schindler told him was not startling simply in moral terms: one was asked to believe that in the midst of a desperate battle, the National Socialists would devote thousands of men, the resources of precious railways, an enormous cubic footage of cargo space, expensive techniques of engineering, a fatal margin of their research and development scientists, a substantial bureaucracy, whole arsenals of automatic weapons, whole magazines of ammunition, all to an extermination

162

which had no military or economic meaning but merely a psychological one. Dr. Sedlacek had expected mere horror stories – hunger, economic strictures, violent pogroms in this city or that, violations of ownership – all the historically accustomed things.

Oskar's summary of events in Poland convinced Sedlacek precisely because of the sort of man Oskar was. He had done well from the occupation, he sat at the heart of his own hive with a glass of brandy in his hand. There was both an impressive surface calm and a fundamental anger in him. He was like a man who had, to his regret, found it impossible to disbelieve the worst. He showed no tendency to be extravagant in the facts he relayed.

If I can arrange your visa, said Sedlacek, would you come to Budapest and pass on what you have just told me to my principal and the others?

Schindler seemed momentarily surprised. You can write a report, he said. And surely you've heard this sort of thing from other sources. But Sedlacek told him no, there had been individual stories, details of this incident and that. No comprehensive picture. Come to Budapest, said Sedlacek. Mind you, it might be uncomfortable travelling.

Do you mean, asked Schindler, that I have to cross the border on foot?

Not as bad as that, said the dentist. You might have to travel in a goods train.

I'll come, said Oskar Schindler.

Dr. Sedlacek asked him about the other names on the Istanbul list. At the head of the list, for instance, stood a Cracow dentist. Dentists were always easy to visit, said Sedlacek, since everyone on earth has at least one *bona fide* cavity. No, said Herr Schindler. Don't visit this man. He's been compromised by the SS.

Before he left Cracow to return to Mr. Springmann in Budapest, Dr. Sedlacek arranged another meeting with Schindler. In Oskar's office at DEF, he handed over nearly all the currency Springmann had given him to bring to Poland. There was always some risk, in view of Schindler's hedonist taste, that he would spend it on black-market jewellery. But neither Springmann nor Istanbul required any assurances. They could never hope to play the auditor.

It must be stated that Oskar behaved impeccably and gave the cash to his contacts in the Jewish community to spend according to their judgment.

Mordecai Wulkan, who like Mrs. Dresner would come to know Herr Oskar Schindler in time, was a jeweller by trade. Now, late in the year, he was visited at home by one of Spira's political OD. This wasn't trouble, the OD man said. Certainly Wulkan had a record. A year ago he had been picked up by the OD for selling currency on the black market. When he had refused to work as an agent for the Currency Control Bureau, he had been beaten up by the SS, and Mrs. Wulkan had had to visit Wachtmeister Beck in the ghetto police office and pay a bribe for his release.

This June he'd been rounded up for transport to Belzec, but an OD man he'd known had led him straight back out of the Optima yard. Even in the OD there were Zionists, however small their chances of ever beholding Jerusalem might be.

The OD man who visited him this time was no Zionist. The SS, he told Wulkan, urgently needed four jewellers. Symche Spira had been given three hours to find them. In this way Herzog, Friedner, Grüner and Wulkan, four jewellers, were assembled at the OD station and marched out of the ghetto to the old Technical Academy, now a warehouse for the SS Economic and Administrative Main Office.

It was obvious to Wulkan as he entered the Academy that a great security operated here. At every door stood a guard. In the front hall an SS officer told the four jewellers that should they speak to anyone about their work here they could expect to be sent to a labour camp. They were to bring with them, he said, every day, their diamond-grading kits, their implements for assessing the karat value of gold.

They were led down into the basement. Around the walls stood racks laden with suitcases, and towering layers of portmanteaus, each with a name studiously and futilely printed on it by its past owner. Beneath the high-up windows stood a line of wooden crates. As the four jewellers squatted in a space cleared in the middle of the floor, two SS men took down a suitcase, laboured across the cellar with it and emptied it in front of Herzog. They returned to the rack for another, which they emptied in front of Grüner. Then they brought a cascade of gold for Friedner, then for Wulkan. It was old gold – rings, brooches, bracelets, watches, lorgnettes, cigarette holders. The jewellers were to grade the gold, separate the gold plate from the solid. Diamonds and pearls were to be valued. They were to classify everything, according to value and karat weight, in separate heaps.

At first they picked up individual pieces tentatively but then worked faster as old professional habits asserted themselves. As the gold and jewellery went into their heaps, the SS men loaded the stuff into its appropriate crate. Every time a crate was filled, it was labelled in black paint – 'SS Reichsführer Berlin'. There were quantities of children's rings and one had to keep a cool rational control of one's knowledge of their provenance. Only once did the jewellers falter, when the SS men opened a suitcase and out of it tumbled gold teeth still smeared with blood. There in a pile at Wulkan's knees, the mouths of a thousand dead were presented, each one calling for him to join them by standing and flinging his instruments and eye piece across the room and declaring the tainted origin of all this precious stuff. Then, after the hiatus, Herzog and Grüner, Wulkan and Friedner commenced to grade again, aware now of course of the radiant value of whatever gold they themselves carried in their mouths, fearful that the SS would come prospecting for it.

It took six weeks for them to work through the treasures of the Technical Academy. After they had finished there, they were taken to a disused garage which had been converted to a silver warehouse. The lubrication pits were filled to spilling over with solid silver – rings, pendants, Passover platters, *yad* pointers, breastplates, crowns, candelabra. They separated the solid silver from the silver plate, they weighed it all. The SS officer in charge complained that some of these objects were awkward to pack, and Mordecai Wulkan suggested that perhaps they might consider melting them down. It seemed to Wulkan, though he was not pious, that it would be somehow better, a minor triumph, if the Reich inherited silver from which the Judaic form had been removed. But for some reason the SS officer refused. Perhaps the objects were intended for some didactic museum inside the Reich. Or perhaps the SS liked the artistry of synagogue silverware.

When this valuing work ran out, Wulkan was again at a loss for employment. He needed to leave the ghetto regularly to find enough food for his family, especially for his bronchitic daughter. For a time he worked at a metalworks in Kazimierz, getting to know an SS moderate, Oberscharführer Gola. Gola found him work as a maintenance man at the SA barracks near Wawel. As Wulkan entered the mess with his wrenches, he saw above the door the inscription, *Fur Juden und Hunde Eintritt Verbotten – Entrance forbidden to Jews and dogs.* This sign, together with the hundred thousand teeth he had valued at the Technical Academy, convinced him that deliverance could not in the end be expected from the offhand favour of Oberscharführer Gola. Gola drank here without noticing the sign and neither would he notice the absence of the Wulkan family on the day they were taken to Belzec or some place of like efficacy. Therefore Wulkan, like Mrs. Dresner and some fifteen thousand other ghetto dwellers, knew that what was needed was a special and startling deliverance. They did not believe for a moment that it would be provided.

18

Dr. Sedlacek had promised an uncomfortable journey and so it was. Oskar journeyed in a good overcoat with a suitcase and a bag full of sundry comforts which he badly needed by the end of the trip. Though he had the appropriate travel documents, he did not want to have to use them. It was considered better if he did not have to present them at the border. He could always deny that he had been to Hungary that December.

He travelled in a goods van filled with bundles of the Party newspaper, *Voelkischer Beobachter*, for sale in Hungary. Closeted amidst the heavy Gothic print of Germany's official newspaper, the reek of printer's ink, he was rocked south over the winter-sharp mountains of Slovakia, across the Hungarian border and down to the valley of the Danube.

A reservation had been made for him at the Pannonia near the university, and on the afternoon of his arrival, little Samu Springmann and an associate of his, Dr. Rezso Kastner, came to see him. The two men who rose to Schindler's floor in the lift had heard fragments of news from refugees. But refugees could give you little but threads. The fact that they had avoided the threat meant that they knew little of its geography, its intimate functioning, the numbers it ran to. Kastner and Springmann were full of anticipation, since – if Sedlacek could be believed – the Sudeten German upstairs could give them the whole cloth, the first full-bodied report on the Polish havoc.

In the room the introductions were brief, for Springmann and Kastner had come to listen and they could tell that Schindler was anxious to talk. There was no effort, in this city obsessed with coffee, to formalise the event by calling room service for coffe and cakes. Kastner and Springmann, after shaking the enormous German by the hand, sat down. But Schindler paced. It seemed that far from Cracow and the realities of Aktion and ghetto, his knowledge disturbed him more than it had when he'd briefly informed Sedlacek. He rampaged across the carpet. They would have heard his steps in the room below, their chandelier would have shaken when he stamped his foot, miming the action of the SS man in the execution squad in Krakusa, the one who'd pinned his victim's head down with a boot in full sight of the red innocent at the tail of the departing column.

He began with personal images of the cruel parishes of Cracow, what he had beheld in the streets or heard from either side of the wall, from Jews and from the SS. In that connection, he said, he was carrying letters from members of the ghetto, from the physician Chaim Hilfstein, from Dr. Leon Salpeter, from Itzhak Stern. Dr. Hilfstein's letter, said Schindler, was a report on hunger. "Once the body fat's gone," said Oskar, "it starts to work on the brain."

The ghettos were being wound down, Oskar told them. It was true equally of Warsaw as of Lódź and of Cracow. The population of the Warsaw ghetto had been reduced by four-fifths, Lódź by two-thirds, Cracow by half. Where were the people who had been transferred? Some were in work camps, but the gentlemen here this afternoon had to accept that at least three-fifths of them had disappeared into camps that used the new scientific methods. Such camps were not exceptional. They had an official name – Vernichtungslager, extermination camp.

In the past few weeks, said Oskar, some two thousand Cracow ghetto dwellers had been rounded up and sent, not to the chambers of Belzec, but to labour camps near the city. One was at Wieliczka, one at Prokocim, both of these being railway stations on the Ostbahn line which ran towards the Russian front. From Wieliczka and Prokocim these prisoners were being marched every day to a site at the village of Plaszów, on the edge of the city, where the foundations for a vast labour camp were being laid. Their life in such a labour camp, said Schindler, would be no holiday – the barracks of Wieliczka and Prokocim were under the command of an SS man called Horst Pilarzik who had earned a reputation last June when he had helped clear from the ghetto some seven thousand people, of whom only one, a chemist, returned. The proposed camp at Plaszów would be under a man of the same calibre. What was in favour of the labour camps was that they lacked the technical apparatus for methodical slaughter. There was a different rationale behind them. They had economic reasons for existing – prisoners from Wieliczka and Prokocim were marched out every day to work on various projects, just as they were from the ghetto. Wieliczka, Prokocim and the proposed camp at Plaszów were under the control of the chiefs of police for Cracow, Julian Scherner and Rolf Czurda, whereas the Vernicht-ungslagers were run by the central management of the SS Administrative and Economic Main Office at Oranien-burg near Berlin. The Vernichtungslagers also used people as labour for a time, but their ultimate industry was death and its by-products – recycling of the clothes, the remaining jewellery or spectacles, the toys, and even the skin and hair of the dead.

In the midst of explaining the distinction between extermination camps and those for forced labour, Schindler suddenly sidestepped towards the door, wrenched it open, and looked up and down the empty hallway. I know the reputation of this city for eavesdropping, he explained. Little Mr. Springmann rose and came to his elbow. "The Pannonia isn't so bad," he told Oskar in a low voice. "It's the Victoria that's the Gestapo hotbed."

Schindler surveyed the hallway once more, closed the door and returned across the room. He stood by the windows and continued his grim report. The forced labour camps would be run by men appointed for their severity and efficiency in clearing the ghettos. There would be sporadic murders and beatings, and there would certainly be corruption involving food and therefore short rations for the prisoners. But that was preferable to the assured death of the Vernichtungslagers. People in the labour camps could get access to extra comforts, and individuals could be taken out and smuggled to Hungary.

These SS men are as corruptible as any other police force then? the gentleman of the Budapest rescue committee asked Oskar. "In my experience," growled Oskar, "there isn't one of them that isn't."

When Oskar finished there was silence. Kastner and Springmann were not readily astounded. All their lives they'd lived under the intimidation of the secret police. Their present activities were both vaguely suspected by the Hungarian police – rendered safe only by Samu's contacts and bribes – and at the same time disdained by respectable Jewry. Samuel Stern, for example, president of the Jewish council, member of the Hungarian senate, would dismiss this afternoon's report by Oskar Schindler as pernicious fantasy, an insult to German culture, a reflection on the decency of the intentions of the Hungarian government. So it was not that Springmann and Kastner were unmanned by Schindler's testimony as much as that their minds were painfully expanding. Their resources seemed minute now that they knew what they were set against: not just any average and predictable Philistine giant but the behemoth itself. Perhaps already they were reaching for the idea that as well as individual bargaining – some extra food for *this* camp, rescue for *this* intellectual, a bribe to temper the professional ardour of *this* SS man – some vaster rescue scheme would have to be arranged at breathtaking expense.

Schindler threw himself into a chair. Samu Springmann looked across at the now reposeful industrialist. He had made an enormous impression on them, said Springmann. They would of course send a report to Istanbul on all Oskar had told them. It would be used to stir the Palestinian Zionists and the Joint Distribution Committee to greater action. At the same time it would be fed to the governments of Churchill and Roosevelt. Springmann said that he thought Oskar was right to worry about people's belief in what he'd say, he was right to say it was all incredible. "Therefore," said Samu Springmann, "I urge you to go to Istanbul yourself and speak to the people there."

After a little hesitation – whether to do with the demands of the enamelware business or with the dangers of crossing so many borders – Schindler agreed. Towards the end of the year, said Springmann. "In the meantime you will see Dr. Sedlacek in Cracow regularly."

They stood up, and Oskar could see that they were changed men. They thanked him and left, becoming simply, on the way downstairs, two pensive Budapest professional men who'd heard disturbing news of mismanagement in the branch offices.

That night Dr. Sedlacek called at Oskar's hotel and took him out into the brisk streets to dinner at the Hotel Gellert. From their table they could see the Danube, its illuminated barges, the city glowing on the far side of the water. It was like a pre-war city, and Schindler began to feel like a tourist again. After his afternoon's temperance, he drank the dense, native burgundy, Bull's Blood, with a slow, assiduous thirst, and created a series of empty bottles at their table.

Halfway through their meal they were joined by an Austrian journalist, Dr. Schmidt, who'd brought with him his mistress, an exquisite, golden Hungarian girl. Schindler admired the girl's jewellery and told her that he was a great fancier of jewellery himself. But over apricot brandy he became less friendly. He sat with a mild frown, listening to Schmidt talk of real estate prices and car dealings and horse races. The girl listened raptly to Schmidt, since she wore the results of his business coups around her neck and at her wrists. But Oskar's surprising disapproval was clear. Dr. Sedlacek was secretly amused: perhaps Oskar was seeing a partial reflection of his own new wealth, his own tendencies towards trading on the fringes.

When the dinner was over, Schmidt and his girl left for some nightclub, and Sedlacek made sure he took Schindler to a different one. They sat drinking unwise further quantities of brandy and watching the floor show.

"That Schmidt," said Schindler, wanting to clear up the question so that he could enjoy the small hours. "Do you use him?"

"Yes."

"I don't think you ought to use men like that," said Oskar. "He's a thief."

Dr. Sedlacek turned his face, and its half smile, away.

"How can you be sure he delivers any of the money you give him?" Oskar asked.

"We let him keep a percentage," said Dr. Sedlacek.

Oskar thought about it for a full half minute. Then he murmured, "I don't want a damned percentage. I don't want to be offered one."

"Very well," said Sedlacek.

"Let's watch the girls," said Oskar.

19

Even as Oskar Schindler returned by freight car from Budapest, where he'd predicted that the ghetto would soon be closed, Untersturmführer Amon Goeth was on his way from Lublin to bring about that liquidation, and to take command of the resultant Zwangsarbeitslager (Forced Labour Camp) at Plaszów. Goeth was some eight months younger than Schindler, but shared more with him than the mere year of birth. Like Oskar he had been raised a Catholic and had ceased observing the rites of the Church as late as 1938, when his first marriage had broken up. Like Oskar, too, he had graduated from high school in the Realgymnasium – Engineering, Physics, Maths. He was therefore a practical man, no thinker but considered himself a philosopher. A Viennese, he had joined the National Socialist Party early, in 1930. When the nervous Austrian Republic banned the party in 1933, he was already a member of its security force, the SS. Driven underground, he had emerged on to the streets of Vienna after the Anschluss of 1938 in the uniform of an SS non-commissioned officer. In 1940 he had been raised to the rank of SS Oberscharführer and in 1941 achieved the honour of commissioned rank, immensely harder to come by in the SS than in Wehrmacht units. After training in infantry tactics, he was put in charge of Sonderkommandos during Aktions in the populous ghetto of Lublin and, by his performance there, earned the right to liquidate Cracow.

Untersturmführer Goeth, then, speeding on the Wehrmacht special between Lublin and Cracow, there to take command of well-tried Sonderkommandos, shared with Oskar not only his year of birth, his religion, his weakness for drink, but a massive physique as well. Goeth's face was open and pleasant, rather longer than Schindler's. His hands, though large but muscular, were long fingered. He was sentimental about his children, the children of his second marriage, whom he had not seen often in the past three years. As a substitute, he was sometimes attentive to the children of brother-officers. He could be a sentimental lover too, a cooer, but though he resembled Oskar in terms of general sexual voraciousness, his tastes were less conventional, running sometimes to his brother SS men, frequently to the beating of women. Once the first blaze of infatuation had died, he could start throwing punches. He considered himself a sensitive man, and thought that his family's trade proved it. His father and grandfather were printers and binders of books in Vienna and he liked to list himself on official papers as a Literat, a man of letters. And though, at this moment, he would have told you that he looked forward to his taking control of the liquidation operation – that this was the major chance of his career and carried with it the promise of promotion – his service in Special Actions seemed to him to have altered the flow of his nervous energies. He had been plagued with insomnia for two years now and, if he had his way, stayed up till three or four and slept late in the mornings. He had become a reckless drinker and believed he carried his drink with an ease he had not known in his youth. Again like Oskar, he never suffered the hangovers he deserved. He thanked his hard-working kidneys for this benefit.

His orders, entrusting him with the extinction of the ghetto and the kingship of Plaszów camp, were dated February 12th, 1943. He hoped that after consulting with his senior NCOs, with Wilhelm Kunde, commander of the SS guard for the ghetto, and with Willi Haase, Scherner's deputy, it would be possible to begin the clearing of the ghetto within a month of the date of his commission.

Commandant Goeth was met at Cracow Central Station by Kunde himself and by the tall young SS man, Horst Pilarzik, who was temporarily in charge of the work camps at Prokocim and Wieliczka. They piled into the back of a Mercedes and were driven off for a reconnaissance of the ghetto and the site of the new camp. It was a bitter day and snow began to fall as they crossed the Vistula. Untersturm-führer Goeth was pleased for a pull on a flask of schnaps Pilarzik carried with him. They passed through the fake Oriental portals and down the tramlines of Lwówska Street, which cut the ghetto into two icy portions. The dapper Kunde, who had been a Customs agent in civilian life and was adept at reporting to superiors, gave a deft sketch of the ghetto. The portion on their left was Ghetto B, said Kunde. Its inhabitants, about two thousand of them, had escaped earlier Aktions or had been previously employed in indus-try. But new identification cards had been issued since then, with appropriate initials – either W for army employees, Z for employees of the civil authorities, or R for workers in essential industries. The inhabitants of Ghetto B lacked these new cards and were to be shipped away for Sonderbe-handlung. In clearing the ghetto, it might be preferable to start on that side first, though that sort of tactical decision was entirely up to the Herr Commandant.

The greater portion of the ghetto stood to the right and contained some ten thousand people still. They would of course be the initial labour force for the factories of Plaszów camp. It was expected that the German entrepreneurs and supervisors, Bosch, Madritsch, Beckmann, the Sudetenlan-der Oskar Schindler, would want to move all or part of their operations out of town into the camp. As well as that there was a cable-making plant just over a kilometre from the proposed camp, and labourers would be marched there and back each day.

Would the Herr Commandant, asked Kunde, care to continue down the road a few kilometres and have a look at the camp site itself?

Oh yes, said Amon, I think that would be advisable.

They turned off the highway where the cable factory yard, snow lying on the giant spools, marked the beginning of Jerozolimska Street. Amon Goeth had a glimpse of a few groups of hunched and bescarfed women dragging seg-ments of huts – a wall panel, an eaves section – across the highway and up Jerozolimska from the direction of the railway station at Cracow-Plaszów. They were women from Prokocim camp, Pilarzik explained. When Plaszów was ready, Prokocim would of course be disbanded and these labouring women would come under the management of the Herr Commandant.

Goeth estimated the distance the women had to carry the frames to be some three-quarters of a kilometre. "All up hill," said Kunde, putting his head on one shoulder then on the other, as if to say, so it's a satisfactory form of discipline but it slows up construction.

The camp would need a railway spur, said Untersturmführer Goeth. He would make an approach to the Ostbahn.

They passed on the right a synagogue and its mortuary buildings, and a half-tumbled wall showed its gravestones like teeth in the cruelly exposed mouth of winter. Part of the camp site had been until last year a Jewish cemetery. "Quite extensive," said Wilhelm Kunde. The Herr Commandant uttered a witticism which would come to his lips often during his residency at Plaszów. "They won't have to go far to get buried."

There was a house to the right which would be suitable as a temporary residence for the commandant, and then a large new building to serve as an administration block. The synagogue mortuary, already partly dynamited, would become the camp stables. Kunde pointed out that the two limestone quarries within the camp area could be seen from here. One stood in the bottom of the little valley, the other up on the hill behind the synagogue. The Herr Commandant might be able to notice the tracks being laid for trolley which would be used in hauling stones. Once the heavy weather let up, the construction of the track would continue.

They drove to the south-east end of the proposed camp and a track, just passable in the snow, took them along the skyline. The track ended at what had once been an Austrian earth fort. A circular mound surrounding a deep and broad indentation. To an artillery man it would have appeared an important redoubt from which cannon could be sighted to enfilade the road from Russia. To Untersturmführer Goeth it was a place suited for disciplinary punishment.

From up here, the camp area could be seen whole. It was a rural stretch, graced with the Jewish cemetery, and folded between two hills. It was in this weather two pages of a largely blank book opened and held at an angle, sideways, to the observer on the fort hill. A grey stone country dwelling was stuck at the entrance to the valley and past it, along the far slope and among the few finished barracks, moved teams of women, black as bunches of musical notations, in the strange darkling luminescence of a snowy evening. Emerging from the icy alleys beyond Jerozolimska, they toiled up the white slope under the urgings of Ukrainian guards and dropped the sections of frames as instructed by the SS engineers in homburgs and civilian clothes.

Untersturmführer Goeth remarked confidingly that he had no complaints about the pace at which the prisoners on the far hill were working. He was in fact secretly impressed that, so late on a biting day, the SS men and Ukrainians on the far slope were not letting the thought of supper and warm barracks slow the pace of operations.

Horst Pilarzik assured him that it was all closer to completion than it looked: the land had been terraced, the foundations dug despite the cold, and a great quantity of prefabricated sections carried up from the railway station. The Herr Untersturmführer would be able to consult with the entrepreneurs tomorrow – a meeting had been arranged for 10 a.m. But modern methods combined with a copious supply of labour meant that these places could be put up almost overnight, weather permitting.

Pilarzik seemed to believe that Goeth was in genuine danger of demoralisation. In fact Amon was exhilarated. From what he could see here, he could make out the final shape of the place. Nor was he worried about fences, which would be a mental comfort for the prisoners rather than an essential precaution. For after the established methodology of SS liquidation had been applied to the Podgórze ghetto, people would be grateful for the barracks of Plaszów. Even those with Aryan papers would come crawling in here, seeking an obscure berth high up in the green, hoar-frosted rooftrees. For most of them, the wire was needed only as a prop, so that they might reassure themselves that they were prisoners against their will.

The meeting with the local factory owners and Treuhänders took place in Julian Scherner's office in central Cracow early the following afternoon. Amon Goeth arrived smiling fraternally and, in his freshly tailored Waffen SS uniform, crafted precisely for his enormous frame, seemed to dominate the room. He was sure he could charm the independents, Bosch and Madritsch and Schindler, into transferring their Jewish labour behind the wire of Plaszów. Besides that, an investigation of the skills available among the ghetto dwellers helped him to see that Plaszów could become quite a business. There were jewellers, upholsterers, tailors who could be used for special enterprises under the commandant's direction, filling orders for the SS, the Wehrmacht, the wealthy German officialdom. There would be the clothing workshops of Madritsch, the enamelworks of Schindler, a proposed metalworks, a brush factory, a warehouse for recycling used, damaged or stained Wehrmacht uniforms from the Russian front, a further warehouse for recycling Jewish clothing from the ghettos and despatching it for the use of bombed-out families at home. He knew from his experiences of the SS jewellery and fur warehouses of Lublin, having seen his superiors at work there and taken his proper cut, that from most of these prison enterprises he could expect a personal percentage. He had reached that happy point in his career at which duty and financial opportunity coincide. The convivial SS police chief, Julian Scherner, over dinner last night, had talked to Amon about what a great opportunity Plaszów would be for a young officer – for them both.

Scherner spoke solemnly about the 'concentration of labour', as if it were a great economic principle new-hatched by the SS bureaucracy. You'll have your labour on site, said Scherner. All factory maintenance will be undertaken at no cost to you and there will be no rent. All the gentlemen were

178

invited to inspect the workshop sites inside Plaszów that afternoon.

The new commandant was introduced. He said how pleased he was to be associated with these businessmen whose valuable contributions to the war effort were already widely known.

Amon pointed out on a map of the camp area the section set aside for the factories. It was next to the men's camp; the women – he told them with an easy and quite charming smile – would have to walk a little further, one or two hundred metres downhill, to reach the workshops. He assured the gentlemen that his main task was to oversee the smooth functioning of the camp and that he had no wish to interfere with their factory policies or to alter the managerial autonomy which they enjoyed here in Cracow. His orders, as Oberführer Scherner could verify, forbade in so many words that sort of intrusion. But the Oberführer had been correct in pointing out the mutual advantages of moving an industry inside the camp perimeter. The factory owners did not have to pay for the premises and he, the commandant, did not have to provide a guard to march the prisoners to town and back. They could understand how the length of the journey and the hostility of the Poles to a column of Jews would erode the worth of the workers.

Throughout this speech, Commandant Goeth glanced frequently at Madritsch and Schindler, the two he particularly wished to win over. He knew he could already depend on Bosch's local knowledge and advice. But Herr Schindler, for example, had a munitions section, small and merely in the developmental stage as yet. It would, however, if transferred, give Plaszów a respectability with the Armaments Inspectorate.

Herr Madritsch listened with a considered frown, and Herr Schindler, head on side, watched the speaker with an acquiescent half smile. Commandant Goeth could tell instinctively, even before he'd finished speaking, that Madritsch would be reasonable and move in, that Schindler would refuse. It was hard to judge by these separate decisions which one of the two felt more paternal towards his

Jews – Madritsch who wanted to be inside Plaszów with them, or Schindler who wanted to have his with him in Emalia.

Oskar Schindler, wearing that same face of avid toler-ance, went with the party to inspect the camp site. Plaszów had the form of a camp now – an improvement in the weather had allowed the assembly of barracks, a thawing of the ground permitted the digging of latrines and post holes. A Polish construction company had installed the kilometres of perimeter fence. Thick-legged watchtowers were going up along the skyline towards Cracow, and also at the mouth of the valley down towards Wieliczka Street, away at the far end of the camp, and up here on this eastern hill where the official party, in the shadow of the Austrian hill fort, watched the fast work of this new creation. Away to the right, Oskar noticed, women were hustling up muddy tracks in the direction of the railway, heavy sections of barracks tilted between them. Below, from the lowest point of the valley and all the way up the far side, the terraced barracks ran, assembled by male prisoners who raised and slotted and hammered with an energy which at this distance resembled willingness.

On the choicest, most level ground beneath the official party, a number of long wooden structures were available for industrial occupation. Cement floors could be poured should heavy machinery need to be installed. The transfer of all plant would be handled by the SS. The road that serviced the area was admittedly little more than a country track, but the engineering firm of Klug had been approached to build a central street for the camp, and the Ostbahn had promised to provide a spur to the camp gate itself, to the quarry down there on the right. Limestone from the quarries and some of what Goeth called "Polish-defaced" gravestones from over in the cemetery would be broken up to provide other interior roads. The gentlemen should not worry about roads, said Goeth, for he intended to maintain a perma-nently strong quarrying and road-building team.

A small railway ran from the quarry up past the adminis-tration building and the large stone barracks that were being built for the SS and Ukrainian garrison. Trolleys of limestone, each weighing six tonnes, were hauled by teams of women, thirty-five or forty of them to a team, dragging on cables set either side of the rock truck, doubled up to compensate for the unevenness in the railway track. Those who tripped or stumbled were trampled or else rolled out of the way, for the teams had their own organic momentum and no individual could deviate from it. Watching this insidious Egyptian looking industry, Oskar felt the same surge of nausea, the same prickling of the blood he had experienced on the hill above Krakusa Street. Goeth had assumed the businessmen were a safe audience, that they were all kinsfolk of his. He was not embarrassed by that savage hauling down there. The question arose, as it had in Krakusa Street. What could embarrass the SS? What could embarrass Amon?

The energy of the barrack builders had, even to an informed observer like Oskar, the specious appearance of men working hard to put up shelter for their women. But, though Oskar had not yet heard the rumour of it, Amon had performed a summary execution in front of those men this morning, so that now they knew what the terms of their labour were. After the early morning meeting with the engineers, Amon had been strolling down Jerozolimska and had come to the SS barracks where the work was under the supervision of an excellent NCO, soon to be promoted to officer rank, called Albert Hujar. Hujar had marched up and made his report. A section of the foundations of the barracks had collapsed, said Hujar, his face flushed. While Hujar spoke, Amon had noticed a girl walking around the half-finished building, speaking to teams of men, pointing, directing. Who was that? he asked Hujar. She was a prisoner named Diana Reiter, said Hujar, an architectural engineer who had been assigned to the construction of the barracks. She was claiming that the foundations hadn't been correctly excavated, and she wanted all the stone and cement dug up and the work on that section of the building to begin again from scratch.

Goeth had been able to tell from the colour of Hujar's

face that he had had a tough argument with the woman. Hujar had in fact been reduced to screaming at her, "You're building barracks, not the sodding Hotel Europa!"

Now Amon half smiled at Hujar. We're not going to have arguments with these people, he said, as if it were a promise. Get the girl.

Amon could tell, from the way she walked towards him, the bogus elegance with which her middle-class parents had raised her, the European manners they had imbued her with, sending her – when the honest Poles wouldn't take her in their universities – off to Vienna or Milan to give her a profession and a heightened protective colouring. She walked towards him as if his rank and hers would bind them in the battle against oafish NCOs and against the inferior craft of whichever SS engineer had supervised the digging of the foundations. She did not know that he hated her the worst – the type who thought, even against the evidence of his SS uniform, of these rising structures, that their Jewishness was not visible.

"You've had occasion to quarrel with Oberscharführer Hujar," Goeth told her as a fact. She nodded firmly. The Herr Commandant would understand, the nod suggested, even though that idiot Hujar couldn't. The entire foundations at that end must be re-dug, she told him energetically. Of course, Amon knew they were like that, they liked to string out tasks and so ensure that the labour force was safe for the duration of the project. If everything is not re-dug, she told him, there will be at least subsidence at the southern end of the barracks. There could be collapse.

She went on arguing the case, and Amon nodded and presumed she must be lying. It was a first principle that you never listened to a Jewish specialist. Jewish specialists were in the mould of Marx, whose theories were aimed at the integrity of government, and of Freud, who had assaulted the integrity of the Aryan mind. Amon felt that this girl's argument threatened his personal integrity.

He called Hujar. The NCO returned uneasily. He thought he was going to be told to take the girl's advice. The girl did too. Shoot her, Amon told Hujar. There was of course a pause while Hujar digested the order. Shoot her, Amon repeated.

Hujar took the girl's elbow to lead her away to some place of private execution.

Here! said Amon. Shoot her here! On my authority, said Amon.

Hujar knew how it was done. He gripped her by the elbow, pushed her a little to his front, took the Mauser from his holster and shot her in the back of the neck.

The sound appalled everyone on the work site, except – it seemed – the executioners and the dying Diana Reiter herself. She knelt and looked up from under her bowed head once. It will take more than that, she was saying. The knowingness of her eyes frightened Amon, justified him, elevated him. He had no idea and would not have believed that these reactions had clinical labels. He believed in fact that he was being awarded the inevitable exaltation that follows an act of political, racial and moral justice. Even so, a man must pay for that, for by evening the fullness of this hour would be followed by such emptiness that he would need, to avoid being blown away like a husk, to augment his size and permanence by food, booze, contact with a woman.

Apart from these considerations, the shooting of this Diana Reiter, the cancelling of her Western European diploma, had this practical value, that no erector of huts or roads in Plaszów would consider himself essential to the task, that if Miss Diana Reiter could not save herself with all her professional skill, the only chance for the others was prompt and anonymous labour. Therefore the women lugging frames up from Cracow-Plaszów railway station, the quarry teams, the men assembling the huts, all worked with an energy appropriate to what they'd learned from Miss Reiter's assassination.

As for Hujar and his colleagues, they knew now that instantaneous execution was to be the permitted style of Plaszów.

20

Two days after the visit of the factory heads to Plaszów, Schindler turned up at Commandant Goeth's temporary office in the city, bringing with him the compliments of a bottle of brandy. The news of Diana Reiter's assassination had by this time reached the front office of Emalia and was the sort of item that confirmed Oskar in his intention to keep his factory clear of Plaszów.

The two big men sat opposite each other and there was a mutual knowingness between them too, just as there had been in the brief relationship between Amon and Miss Reiter. What they knew was that each of them was in Cracow to make a fortune; that Oskar would therefore pay for favours. At that level Oskar and the commandant understood each other. Oskar had the characteristic salesman's gift of treating men he abhorred as if they were soul brothers, and it would deceive the Herr Commandant so completely that Amon would always believe Oskar a friend.

But from the evidence of Stern and others it is obvious that, from the time of their earlier contacts, Oskar abominated Goeth as a man who went to the work of murder as calmly as a clerk goes to his office. Oskar could speak to Amon the administrator, Amon the speculator, but knew at the same time that nine-tenths of the commandant's being lay beyond the normal rationalities of humans. The business and social connections between Oskar and Amon worked well enough to tempt the supposition that Oskar was somehow and despite himself fascinated by the evil of the man. In fact, no one who knew Oskar at this time or later saw a sign of any such enthralment. Oskar despised Goeth in the simplest and most passionate terms. His contempt would grow without limit and his career would dramatically demonstrate it. Just the same, the reflection can hardly be avoided that Amon was Oskar's dark brother, was the berserk and fanatic executioner Oskar might, by some unhappy reversal of his appetites, have become.

With a bottle of brandy between them, Oskar explained to Amon why it was impossible for him to move into Plaszów. His plant was too substantial to be shifted. He believed his friend Madritsch intended to move his Jewish workers in, but Madritsch's machinery was more easily transferred – it was basically a series of sewing machines. There were different problems involved in moving heavy metal presses, each of which, as a sophisticated machine will, had developed special quirks. His skilled workers had become accustomed to these quirks. But on a new factory floor the machines would display an entirely new set of eccentricities. There'd be delays, the settling-in period would take longer than it would for his esteemed friend Julian Madritsch. The Untersturmführer would understand that with important war contracts to fulfil, DEF could not spare such a lapse of time. Herr Beckmann, who had the same sort of problem, was sacking all his Jews over at the Corona works. He didn't want the fuss of the Jews marching out from Plaszów to the factory in the morning and back in the evenings. Unfortunately he, Schindler, had hundreds more *skilled* Jewish workers than Beckmann did. If he got rid of them, Poles would have to be trained in their place and there would again be a delay in production, an even greater one than if he accepted Goeth's attractive offer and moved into Plaszów.

Amon secretly thought that Oskar might be worried that a move into Plaszów would impinge on any sweetly running little deals he had set up in Cracow. The commandant therefore hurried to reassure Herr Schindler that there'd be no interference in the management of the enamelworks. "It's purely the industrial problems that worry me," said Schindler piously. He didn't want to inconvenience the commandant, but he would be grateful, and he was sure the Armaments Inspectorate would also be grateful, if DEF were permitted to stay in its present location.

Among men like Goeth and Oskar the word *gratitude* did not have an abstract meaning. Gratitude was a pay-off. Gratitude was drink and diamonds. I understand your problems, Herr Schindler, said Amon. I shall be happy, once the ghetto is liquidated, to provide a guard to escort your workers from Plaszów to Zablocie.

Itzhak Stern, coming to Zablocie one afternoon on business for the Progress factory, found Oskar depressed and sensed in him a dangerous feeling of impotence. After Klonowska had brought in the coffee, which the Herr Direktor drank as always with a shot of cognac, Oskar told Stern that he'd been to Plaszów again, ostensibly to look at the facilities, in fact to gauge when it would be ready for the Ghetto-menschen. "I made a count," said Oskar. He'd counted the terraced barracks on the far hill and found that if Amon intended to cram two hundred women into each, as was likely, there was now room for some six thousand women up there in the top compound. The men's sector down the hill did not have so many finished buildings, but at the rate things were done at Plaszów it could be finished in days.

Everyone on the factory floor knows what's going to happen, said Oskar. And it's no use keeping the nightshift on the premises here, because after this one, there'll be no ghetto to go back to. All I can tell them, said Oskar, taking a second slug of cognac, is that they shouldn't try to hide unless they're sure of the hiding place. He'd heard that the pattern was to tear the ghetto apart after it had been cleared. Every wall cavity would be probed, every attic carpet taken up, every niche revealed, every cellar plumbed. All I can tell them, said Oskar, is not to resist.

So it happened oddly that Stern, one of the targets of the coming Aktion, sat comforting Herr Direktor Schindler, a mere witness. Oskar's attention to his Jewish labourers was being diffused, tempted away by the wider tragedy of the ghetto's coming end. Plaszów was a labour institution, said Stern. Like all institutions, it could be outlived. It wasn't like Belzec where they made death in the same manner in which Henry Ford made cars. It was degrading to have to line up

186

for Plaszów on orders, but it wasn't the end of things. When Stern had finished arguing, Oskar put both thumbs under the bevelled top of his desk and seemed for a few seconds to want to tear it off, by the nails, like a lid. You know, Stern, he said, that that's not damn well good enough!

It is, said Stern. It's the only course. And he went on arguing, quoting and hairsplitting, and was himself frightened. For Oskar seemed to be in crisis. If Oskar lost hope, Stern knew, all the Jewish workers of Emalia would be sacked, for Oskar would wish to be purified of the entire dirty business.

There'll be time to do something more positive, said Stern. But not yet.

Abandoning the attempt to tear the lid from his desk, Oskar sat back in his chair and resumed his depression. You know that Amon Goeth, he said. He's got charm. He could come in here now and charm you. But he's a lunatic.

On the ghetto's last morning – a *Shabbat*, as it happened, March 13th 1943 – Amon Goeth arrived in Plac Zgody, the Square of Peace, at an hour which officially preceded dawn. Low clouds obscured any sharp distinctions between night and day. He saw that the men of the Sonderkommando had already arrived and stood about on the frozen earth of the small park in the middle, smoking and laughing low, keeping their presence a secret from the ghetto dwellers in the streets beyond Herr Pankiewicz's pharmacy. The roads down which they'd move were clear, as in a model municipality. The remaining snow lay heaped and tarnished in gutters and against walls. It is safe to guess that sentimental Goeth felt paternal as he looked out at the orderly scene and saw the young men, comradely before action, in the middle of the square.

Amon took a pull of cognac while he waited there for the middle-aged Sturmbannführer Wilhelm Haase, who would have strategic though not tactical control of today's Aktion. Today Ghetto A, from Plac Zgody westwards, the major section of the ghetto, the one where all the working (healthy, hoping, opinionated) Jews dwelt, would be emptied.

Ghetto B, the small compound a few blocks square at the eastern end of the ghetto containing the old, the last of the employable, would be uprooted overnight, or tomorrow. They were slated for Commandant Rudolf Höss's greatly expanded extermination camp at Auschwitz. Ghetto B was straightforward, honest work. Ghetto A was the challenge.

Everyone wanted to be here today, for today was history. There had been for more than seven centuries a Jewish Cracow, and by this evening – or at least by tomorrow – those seven centuries would have become a rumour, and Cracow would be *judenfrei*. And every petty SS official wanted to be able to say that he had seen it happen. Even Unkelbach, the Treuhänder of the Progress cutlery factory, having some sort of reserve SS rank, would put on his NCO's uniform today and move through the ghetto with one of the squads. Therefore the distinguished Willi Haase, being of field rank and involved in the planning, had every right to be counted in.

Amon would be suffering his customary minor headache and be feeling a little drained from the feverish insomnia in which he'd spent the small hours. Now he was here, though, he felt a certain professional exhilaration. It was a great gift which the National Socialist Party had given to the men of the SS, that they could go into battle without physical risk, that they could achieve honour without the contingencies that plagued the whole business of being shot at. Psychological impunity had been harder to achieve. Every SS officer had friends who had committed suicide. SS training documents, written to combat these futile casualties, pointed out the simplemindedness of believing that because the Jew bore no visible weapons he was bereft of social, economic or political arms. He was in fact armed to the teeth. Steel yourself, said the documents, for the Jewish child is a cultural time bomb, the Jewish woman a biology of treasons, the Jewish male a more incontrovertible enemy than any Russian could hope to be.

Amon Goeth was steeled. He knew he could not be touched, and the very thought of that gave him the same delicious excitement a long distance runner might have before an event he feels sure about. Amon despised in a genial sort of way those officers who fastidiously left the act itself to their men and NCOs. He sensed that in some way that might be more dangerous than taking a hand yourself. He would show the way, as he had with Diana Reiter. He knew the euphoria that would build during the day, the gratification that would grow, along with a taste for drink, as noon came and the pace hotted up. Even under the low squalor of those clouds, he knew that this was one of the best days, that when he was old and the race extinct, the young would ask with wonder about days like this.

Less than a kilometre away, a doctor of the ghetto's convalescent hospital, Dr. D, was also up and in an active frame of mind this dull morning of the ghetto's liquidation. The hospital's top floor, where he sat among his last patients, was in darkness, and he was grateful they were isolated like this, high above the street, by pain and fever.

For at street level everyone knew what had happened at the epidemic hospital near Plac Zgody. An SS detachment under Oberscharführer Albert Hujar had entered the hospital to close it down and had found Dr. Rosalia Blau standing among the beds of her scarlet fever and tuberculosis patients, who, she said, should not be moved. The whooping-cough children she had sent home earlier. But the scarlet-fever sufferers were too dangerous to move, both for their own sakes and for the community, and the tuberculosis cases were simply too sick to walk out.

Since scarlet fever is an adolescent disease, many of Dr. Blau's patients were girls between the ages of twelve and sixteen. Faced with Albert Hujar, Dr. Rosalia Blau pointed, as warranty for her professional judgment, to these wide-eyed, feverish girls.

Hujar himself, acting on the mandate he'd received the previous week from Amon Goeth, shot Dr. Blau in the head. The infectious patients, some trying to rise in their beds, some detached in their own delirium, were executed in a rage of automatic fire. When Hujar's squad had finished, a detail of ghetto men was sent up the stairs to deal with the dead, to pile the bloodied linen and to sluice down the walls.

The convalescent hospital was situated in what had been before the war a Polish police station. Throughout the life of the ghetto, its three floors had been cluttered with the sick. Its director was a respected physician named Dr. B. By the dull morning of March 18th, Doctors B and D had reduced its population to four, all of them unmovable. One was a young workman with galloping consumption, the second a talented musician with terminal kidney disease. It seemed important to D that somehow they be spared the final great affright of a mad volley of fire. Even more so the blind man afflicted by a stroke, and the old gentleman whose earlier surgery for an intestinal tumour had left him weakened and burdened with a colostomy.

The medical staff here, including Dr. D, were of the highest calibre. From this ill-equipped ghetto hospital would come the first Polish account of Weil's erythroblastic disease, a condition of the bone marrow, and of the Wolff-Parkinson-White syndrome. This morning, though, D was concerned with the question of cyanide.

With an eye to the option of suicide, D had acquired a supply of cyanic acid solution. He knew that other doctors had too. This past year, depression had been endemic to the ghetto. It had infected D. He was young, he had forearms like hams. Yet history itself seemed to have gone malignant. To know he had access to cyanide had been a comfort for D on his worst days. By this late stage of the ghetto's history, it was the one pharmaceutical left to him and to the other doctors in quantity. There had rarely been any sulpha. Emetics, ether and even aspirin were used up. Cyanide was the single sophisticated drug remaining.

This morning before five, Dr. D had been awakened in his room in Wit Stwosz Street by the noise of trucks pulling up beyond the wall. Looking down from his window, he saw the Sonderkommandos assembling by the river and knew that they had come to take some decisive action in the ghetto. He rushed to the hospital and found Dr. B and the nursing staff already working there on the same premise, arranging for every patient who could move to be taken downstairs and fetched home by relatives or friends. When all except the four had gone, Dr. B told the nurses to leave, and all of them obeyed except for one senior nurse. Now she and Doctors B and D remained with the last four patients in the nearly deserted hospital.

B and D did not speak much as they waited. They each had access to the cyanide, and soon D would be aware that Dr. B's mind was also sadly preoccupied with it.

There was suicide, yes. But there was euthanasia as well. The concept terrified D. He had a sensitive face and a marked delicacy about the eyes. He suffered painfully from a set of ethics as intimate to him as the organs of his own body. He knew that a physician with commonsense and a syringe and little else to guide him could add up like a shopping list the values of either course – to inject the cyanide, or to abandon the patients to the Sonder-kommandos. But D knew these things were never a matter of totting up columns, that ethics was higher and more tortuous than algebra.

Sometimes Dr. B would go to the window, look out to see if anything had begun in the streets, and turn back to D with a level, professional calm in his eyes. B, D could tell, was also running through the options, flicking the faces of the problem like the faces of riffled cards; then starting again. Suicide. Euthanasia. Hydrocyanic acid. One appealing concept: stand and be found among the beds like Rosalia Blau. Another: use the cyanide on oneself as well as on the sick. The second idea appealed to D, seeming not as passive as the first. As well as that, waking depressed these past three nights, he'd felt something like a physical desire for the fast poison, as if it were merely the drug or stiff drink that every victim needed to soften the final hour.

To a serious man like D, this allure was a compelling reason not to take the stuff. For him the precedents for suicide had been set in his scholarly childhood, when his father had read to him in Josephus the account of the Dead Sea Zealots' mass suicide on the eve of capture by the Romans. The principle was, death should not be entered like some snug harbour. It should be an unambiguous refusal to surrender. Principle is principle, of course, and terror in a grey morning is another thing. But D was a man of principle.

And he had a wife. He and his wife could find another exit, and he knew it. It led through the sewers near the corner of Piwna and Krakusa Streets. The sewers and a chancy escape to the forest of Ojców. He feared that more than the easy oblivion of cyanide. If Blue Police or Germans stopped him, however, and dragged his trousers down, he would pass the test, thanks to Dr. Lachs. Lachs was a distinguished plastic surgeon who had taught a number of young Cracow Jews how to lengthen their foreskins bloodlessly by sleeping with a weight – a bottle containing a gradually increasing volume of water – attached to themselves. It was, said Lachs, a device that had been used by Jews in periods of Roman persecution, and the intensity of SS action in Cracow had caused Lachs to revive its use in the past eighteen months. Lachs had taught his young colleague D the method, and the fact that it had worked with some success allowed D even fewer grounds for suicide.

At dawn the nurse, a calm woman of about forty, came to D and made a morning report. The young man was resting well, but the blind man with the stroke-affected speech was in a state of anxiety. The musician and the intestinal tumour case had both had a painful night. It was all very quiet in the convalescent hospital now, however. The patients snuffled in the last of their sleep or the intimacy of their pain, and Dr. D went out on to the freezing balcony above the courtyard to smoke a cigarette and chew over the question once more.

Last year D had been at the old epidemic hospital in Rekawka when the SS decided to close that section of the ghetto and *relocate* the hospital. They had lined the staff up against the wall and dragged the patients downstairs. D had seen old Mrs. Reisman's leg caught between the balusters, and an SS man hauling her by the other leg did not stop and extricate her but pulled until the trapped limb snapped with an audible thud. That was how patients were moved in the ghetto. But last year no one thought of mercy-killing. At that stage everyone still hoped that things might improve.

Now, even if he and Dr. B made their decision, D didn't

know if he had the rigour to feed the cyanide to the ill, or to watch someone else do it and maintain a professional dispassion. It was absurdly like the argument in one's youth, about whether you should approach a girl you were infatuated with. And when you'd decided, it still counted for nothing. The act still had to be faced.

Out there on the balcony he heard the first noise. It began early and came from the eastern end of the ghetto. The Raus! Raus! of megaphones, the customary lie about luggage which some people still chose to believe. In the deserted streets, and among the tenements in which no one moved, you could hear all the way from the cobblestones of Plac Zgody and up by the river in Nadwislanska Street an indefinite terror-sick murmur which made D himself tremble.

Then he heard the first volley, loud enough to wake the patients. And a sudden stridency after the firing, a bull megaphone raging at some plangent feminine voice; and then the wailing snapped off by a further burst of fire, and a different wailing succeeding, the bereaved being hurried along by the SS bullhorns, by anxious OD men and by neighbours, unreasonable grief fading into the far corner of the ghetto where there was a gate. He knew that it might all have cut through even the precomatose state of the musician with the failed kidneys.

When he returned to the ward, he could see that they were watching him – even the musician. He could sense rather than see the way their bodies stiffened in their beds, and the old man with the colostomy cried out with the muscular exertion. "Doctor, doctor!" someone said. "Please!" answered D, by which he meant, *I'm here and they're a long way off yet.* He looked at Dr. B who narrowed his eyes as the noise of evictions broke out again three blocks away. Dr. B nodded at him, walked to the small locked pharmaceutical chest at the end of the ward, and came back with the bottle of hydrocyanic acid. After a pause, D moved to his colleague's side. He could have stood and left it to B. He guessed that the man had the strength to do it alone, without the approval of colleagues. But it would be shameful, D thought, not to cast his own vote, not to take some of the burden. D, though younger than B, had been associated with the Jagiellonian University, was a specialist, a thinker. He wanted to give B the backing of all that.

"Well," said B, displaying the bottle briefly to D. The word was nearly obscured by a woman's screaming and ranting official orders from the far end of Józefińska Street. B called the nurse. "Give each patient forty drops in water." "Forty drops," she repeated. She knew what the medication was. "That's right," said B. D also looked at her. Yes, he wanted to say. I'm strong now, I could give it myself. But if I did it would alarm them. Every patient knows that nurses bring the medicine round.

As the nurse prepared the mixture, D wandered down the ward and laid his hand on the old man's. I have something to help you, Roman, he told him. D sensed with amazement the old man's history through the touch of skin. For a second, like a surge of flame, the young man Roman was there, growing up in Franz Josef's Southern Poland, a ladykiller in the sweet little nougat of a city, the *petit* Wien, the jewel of the Vistula, Cracow. Wearing Franz Josef's uniform and going to the mountains for spring manoeuvres. Chocolate-soldiering in Rynek Glowny with the girls of Kazimierz, in a city of lace and patisseries. Climbing the Kosciuszko Mound and stealing a kiss among the shrubs. How could the world have come so far in one manhood? asked the young man in old Roman. From Franz Josef to the NCO who had had a sanction to put Rosalie Blau and the scarlet-fever girls to death?

"Please, Roman," said the doctor, meaning that the old man should unclench his body. He believed the Sonderkommandos were coming within the hour. D felt, but resisted, a temptation to let him into the secret. Dr. B had been liberal with the dosage. A few seconds of breathlessness and a minor amazement would be no new or intolerable sensation to old Roman.

When the nurse came with four medicine glasses, none of them even asked her what she was bringing them. D would never know if any of them understood. He turned away and looked at his watch. He feared that when they drank it, some noise would begin, something worse than the normal hospital gasps and gaggings. He heard the nurse murmuring, "Here's something for you." He heard an intake of breath. He didn't know if it was patient or nurse. The woman is the hero of this, he thought.

When he looked again, the nurse was waking the kidney patient, the sleepy musician, and offering him the glass. From the far end of the ward, Dr B looked on in a clean white coat. D moved to old Roman and took his pulse. There was none. In a bed at the far end of the ward, the musician forced the almond-smelling mixture down.

It was all as gentle as D had hoped. He looked at them – their mouths agape, but not obscenely so, their eyes glazed and immune, their heads back, their chins pointed at the ceiling – with the envy any ghetto dweller would feel for escapees.

21

Poldek Pfefferberg shared a room on the second floor of a nineteenth-century house at the end of Józefińska Street. Its windows looked down over the ghetto wall at the Vistula, where Polish barges passed up stream and down in ignorance of the ghetto's last day and SS patrol boats puttered as casually as pleasure craft. Here Pfefferberg waited with his wife Mila for the Sonderkommandos to arrive and order them out into the street. Mila was a small, nervous girl of twenty-two years, a refugee from Łódź whom Poldek had married in the first days of the ghetto. She came from generations of physicians, her father being a surgeon who had died young in 1937, her mother a dermatologist who, during an Aktion in the ghetto of Tarnow last year, had suffered the same death as Rosalia Blau of the epidemic hospital, being cut down with automatic fire while standing amid her patients.

Mila had lived a sweet childhood, even in Jew-baiting Łódź, and had begun her own medical education in Vienna the year before the war. They had met when Łódź people were shipped down to Cracow in 1939. Mila had found herself billeted in the same apartment as the lively Poldek Pfefferberg.

Now he was already, like Mila, the last of his family. His mother, who had once redecorated Schindler's Straszewskiego Street apartment, had been shipped with his father to the ghetto of Tarnow. From there, it would be discovered in the end, they were taken to Belzec and murdered. His sister and brother-in-law, on Aryan papers, had vanished in the Pawiak prison in Warsaw. He and Mila had only each other. There was a temperamental gulf between them: Poldek was a neighbourhood boy, a leader, an organiser;

the type who, when authority appeared and asked what in God's name was happening, would step forward and speak up. Mila was quieter, rendered more so by the unspeakable destiny that had swallowed her family. In a peaceable era, the mix between them would have been excellent. She was not only clever but wise; she was a quiet centre. She had a gift for irony, and Poldek Pfefferberg often needed her to restrain his torrents of oratory. Today, however, on this impossible day, they were in conflict.

Though Mila was willing, should the chance come, to leave the ghetto, even to entertain a mental image of herself and Poldek as partisans in the forest, she feared the sewers. Poldek had used them more than once as a means of leaving the ghetto, even though the police were sometimes to be found at one end or the other. His friend and former lecturer, Dr. D, had also mentioned the sewers recently as an escape route which might not be guarded on the day the Sonderkommandos moved in. The thing would be to wait for the early winter dusk. The door of the doctor's house was mere metres from a manhole cover. Once down in there, you took the lefthand tunnel which brought you beneath the streets of non-ghetto Podgórze to an outlet on the embankment of the Vistula near the Zatorska Street canal. Yesterday D had given him the definite news. D and his wife would attempt the sewers exit and the Pfefferbergs were welcome to join them. Poldek could not at that stage commit Mila and himself. Mila had a fear, a reasonable one, that the SS might flood the sewers with gas or might resolve the matter anyhow by arriving early at the Pfefferbergs' room at the far end of Józefińska Street.

It was a slow, tense day up in the attic room, waiting to find out which way to jump. Neighbours must also have been waiting. Perhaps some of them, not wanting to deal with the delay, had marched up the road already with their packages and hopeful suitcases, for in a way it was a mix of sounds fit to draw you down the stairs — violent noise dimly heard from blocks away, and here a silence in which you could hear the ancient, indifferent timbers of the house ticking away the last and worst hours of your tenancy. At murky noon Poldek and Mila chewed on their brown bread, the three-hundred grammes each they had in stock. The recurrent noises of the Aktion swept up to the corner of Wegierska, a long block away, and then, towards mid-afternoon, receded again. There was near silence then. Someone tried uselessly to flush the recalcitrant toilet on the first-floor landing. It was nearly possible at that hour to believe that they had been overlooked.

The last dun afternoon of their life in Number 2 Józefińska refused, in spite of its darkness, to end. The light in fact was poor enough, thought Poldek, for them to try for the sewer earlier than dusk. He wanted, now that it was quiet, to go and consult with Dr. D. *Please*, said Mila. But he soothed her. He would keep off the streets, moving through the network of holes that connected one building with another. He piled up the reassurances. The streets at this end would seem to be clear of patrols. He would evade the occasional OD or wandering SS man at the intersections, and be back within five minutes. Darling, darling, he told her, I have to check with D.

He went down the backstairs and into the yard through the hole in the stables' wall, not emerging into the open street until he'd reached the Labour Office. There he risked crossing the broad carriageway, entering the warren of the triangular block of houses opposite, meeting occasional groups of confused men conveying rumours and discussing options in kitchens, sheds, yards and corridors. He came out into Krakusa Street just across from the doctor's place. He crossed unnoticed by a patrol working down near the southern limit of the ghetto, three blocks away, in the area where Schindler had witnessed his first demonstration of the extremities of Reich racial policy.

D's building was empty, but in the yard Poldek met a dazed middle-aged man who told him that the Sonderkommandos had already visited the place and that D and his wife had first hidden, and then gone for the sewers. Perhaps it's the right thing to do, said the man. They'll be back, the SS. Poldek nodded; he knew now the tactics of the Aktion, having already survived so many.

He went back the way he'd come and again was able to cross the road. But he found Number 2 empty, Mila vanished with their baggage, all doors opened, all rooms vacant. He wondered if in fact they were not all hidden down at the hospital – Dr. D, Mrs. D, Mila. Perhaps the Ds had called for her out of respect for her anxiety and her long medical lineage.

Poldek hurried out through the stables again, and by alternative passageways reached the hospital courtyard. Like disregarded flags of surrender, bloodied bedding hung from the balconies of both the upper floors. On the cobblestones was a mound of victims. They lay, some of them, with their heads split open, their limbs crooked. They were not of course the terminal patients of Doctors B and D. They were people who had been detained here during the day and then executed. Some of them must have been imprisoned upstairs, shot, then tumbled into the yard.

Always thereafter, when questioned about the corpses in the ghetto hospital yard, Poldek would say sixty to seventy, though he had no time to count that tangled pyramid. Cracow being a provincial town and Poldek having been raised as a very sociable child in Podgórze and then in the Centrum, visiting with his mother the affluent and distinguished people of the city, he recognised in that heap familiar faces, old clients of his mother's, people who had asked him about school at the Kosciuszko gymnasium, got precocious answers in reply and fed him cake and sweets for his looks and his charm. Now they were shamefully exposed and jumbled in that blood-red courtyard.

Somehow it did not occur to Pfefferberg to look for the body of his wife and the Ds in that frightful heap. He sensed why he had been placed there. He believed unshakeably in better years to come, years of just tribunals. He had that sense of being a witness which Schindler had experienced on the hill beyond Rekawka.

He was distracted by the sight of a wash of people in Wegierska Street beyond the courtyard. They moved towards the Rekawka gate with the dull but not desperate languor of factory workers on a Monday morning or even of supporters of a defeated football team. Among this wave of people he noticed neighbours from Józefińska Street. He walked out of the yard, carrying like a weapon up his sleeve his memory of it all. What had happened to Mila? Did any of them know? She'd already left, they said. The Sonderkommandos had been through. She'd already be out of the gate, on her way to the place. To Plaszów.

He and Mila of course had a contingency plan for an impasse like this. If one of them ended up in Plaszów, it would be better for the other to attempt to stay out. He knew that Mila had her gift for unobtrusiveness, a good gift for prisoners, but also she could be racked by extraordinary hunger. He'd be her purveyor on the outside. He was sure these things could be managed. It was no soft decision, though – the bemused crowds, barely guarded by the SS, now making for the south gate and the barbed-wire factories of Plaszów, were an indication of where most people, probably quite correctly, considered that long-term safety lay.

The light, though late now, was sharp, as if snow were coming on. Poldek was able to cross the road and enter the empty apartments beyond the pavement. He wondered whether they were in fact empty or full of ghetto dwellers concealed cunningly or naïvely, those who believed that wherever the SS took you, it led in the end to the gas chambers.

Poldek was looking for a first-class hiding place. He came by back passages to the timber yard on Józefińska. Timber was a scarce commodity. There were no great structures of sawn planks to hide behind. The place that looked best was behind the iron gates at the yard entrance. Their size and blackness seemed a promise of the coming night. Later he would not be able to believe that he'd chosen them with such enthusiasm.

He hunched in behind the one that was pushed back against the wall of the abandoned office. Through the crack left between the gate and the gatepost, he could see up Józefińska in the direction he'd come from. Behind that freezing iron leaf he watched the slice of cold evening, a luminous grey, and pulled his coat across his chest. A man and his wife hurried past, rushing for the gate, dodging among the dropped bundles, the suitcases labelled with futile large letters. *Kleinfeld*, they proclaimed in the evening light. *Lehrer, Baume, Weinberg, Smolar, Strus, Rosenthal, Birman, Zeitlin*. Names against which no receipts would be issued. "Heaps of goods laden with memories," the young artist Bau had written of such scenes. "Where are my treasures?"

From beyond this battleground of fallen luggage he could hear the aggressive baying of dogs. Then into Józefińska Street, striding on the far pavement, came three SS men, one of them dragged along by a canine flurry which proved to be two large police dogs. The dogs dragged their handler into Number 41 Józefińska, but the other two waited on the pavement. Poldek had paid most of his attention to the dogs. They looked like a lean cross between Dalmatians and German Shepherds. Pfefferberg still saw Cracow as a genial city, and dogs like that looked foreign, as if they'd been brought in from some other and more savage ghetto. For, even in this last hour, among the litter of packages, behind an iron gate, he was grateful for the city and presumed that the ultimate frightfulness was always performed in some other, less gracious place. This last assumption was wiped away in the next half minute. The worst thing, that is, occurred in Cracow. Through the crack in the gate, he saw the event which revealed that if there was a pole of evil it was not situated in Tarnow, Czestochowa, Lwów or Warsaw as you thought. It was at the north side of Józefińska Street a hundred and twenty paces away. From 41 came a screaming woman and a child. One dog had the woman by the cloth of her dress, the flesh of her hip. The SS man who was the servant of the dogs took the child and flung it against the wall. The sound of it made Pfefferberg close his eyes and he heard the shot which put an end to the woman's howling protest.

Just as Pfefferberg would think of the pile of bodies in the hospital yard as sixty or seventy, he would always testify that the child was two or three years of age.

Perhaps before she was even dead, certainly before he himself even knew he had moved, as if the decision had come from some mettlesome gland behind his forehead, Pfefferberg gave up the freezing iron gate, since it would not protect him from the dogs, and found himself in the open yard. He adopted at once the military bearing he'd learned in the Polish army. He emerged from the timber yard like a man on a ceremonial assignment, and bent and began lifting the bundles of luggage out of the carriageway and heaping them against the walls of the yard. He could hear the three SS men approaching, the dogs' snarling breath was palpable and the whole evening was stretched to breaking by the tension in their leashes. When he believed they were some ten paces off, he straightened and permitted himself, playing the biddable Jew of some European background, to notice them. He saw that their boots and riding britches were splashed with blood, but they were not abashed to appear before other humans dressed that way. The officer in the middle was the tallest. He did not look like a murderer, there was a sensitivity to the large face and a subtle line to the mouth.

Pfefferberg in his shabby suit clicked his cardboard heels in the Polish manner and saluted this tall one in the middle. He had no knowledge of SS ranks and did not know what to call the man. "Herr," he said. "Herr Commandant!"

It was a term his brain, under threat of its extinction, had thrown forth with electric energy. It proved to be the precise word, for the tall man was Amon Goeth in the full vitality of his afternoon, elated at the day's progress and as capable of instant and instinctive exercises of power as Poldek Pfefferberg was of instant and instinctive subterfuge.

"Herr Commandant, I respectfully report to you that I received an order to put all the bundles together to one side of the road so that there will be no obstruction of the thoroughfare."

The dogs were craning towards him through their collars. They expected, on the basis of their black training and the rhythm of today's Aktion, to be let fly at Pfefferberg's wrist and groin. Their snarls were not simply feral, but full of a frightful confidence in the outcome, and the question was whether the SS man on the Herr Commandant's left had enough strength to restrain them. Pfefferberg didn't expect much. He would not be surprised to be buried by dogs and after a time to be delivered from their teeth by a bullet. If the woman hadn't got away with pleading her motherhood, he stood little chance with stories of bundles, of clearing a street in which human traffic had, in any case, been abolished.

But the commandant was more amused by Pfefferberg than he had been by the mother. Here was a little wedge of a Ghettomensch playing soldier in front of three SS officers and making his report, servile if true, and almost endearing if not. His manner was above all a break in style for a victim. Of all today's doomed, not one other had tried heel-clicking. The Herr Commandant could therefore exercise the kingly right to show irrational and unexpected amusement. His head went back, his long upper lip retracted. It was a broad honest laugh and his colleagues smiled and shook their heads at its extent.

In his excellent baritone, Untersturmführer Goeth said, "We're looking after everything. The last group is leaving the ghetto. Verschwinde!" That is, Disappear, little Polish clicking soldier!

Pfefferberg began to run, not looking back, and it would not have surprised him if he had been felled from behind. Running, he got to the corner of Wegierska and rounded it, past the hospital yard where some hours ago he had been a witness. The dark came down as he neared the gate, and the ghetto's last familiar alleys faded. In Podgórze Place, the last official huddle of prisoners stood in a loose cordon of SS men and Ukrainians.

"I must be the last one out alive," he told people in that crowd.

Or if not he it was Wulkan the jeweller and his wife and son. Wulkan had been working these past months in the Progress factory and, knowing what was to happen, had approached Treuhänder Unkelbach with a large diamond concealed for two years in the lining of a coat. Herr Unkelbach, he told the supervisor, I'll go wherever I'm sent, but my wife isn't up to all that noise and violence. Wulkan and his wife and son would wait at the OD police station under the protection of a Jewish policeman they knew and then perhaps during the day Herr Unkelbach would come and convey them bloodlessly to Plaszów.

Since this morning they had sat in a cubicle in the police station, but it had been as frightful a wait as if they'd stayed in their kitchen, the boy alternately bored and terrified, his wife continuing to hiss her reproaches. Where is he? Is he going to come at all? These people, these people! Early in the afternoon, Unkelbach did in fact appear, came into the Ordnungsdienst to use the lavatory and have coffee. Wulkan, emerging from the office in which he'd been waiting, saw a Treuhänder Unkelbach he had never known before, a man in the uniform of an SS NCO, smoking and exchanging sharp animated sentences with another SS man; using one hand to take hungry gulps of coffee, to bite off mouthfuls of smoke, to savage a lump of brown bread while his pistol, still held in the left hand, lay like a resting animal on the police station counter and dark spatters of blood ran across the breast of his uniform. The eyes he turned to meet Wulkan's did not see the jeweller. Wulkan knew at once that Unkelbach was not backing out of the deal, he simply did not remember it. The man was drunk, and not on alcohol. If Wulkan had called to him, the answer would have been a stare of ecstatic incomprehension. Followed, very likely, by something worse.

Wulkan gave it up and returned to his wife. She kept saying, Why don't you talk to him, I'll talk to him if he's still there. But then she saw the shadow in Wulkan's eyes and sneaked a look around the edge of the door. Unkelbach was getting ready to leave. She saw the unaccustomed uniform, the blood of small traders and their wives splashed across its front. She uttered a whimper and returned to her seat.

Like her husband, she now fell into a well-founded despair, and the waiting became somehow easier. The OD man they knew restored them to the usual pulse of hope and anxiety. He told them that all the OD, apart from Spira's praetorians, had to be out of the ghetto by 6 p.m. and on the Wieliczka Road to Plaszów. He would see if there was a way of getting the Wulkans into one of the vehicles.

After dark had fallen in the wake of Pfefferberg's passage up Wegierska, after the last party of prisoners had assembled at the gate into Podgórze Place, while Dr. D and his wife were moving eastward in the company and under the cover of a group of rowdy Polish drunks, and while the squads of the Sonderkommandos were resting and taking a smoke before the last search of the tenements, two horse-drawn carts came to the door of the police station. The Wulkan family were hidden by the OD men under cartons of paperwork and bundles of clothing. Symche Spira and his OD associates were not in sight, were on the job somewhere in the streets, drinking coffee with NCOs, celebrating their permanence within the system.

But before the carts had turned out of the ghetto gate, the Wulkans, flattened to the boards, heard the nearly continuous sound of rifle and small arms fire from the streets behind them. It meant that Amon Goeth and Willi Haase, Albert Hujar, Horst Pilarzik and some hundreds of others were bursting into the attic niches, the false ceilings, the crates in cellars, and finding those who all day had maintained a hopeful silence.

More than four thousand such people were discovered overnight and executed in the streets. In the next two days their bodies were taken to Plaszów on open platformed trucks and buried in two mass graves in the woods beyond the new camp.

22

We do not know in what condition of soul Oskar Schindler spent March 13th, the ghetto's last and worst day. But by the time his workers returned to him under guard from Plaszów he was back in the mood for collecting data to pass on to Dr. Sedlacek on the dentist's next visit. He found out from the prisoners that Zwangsarbeitslager Plaszów – as it was known in SS bureaucratese – was to be no rational kingdom. Goeth had already pursued his passion against engineers by letting the guards beat Zygmunt Grünberg into a coma and bring him so late to the clinic up near the women's camp that his death was assured. From the prisoners who ate their hearty noonday soup at Deutsche Email Fabrik, Oskar heard also that Plaszów was being used not only as a work camp but as a place of execution as well. Though all the camp could hear these executions, some of the prisoners had also been witnesses.

The prisoner M*, for example, who had had a pre-war decorating business in Cracow. In the first days of the camp he was in demand to decorate the houses of the SS, the few small country villas that flanked the lane on the north side of the camp. Like any especially valued artisan he had more freedom of movement, and one afternoon that spring he had been walking from the villa of Untersturmführer Leo John up the track towards the hill called Chujowa Górka on whose crest stood the Austrian fort.

Before he was ready to turn back down the slope towards the factory yard, he had to pause to let an army truck grind past him uphill. M had noticed that beneath its canopy were women under the care of white overalled Ukrainian guards.

* Now living in Vienna, the man does not want his real name used.

He had hidden between stacks of timber and got, through the gap in the mound walls, an incomplete view of the women, disembarked and marched inside the fort, refusing to undress. The man yelling the orders in there was the SS man Edmund Sdrojewski. Ukrainian NCOs marched among the women hitting them with whip handles. M presumed they were Jewish, probably women caught with Aryan papers, brought here from Montelupich prison. Some cried out at the blows, but others were silent, as if to refuse the Ukrainians that much satisfaction. One of them began to intone the *Shema Yisroel*, and the others took it up. The verses rose vigorously above the mound, as if it had just occurred to the girls – who till yesterday had played straight Aryans – that now the pressure was off they were freer than anyone to celebrate their tribal difference in the faces of Sdrojewski and the Ukrainians. Then, huddling for modesty and the bite of the spring air, they were all shot. At night the Ukrainians took them away in barrows and buried them in the woods on the far side.

People in the camp below had also heard that first execution on the hill, now profanely nicknamed Prick Hill. Some told themselves that it was partisans being shot up there, intractable Marxists or crazy nationalists. It was another country up there. If you kept the ordinances within the wire, you need never visit it. But the more clear-headed of Schindler's workers, marched up Wieliczka Street past the cable works and over to Zablocie to work at DEF, *they* knew why prisoners from Montelupich were being shot at the Austrian hill fort, why the SS did not seem alarmed if the truckloads were seen arriving or the noise was heard throughout Plaszów. The reason was that the SS did not look on the prison population as ultimate witnesses. If there had been concern about a time in court, a mass of future testimony, they would have taken the women deeper into the woods. The conclusion to be drawn, Oskar decided, was not that the mound fort was a separate world from Plaszów, but that all of them were under sentence.

The first morning Commandant Goeth stepped out of his

front door and murdered a prisoner at random there was a tendency to see *this* also, like the first execution on the hill fort, as a one-off event, discrete from what would become the customary life of the camp. In fact, of course, the killings on the hill would soon prove to be habitual, and so would Amon's morning routine.

Wearing a shirt and riding britches and boots on which his orderly had put a high shine, he would emerge on the steps of his temporary villa. (They were renovating a better place for him down at the other end of the camp perimeter.) As the season wore on he would appear without his shirt, for he loved the sun. But for the moment he stood in the clothes in which he had eaten breakfast, a pair of binoculars in one hand and a sniper's rifle in the other. He would scan the camp area, the work at the quarry, the prisoners pushing or hauling the quarry trucks on the rails which passed by his door. Those glancing up could see the smoke from the cigarette which he held clamped between his lips, the way a man smokes without hands when he is too busy to put down the tools of his trade. Within the first few days of the camp's life he appeared thus at his front door and shot a prisoner who did not seem to be pushing hard enough at a cart loaded with limestone. No one knew Amon's precise reason for settling on that prisoner – Amon certainly did not have to document his motives. With one blast from the doorstep, the man was plucked out of the group of pushing and pulling captives and hurled sideways in the road. The others stopped pushing of course, their muscles seized in expectation of a general slaughter. But Amon waved them on, frowning, as if to say that he was pleased for the moment with the standard of work he was getting from them.

Apart from such excesses with prisoners, Amon was also breaking one of the promises he'd made to the entrepreneurs. Oskar got a telephone call from Madritsch, who wanted them both to complain. Amon had said he would not interfere in the business of the factories. At least, he was not interfering from within. But he held up shifts by detaining the prison population for hours on the Appellplatz at rollcall. Madritsch mentioned a case in which a potato had been found in a given hut, and therefore every prisoner from that barracks had to be publicly flogged in front of the thousands of inmates. It is no fast matter to have a few hundred people drag their trousers or knickers down, their shirts or dresses up and treat each of them to twenty-five lashes. It was Goeth's rule that the flogged prisoner call out the numbers for the guidance of the Ukrainian orderlies who did the flogging. If the victim lost track of the count, it was to begin again. Commandant Goeth's rollcalls on the Appellplatz were full of just such time-consuming trickery.

Therefore shifts would arrive hours late at the Madritsch clothing works in Plaszów camp, and an hour later still at Oskar's place in Lipowa Street. They would arrive shocked, too, unable to apply their minds, muttering stories of what Amon or John or Scheidt or some other officer had done that morning. Oskar complained to an engineer he knew at the Armaments Inspectorate. It's no use complaining to the police chiefs, said the engineer. They're not involved in the same war as us. What I ought to do, said Oskar, is keep the people on the premises. Make my own camp.

The idea amused the engineer. Where would you put them, old man? he asked. You don't have much room.

If I can acquire the space, said Oskar, would you write a supporting letter?

When the engineer agreed, Oskar telephoned the elderly Bielski couple who lived in Stradom Street. He wondered if they would consider an offer for the land abutting his factory. He drove across the river to see them. They were delighted by his manner. Because he had always been bored by the rituals of haggling, he began by offering them a boomtime price. They gave him tea and, in a state of high excitement, called their lawyer to draw up the papers while Oskar was still on the premises. From their apartment, Oskar drove out and told Amon, as a matter of courtesy, that he intended to make a subcamp of Plaszów in his own factory yard. Amon was quite taken with the idea. If the SS chiefs approved, he said, you can expect my cooperation. As long as you don't want my musicians or my maid.

The next day a full scale appointment was arranged with

Oberführer Scherner at Pomorska Street. Somehow both Amon and General Scherner knew that Oskar could be made to foot the whole bill for a new camp. They could detect that when Oskar pushed the industrial argument – "I want my workers on the premises so that their labour can be more fully exploited" – he was at the same time pushing some other intimate craze of his of which expense was not a consideration. They thought of him as a good enough fellow who'd been stricken with a form of Jew-love as with a virus. It was a corollary to SS theory that the Jewish genius so pervaded the world, could achieve such magical effects, that Herr Schindler was to be pitied as much as was a prince turned into a frog. But he would have to pay for his disease.

The requirements of Obergruppenführer Friedrich-Wilhelm Krüger, police chief of the Government General and superior of Scherner and Czurda, were based on the regulations set down by the Concentration Camp Section of General Oswald Pohl's SS Main Administrative and Economic Office, even though as yet Plaszów was run independently of Pohl's bureau. The basic stipulations for an SS Forced Labour Subcamp involved the erection of fences nine feet tall, of watchtowers at given intervals according to the length of the camp perimeter, of latrines, barracks, a clinic, a dental surgery, a bath house and delousing complex, a barber shop, a food store, a laundry, a barracks office, a guard block of somewhat better construction than the barracks themselves, and all the accessories. What had occurred to Amon, Scherner and Czurda was that Oskar, as was only proper, would meet the expenses either out of economic motives or because of the cabalistic enchantment he lay under.

And even though they would make Oskar pay, his proposal suited them. There was still a ghetto in Tarnow, forty-five miles east, and when it was abolished the population would need to be absorbed into Plaszów. Likewise the thousands of Jews now arriving at Plaszów from the shtetls of south Poland. A subcamp in Lipowa Street would ease that pressure.

Amon also understood, though he would never say it

aloud to the police chiefs, that there would be no need to supply a Lipowa Street camp too precisely with the minimum food requirements as laid down in General Pohl's directive. Amon, who could hurl thunderbolts from his doorstep without meeting protest, who believed in any case in the official idea that a certain attrition should take place in Plaszów, was already selling a percentage of the prison rations on the open market in Cracow through an agent of his, a Jew called Wilek Chilowicz who had contacts with factory managements, merchants and even restaurants in Cracow.

Dr. Alexander Biberstein, now a Plaszów prisoner himself, found that the daily ration varied between seven hundred and eleven hundred calories. At breakfast a prisoner received a half litre of black coffee, tasting of acorns, and a lump of rye bread weighing a hundred and seventy-five grammes, an eighth of one of the round loaves collected by barracks mess orderlies each morning at the bakery. Hunger being such a disruptive force, each mess orderly cut up the loaf with his back to the others and called, "Who wants this piece? Who wants that?" At midday a soup was distributed – carrots, beets, sago substitute. Some days it had a fuller body than on others. Better food came in with the work parties who returned each evening. A small chicken could be carried under a coat, a french roll down a trouser leg. Yet Amon tried to prevent this by having the guards search returning details at dusk in front of the Administration Block. He did not want the work of natural wastage to be frustrated, nor the ideological wind to be taken out of his food dealings through Chilowicz. Since, therefore, he did not indulge his own prisoners, he felt that if Oskar chose to take a thousand Jews, he could indulge them at his own expense, without too regular a supply of bread and beets from the food stores of Plaszów.

That spring, it was not only the police chiefs of the Cracow region whom Oskar had to talk to. He went into his backyard, persuading the neighbours. Beyond the two shabby huts constructed of Jereth's wood, he came to the radiator factory run by Kurt Hoderman. It employed a horde of Poles and about a hundred Plaszów inmates. In the other direction was Jereth's box works, supervised by the German engineer Kuhnpast. Since the Plaszów people were such a small part of their staff, they didn't take to the idea with any passion, but they weren't against it. For Oskar was offering to house their Jews fifty metres from work instead of five kilometres.

Next Oskar moved out into the neighbourhood to talk to Engineer Schmilewski at the Wehrmacht garrison office a few streets away. He employed a squad of Plaszów prisoners. Schmilewski had no objections. His name, with Kuhnpast's and Hoderman's, was appended to the application Schindler sent off to Pomorska Street.

SS surveyors visited Emalia and conferred with Surveyor Steinhauser, an old friend of Oskar's from the Armaments Inspectorate. They stood and frowned at the site, as surveyors will, and asked questions about drainage. Oskar had them all into his office upstairs for a morning coffee and a cognac, and then everyone parted amiably. Within a few days the application to establish a Forced Labour Camp in the factory backyard was accepted.

That year Deutsche Email Fabrik would enjoy a turnover of 15.8 million Reichsmarks. It might be thought that the three-hundred thousand Reichsmarks Oskar now spent on building materials for the Emalia camp was a large but not fatal overhead. The truth was though that he was only beginning to pay.

Oskar sent a plea to the Bauleitung or Construction Office of Plaszów for the help of a young engineer called Adam Garde. Garde was still working on the barracks of Amon's camp and, after leaving instructions for the barrack builders, would be marched under individual guard from Plaszów to Lipowa Street to supervise the setting up of Oskar's compound. When Garde first turned up in Zablocie, he found two rudimentary huts already occupied by close to four hundred prisoners. There was a fence patrolled by an SS squad, but the inmates told Garde that Oskar did not let the SS into the encampment or on to the factory floor, except of course when senior inspectors came to look over the place. Oskar, they said, kept the small SS garrison of the Emalia factory well liquored and happy with their lot. Garde could see that the Emalia prisoners themselves were content between the shrinking fragile boards of their two huts, the men's and the women's. Already they called themselves Schindlerjuden using the term in a mood of cautious self-congratulation, the way a man recovering from a heart attack might describe himself as a lucky beggar.

They'd already dug some primitive latrines which engineer Garde, much as he approved the impulse behind the work, could smell from the factory entrance. They washed at a pump in the DEF yard.

Oskar asked him to come up to the office and look at the plans. Six barracks for up to twelve hundred people. The cookhouse at this end, the SS barracks – Oskar was temporarily accommodating the SS in a part of the factory – beyond the wire at the far end. I want a really first-class shower block and laundry, Oskar told him. I have the welders who can put it together under your direction. Typhus, he growled, half smiling at Garde. None of us wants typhus. The lice are already biting in Plaszów. We need to be able to boil up clothes.

Adam Garde was delighted to go to Lipowa Street each day. Two engineers had already been punished at Plaszów for possessing diplomas, but at Deutsche Email Fabrik experts were still experts. One morning, as he was marching up Wieliczka Street towards Zablocie, neither he nor the Ukrainian pushing the pace and only peasant carts apparent on the road, a black limousine materialised, braking hard at their heels. From it emerged Untersturmführer Goeth. He had that look about him, as if he would not be slothful in his enquiries.

One prisoner, one guard, he observed. What does it mean? The Ukrainian begged to inform the Herr Commandant that he had orders to escort this prisoner each morning to Herr Oskar Schindler's Emalia. They both hoped, Garde and the Ukrainian, that the mention of Oskar's name would give them immunity. One guard, one prisoner? asked the commandant again, but he was appeased and got back into his car without resolving the matter in any radical way.

Later in the day he approached Wilek Chilowicz, who besides being his agent was also chief of the Jewish camp police or 'firemen', as they were called. Symche Spira, recently the Napoleon of the ghetto, still lived there and spent each day supervising the searching out and the digging up of the diamonds, gold and cash hidden away and unrecorded by people who were now ashes on the pineneedles of Belzec. In Plaszów, however, Spira had no power, the centre of prison power being Chilowicz, although no one knew from where his authority derived. Perhaps Willi Kunde had mentioned his name to Amon, perhaps Amon had recognised and liked his style. But, all at once, here he was chief of firemen in Plaszów, hander-out of the caps and armbands of authority in that debased kingdom and, like Symche, limited enough in imagination to equate his power with that of tsars.

Goeth approached this cut-rate Sejanus and said that he had better send Adam Garde to Schindler full time and be done with it. We have engineers to burn, said Goeth with distaste. He meant that engineering had been a soft option for Jews who weren't allowed into the medical faculties of the Polish universities. First, though, said Amon, before he goes to Emalia, he has to finish the work on my conservatory.

This news came to Adam Garde in his barracks, at his place in the four-tiered bunks of hut 21. He would be delivered to Zablocie at the end of a trial. He would be building at Goeth's back door where, as Reiter and Grünberg might have told him, the rules were unpredictable.

In the midst of his work for the commandant, a large beam was lifted to its place in the roof tree of Amon's conservatory. As he worked Adam Garde could hear the commandant's two dogs, named Rolf and Ralf, names from a newspaper cartoon – laughable, except that Amon had permitted them in the past week to rip the breast from a female prisoner suspected of idling. Amon himself, with his half-completed technical education, would return again and again to take a professional stance and watch the roof beams lifted by pulley. He came to ask questions when the centrebeam was being slotted into place. It was an immense length of heavy pine and across it Goeth called his question. Adam Garde could not catch the meaning and put his hand to his ear. Again Goeth asked it and, worse than not hearing it, Garde could not understand it. I don't understand, Herr Commandant, he admitted. Amon grabbed the rising beam with both long fingered hands, dragged back the end of it and swung it towards the engineer. Garde saw the massive swatting timber spinning towards his head and understood that it was a mortal instrument. He lifted his right hand and the beam took it, shattering the knuckles and the metacarpi and hurling him to the ground. When he could see again through the fog of pain and nausea, Amon had turned and walked away. Perhaps he would come again tomorrow for a satisfactory answer.

Lest he be seen as deformed and unfit, engineer Garde avoided favouring his shattered hand on the way to the Krankenstube, or clinic. Carried normally, it weighed at his side, a bladder of torment. He let Dr. Hilfstein talk him into accepting a plaster cast. So he continued to supervise the construction of the conservatory and each day marched to the Emalia works, hoping that the long sleeve of his coat helped conceal the plaster cast. When he was unsure about this, he cut his hand free. Let the hand mend crookedly. He wanted to ensure his transfer to Schindler's subcamp by presenting an unmaimed appearance.

Within a week, carrying a shirt and some books in a bundle, he was marched to Lipowa Street for good.

23

Among prisoners who knew, there was already competition to get into Emalia. Prisoner Dolek Horowitz, a purchasing officer inside the Plaszów camp, knew that he would not be allowed to go to Schindler's place himself. But he had a wife and two children.

Richard, the younger of the children, woke up early these spring mornings as the earth gave off its last winter humour in vapour, got down from his mother's bunk in the women's quarters, and ran down the hillside to the men's camp, his mind on the coarse morning bread. He had to be with his father for morning rollcall on the Appellplatz. His path took him past Chilowicz's Jewish police post and, even on foggy mornings, within sight of two watchtowers. But he was safe because he was known. He was a Horowitz child. His father was considered invaluable by Herr Bosch, who in turn was a drinking companion of the commandant's. Richard's unselfconscious freedom of movement derived from his father's expertise, he moved charmed under the eyes in the towers, finding his father's barracks and climbing to his cot and waking him with questions. Why is there mist in the mornings and not in the afternoons? Will there be trucks? Will it take long on the Appellplatz today? Will there be floggings? Floggings delayed mess call.

Through Richard's morning questions, Dolek Horowitz had it borne in on him that Plaszów was unfit even for privileged children. Perhaps he could contact Schindler – Schindler came out here now and then and walked around the Administrative Block and workshops, under the guise of doing business, to leave small gifts and exchange news with old friends like Stern and Roman Ginter and Poldek Pfeffer-berg. When Dolek did not seem to be able to make contact this way, it struck him that perhaps Schindler could be approached through Bosch. Dolek believed they met a lot. Not out here so much, but perhaps in offices in town and at parties. You could tell they were not friends, but were bound together by dealings, by mutual favours.

It was not only and perhaps not mainly Richard whom Dolek wanted to get into Schindler's compound. Richard could diffuse his terror in clouds of questions. It was his ten-year-old daughter Niusia, who no longer asked questions, who was just another thin child past the age of frankness, who – from a window in the brushworks shop where she sewed the bristles into the wooden backs – saw the daily truckloads arriving at the Austrian hill fort and carried her terror insupportably, the way adults will, unable to climb on to a parental chest and transfer the fear. To soothe her hunger in Plaszów, Niusia had taken to smoking onion leaves in newspaper wrappings. According to solid rumours about Emalia such precocious methods were unnecessary there.

So Dolek appealed to Herr Bosch during one of his tours of the clothing warehouse. He presumed on Herr Bosch's earlier kindnesses, he said, to beg him to talk to Herr Schindler. He repeated his pleadings and repeated the children's names again so that Bosch, whose memory was part atrophied by schnaps, might still remember. Herr Schindler is probably my best friend, said Bosch. He'll do anything for me.

Dolek expected little from the talk. His wife, Regina, had no experience of making shells or enamelware. Bosch himself never mentioned the request again. Yet within the week they marched out on the next Emalia list, cleared by Commandant Goeth in return for a little envelope of jewellery. Niusia looked like a thin and reserved adult in the women's barracks in Zablocie, and Richard moved as he had in Plaszów, everyone knowing him in the munitions hall and the enamel shops, the guards accepting his familiarity. Regina kept expecting Oskar to come up to her in the enamelworks and say, "So you're Dolek Horowitz's wife?" Then the only question would be how to frame her thanks.

But he never did. She was delighted to find that neither she nor Niusia was very visible at Lipowa Street. They understood that Oskar knew who they were, since he often chatted with Richard by name. They knew too by the altered nature of Richard's questions the extent of what they had been given.

The Emalia camp had no resident SS commandant to tyrannise the inmates. There were no permanent guards. The garrison was changed every two days, two truckloads of SS and Ukrainians coming up to Zablocie from Plaszów to take over the security of the subcamp. The Plaszów soldiers liked their occasional duty at Emalia. The Herr Direktor's kitchens, more primitive even than Plaszów's, turned out better meals. Since the Herr Direktor started raging and making phone calls to Oberführer Scherner if any guard entered the camp instead of just patrolling the perimeter, the garrison kept to their side of the fence. Duty in Zablocie was pleasurably dull.

Except for inspection by senior SS men, the prisoners who worked at DEF rarely got a close view of their guards. One barbed-wire passageway took the inmates to their work in the enamel plant, another ran to the door of the armaments hall. Those Emalia Jews who worked at the box factory, the radiator plant, the garrison office, were marched to work and back by Ukrainians – different Ukrainians every second day. No guard had the time to develop a fatal grudge against a prisoner.

Therefore, though the SS may have set the limits to the life people led in Emalia, Oskar set its tone. The tone was one of fragile permanence. There were no dogs. There were no beatings. The soup and the bread were better and more plentiful than in Plaszów – about two thousand calories a day according to a doctor who worked in Emalia as a factory hand. The shifts were long, often twelve hours, for Oskar was still a businessman with war contracts to fill and a conventional desire for profit. It must be said, though, that no shift was arduous and that many of his prisoners seem to have believed at the time that their labour was making a contribution in measurable terms to their survival. According to accounts Oskar presented after the war to the Joint Distribution Committee, he spent one million, eight-hundred thousand zloty (three hundred and sixty thousand dollars) on food for the Emalia camp. Cosmetic entries could be found, written off to similar expenditure, in the books of Farben and Krupp – though nowhere near as high a percentage of the profit as in Oskar's accounts. In Emalia no one collapsed and died of overwork, beatings or hunger, whereas at I. G. Farben's Buna plant alone, twenty-five thousand prisoners out of a work force of thirty-five thousand would perish at their labour.

Long afterwards, Emalia people would call the Schindler camp a paradise. Since they were by then widely scattered, it cannot have been a description they decided on after the fact. The term must have had some currency while they were in Emalia. It was of course only a relative paradise, a heaven by contrast to Plaszów. What it inspired in its people was a sense of almost surreal deliverance, something preposterous which they didn't want to look at too closely for fear it would evaporate. New DEF hands knew of Oskar only by report. They did not want to put themselves in the Herr Direktor's path or risk speaking to him. They needed time for recovery and for adjustment to Schindler's unorthodox prison system.

A girl named Lusia, for example. Her husband had recently been picked out from the mass of prisoners on the Appellplatz at Plaszów and shipped off with others to Mauthausen. With what would turn out to be mere realism, she grieved like a widow. Grieving, she'd been marched to Emalia. She worked at carrying dipped enamelware to the furnaces. You were permitted to heat up water on the warm surfaces of machinery, and the floor was warm. For her, hot water was Emalia's first beneficence.

She saw Oskar at first only as a large shape moving down an aisle of metal presses or traversing a catwalk. It was somehow not a threatening shape. She sensed that if she were noticed the nature of the place – the lack of beatings, the food, the absence of guards in the camp – might somehow reverse itself. She wanted only to work her shift unobtrusively and return down the barbed-wire tunnel to her hut in the compound.

After a while she found herself giving an answering nod of the head to Oskar and even telling him that, Yes thank you, Herr Direktor, she was quite well. Once he gave her some cigarettes, better than gold both as a comfort and as a means of trading with the Polish workers. Since she knew that friends vanished, she feared his friendship; she wanted him to continue to be a presence, a magical parent. A paradise run by a friend was too fragile. To manage an enduring heaven, you needed someone both more authoritative and more mysterious than that.

Many of the Emalia prisoners felt the same.

There was a girl called Regina Perlman living, at the time Oskar's factory camp came into existence, in the city of Cracow on forged South American papers. Her dark complexion made the papers credible, and under them she worked as an Aryan in the office of a factory in Podgórze. She would have been safer from blackmailers if she'd gone to Warsaw, Lódź or Gdansk. But her parents were in Plaszów and she carried forged papers for their sakes too, so that she could supply them with food, comforts, medicine. She knew from the days in the ghetto that it was an adage in the Jewish mythology of Cracow that Herr Schindler could be expected to take extreme pains. She also knew the reports from Plaszów, from the quarry, the commandant's front steps. She would have to break cover to do it, but she believed it essential that she get her parents into Schindler's backyard camp.

The first time she visited Deutsche Email Fabrik she wore a safely anonymous faded floral dress and no stockings. The Polish gateman went through the business of calling Herr Schindler's office upstairs, and through the glass she could see him disapproving of her. It's nobody – some grubby girl from one of the other factories. She had the normal fear of people on Aryan papers, that a hostile Pole would somehow spot her Jewishness. This one looked hostile.

It's of no great importance, she told him when he returned

shaking his head. She wanted to put him off her track. But the Pole did not even bother to lie to her. He won't see you, he said. The hood of a BMW glowered in the factory yard, she could see it, and it could only belong to Herr Schindler. He was in, but not to visitors who couldn't afford stockings. She went away trembling at her escape. She'd been saved from making to Herr Schindler a confession which, even in her sleep, she feared making to anyone.

She waited a week before she could get more time off from the factory in Podgórze. She devoted an entire half day to her approach. She bathed and got black-market stockings. From one of her few friends – a Jewish girl on Aryan papers could not risk having many friends – she borrowed a blouse. She had an excellent jacket of her own and bought a lacquered straw hat with a veil. She made up her face, achieving a dark radiance appropriate to a woman living beyond threat. In the mirror she looked like her pre-war self, an elegant Cracovienne of exotic racial derivation, Hungarian businessman father perhaps and a mother from Rio.

This time, as she had intended, the Pole in the gatehouse did not even recognise her. He let her inside while he rang Miss Klonowska, the Herr Direktor's secretary, and then was put on to speak to the Herr Direktor himself. Herr Direktor, said the Pole, there is a lady here to see you on important business. Herr Schindler seemed to want details. A very well-dressed young lady, said the Pole, and then, bowing while holding the telephone, a very beautiful young lady, he said. As if he had a hunger to see her, or perhaps as if she might be some forgotten girl who'd embarrass him in the outer office, Schindler met her on the steps. He smiled when he saw he did not know her. He was very pleased to meet her, this Miss Rodriguez. She could see that he had a respect for pretty women, that it was at the same time childlike and yet sophisticated. With flourishes like those of a matinee idol, he indicated she should follow him upstairs. She wanted to talk to him in confidence? Of course she should. He led her past Klonowska. Klonowska took it calmly. The girl could mean anything – black market or currency business. She could even be a chic partisan. Love might be the least of motivations. In any case, a worldly girl such as Klonowska didn't expect to own Oskar, or to be owned in return.

Inside the office, Schindler placed a chair for her and walked behind his desk beneath the ritual portrait of the Führer. Would she like a cigarette? Perhaps a Pernod or a cognac? No, she said, but he must of course feel free to take a drink. He poured himself one from his cocktail cabinet. What's this very important business? he asked, not quite with that crisp grace he'd shown on the stairs. For her demeanour had changed now the door to the outer office was closed. He could tell she'd come to do hard business. She leaned forward. For a second it seemed ridiculous for her, a girl whose father had paid fifty thousand zloty for Aryan papers, to say it without a pause, to give it all away to a half ironic, half worried Sudetendeutscher with a glass of cognac in his hand. Yet in some ways it was the easiest thing she'd ever done.

I have to tell you, Herr Schindler, I'm not a Polish Aryan. My real name is Perlman. My parents are in Plaszów. They say, and I believe it, that coming here is the same as being given a Lebenskarte – a card of life. I have nothing I can give you, I borrowed clothes to get inside your factory. Will you bring them here for me?

Schindler put down his drink and stood up. You want to make a secret arrangement? I don't make secret arrangements. What you suggest, Miss Perlman, is illegal. I have a factory here in Zablocie and the only question I ask is whether or not a person has certain skills. If you care to leave your Aryan name and address it might be possible to write to you at some stage and inform you that I need your parents for their work skills. But not now and not on any other grounds.

But they can't come as skilled workers, she said. My father's an importer, not a metalworker.

We have an office staff, said Schindler. But mainly we need skills on the factory floor.

She was defeated. Half blind with tears, she wrote her false name and real address – he could do with it whatever he wanted. But on the street she understood and began to revive. Maybe Schindler thought she might be an agent, that she might have been there for entrapment. Just the same, he'd been cold. There hadn't even been an ambiguous non-indictable gesture of kindness in the manner with which he'd thrown her out of his office.

Within a month Mr. and Mrs. Perlman came to Emalia from Plaszów. Not on their own, as Regina Perlman had imagined it would happen should Herr Oskar Schindler decide to be merciful, but as part of a new detail of thirty workers. Sometimes she would go around to Lipowa Street and bribe her way on to the factory floor to see them. Her father worked dipping the enamel, shovelling coal, clearing the floor of scrap. But he talks again, said Mrs. Perlman to her daughter. For in Plaszów he'd grown silent.

In fact, despite the draughty huts, the plumbing, here at Emalia there was a certain mood, a fragile confidence, a presumption of permanence such as she, living on risky papers in sullen Cracow, could not hope to feel until the day the madness stopped.

Miss Perlman-Rodriguez did not complicate Herr Schindler's life by storming his office in gratitude or writing effusive letters. Yet she always left the yellow gate of Deutsche Email Fabrik with an unquenchable envy for those who stayed inside.

Then there was a campaign to get Rabbi Menasha Levartov, masquerading as a metalworker in Plaszów, into Emalia. Levartov was a scholarly city rabbi, young and black-bearded. He was more liberal than the rabbis from the shtetls of Poland, the ones who believed the Sabbath was more important even than life and who, throughout 1942 and 1943, were shot by the hundreds every Friday evening for refusing to work in the forced labour cantonments of Poland. He was one of those men who, even in the years of peace, would have advised his congregation that while God may well be honoured by the inflexibility of the pious, he might also be honoured by the flexibility of the sensible.

Levartov had always been admired by Itzhak Stern, who

now worked in the Building Office in Amon Goeth's Administration Block. Stern and Levartov would, if given the leisure, have sat together for hours over a glass of herbata, letting it grow cold while they talked about the influence of Zoroaster on Judaism, or the other way round, or the concept of the natural world in Taoism. Stern, when it came to comparative religion, got greater pleasure out of talking to Levartov than he could ever have received from bluff Oskar Schindler, who nonetheless had a fatal weakness for vapouring on the same subject.

During one of Oskar's visits to Plaszów, Stern told him that somehow Menasha Levartov had to be got into Emalia, or else Goeth would surely kill him. For Levartov had a sort of visibility – it was a matter of presence. Goeth was drawn to people of presence, they were, like idlers, another class with high priority as targets. Stern told Oskar how Goeth had attempted to murder Levartov.

Amon Goeth's camp now held more than thirty thousand people. On the near side of the Appellplatz, near the stables made from the Jewish Mortuary Chapel, stood a Polish compound that could hold some twelve hundred prisoners. Obergruppenführer Krüger was so pleased by his inspection of the new, booming camp that he promoted the commandant two SS grades to the rank of Hauptsturmführer.

As well as the crowd of Poles, Jews from the East and from Czechoslovakia would be held in Plaszów while space was made for them further west in Auschwitz-Birkenau or Gröss-Rosen. Sometimes the population rose above thirty-five thousand and the Appellplatz teemed at rollcall. Amon therefore had often to cull his early comers to make way for new prisoners. And Oskar knew that the commandant's quick method was to enter one of the camp offices or workshops, form up two lines, and march one of them away. The line marched away would be taken either to the Austrian hill fort and executed by Horst Pilarzik's firing squads, or else taken to the cattle wagons at Cracow Plaszów station or, when it was laid down in the autumn of 1943, to the railway siding by the fortified SS barracks.

On just such a culling exercise, Stern told Oskar, Amon

had entered the metalworks in the factory enclosure some days past. The supervisors had come to attention like soldiers and made their eager reports, knowing that they could die for an unwise choice of words. I need twenty-five metalworkers, Amon told the supervisors when the reports were finished. Twenty-five and no more. Point out to me the ones who are skilled.

One of the supervisors pointed to Levartov and he joined the line, though he could see that Amon took a special note of his selection. Of course one never knew which line would be moved out or where it would be moved to, but it was in most cases a safer bet to be on the line of the skilled.

So the selection continued. Levartov had noticed that the metal shops were strangely empty that morning, since a number of those who worked or filled in time by the door had got forewarning of Goeth's approach and had slipped over to the Madritsch garment factory to hide among the bolts of linen or appear to be mending sewing machines. The forty or so slow or inadvertent who had stayed on in the metalworks were now in two lines between the benches and the lathes. Everyone was fearful, but those in the smaller line were the more uneasy.

Then a boy of indeterminate age, perhaps as young as sixteen or as old as nineteen, had called from the midst of the shorter line, "But Herr Commandant, I'm a metal specialist too."

"Yes, Liebchen?" murmured Amon, drawing his service revolver, stepping to the boy and shooting him in the head. The enormous blast in this place of metal threw the lad against the wall. He was dead, the appalled Levartov believed, before he fell to the workshop floor.

The even shorter line was now marched out to the railway depot, the boy's corpse was taken over the hill in a barrow, the floor was washed, the lathes returned to operation. But Levartov, making gate hinges slowly at his bench, was aware of the recognition that had flashed for an instant in Amon's eye, the look that had said, there's one. It seemed to the rabbi that the boy had, by crying out, distracted Amon from Levartov himself, the more obvious target. That the youngster's pitiable death was not simply murder but a pledge that he, Levartov, would soon be likewise attended to.

A few days passed, Stern told Schindler, before Amon returned to the metalworks and found it crowded, and went around making his own selections for the hill or the transports. Then he'd halted by Levartov's bench, as Levartov knew he would. Levartov could smell Amon's after-shave. He could see the starched cuff of Amon's shirt. Amon was a splendid dresser.

"What are you making?" asked the commandant.

"Herr Commandant," said Levartov, "I am making hinges." The rabbi pointed in fact to the small heap of hinges on the floor.

"Make me one now," Amon ordered. He drew a watch from his pocket and began timing. Levartov earnestly cut a hinge, his fingers urging the metal, pressuring the lathe; convinced labouring fingers, delighted to be skilled. Keeping tremulous count in his head, he turned out a hinge in what he believed was fifty-eight seconds, and let it fall at his feet.

"Another," murmured Amon. After his speed trial, the rabbi was now more assured and worked with confidence. In perhaps another minute the second hinge slid to his feet.

Amon considered the heap. "You've been working here since six this morning," said Amon, not raising his eyes from the floor. "And can work at a rate you've just shown me and yet, such a mean little pile of hinges?" Levartov knew, of course, that he had crafted his own death. Amon walked him down the aisle, no one bothering or brave enough to look up from his bench. To see what? A death walk. Death walks were prosaic in Plaszów.

Outside, in the midday air of spring, Amon stood Menasha Levartov against the workshop wall, adjusting him by the shoulder, and took out the pistol with which he'd slaughtered the boy two days ago.

Levartov blinked and watched the other prisoners hurry by, wheeling and toting the raw materials of Plaszów camp, concerned to be out of range. The Cracovians among them thinking, My God, it's Levartov's turn. Privately he murmured the *Shema Yisroel* and heard the mechanisms of the pistol. But the small internal stirrings of metal ended not in a roar but in a click like that of a cigarette lighter which won't give a flame. And like a dissatisfied smoker, with just such a banal level of annoyance, Amon Goeth extracted and replaced the magazine of bullets from the butt of the pistol, again took his aim, and fired. As the rabbi's head swayed to the normal human suspicion that the impact of the bullet could be absorbed as could a punch, all that emerged from Goeth's pistol was another click.

Herr Commandant Goeth began cursing prosaically. "Donnerwetter! Zum-Teufel!" It seemed to Levartov that at any second Amon would begin to run down faulty modern workmanship, as if they were two tradesmen trying to bring off some simple effect, the threading of a pipe, a drill hole in the wall. Amon put the faulty pistol away in its black holster and withdrew from a jacket pocket a pearl-handled revolver, of a type Rabbi Levartov had only read of in theWesterns of his boyhood. Clearly, he thought, there are going to be no remissions due to technical failure. He'll keep on. I'll die by cowboy revolver, and even if all the firing pins are filed down, Hauptsturmführer Goeth will fall back on more primitive weapons.

As Stern relayed it to Schindler, when Goeth aimed again and fired, Menasha Levartov had already begun to look about in case there was some object in the neighbourhood that could be used, together with these two astounding failures of Goeth's service pistol, as a lever. By the corner of the wall stood a pile of coal, an unpromising item in itself. "Herr Commandant," Levartov began to say, but he could already hear the small murderous hammers and springs of the bar-room pistol acting on each other. And again the click of a failing cigarette lighter. Amon, raging, seemed to be attempting to tear the barrel of the thing from its socket.

Now Rabbi Levartov adopted the stance he had seen the supervisors in the metalworks assume. "Herr Commandant, I would beg to report that my heap of hinges was so unsatisfactory for the reason that the machines were being re-calibrated this morning. And therefore instead of hinge-work I was put on to shovelling that coal."

It seemed to Levartov that he had violated the rules of the game they had been playing together, the game that was to be closed by Levartov's reasonable death just as surely as Snakes and Ladders ends with the throwing of a six. It was as if the rabbi had hidden the dice and now there could be no conclusion. Amon hit him on the face with a free left hand and Levartov tasted blood in his mouth, lying on the tongue like a guarantee.

Hauptsturmführer Goeth then simply abandoned Levartov against the wall. The contest, however, as both Levartov and Stern could tell, had merely been suspended.

Stern whispered this narrative to Oskar in the Building Office of Plaszów. Stern, stooping, eyes raised, hands joined, was as generous with detail as ever. "It's no problem," Oskar murmured. He liked to tease Stern. "Why the long story? There's always room at Emalia for someone who can turn out a hinge in less than a minute."

When Levartov and his wife came to the Emalia factory camp in the summer of 1943 he had to suffer what at first he believed to be Schindler's little religious witticisms. On Friday afternoons, in the munitions hall of DEF where Levartov worked a lathe, Schindler would say, "You shouldn't be here, Rabbi. You should be preparing for *Shabbat*." But when Oskar slipped him a bottle of wine for use in the ceremonies, Levartov knew that the Herr Direktor was not joking. Before dusk on Fridays, the rabbi would be dismissed from his workbench and would go to his barracks behind the wire in the backyard of DEF. There, under the strings of sourly drying laundry, he would recite *Kiddush* over a cup of wine among the roof-high tiers of bunks. Under, of course, the bulk of an SS watchtower.

24

The Oskar Schindler who dismounted from his horse these days in the factory yard of Emalia was still a boomtime businessman. He looked sleekly handsome in the style of the film stars George Sanders and Curd Jurgens, to both of whom he would always be compared. His hacking jacket and jodhpurs were tailored, his riding boots had a high shine. He looked like a man to whom it was profit all the way.

Yet he would return from his rural rides and go upstairs to face the sort of bills novel even to the history of an eccentric enterprise such as Deutsche Email Fabrik.

Bread shipments from the bakery at Plaszów to the factory camp in Lipowa Street Zablocie were a few hundred loaves delivered twice a week and an occasional token half truckload of turnips. These few high-backed and lightly laden trucks were no doubt written large and multiplied in Commandant Goeth's books, and such trusties as Chilowicz sold off on behalf of the Herr Hauptsturmführer the difference between the mean supplies that arrived at Lipowa Street and the plenteous and phantom convoys which Goeth put down on paper. If Oskar had depended on Amon for prison food, his nine hundred internees would each have been fed perhaps three-quarters of a kilo of bread a week and soup every third day. On missions of his own and through his manager Oskar was spending fifty thousand zloty a month on black-market food for his camp kitchen. Some weeks he had to find over three thousand round loaves. He went to town and spoke to the German supervisors in the big bakeries, and had Reichsmarks and two or three bottles in his briefcase.

Oskar did not seem to realise that throughout Poland that

summer of 1943 he was one of the champion illicit feeders of prisoners, that the pall of hunger which should by SS policy hang over the great death factories and over every one of the little, barbed-wire forced-labour slums was lacking in Lipowa Street in a way that was dangerously visible.

That summer a host of incidents occurred which augmented the Schindler mythology, the almost religious supposition among many prisoners of Plaszów and the entire population of Emalia that Oskar was a provider of outrageous salvation.

Early in the career of every subcamp, senior officers from the parent Lager paid a visit to ensure that the energy of the slave labourers was stimulated in the most radical and exemplary manner. It is not certain exactly which members of Plaszów's senior staff visited Emalia, but some prisoners and Oskar himself would always say that Goeth was one of them. And if not Goeth it was Leo John, or Scheidt. Or else Josef Neuschel, Goeth's protégé. It is no injustice to mention any of their names in connection with 'stimulating energy in a radical and exemplary manner'. Whoever they were, they had already in the history of Plaszów taken or condoned fierce action. And now, visiting Emalia, they spotted in the yard a prisoner called Lamus pushing a barrow too slowly across the factory yard. Oskar himself later declared that it was Goeth who was there that day and saw Lamus's slow trundling and turned to a young NCO called Grün – Grün being another Goeth protégé, his bodyguard, a former wrestler. It was certainly Grün who was ordered to execute Lamus.

So Grün made the arrest and the inspectors continued on into other parts of the factory camp. It was someone from the metal hall who rushed up to the Herr Direktor's office and alerted Schindler. Oskar came roaring down the stairs even faster than on the day Miss Regina Perlman had visited, and reached the yard just as Grün was positioning Lamus against the wall.

Oskar called out. You can't do that here. I won't get work out of my people if you start shooting. I've got high priority war contracts, etc. etc. It was the standard Schindler argument and carried the suggestion that there were senior officers known to Oskar to whom Grün's name would be given if he impeded production in Emalia.

Grün was cunning. He knew the other inspectors had passed on to the workshops where the whumping of metal presses and the roaring of lathes would cover any noise he chose, or failed, to make. Lamus was such a small concern to men like Goeth and John that no enquiry would be made afterwards. What's in it for me? the SS youth asked Oskar. Would vodka do? said Oskar. A litre and a half?

To Grün it was a substantial prize. For working all day behind the machine guns during Einsatzaktions, the massed and daily executions in the East – for shooting hundreds, that is – you were given half a litre of vodka. The boys lined up to be on the squad so that they could take that prize of liquor back to their messes in the evening. And here the Herr Direktor offered him three times that for one act of omission.

I don't see the bottle, he said nonetheless. Herr Schindler was already nudging Lamus away from the wall and pushing him out of range. Disappear, Grün yelled at the wheelbarrow man. You may collect the bottle, said Oskar, from my office at the end of the inspection.

Oskar took part in a similar transaction when the Gestapo raided the apartment of a forger and discovered, among other false documents completed or near completed, a set of Aryan papers for a family called the Wohlfeilers, mother, father, three adolescent children, all of them workers at Schindler's camp. Two Gestapo men therefore came to Lipowa Street to collect the family for an interrogation which would lead, through Montelupich prison, to that grim hill fort. Three hours after entering Oskar's office both men left Deutsche Email Fabrik, reeling on the stairs, beaming with the temporary bonhomie of cognac and, for all anyone knew, of a pay-off. The confiscated papers now lay on Oskar's desk and he picked them up and put them in the fire.

Next, the brothers Danziger, who cracked a metal press one Friday. Honest bemused men, half skilled, looking up with staring shtetl eyes from the machine they had just loudly shattered. The Herr Direktor was away on business and someone – a factory spy, Oskar would always say – denounced the Danzigers to the administration in Plaszów. The brothers were taken from Emalia and their hanging advertised in the next morning's rollcall in Plaszów. *Tonight*, (it was announced) *the people of Plaszów will witness the execution of two saboteurs*. What of course qualified the Danzigers above all for execution was their orthodox aura.

Oskar returned from his business trip to Sosnowiec at three o'clock on Saturday afternoon, three hours before the promised execution. News of the sentence was waiting on his desk. He drove out through the suburbs to Plaszów at once, taking cognac with him and some fine kielbasa sausage. He parked by the Administration Block of Plaszów and found Goeth in his office. He was pleased not to have to rouse the commandant from an afternoon nap. No one knows the extent of the deal that was struck in Goeth's office that afternoon, in that office akin to Torquemada's, where Goeth had had ringbolts attached to the wall from which people could be hanged for discipline or instruction. It is hard to believe, though, that Amon was satisfied simply with cognac and sausage. In any case, his concern for the integrity of the Reich's metal presses was soothed by the interview, and at six o'clock, the hour of their execution, the Danziger brothers returned in the back seat of Oskar's plush limousine to the sweet squalor of Emalia.

All these triumphs were, of course, partial. It is an aspect of Caesars, Oskar knew, to remit as irrationally as they condemn. Emil Krautwirt, by day an engineer in the radiator factory beyond the Emalia barracks, was an inmate of Oskar's SS subcamp. He was young, having got his diploma in the late 1930s. Krautwirt, like other natives of Emalia, called the place Schindler's camp, but by taking Krautwirt away to Plaszów for an exemplary hanging the SS demonstrated whose camp it really was, at least for some aspects of its existence.

For the fraction of the Plaszów people who would live on

into the peace, the hanging of engineer Krautwirt was the first story, other than their own intimate stories of pain and humiliation, which they would relate. The SS were ever economical with their scaffolds, and at Plaszów the gallows resembled a long low set of goalposts, lacking the majesty of the gibbets of history, of the Revolutionary guillotine, the Elizabethan scaffold, the tall solemnity of jailhouse gallows in the sheriff's backyard. Seen in peacetime, the gallows of Plaszów and Auschwitz would intimidate not by their solemnity but by their ordinariness. But as mothers would discover in Plaszów, it was still possible, even with such a banal structure, for their children to see too much of an execution from within the mass of prisoners on the Appell-platz. A sixteen-year-old boy called Haubenstock was to be hanged with Krautwirt. Krautwirt had been condemned for some letters he had written to seditious persons in the city of Cracow. But with Haubenstock it was that he had been heard singing *Volga, Volga, Kalinka Maya*, and other ban-ned Russian songs with the intention – according to his death sentence – of winning the Ukrainian guards over to Bolshevism.

The rules for the rite of execution inside Plaszów involved silence. Unlike the festive hangings of earlier times, the drop was performed in a church stillness. The prisoners stood in phalanxes, and were patrolled by men and women who knew the extent of their power, by Hujar and John, Amthor and Scheidt, by Grimm and by Grün, by the SS women supervisors recently posted to Plaszów, both of them energetic with the baton – Alice Orlowski, and Luise Danz – and by Ritschek, and Schreiber. Under such super-vision, the pleadings of the condemned were heard in silence.

Engineer Krautwirt himself seemed at first stunned and had nothing to say, but the boy was vocal. In an uneven voice he reasoned with the Hauptsturmführer, who stood beside the scaffold. I am not a Communist, Herr Comman-dant. I hate Communism. They were just songs. Ordinary songs. The hangman, a Jewish butcher of Cracow, par-doned for some earlier crime on condition that he undertake this work, stood Haubenstock on a stool and placed the noose around his neck. He could tell Amon wanted the boy done first, didn't want the debate to drag on. When the butcher kicked the support out from beneath Haubenstock, the rope broke and the boy, purple and gagging, noose around his neck, crawled on his hands and knees to Goeth, continuing his pleadings, ramming his head against the commandant's ankles and hugging his legs. It was the most extreme submission, it conferred on Goeth again the king-ship he'd been exercising these fevered months past. Amon, in an Appellplatz of gaping mouths uttering no sound but a low hiss, a susurrus like a wind in sand dunes, took his pistol from his holster, kicked the boy away and shot him through the head.

When poor engineer Krautwirt saw the horror of the boy's execution, he took a razor blade that he'd concealed in his pocket and slashed his wrists. Those prisoners at the front could tell that Krautwirt had injured himself terribly in both arms. But Goeth ordered the hangman to proceed in any case, and splashed with the gore from Krautwirt's injuries, two Ukrainians lifted him to the scaffold, where, gushing from both wrists, he strangled in front of the Jews of southern Poland.

It was natural for the internees of Plaszów to believe with one part of the mind that each such barbarous exhibition might be the last, that there might be a reversal of the methods and attitudes even in Amon, or if not in him, then in those unseen officials who, in some high office with French windows and waxed floors overlooking a square where old women sold flowers, must formulate half of what happened in Plaszów and condone the rest.

On the second visit of Dr. Sedlacek from Budapest to Cracow, Oskar and the dentist devised a scheme which might to a more introverted man than Schindler have seemed naïve. Oskar suggested to Sedlacek that perhaps one of the reasons Amon Goeth behaved so savagely was the bad alcohol he imbibed, the buckets of ninety-six per cent proof local so-called 'cognac' which further weakened

Amon's faulty sense of ultimate consequences. With a portion of the Reichsmarks Dr. Sedlacek had just brought to Emalia and handed to Oskar, a crate of first-rate cognac should be bought – not such an easy or inexpensive item in post-Stalingrad Poland. Oskar should deliver it to Amon, and in the progress of conversation suggest to Goeth that one way or another the war would end at some time, and that there would be investigations into the actions of individuals. That perhaps even Amon's friends would remember the times he'd been too zealous.

It was Oskar's nature to believe that you could drink with the devil and adjust the balance of evil over a tumbler of cognac. It was not that he found more radical methods frightening. It was that they did not occur to him. He'd always been a man of transactions.

Wachtmeister Oswald Bosko who had earlier had control of the ghetto perimeter, was, by contrast, a man of ideas. It had become impossible for him to work within the SS scheme, passing a bribe here, a forged paper there, placing a dozen children under the patronage of his rank while a hundred more were marched out of the ghetto gate. Bosko had absconded from his police station in Podgórze and vanished into the partisan forests of Niepolomice. In the People's Army he would try to expiate the callow enthusiasm he'd felt for Nazism in the summer of 1938. Dressed as a Polish farmer, he'd be recognised in the end in a village west of Cracow and shot for treason. Bosko would therefore become a martyr.

Bosko had gone to the forest because he had no other option. He lacked the financial resources with which Oskar greased the system. But it accorded with the natures of both men that one be found with nothing but a cast-off rank and uniform and the other would make certain he had cash and trade goods. It is not to praise Bosko or denigrate Schindler that one says that if ever Oskar suffered martyrdom, it would be by accident, because some business he had on hand had turned sour on him. But there were people who still drew breath – the Wohlfeilers, the Danziger brothers,

Lamus – because Oskar worked that way. Because Oskar worked that way, the unlikely camp of Emalia stood in Lipowa Street, and there, on most days, a thousand were safe from seizure, and the SS stayed outside the wire. No one was beaten there, and the soup was thick enough to sustain life. In proportion to their natures, the moral disgust of both Party members, Bosko and Schindler, was equal, even if Bosko manifested his by leaving his empty uniform on a coat-hanger in Podgórze, while Oskar put on his big Party pin and went to deliver high-class booze to mad Amon in Plaszów.

It was late afternoon, and Oskar and Goeth sat in the salon of Goeth's white villa. Goeth's girlfriend Majola looked in, a small-boned woman, a secretary at the Wagner factory in town. She did not spend all her days in the excessive air of Plaszów. She had sensitive manners, and this delicacy helped a rumour to emerge, that Majola had threatened not to sleep with Goeth if he continued gunning people down. But no one knew whether that was the truth or just one of those therapeutic interpretations that arise in the minds of prisoners desperate to make the earth habitable.

Majola did not stay long with Amon and Oskar that afternoon. She could tell there would be a drinking session. Helen Hirsch, pale and in black, brought them the necessary accompaniments – cakes, canapés, sausage. She reeled with exhaustion. Last night Amon had beaten her for preparing food for Majola without his permission, this morning he had made her run up and down the villa's three flights of stairs fifty times on the double because of a fly speck on one of the pictures in the corridor. She had heard certain rumours about Herr Schindler but had not met him until now. This afternoon she took no comfort from the sight of these two big men, seated either side of the low table, fraternal and in apparent concord. There was nothing here to interest her, for the certainty of her own death was a first premise. She thought only about the survival of her young sister, who worked in the camp's general kitchen. She kept a sum of money hidden in the hope that it would effect her sister's survival. There was no sum, she believed, no deal, that could influence her own prospects.

So they drank through the camp's twilight and into the dark. Long after the prisoner Tosia Lieberman's nightly rendition of Brahms's *Lullaby* had calmed the women's camp and insinuated itself between the timbers of the men's, the two big men sat on. Their prodigious livers glowed hot as furnaces. And at the right hour, Oskar leaned across the table and acting out of an amity which, even with this much cognac aboard, did not go beyond the surface of the skin, was merely a sort of frisson, a phantom shiver of brotherhood running along the pores, nothing more – Oskar, leaning towards Amon and cunning as a demon, began to tempt him towards restraint.

Amon took it well. It seemed to Oskar that he was attracted by the thought of moderation – a temptation worthy of an emperor. Amon could imagine a sick slave on the trolleys, a returning prisoner from Kabelwerke, staggering – in that put-upon way one found so hard to tolerate – under a load of clothing or timber picked up at the prison gate. And the fantasy ran with a strange warmth in Amon's belly that he would forgive that laggard, that pathetic actor. As Caligula might have been tempted to see himself as Caligula the Good, so the image of Amon the Good exercised the commandant's imagination for a time. He would, in fact, always have a weakness for it. Tonight, his blood running golden with cognac and nearly all the camp asleep beyond his steps, Amon was more definitely seduced by mercy than by the fear of reprisal. But in the morning he would remember Oskar's warning and combine it with the day's news, that Russian threats were developing to the front at Kiev. Stalingrad had been an inconceivable distance from Plaszów. But the distance to Kiev was imaginable.

For some days after Oskar's bout with Amon, news came to Emalia that the double temptation of mercy and discretion was having its result with the commandant. Dr. Sedlacek, going back to Budapest, would report to Samu Springmann that Amon had given up, for the time being at least, arbitrarily murdering people. And gentle Samu, among the diverse cares he had in the list of places from Dachau and Drancy in the west to Sobibor and Belzec in the east, hoped for a time that the hole at Plaszów had been plugged. But the allure of clemency vanished quickly. If there was a brief respite, those who were to survive and give testimony of their days in Plaszów would not be aware of it. The summary assassinations would seem continual to them. If Amon did not appear on his balcony this morning or the next, it did not mean he would not appear the morning after that. It took much more than Goeth's temporary non-appearance to give even the most deluded prisoner some hope of a fundamental change in the commandant's nature. And then, in any case, there he would be, on the steps in the Austrian-style cap he wore to murders, looking through his binoculars for a culprit.

Dr. Sedlacek would return to Budapest not only with overly hopeful news of a reform in Amon but with more reliable data on the camp at Plaszów.

One afternoon a guard from Emalia turned up at Plaszów to summon Stern to Zablocie. Once Stern arrived at the front gate, he was led upstairs into Oskar's new apartment. There Oskar introduced him to two men in good suits. One was Dr. Sedlacek, the other a Jew – equipped with a Swiss passport – who introduced himself as Babar. My dear friend, Oskar told Stern, I want you to write as full a report on the situation in Plaszów as you can manage in an afternoon. Stern had never seen Sedlacek or Babar before this and thought that Oskar was being indiscreet. He bent over his hands, murmuring that before he undertook a task like that he would like a word in private with the Herr Direktor.

Oskar used to say that Itzhak Stern could never make a straight statement or request unless it arrived smuggled under a baggage of talk of the Babylonian Talmud and purification rites. But now he was more direct. "Tell me please, Herr Schindler," he asked, "don't you believe this is a dreadful risk?"

Oskar exploded. Before he got control of himself, the

strangers would have heard him in the other room. "Do you think I'd ask you, if there was a risk?" Then he calmed and said, "There's always risk, as you know better than I. But not with these two men. These two are safe."

In the end Stern spent all afternoon on his report. He was a scholar and accustomed to writing in exact prose. The rescue organisation in Budapest, the Zionists in Istanbul would receive from Stern a report they could rely on. Multiply Stern's summary by the seventeen hundred large and small forced labour camps of Poland and then you had a tapestry to stun the world.

Sedlacek and Oskar wanted more than that of Stern. On the morning after his binge with Amon, Oskar dragged his heroic liver back out to Plaszów before office-opening time. In between the suggestions of tolerance Oskar had tried to drop in Amon's ear the night before, he'd also got a written permit to take two 'brother-industrialists' on a tour of this model industrialist community. Oskar brought the two captains of manufacture into the grey Administration Building that morning and demanded the services of Haftling (prisoner) Itzhak Stern for a tour of the camp. Sedlacek's friend Babar had some sort of miniature camera, but he carried it openly in his hand. It was almost possible to believe that if an SS man had challenged him, he would have welcomed the chance to stand and boast for five minutes about this little gadget he'd got on a recent business trip to Brussels or Stockholm.

As Oskar and the visitors from Budapest emerged from the Administration Building, Oskar took the thin clerkly Stern by the shoulder. His friends would be happy to see the workshops and the living quarters, said Oskar. But if there was anything Stern thought they were missing out on, he was just to bend down and tie his shoestring.

On Goeth's great road they moved past the SS barracks. Here, almost at once, prisoner Stern's shoestring needed tying. Sedlacek's associate snapped the teams hauling truckloads of rock up from the quarry, while Stern murmured, "Forgive me, gentlemen." Yet he took his time with the tying so that they could look down and read the monumental fragments that paved the road. Here were the grave-stones of Bluma Gemeinerowa (1859–1927), of Matylde Liebeskind, deceased at the age of ninety in 1912, of Helena Wachsberg, who died in childbirth in 1911, of Rozia Groder, a thirteen year old who had passed on in 1931, of Sofia Rosner and Adolf Gottlieb, who had died in the reign of Franz Josef. Stern wanted them to see that the names of the honourable dead had been made into paving stones.

Moving on, they passed the Puffhaus, the SS and Ukrainian brothel staffed by Polish girls, before reaching the quarry, the excavations running back into the limestone cliff. Stern's shoelaces required reef knots here; he wanted this recorded. They destroyed men at this rock face, working them on the hammers and wedges. None of the scarred men of the quarry parties showed any curiosity towards their visitors this morning. Ivan, Amon Goeth's Ukrainian driver, was on duty here, and the supervisor was a bullet-headed German criminal called Erik. Erik had already demonstrated a capacity for murdering families, having killed his own mother, father, sister. He might by now have hanged or at least been put in a dungeon if the SS had not realised that there were worse criminals still than patricides and that Erik should be employed as a stick to beat them with. As Stern had mentioned in his report, a Cracow physician called Edward Goldblatt had been sent here from the clinic by SS Dr. Blancke and his Jewish protégé, Dr. Leon Gross. Erik loved to see a man of culture and speciality enter the quarry and report soft-handed for work, and in Gold-blatt's case the beatings began with the first display of uncertainty in handling the hammer and spikes. Over a period of days, Erik and sundry SS and Ukrainian rankers beat Goldblatt. The doctor was forced to work with a ballooning face, now half again its normal size, with one eye sealed up. No one knew what error of quarry technique set Erik to give Dr. Goldblatt his final beating. Long after the doctor lost consciousness, Erik permitted him to be carried to the Krankenstube where Dr. Leon Gross refused to admit him. With this medical sanction Erik and an SS enlisted man continued to boot the dying Goldblatt as he lay, rejected for treatment, on the threshold of the hospital.

Stern bent and tied his shoelace at the quarry because, like Oskar and some others in the Plaszów complex, he believed in a future of judges who might ask, Where – in a word – did this act occur?

That morning Oskar was able to give his colleagues an overview of the camp, taking them up to Chujowa Górka where the bloodied wheelbarrows used to transport the dead to the woods stood unabashedly at the mouth of the fort. Already thousands were buried down there in mass graves in or on the verges of those eastern pinewoods. When the Russians came from the east, that wood with its population of victims would fall to them before half-dying Plaszów.

25

To some people it now seemed that Oskar was spending like a man with a gambling madness. Even from the little they knew of him, his prisoners could sense that he would ruin himself for them if that was the price. Later – not now, for now they accepted his mercies in the same spirit in which a child accepts Christmas presents from its parents – they would say, Thank God he was more faithful to us than to his wife. And like the prisoners, sundry officials could also sniff out Oskar's passion.

One such official, Dr. Sopp, physician to the SS prisons in Cracow and to the SS Court in Pomorska, let Herr Schindler know through a Polish messenger that he was willing to do a brand of business. In Montelupich prison was a woman named Frau Helene Schindler. Dr. Sopp knew she was no relative of Oskar's, but her husband had invested some money in Emalia. She had questionable Aryan papers. Dr. Sopp did not need to say that for Mrs. Schindler this portended a truck ride to Chujowa Górka. But if Oskar would put up certain amounts, said Sopp, the doctor was willing to issue a medical certificate saying that, in view of her condition, Mrs. Schindler should be permitted to take the cure indefinitely at Marienbad, down in Bohemia.

Oskar went to Sopp's office, where he found out that the doctor wanted fifty thousand zloty for the certificate. It was no use arguing. After three years of practice, a man like Sopp could tell to within a few zloty the price to put on favours. During the afternoon, Oskar found the money. Sopp knew he could, knew that Oskar was the sort of man who had black-market money stashed, money with no recorded history.

Before making the payment, Oskar set some conditions. He would need to go to Montelupich with Dr. Sopp to collect the woman from her cell. He would himself deliver her to mutual friends in the city. Sopp did not object. Under a bare light bulb in freezing Montelupich, Mrs. Schindler was handed her costly documents.

A more careful man, a man with an accountant's mind, might reasonably have repaid himself for his trouble from the money Sedlacek brought from Budapest. Altogether, Oskar would be handed nearly a hundred and fifty thousand Reichsmarks carried to Cracow as before in false-bottomed suitcases and in the lining of clothes. But Oskar, partly because his sense of money (whether owed or owing) was so inexact, partly because of his sense of honour, passed on to his Jewish contacts all the money he ever received from Sedlacek, except for the sum spent on Amon's cognac.

It was not always a straightforward business. When in the summer of 1943 Sedlacek arrived in Cracow with fifty thousand Reichsmarks, the Zionists inside Plaszów to whom Oskar offered the cash feared it might be a frame-up.

Oskar first approached Henry Mandel, a welder in the Plaszów garage and a member of Hitach Dut, a Zionist youth and labour movement. Mandel did not want to touch the money. Look, said Schindler, I've got a letter in Hebrew to go with it, a letter from Palestine. But, of course, if it was a frame-up, if Oskar had been compromised and was being used, he *would* have a letter from Palestine; and when you hadn't enough bread for breakfast, it was quite a sum to be offered, fifty thousand Reichsmarks, a hundred thousand zloty. To be offered that for your discretionary use. It just wasn't credible.

Schindler then tried to pass the money, which was sitting there, inside the boundary of Plaszów in the trunk of his car, to another member of Hitach Dut, a woman named Alta Rubner. She had some contacts, through prisoners who went to work in the cable factory, through some of the Poles in the Polish prison, with the underground in Sosnowiec. Perhaps, she said to Mandel, it would be best to refer the whole business to the underground, and let them decide on the provenance of the money Herr Oskar Schindler was offering.

Oskar kept trying to persuade her, raising his voice at her under cover of the chattering sewing machines in the Madritsch factory. "I guarantee with all my heart that this isn't a trap!" *With all my heart.* Exactly the sentiment one would expect from an agent provocateur!

Yet after Oskar had gone away and Mandel had spoken to Stern, who declared the letter authentic, and then conferred again with the girl, a decision was made to take the money. They found now, however, that Oskar wouldn't be back with it. Mandel went to Marcel Goldberg at the Administration Office. Goldberg had also been a member of Hitach Dut but, after becoming the clerk in charge of lists, of labour and transport lists, of the lists of living and dead, he had begun taking bribes. Mandel could put pressure on him, though. One of the lists Goldberg could draw up – or at least add to and subtract from – was the list of those who went to Emalia to collect scrap metal for use in the workshops of Plaszów. For old times' sake, and without having to disclose his reasons for wanting to visit Emalia, Mandel was put on *this* list.

But arriving in Zablocie and sneaking away from the scrap detail to get to Oskar, he'd been blocked in the front office by Bankier. Herr Schindler was too busy, said Bankier.

A week later Mandel was back. Again Bankier wouldn't let him in to speak to Oskar. The third time Bankier was more specific. You want that Zionist money? You didn't want it before. And now you want it. Well, you can't have it. That's the way life goes, Mr. Mandel!

Mandel nodded and left. He presumed that Bankier had already lifted at least a fraction of the cash. In fact Bankier was being careful. The money did finish in the hands of Zionist prisoners in Plaszów – Alta Rubner's receipt for the funds was delivered to Springmann by Sedlacek. It seems that the amount was used in part to help Jews from cities other than Cracow and who therefore had no local sources of support.

Whether the funds that came to Oskar and were passed on by him were spent mainly on food, as Stern would have preferred, or largely on underground resistance – the purchase of passes or weapons – is a question that Oskar never examined. None of this money however went to buy Mrs. Schindler out of Montelupich prison or to save the lives of such people as the Danziger brothers. Nor was the Sedlacek money used to replace the thirty thousand kilos of enamelware which Oskar would pay out to major and minor SS officials during 1943 to prevent them from recommending the closure of the Emalia camp.

None of it was spent on the sixteen thousand zloty set of gynaecological instruments that Oskar had to buy on the black market when one of the Emalia girls fell pregnant, pregnancy being, of course, an immediate ticket to Auschwitz. Nor did any of it go to purchase the broken-down Mercedes from Untersturmführer John. John offered Oskar the Mercedes for sale at the same time as Oskar presented a request for thirty Plaszów people to be transferred to Emalia. The car, bought by Oskar one day for twelve thousand zloty, was requisitioned the next by Leo John's friend and brother officer, Untersturmführer Scheidt, to be used in the construction of field works on the camp perimeter. Perhaps they'll carry soil in the trunk, Oskar raged to Ingrid at the supper table. In a later informal account of the incident, he commented that he was glad to be of assistance to both gentlemen.

26

Raimund Titsch was making payments of a different order. Titsch was a quiet, clerkly Austrian Catholic with a limp that some said came from the first war and others from a childhood accident. He was ten years or more older than either Amon or Oskar. Inside Plaszów camp, he managed Julius Madritsch's uniform factory, a business of three thousand seamstresses and mechanics.

One way he paid was through his bouts of chess with Amon Goeth. The Administration Block was connected with the Madritsch works by telephone, and Amon would often call Titsch up to his office for a game. The first time Raimund had played Amon, the game had ended in half an hour and not in the commandant's favour. Titsch, with the restrained and not so very triumphal "Mate!" dying on his lips, had been amazed at the tantrum Amon had thrown. The commandant had grabbed for his coat and gun belt, buttoning and buckling them on, ramming his cap on his head. Raimund Titsch, appalled, believed that Amon was about to go down to the trolley line looking for a prisoner to chastise for his, for Raimund Titsch's, minor accomplishment at chess. Since that first afternoon, Titsch had taken a new direction. Now he could take as long as three hours to lose to the commandant. When workers in the Administration Block saw Titsch limping up Jerozolimska to do this chess duty, they knew the afternoon would be saner for it. A modest sense of security spread from them down to the workshops and even to the miserable trolley pushers.

But Raimund Titsch did not only play preventative chess. Independently of Sedlacek and of the man with the pocket camera whom Oskar had brought to Plaszów, Titsch had begun photographing. Sometimes from his office window, sometimes from the corners of workshops, he photographed the stripe-uniformed prisoners in the trolley-line, the distribution of bread and soup, the digging of drains and foundations. Some of these photographs of Titsch's are probably of the illegal supply of bread to the Madritsch workshop. Certainly round brown loaves were bought by Raimund himself, with Julius Madritsch's consent and money, and delivered to Plaszów by truck beneath bales of rags and bolts of cloth. Titsch photographed round rye being carried from hand to hand into the Madritsch factory storeroom, on its relatively blind side, the side away from the towers and screened from the main access road by the bulk of the camp stationery plant. He photographed the SS and the Ukrainians marching, at play, at work. He photographed a work party under the supervision of Engineer Karp, who was soon to be set on by the killer dogs, his thigh ripped open, his genitals torn off. In a long shot of Plaszów, he intimated the size of the camp, its desolation. It seems that on Amon's sundeck he even took close-ups of the commandant at rest in a deckchair, a hefty Amon approaching now the hundred and twenty kilos at which newly arrived SS Dr. Blancke will say to him, "Enough, Amon; you have to take some weight off." Titsch also photographed Rolf and Ralf loping and sunning, and Majola holding one of the dogs by the collar and pretending to enjoy it. He also took Amon in full majesty on his big white horse.

As the reels were shot, Titsch did not have them developed. As an archive, they were safer and more portable in roll form. He hid them in a steel box in his Cracow apartment. There also he kept some of the remaining goods of the Madritsch Jews. Throughout Plaszów you found people who had a final treasure, something to offer – at the moment of greatest danger – to the man with the list, the man who opened and closed the doors on the cattle wagons. Titsch understood that only the desperate deposited goods with him. That prison minority who had a stock of rings and watches and jewellery hidden somewhere in Plaszów didn't need him. *They* traded regularly for favours and comforts.

But into the same hiding as Titsch's photographs went the final resources of a dozen families – Auntie Yanka's brooch, Uncle Mordche's watch.

In fact, when the Plaszów regimen passed, when Scherner and Czurda had fled, and when the impeccable files of the SS Main Economic and Administrative Office had been baled up in trucks and moved away as evidence, Titsch had no need to develop the photographs, and every reason not to. On the files of ODESSA, the postwar secret society of former SS men, he would be listed as a traitor. The fact that he'd supplied the Madritsch people with some thirty thousand loaves of bread, as well as many chickens and some kilos of butter, and that for his humanity he had been honoured by the Israeli government, had received some publicity in the press. Some people made threats and hissed at him as he passed in the streets of Vienna. "Jew-kisser." So the Plaszów reels would lie for twenty years in the soil of a small park in the suburbs of Vienna where Titsch had buried them, and might well have stayed there for ever, the emulsion drying on the dark and secret images of Amon's love, Majola, his killing dogs, his nameless slave labourers. It might therefore have been seen as a sort of triumph for the population of Plaszów when, in November 1963, a Schindler survivor (Leopold Pfefferberg) secretly bought the box and its contents from Raimund Titsch, who was then suffering from terminal heart disease. Even then, Raimund didn't want the rolls developed until after his death. The anonymous shadow of ODESSA frightened him more than had the names of Amon Goeth, of Scherner, of Auschwitz in the days of Plaszów.

After his burial, the reels were developed. Nearly all the pictures came out.

Not one of that small body of Plaszów inmates who would survive Amon and the camp itself would ever have anything accusatory to say of Raimund Titsch. But he was never the sort of man concerning whom mythologies arose. Oskar was. From late 1943, there is a story about Schindler which runs among the Plaszów survivors with the electric excitement of a myth. For the thing about a myth is not whether it is true or not, nor whether it *should* be true, but that it is somehow truer than truth itself. Through listening to such stories, one can see that to the Plaszów people, while Titsch may have been the good hermit, Oskar had become a minor god of deliverance, double-faced – in the Greek manner – as any small god, endowed with all the human vices, many-handed, subtly powerful, capable of bringing gratuitous but secure salvation.

One story concerns the time when the SS police chiefs were under pressure to close Plaszów, as its reputation as an efficient industrial complex was not high with the Armaments Inspectorate. Helen Hirsch, Goeth's maid, often encountered officers, dinner guests, who wandered into the hallway or kitchen of the villa to escape Amon for a while and to shake their heads. An SS officer called Tibritsch, turning up in the kitchen, had said to Helen, "Doesn't he know there are men giving their lives?" He meant on the Eastern Front, of course, not out there in the dark of Plaszów. Officers with less imperial lives than Amon were becoming outraged by what they saw at the villa or, perhaps more dangerously, envious.

As the legend has it, it was on a Sunday evening that General Julius Schindler himself visited Plaszów to decide whether its existence was of any real value to the war effort. It was an odd hour for a grand bureaucrat to be visiting plant, but perhaps the Armaments Inspectorate, in view of the perilous winter now falling on the Eastern Front, were working desperate hours. The inspection had been preceded by dinner at Emalia, at which wine and cognac flowed, for Oskar is associated like Bacchus with the Dionysian line of gods.

Because of the dinner, the inspection party rolling out to Plaszów in their Mercedes were in a mood of less than professional detachment. In making this claim, the story ignores the fact that Schindler and his officers were all production experts and engineers with nearly four years of detached professionalism behind them. But Oskar would be the last to be awed by that fact.

The inspection started at the Madritsch works. This was Plaszów's showplace. During 1943, it had produced Wehrmacht uniforms at a monthly rate of something over twenty thousand. But the question was whether Herr Madritsch would do better to forget Plaszów, to spend his capital on expanding his more efficient and better supplied Polish factories in Podgórze and Tarnow. The ramshackle conditions of Plaszów were no encouragement to Madritsch or any other investor to install the sort of machinery a sophisticated works would need.

The official party had just begun its inspection when all the lights in all the workshops went out, the power circuit broken by friends of Itzhak Stern in Plaszów's generator shed. To the handicaps of drink and indigestion which Oskar had imposed on the gentlemen of the Armaments Inspectorate were now added the limitations of bad light. The inspection went ahead by flashlight, in fact, and the machinery on the benches remained inoperative and therefore less of a provocation to the inspectors' professional feelings.

As General Schindler squinted along the beam of a flashlight at the presses and lathes in the metalworks, thirty thousand Plaszóvians, restless in tiered bunks, waited on his word. Even on the overladen lines of the Ostbahn, the higher technology of Auschwitz was but a few hours' journey west, they knew. They understood that they could not expect from General Schindler compassion as such. *Production* was his speciality. For him, *Production* was meant to be an overriding value.

Because of Schindler's dinner and the power failure, says the myth, the people of Plaszów were saved. It is a generous fable, because in fact only a tithe of Plaszów people would be alive at the end. But Stern and others would later celebrate the story, and most of its details are probably true. For Oskar always had recourse to alcohol when puzzled as to how to treat officials, and he would have liked the trickery of plunging them into darkness. "You have to remember," said a boy whom Oskar would later save, "that Oskar had a German side but a Czech side too. He was the good soldier Schweik. He loved to foul up the system.''

It is ungracious to the myth to ask what the exacting Goeth thought when the lights went out. Maybe, even on the level of literal event, he was drunk or dining elsewhere. It could justly be asked whether Plaszów survived because General Schindler was deceived by dim light and alcohol-dimmed vision, or whether it continued because it was such an excellent holding centre for those weeks when the great terminus at Auschwitz-Birkenau was overcrowded. But the story says more of people's expectations of Oskar than it does of the frightful compound of Plaszów or the final end of most of its inmates.

And while the SS and the Armaments Inspectorate considered the future of Plaszów, Josef Bau – a young artist from Cracow, whom Oskar would in the end come to know well – was falling into conspicuous and unconditional love with a girl called Rebecca Tannenbaum. Bau worked in the Construction Office as a draughtsman. He was a solemn boy with an artist's sense of destiny. He had – so to speak – *escaped* into Plaszów, because he had never held the correct ghetto papers. Since he had had no trade of use to the ghetto factories, he had been hidden by his mother and by friends. During the liquidation in March 1943, he'd escaped out of the walls and attached himself to the tail of a labour detail going to Plaszów. For in Plaszów there was a new industry which had had no place in the ghetto. Building. In the same sombre, two-winged building blockhouse in which Amon had his office, Josef Bau worked on blueprints. He was a protégé of Itzhak Stern, and Stern had mentioned him to Oskar as an accomplished draughtsman and as a boy who had, potentially at least, skills as a forger.

He was lucky not to come into too much contact with Amon, because he displayed that air of genuine sensibility which had until now always caused Amon to reach for his revolver.

Bau's office was on the far side of the building from Amon's. Some prisoners worked on the ground floor, with offices near the commandant's. There were the purchasing officers, the clerks, Mietek Pemper the stenographer. They faced not only a daily risk of an unexpected bullet but, more certainly than that, assaults on their sense of outrage. Mundek Korn, for example, who had been a buyer for a string of Rothschild subsidiaries before the war, and who now bought the fabrics, seagrass, lumber and iron for the prison workshop, had to work not only in the Administration Building but in the same wing as Amon had his office. One morning Korn looked up from his desk and saw through the window, across Jerozolimska Street and by the SS barracks, a boy of twenty years or so, a Cracovian of his acquaintance, urinating against the base of one of the stacks of timber there. At the same time he saw white-shirted arms and two ham fists appear through the bathroom window. The right hand held a revolver. There were two quick shots, at least one of which entered the boy's head and drove him forward against the pile of cut wood. When Korn looked once more at the bathroom window, one white-shirted arm and free hand were engaged in closing the window.

On Korn's desk that morning were requisition forms signed with Amon's open vowelled but not deranged scrawl. His gaze ranged from the signature to the unbuttoned corpse at the box of timber. Not only did he wonder if he had seen what he had seen. He sensed the seductive concept inherent in Amon's methods. That is, the temptation to agree that if murder was no more than a visit to the bathroom, a mere pulse in the monotony of form signing, then perhaps all death should now be accepted – with whatever despair – as routine.

It does not seem that Josef Bau was exposed to such radical persuasion. He missed too the purge of the administrative staff on the ground floor right and centre. It had begun when Josef Neuschel, Goeth's protégé, complained to the commandant that a girl in the office had acquired a rind of bacon. Amon had come raging down the corridor from his office. You're all getting fat, he had screamed. He had divided the office staff into two lines then. It had been to Korn like a scene from the Podgórze gymnasium, the girls in the other line so familiar to him, daughters of families he'd grown up with, Podgórze families. It could have been that a teacher was sorting them out into those who would visit the Kosciuszko Monument and those for the museum at the Wawel. In fact, the girls in the other line were taken straight from their desks to Chujowa Górka and, for the decadence of that bacon rind, gunned down by one of Pilarzik's squads.

Though Josef Bau was not involved in such office turmoil, no one could have said that he was leading a sheltered life in Plaszów. But it had been less perilous than the experience of the girl he had fallen for. Rebecca Tannenbaum was an orphan, though in the clannish life of Jewish Cracow she had not been bereft of kindly aunts and uncles. She was nineteen, sweet-faced and neatly built. She could speak German well and made pleasant and generous conversation. Recently she'd begun to work in Itzhak Stern's office at the rear of the Administration Building – upstairs, away from the immediate environs of the commandant's berserk interference. But her job in the Construction Office was only half her labour. She was a manicurist. She treated Amon weekly, she tended the hands of Untersturmführer Leo John, those of Dr. Blancke and of his SS lover, the harshly pretty Alice Orlowski. Taking Amon's hands, she had found them long and well made with tapering fingers, not a fat man's hands at all; certainly not those of a savage.

When a prisoner had first come to her and told her that the Herr Commandant wanted to see her, she had begun to run away, fleeing among the desks and down the back stairs. The prisoner had followed and cried after her, "For God's sake, don't. He'll punish *me* if I don't bring you back."

So she had followed the man down to Goeth's villa. But before going into the salon, she first visited the stinking cellar – this was in Goeth's first residence, and the cellar had been dug into the boundaries of an ancient Jewish graveyard. Down among the grave soil, Rebecca's friend Helen Hirsch had been nursing bruises. You have a problem, Helen admitted. But just do the job and see. That's all you can do. Some people he likes a professional manner from, some people he doesn't. And I'll give you cake and sausage when you come. But don't just take food. Ask me first. Some people take food without asking, and I don' know what I have to cover up for.

Amon did accept Rebecca's professional manner, pre senting his fingers and chatting in German. It could have been the Hotel Cracovia again, and Amon a crisp-shirted overweight young German tycoon come to Cracow to sel textiles or steel or chemicals. There were, however, two aspects to these meetings that detracted from their air o timeless geniality. The commandant always kept his service revolver at his right elbow, and frequently one or other o the dogs drowsed in the salon. She had seen them, on the Appellplatz, tear the flesh of engineer Karp. Yet sometimes as a dog snuffled in sleep and she and Amon compared note on pre-war visits to the spa at Carlsbad, the rollcall horror seemed remote and beyond belief. One day she felt con fident enough to ask him why the revolver was always at hi elbow. His answer chilled the back of her neck as she ben over his hand. "That's in case you ever nick me," he told her.

If she ever needed proof that a chat about spas was all the same to Amon as an act of madness, she had it the day she entered the hallway and saw him dragging her friend Helen Hirsch out of the salon by the hair – Helen striving to keep her balance and her auburn hair coming out by the roots and Amon, if he lost his grip one second, regaining it th next in his giant, well-tended hands. And further proo came on the evening she entered the salon and one of thos dogs – Rolf or Ralf – materialised, jumped at her and holding her by the shoulders, took her breast in its jaw. She looked across the room and saw Amon lolling on the sofa and smiling. "Stop shaking, you stupid girl," he told her "or I won't be able to save you from the hound."

During the time she tended the commandant's hands h would shoot his shoe-shine boy for faulty work, suspend hi fifteen-year-old orderly, Poldek Dereshowitz, from the ring bolts in his office because a flea had been found on one of th dogs, and execute his servant Lisiek, for lending a *drozk* and horse to Bosch without first checking. Yet twice a week the pretty orphan entered the salon and philosophically took the beast by the hand.

She met Josef Bau one grey morning when he stood outside the Construction Office holding up a blueprint frame towards the low autumn cloud. His thin body seemed overburdened by the weight of it. She asked if she could help him. No, he said. I'm just waiting for the sunshine. Why? she asked. He explained how his transparency drawings for a new building were clamped in the frame beside sensitised blueprint paper. If the sun were only to shine harder, he said, a mysterious chemical union would transfer the drawing from the transparency to the blueprint. Then he said, Why don't you be my magical sunshine?

Pretty girls weren't used to delicacy from boys in Plaszów. Sexuality took its harsh impetus from the volleys heard on Chujowa Górka, the executions on the Appellplatz. Imagine a day, for instance, when a chicken is found among the work party returning from the cable factory on Wieliczka. Amon is ranting on the Appellplatz, for the chicken was discovered lying in a bag in front of the camp gate during a spot check. Whose bag was it? Amon wants to know. Whose chicken? Since no one on the Appellplatz will admit anything, Amon takes a rifle from an SS man and shoots the prisoner at the head of the line. The bullet, passing through the body, also fells the man behind. No one speaks though. How you love one another! roars Amon, and prepares to execute the next man in line. A boy of fourteen steps forward. He is shuddering and weeping. He can say who brought the chicken in, he tells the Herr Commandant. Who then?

The boy points to one of the two dead men. That one, the boy screams. Amon astonishes the entire Appellplatz by believing the boy and puts his head back and laughs with the sort of classroom incredulity teachers like to exhibit. These people, he's saying. Can't they understand now why they're all forfeit?

After an evening like that, in the hours of free movement between 7 and 9 p.m., most prisoners felt that there was no time for leisurely courtship. The lice which plagued your groin and armpits made a mockery of formality. Young males jumped on girls without ceremony. In the women's camp they sang a song which asked the virgin why she'd bound herself up with string and for whom she thought she was saving herself.

The atmosphere at Emalia was not as desperate. In the enamel workshop niches had been designed among machinery on the factory floor to permit lovers to meet at greater length. There was only a theoretic segregation in the cramped barracks. The absence of daily fear, the fuller ration of daily bread made for a little less frenzy. Besides, Oskar would not let the SS garrison go inside the prison without his permission.

One prisoner recalls wiring installed in Oskar's office in case any SS official did demand entry to the barracks. While the SS man was on his way downstairs, Oskar could punch a button connected to a bell inside the camp. It gave men and women warning to stub out the illicit cigarettes supplied daily by Oskar. ("Go to my apartment," he would tell someone on the factory floor almost daily, "and fill this cigarette case." He would wink significantly.) The bell also warned men and women to get back to their appointed bunks.

To Rebecca though, in Plaszów, it was something close to a shock, a remembrance of a vanished culture, to meet a boy who courted as if he'd met her in a patisserie in the Rynek.

Another morning when she came downstairs from Stern's office, Josef showed her his work desk. He was drawing plans for yet more barracks. What's your barrack number and who's your barrack Alteste? She let him know with the correct reluctance. She had seen Helen Hirsch dragged down the hallway by the hair and would die if she accidentally jabbed the cuticle of Amon's thumb, yet this boy had restored her to coyness, to girlhood. I'll come and speak to your mother, he promised. I don't have a mother, said Rebecca. Then I'll speak to the Alteste.

That was how the courting began, with the permission of elders and as if there *were* world enough and time. Because he was such a fantastical and ceremonious boy, they did not kiss. It was in fact under Amon's roof that they first managed a proper embrace. It was after a manicure session. Rebecca had collected hot water and soap from Helen and crept up to the top floor, vacant because of renovations pending, to wash her blouse and her change of underwear. Her washtub was her mess can. It would be needed tomorrow noon to hold her soup.

She was working away on that small bucket of suds when Josef appeared. Why are you here? she asked him. I'm measuring for my drawings, for the renovations, he told her. And why are you here yourself? You can see, she told him. And please don't talk too loudly.

He danced around the room, flashing the tape-measure up walls and along skirting boards. Do it carefully, she told him, anxious, aware of Amon's exacting standards.

While I'm here, he told her, I might as well measure you. He ran the tape along her arms and down from the nape of her neck to the small of her spine. She did not resist the way his thumb touched her, marking her dimensions. But when they had embraced each other thoroughly for a while, she ordered him out. This was no place for a languorous afternoon.

There were other desperate romances in Plaszów, even among the SS, but they proceeded less sunnily than this very proper romance between Josef Bau and the manicurist. Oberscharführer Albert Hujar, for example, who had shot Dr. Rosalia Blau in the ghetto and Diana Reiter after the foundations of the barracks collapsed, had fallen in love with a Jewish prisoner. Madritsch's daughter had been captivated by a Jewish boy from the Tarnow ghetto – he had of course worked in Madritsch's Tarnow plant until the expert ghetto-liquidator, Amon, had been brought in at the end of the summer to close down Tarnow as he had Cracow. Now he was in the Madritsch workshop inside Plaszów, the girl could visit him there. But nothing could come of it. The prisoners themselves had niches and shelters where lovers and spouses could meet. But everything – the law of the Reich and the strange code of the prisoners – resisted the affair between Fraülein Madritsch and her young man.

Similarly, honest Raimund Titsch had fallen in love with one of his machinists. That too was a gentle, secretive and largely abortive love. As for Oberscharführer Hujar, he was ordered by Amon himself to stop being a fool. So Albert took the girl for a walk in the woods and with fondest regrets shot her through the nape of the neck.

It seemed, in fact, that death hung over the passions of the SS. Henry and Leopold Rosner, spreading Viennese melodies around Goeth's dinner table, were aware of it. One night a tall, slim, grey officer in the Waffen SS had visited Amon for dinner and, drinking a lot, had kept asking the Rosners for the Hungarian song, *Gloomy Sunday*, a syrupy love ballad in which a boy is about to commit suicide for love. It had exactly the sort of excessive feeling which, Henry had noticed, appealed to SS men at their leisure. It had, in fact, enjoyed notoriety in the thirties – governments in Hungary, Poland and Czechoslovakia had considered banning it because its popularity had brought on a rash of thwarted-love suicides. Young men about to blow their heads off would sometimes quote its lyrics in their suicide notes. It had long been a song proscribed by the Reich Propaganda Office. Now this tall elegant officer, old enough to have teenage sons and daughters, themselves caught up in the excesses of calf-love, kept walking up to the Rosner boys and saying, play *Gloomy Sunday*. And though Dr. Goebbels would not have permitted it, no one in the wilds of Southern Poland was going to argue with an SS field officer with unhappy memories of an affair.

After the guest had demanded the song four or five times, an unearthly conviction took hold of Henry Rosner. In its tribal origins, music was always magic and always looked to a result. And no one in Europe had a better sense of the potency of the violin than a Cracovian Jew like Henry, who came from the sort of family in which music is not so much learned as inherited, in the same way as the status of *Kohen* or hereditary priest. It came to Henry now that, as he would say later – "God, if I have the power, maybe this son of a bitch will kill himself."

The proscribed music of *Gloomy Sunday* had gained

legitimacy in Amon's dining room through being repeated, and now Henry declared war with it, Leopold playing with him and reassured by the stares of almost grateful melancholy which the handsome officer directed at them. Henry sweated, believing that he was so visibly fiddling up the SS man's death that at any moment Amon would notice and come and take him behind the villa for execution. As for the standard of Henry's performance, it is not relevant to ask was it good or bad. It was possessed. And only one man, the SS officer noticed and assented and, across the hubbub of drunken Bosch and Scherner, Czurda and Amon, continued to look up from his chair directly into Henry's eyes, as if he were going to jump up at any second and say, "Of course, gentlemen. The violinist is absolutely right. There's no sense in carrying a grief like this."

The Rosners went on repeating the song beyond the limit at which Amon would normally have shouted, "Enough!" Then the officer stood up and went out on to the balcony. Henry knew at once that everything he could do to the man had been done. He and his brother slid into some von Suppé and Lehar, covering their tracks with full-bodied operetta. The guest remained alone on the balcony and after half an hour interrupted a good party by shooting himself through the head.

Such was sex in Plaszów. Lice, crabs and urgency inside the wire, murder and lunacy on its fringes. And in its midst Josef Bau and Rebecca Tannenbaum were pursuing a ritual dance of courtship.

In the midst of the snows that year, Plaszów underwent a change of status adverse to all lovers inside the wire. In the early days of January 1944, it was designated a Konzentrationslager under the central authority of General Oswald Pohl's SS Main Economic and Administrative Office in Oranienburg on the outskirts of Berlin. Subcamps of Plaszów – such as Oskar Schindler's Emalia – now also came under Oranienburg's control. Police chiefs Scherner and Czurda lost their direct authority. The labour fees of all those prisoners employed by Oskar and Madritsch no longer went to Pomorska Street, but to the office of General Richard Glücks, head of Pohl's Section D (Concentration Camps). Oskar, if he wanted favours now, had not only to drive out to Plaszów and sweeten Amon, not only to have Julian Scherner to dinner, but also to reach certain officials in the grand bureaucratic complex of Oranienburg.

Oskar took an early opportunity to travel to Berlin and meet the people who would be dealing with his files. Oranienburg had begun as a concentration camp. Now it had become a sprawl of administrative barracks. From the offices of Section D, every aspect of prison life and death was regulated. Its chief, Richard Glücks, had responsibility as well, in consultation with Pohl, for establishing the balance between labourers and candidates for the chambers, for the equation in which X represented slave labour and Y represented the more immediately condemned.

Glücks had laid down procedures for every event and from his department came memos drafted in the anaesthetic verbiage of the planner, the paper shuffler, the detached specialist.

SS Main Office of Economics
and Administration
Section Chief D (Concentration
Camps)
D1-AZ:14fl-ot-S-GEH TGB NO 453–44

To the Commandants of Concentration Camps
Da, Sah, Bu, Mau, Slo, Neu, Au l-III,
Gr-Ro, Natz, Stu, Rav, Herz, A-L-Bels,
Gruppenl. D. Riga, Gruppenl.D.Cracow (Plaszów).

Applications from Camp Commandants for punishment by flogging in cases of sabotage by prisoners in the war production industries are increasing.

I request that in future in all *proven* cases of sabotage (a report from the management must be enclosed), an application for execution by hanging should be made. The execution should take place before the assembled members of the work detachment concerned. The reason for the execution is to be made known so as to act as a deterrent.

Signed SS Obersturmführer.

In this eerie chancellory, some files discussed the length a prisoner's hair should be before it was considered of economic use for "the manufacture of hair-yarn socks for U-boat crews and hair-felt footwear for the Reich's railway," while others debated whether the form registering 'death cases' should be filed by eight departments or merely covered by letter and appended to the personal records as soon as the index card had been brought up to date.

And here came Herr Schindler of Cracow to talk about his little industrial compound in Zablocie. They appointed someone of middle status to handle him, a personnel officer of field rank.

Oskar wasn't distressed. There were larger employers of Jewish prison labour than he. There were the megaliths, Krupp, of course, and I. G. Farben. There was the cable works at Plaszów. Walter C. Toebbens, the Warsaw industrialist whom Himmler had tried to force into the Wehrmacht, was a heavier employer of labour than Herr Schindler. Then there were the steelworks at Stalowa Wola, the aircraft factories at Budzyn and Zakopane, the Steyr-Daimler-Puch works at Radom.

The personnel officer had the plans of Emalia on his desk. I hope, he said curtly, you don't want to increase the size of your camp. It would be impossible to do it without courting a typhus epidemic.

Oskar waved that suggestion aside. He was interested in the permanence of his labour force, he said. He had had a talk on that matter, he told the officer, with a friend of his, Colonel Erich Lange. The name, Oskar could tell, meant something to the SS man. Oskar produced a letter from the colonel, and the personnel officer sat back reading it. The office was so silent, all you could hear from other rooms was pen-scratch and the whisper of papers and quiet, earnest talk, as if none here knew that they lay at the core of a network of screams.

Colonel Lange was a man of influence, Chief-of-Staff of the Armaments Inspectorate at Army Headquarters, Berlin. Oskar had met him at a party at General Schindler's office in Cracow. They had liked each other almost at once. It happened a lot at parties that two people could sense in each other a certain resistance to the régime and might retire to a corner to test each other out and perhaps establish a friendship. Erich Lange had been appalled by the factory camps of Poland, by the I. G. Farben works at Buna, for example, where foremen adopted the SS 'work tempo' and made prisoners unload cement on the run, where the corpses of the starved, the broken, were hurled into ditches built for cables and covered, together with the cables, with cement. "You are not here to live but to perish in concrete," a works manager had told newcomers, and Lange had heard the speech and felt damned.

The letter Schindler carried had been preceded by some phone calls, and both calls and letter pushed the same proposition. Herr Schindler, with his messkits and his 45mm anti-tank shells, is considered by this Inspectorate to be a major contributor to the struggle for our national survival. He has built up a staff of skilled specialists, and nothing should be done to disrupt the work they perform under the Herr Direktor Schindler's supervision.

The personnel officer was impressed, and said he would speak frankly to Herr Schindler. There were no plans to alter the status or interfere with the population of the camp in Zablocie. However, the Herr Direktor had to understand that the situation of Jews, even skilled armaments-workers, was always risky. Take the case of our own SS enterprises. Ostindustrie, the SS company, employs prisoners at a peat works, a brush factory and iron foundry in Lublin, an equipment works in Radom, a fur works in Trawniki. But other branches of the SS shoot the work force continually, and now Osti is for all practical purposes out of business. Likewise, at the killing centres, the staff never retain a sufficient percentage of prisoners for factory work. This has been a matter of frequent correspondence, but they're intransigent, those people in the field. Of course, said the personnel officer, tapping the letter, I'll do what I can for you.

I understand the problem, said Oskar, looking up at the SS man with that radiant smile. If there is any way I can express my gratitude. . .

In the end, Oskar left Oranienburg with at least some guarantees about the continuity of his backyard camp in Cracow.

The manner in which the new status of Plaszów impinged on lovers was that a proper penal separation of the sexes – such as was provided for in a series of SS Main Office of Economics and Administration memos – was created. The fences between the men's prison and the women's, the perimeter fence, the fence around the industrial sector were all electrified. The voltage, the spacing of wires, the number of electrified strands and insulators were all provided for by Main Office directives. Amon and his officers were not slow to notice the disciplinary possibilities involved. Now you could stand people for twenty-four hours at a time between the electrified outer fence and the inner, neutral, original fence. If they staggered with weariness, they knew that inches behind their backs ran the hundreds of volts. Mundek Korn, for example, found himself, on returning to camp with a work party from which one prisoner was missing, standing in that narrow gulf for a day and a night.

But perhaps worse than the risk of falling against the wire was the way the current ran, from the end of evening rollcall to reveille in the morning, like a moat between man and woman. Time for contact was now reduced to the short phase of milling on the Appellplatz, before the orders for falling into line were shouted. Each couple devised a tune, whistling it among the crowds, straining to pick up the answering refrain among a forest of sibilance. Rebecca Tannenbaum also settled on a code tune. The requirements of General Pohl's Main SS Office had forced the prisoners of Plaszów to adopt the mating stratagems of birds. And by these means, the formal romance of Rebecca and Josef went forward.

Then Josef somehow got a dead woman's dress from the clothing warehouse. Often, after rollcall in the men's lines, he would go to the latrines, put on the long gown, and place an orthodox bonnet on his hair. Then he would come out and join the women's lines. His short hair would not have amazed any SS guard, since most of the women had been shorn because of lice. So, with thirteen thousand women prisoners, he would pass into the women's compound and spend the night sitting up in hut 57 keeping Rebecca company.

In Rebecca's barracks, the older women took Josef at his word. If Josef required a traditional courtship, they would fall into their traditional rôle as chaperones. Josef was a gift to them too, a licence to play their pre-war ceremonious selves. From their four-tiered bunks they looked down on the two children until everyone fell asleep. If any one of them thought, Let's not be too fussy in times like these about what the children get up to at dead of night, it was never said. In fact, two of the older women would crowd into the one narrow ledge so that Josef could have a bunk of his own. The discomfort, the smell of the other body, the risk of the migration of lice from your friend to yourself – none of that was as important, as crucial to self-respect, as that the courtship should be fulfilled according to the norms.

At the end of winter, Josef, wearing the armband of the Construction Office, went out into the strangely immaculate snow in the strip between the inner fence and the electrified barrier and, steel measure in hand, under the eyes of the domed watchtowers, pretended to be sizing up no man's land for some architectural reason.

At the base of the concrete stanchions studded with porcelain insulators grew the first pigmy flowers of that year. Flashing his steel ruler, he picked them and shoved them into his jacket. He brought the flowers across the camp, up Jerozolimska Street. He was passing Amon's villa, his chest stuffed with blossoms, when Amon himself appeared from the front door and advanced, towering, down the steps. Josef Bau stopped. It was most dangerous to stop, to appear to be in arrested motion in front of Amon. But having stopped, he seemed frozen there. He feared that the heart he'd so energetically and honestly signed over to the orphan Rebecca would likely now become just another of Amon's targets.

But when Amon walked past him, not noticing him, not objecting to his standing there with an idle ruler in his hands, Josef Bau concluded that it meant some kind of guarantee. No one escaped Amon unless it was a sort of destiny. All dolled up in his shooting uniform, Amon had entered the camp unexpectedly one day through the back gate and had found the Warrenhaupt girl lolling in a limousine at the garage, staring at herself in the rear-view mirror. The car windows she'd been assigned to clean were still smudged. He had killed her for that. And there was that mother and daughter Amon had noticed through a kitchen window. They had been peeling potatoes too slowly. So he'd leaned in on the sill and shot both of them. Yet here at his steps was something he hated, a stockstill Jewish lover and draughtsman, steel rule dangling in his hands. And Amon had walked by. Bau felt the urge to confirm this outrageous good luck by some emphatic act. Marriage was, of course, the most emphatic act of all.

He got back to the Administration Block, climbed the stairs to Stern's office and, finding Rebecca, asked her to marry him. Urgency, Rebecca was pleased and concerned to notice, had entered the business now.

That evening, in the dead woman's dress, he visited his mother again and the council of chaperones in hut 57. They awaited only the arrival of a rabbi. But if rabbis came, they remained only a few days on their way to Auschwitz, not long enough for people requiring the rites of *kiddushin* and *nissuin*, to locate them and ask them, before they stepped into the furnace, for a final exercise of their priesthood.

Josef married Rebecca on a Sunday night of fierce cold in February. There was no rabbi. Mrs. Bau, Josef's mother, officiated. They were Reformed Jews, so that they could do without a *ketubbah* written in Aramaic. In the workshop of

Wulkan the jeweller someone had made up two rings out of a silver spoon Mrs. Bau had had hidden in the rafters. On the barrack floor, Rebecca circled Josef seven times and Josef crushed glass – a spent light bulb from the Construction Office – beneath his heel.

The couple had been given the top bunk of the tier. For the sake of privacy, it had been hung with blankets. In darkness Josef and Rebecca climbed to it, and all around them the earthy jokes were running. At weddings in Poland there was always a period of truce where profane love was given its chance to speak. If the wedding guests didn't wish to voice the traditional *double entendres* themselves, they could get in a professional wedding jester. Women who might in the twenties and thirties have sat up at weddings making disapproving faces at the risqué hired jester and the belly-laughing men, only now and then permitting themselves – as mature women – to be overcome with amusement, stepped tonight into the place of all the absent and dead wedding jesters of southern Poland.

Josef and Rebecca had not been together more than ten minutes on the upper bunk when the barrack lights came on. Looking through the blankets, Josef saw Untersturmführer Scheidt patrolling the tiers of bunks. The same old fearful sense of destiny overcame Josef. They'd found he was missing from his barracks, of course, and sent one of the worst of the officers to look for him in his mother's hut. Amon had been blinded to him that day outside the villa only so that Scheidt, who was quick on the trigger, could come and kill him on his wedding night!

He knew too that all the women were compromised – his mother, his bride, the witnesses, the ones who'd uttered the most exquisitely embarrassing jokes. He began murmuring apologies, pleas to be forgiven. Rebecca told him to be quiet. She took down the screen of blankets. At this time of night, she reasoned, Scheidt wasn't going to climb to a top bunk unless provoked. The women on the lower bunks were passing their small straw-filled pillows to her. Josef might well have orchestrated the courtship, but he was now the child to be concealed. Rebecca pushed him hard up into the corner of the bunk and covered him with pillows. She watched Scheidt pass below her, leave the barracks by its back door. The lights went out. Among a last spatter of dark, earthy jokes, the Baus were restored to their privacy.

Within minutes, the sirens began to sound. Everyone sat up in the darkness. The noise meant to Bau that yes, they *were* determined to crush this ritual marriage. They *had* found his empty bunk over in the men's quarters and were now seriously hunting him.

In the dark aisle, the women were milling. They knew it too. From the top bunk he could hear them saying it. His old-fashioned love would kill them all. The barrack Alteste, who'd been so decent about the whole thing, would be shot first once the lights came on and they found a bridegroom there in token female rags.

Josef Bau grabbed his clothes. He kissed his wife perfunctorily, slid to the floor and ran from the hut. In the darkness outside, the wail of the sirens pierced him. He ran in dirty snow, with his jacket and old dress bundled up under his armpits. When the lights came on, he would be seen by the towers. But he had the berserk idea that he could beat the lights over the fence, that he could even climb it between the alternations of its current. Once back in the men's camp, he could make up some story about diarrhoea, about having gone to the latrines and collapsed on the floor, being brought back to consciousness by the noise of sirens.

If electrocuted, he understood as he sprinted, he could not then confess what woman he was visiting. Racing for the immolatory wire he did not understand that there would have to be a classroom-like scene on the Appellplatz and that Rebecca would be made, one way or another, to step forward.

In the fence between the men's and women's camps in Plaszów ran nine electrified strands. Josef Bau launched himself high, so that his feet would find purchase on the third of the strands and his hands, at the stretch, might reach the second top. He imagined himself then as racing over the strands with a ratlike quickness. In fact he landed in the mesh of wire and simply hung there. He thought the coldness of the metal in his hands was the first message of the current. But there was no current. There were no lights. Josef Bau, stretched on the fence, did not speculate on the reason there wasn't any voltage. He got to the top and vaulted into the men's camp. You're a married man, he told himself. He slid into the latrines by the wash houses. "A frightful diarrhoea, Herr Oberscharführer." He stood gasping in the stench. Amon's blindness on the day of the flowers . . . the consummation, waited for with an untoward patience, twice interrupted . . . Scheidt and the sirens . . . a problem with the lights and the wire. Staggering and gagging, he wondered if he could support the ambiguity of his life. Like others, he wanted a more definite rescue.

He wandered out to be one of the last to join the lines in front of his hut. He was trembling but sure the Alteste would cover up for him. "Yes, Herr Untersturmführer, I gave Haftling Bau permission to visit the latrines."

They weren't looking for him at all. They were looking for three young Zionists who'd escaped in a truckload of products from the upholstery works, where they made Wehrmacht mattresses out of seagrass.

27

On April 28th 1944, Oskar – by looking sideways at himself in a mirror – was able to tell that his waist had thickened for his thirty-sixth birthday. But at least today, when he embraced the girls, no one bothered to denounce him. Any informer among the German technicians must have been demoralised, since the SS had let Oskar out of Pomorska and Montelupich, both centres supposedly impregnable to influence.

To mark the day, Emilie sent the usual greetings from Czechoslovakia, and Ingrid and Klonowska gave him gifts. His domestic arrangements had scarcely changed in the four and a half years he had spent in Cracow. Ingrid was still a consort, Klonowska a girlfriend, Emilie an understandably absent wife. Whatever grievances and bewilderment each suffered goes unrecorded, but it would become obvious in this his thirty-seventh year that some coolness had entered his relations with Ingrid, that Klonowska, always a loyal friend, was content with a merely sporadic liaison, and that Emilie still considered their marriage indissoluble. For the moment, they gave their presents and kept their counsel.

Others took a hand in the celebration. Amon permitted Henry Rosner to bring his violin to Lipowa Street in the evening under the guard of the best baritone in the Ukrainian garrison. Amon was, at this stage, very pleased with his association with Schindler. In return for his continuing support for the Emalia camp, Amon had one day recently requested and got the permanent use of Oskar's Mercedes – not the jalopy Oskar had bought from John for a day, but the most elegant car in the Emalia garage.

The recital took place in Oskar's office. No one attended

except Oskar. It was as if the rowdy tycoon was tired of company.

When the Ukrainian went to the lavatory, Oskar exposed his depression to Henry. He was upset about the war news. His birthday had come in a hiatus. The Russian armies had halted behind the Pripet Marshes in Belorussia and in front of Lwów. Oskar's fears puzzled Henry a little. Doesn't he understand, he wondered, that if the Russians aren't held up, it's the end of his operation here?

I've often asked Amon to let you come here permanently, Oskar told Rosner. You and your wife and child. He won't hear of it. He appreciates you too much. But eventually . . .

Henry was grateful. But he felt he had to point out that his family might be as safe as any in Plaszów. His sister-in-law, for example, had been discovered by Goeth smoking at work, and he had ordered her execution. But one of the NCOs had begged to put before the Herr Commandant's notice the fact that this woman was Mrs. Rosner, wife of Rosner the accordionist. Oh, Amon had said, pardoning her. Well, remember, girl, I won't have smoking on the job.

Henry told Oskar that night that it had been this attitude of Amon's – that the Rosners were immune because of their musical talent – which had persuaded Manci and himself to bring their eight-year-old son, Olek, into the camp. He had been hiding with friends in Cracow, but that was daily becoming a less and less secure business. Once inside, Olek could blend into that small crowd of children, many unregistered in the prison records, whose presence in Plaszów was connived at by prisoners and tolerated by some of the junior camp officials. Getting Olek into the place, however, had been the risky part. Poldek Pfefferberg, who'd had to drive a truck to town to pick up toolboxes, had smuggled the boy in. The Ukrainians had nearly discovered him at the gate while he was still an outsider and living in contravention of every racial statute of the Reich Government General. His feet had burst out of the end of the box that lay between Pfefferberg's ankles. "Mr. Pfefferberg, Mr. Pfefferberg," Poldek had heard while the Ukrainians searched the back of the truck. "My feet are sticking out."

Henry could laugh at that now, though warily, since there were still rivers to be crossed. But Schindler reacted dramatically with a gesture that seemed to grow from the slightly alcoholic melancholy which had beset him on this evening of his birthday. He lifted his office chair by its back and raised it to the portrait of the Führer. It seemed for a second that he was about to lash into the icon. But he spun again on his heel, lowered the chair deliberately until its four legs hung equidistant from the floor, and rammed them down into the carpet at a rate which shook the wall.

Then he said, "They're burning bodies out there, aren't they?"

Henry grimaced as if the stench were in the room. "They've started," he admitted.

Now that Plaszów was – in the language of the bureaucrats – a KL (Konzentrationslager) its inmates found that it was safer to encounter Amon. The chiefs in Oranienburg did not permit summary execution. The days when slow potato-peelers could be expunged on the spot were gone. They could now only be destroyed by due process. There had to be a hearing, the record of which was to be sent in triplicate to Oranienburg. The sentence had to be confirmed not only by General Glücks's office but also by General Pohl's Department W (Economic Enterprises). For if a commandant killed essential workers, Department W could find itself hit with claims for compensation. Allach-Munich Ltd, for example, porcelain manufacturers using slave labour from Dachau, had recently filed a claim for thirty-one thousand, eight hundred Reichsmarks because "as a result of the typhoid epidemic which broke out in January 1943, we had no prison labour at our disposal from January 26th 1943 until March 3rd 1943. In our opinion we are entitled to compensation under Clause 2 of the Businesses Compensation Settlement Fund . . ."

Department W was all the more liable for compensation if the loss of skilled labour arose from the zeal of a trigger-happy SS officer.

So, to avoid the paper work and the departmental complications, Amon held his hand on most days. The people who appeared within his range in the spring and early summer of 1944 somehow understood it was safer, though they knew nothing of Department W and Generals Pohl and Glücks. It was to them a remission as mysterious as Amon's madness itself.

Yet, as Oskar had mentioned to Henry Rosner, they were now burning bodies at Plaszów. In preparation for the Russian offensive, the SS was abolishing its institutions in the East. Treblinka, Sobibor and Belzec had been evacuated the previous autumn. The Waffen SS who had run them had been ordered to dynamite the chambers and the crematoria, to leave no recognisable trace, and had then been posted to Italy to fight partisans. The immense complex at Auschwitz, in its safe ground in Upper Silesia, would complete the great task in the East, and, once that was concluded, the crematoria would be ploughed under the earth. For without the evidence of the crematoria, the dead could offer no witness, were a whisper behind the wind, an inconsequential dust on the aspen leaves.

Plaszów was not as simple a case, for its dead lay everywhere around it. In the enthusiasm of the spring of 1943, bodies – notably the bodies of those killed in the ghetto's last two days – were thrown randomly into mass graves in the wood. Now Department D charged Amon with finding them all.

Estimates of the numbers of bodies vary widely. Polish publications, based on the work of the Main Commission for the Investigation of Nazi Crimes in Poland and on other sources, claim that a hundred and fifty thousand prisoners, many of them in transit to other places, went through Plaszów and its five subcamps. Of these, the Poles believe that eighty thousand died there, mainly in mass executions on Chujowa Górka or else in epidemics.

These figures baffle the surviving Plaszów inmates who remember the fearsome work of burning the dead. They say the number they exhumed was somewhere between eight and ten thousand, a multitude frightful in itself and which they have no desire to exaggerate. The distance between the two estimates looks narrower when it is remembered that executions of Poles, Gypsies and Jews would continue at Chujowa Górka and at other points around Plaszów throughout most of that year, and that the SS themselves took up the practice of burning bodies immediately after mass killings in the Austrian hill fort. Besides, Amon would not succeed in his intention of removing all the bodies from the woods. Some thousands more would be found in post-war exhumations, and today, as the suburbs of Cracow close Plaszów in, bones are still discovered during the digging of foundations.

Oskar saw the line of pyres on the ridge above the workshops during a visit he made to Plaszów just before his birthday. When he came back a week later the activity had increased. The bodies were dug up by male prisoners who worked masked and gagging. On blankets and barrows and litters the dead were brought to the burning site and laid on log frames. So the pyre was built, layer by layer, and when it reached the height of a man's shoulder was doused in fuel and lit. Pfefferberg was horrified to see the temporary life the flames gave to the dead, the way the corpses sat forward, throwing the burning logs away, their limbs reaching, their mouths opening for a last utterance. A young SS man from the delousing station ran among the pyres waving a pistol and roaring frenetic orders. The dust of the dead fell in hair and on the clothing hung in the back gardens of junior officers' villas. Oskar was bemused to see the way the personnel reacted to the smoke, as if the grit in the air were some sort of inevitable industrial fallout. And through the fogs caused by the pyres, Amon went riding with Majola, both of them calm in the saddle. Leo John took his twelve-year-old boy off to catch tadpoles in the marshy ground in the wood. The flames and the stench did not distract them from their daily lives.

Oskar, leaning back in the driver's seat of his BMW, the windows up and a handkerchief clamped over his mouth and nose, thought how they must be burning the Spiras with all the rest. He'd been astounded when they'd executed all the ghetto policemen and their families last Christmas, as soon as Symche Spira had finished directing the dismantling of the ghetto. They had brought them all, and their wives and children, up here in the afternoon and shot them as the cold sun vanished. They'd shot the most faithful (Spira and Zellinger) as well as the most grudging. Spira and bashful Mrs. Spira and the ungifted Spira children whom Pfefferberg had tutored – they'd all stood naked amid a circle of rifles, shivering against each other's flanks; Spira's Napoleonic OD uniform now just a heap of clothing for recycling, flung down at the fort entrance. And Spira still assuring everyone that it could not happen.

That execution had shocked Oskar because it showed that there was no obedience or obeisance a Jew could make to guarantee survival. And now they were burning the Spiras as anonymously, as ungratefully, as they had executed them.

Even the Gutters! It had happened after a dinner at Amon's the year before. Oskar had gone home early, but later heard what had happened after he left. John and Neuschel had started in on Bosch. They thought he was squeamish. He'd made a fuss about being a veteran of the trenches. But they had not seen him perform any executions. They kept it going for hours – the joke of the evening. In the end, Bosch had ordered David Gutter and his son roused in their barracks and Mrs. Gutter and the Gutter girl fetched from theirs. Again, it was a matter of faithful servants. David Gutter had been the last president of the Judenrat and had cooperated in everything, had never gone to Pomorska Street and tried to start any argument over the scope of the SS Aktions or the size of transports sent to Belzec. Gutter had signed everything and thought every German demand reasonable. Besides that, Bosch had used Gutter as an agent inside and outside Plaszów, sending him up to Cracow with truckloads of newly-upholstered furniture or pocketfuls of jewellery to sell on the black market. And Gutter had done it partly because he was a scoundrel anyhow, but mainly because he believed it would make his wife and children immune.

At two o'clock that polar morning, a Jewish policeman,

Zauder, a friend of Pfefferberg and of Stern, later to be shot by Pilarzik during one of that officer's drunken rampages, on duty at the women's gate that night, heard it – Bosch ordering the Gutters into position in a depression in the ground near the women's camp, the children pleading, but David and Mrs. Gutter taking it calmly, knowing there was no argument. And now as Oskar watched, all of that evidence – the Gutters, the Spiras, the rebels, the priests, the children, the pretty girls found on Aryan papers – all of it was returning to that mad hill to be obliterated in case the Russians came to Plaszów and made too much of it.

Care, said Oranienburg in a letter to Amon, is to be taken in the future over the disposal of all bodies, and for that purpose they were sending a representative of a Hamburg engineering firm to survey the site for crematoria. In the meantime, the dead were to be kept, awaiting retrieval, at well-marked burial sites.

When, on that second visit, Oskar saw the extent of the fires on Chujowa Górka, his first impulse was to stay in the car, that sane German mechanism, and drive home. Instead he went calling on friends of his in the workshop, and then visited Stern's office. He thought that with all that grit falling on the windows, it wasn't out of the question that people inside Plaszów would consider suicide. Yet he was the one who seemed depressed. He didn't ask any of his usual questions, such as, "All right, Herr Stern, if God made man in his image, which race is most like him? Is a Pole more like him than a Czech?" There was none of that whimsy today. Instead he growled, "What does everyone think?" Stern told him that the prisoners were like prisoners. They did their work and hoped for survival.

"I'm going to get you out," Oskar grunted all at once. He put a balled fist on the desk. "I'm going to get you *all* out."

"All?" asked Stern. He couldn't help himself. Such massive biblical rescues didn't suit the era.

"You, anyhow," said Oskar. "*You*."

28

In Amon's office in the Administration Block there were two typists. One was a German girl called Frau Kochmann, the other the studious young prisoner, Mietek Pemper. Pemper would one day become secretary to Oskar, but in the summer of 1944 he still worked with Amon, and like anyone else in that situation was not too sanguine about his chances.

He first came into close contact with Amon as accidentally as had Helen Hirsch the maid. Pemper was summoned to Amon's office after someone had recommended him to the commandant. The young prisoner was a student of accounting, a touch typist, and could take dictation in both Polish and German. His powers of memory were said to be prodigious. Therefore, captive of his own skills, Pemper found himself in Plaszów's main office with Amon, and would also sometimes go to the villa to take dictation from the commandant there.

The irony was that, in the end – out of all the prisoners' testimony – it would be Pemper's photographic memory that would most effectively bring about Amon's hanging.

Pemper was meant to be the second typist. For confidential documents, Amon was to use his German secretary, Frau Kochmann, a girl not nearly as competent as Mietek and slow at dictation. Sometimes Amon would break the rule and let young Pemper take confidential dictation. And Mietek, even while he sat across Amon's desk with the pad on his knee, could not stop contradictory suspicions from distracting him. The first was that all these inside reports and memoranda, whose details he was storing in his remarkable mind, would make him a prime witness on the remote day when he and Amon stood before a tribunal. The other suspicion was that Amon would, in the end, have to erase him as one would a classified tape.

Nonetheless, each morning Mietek prepared not only his own sets of typing paper, carbons and duplicates, but a dozen for the German girl. After the girl had done her typing, Pemper would undertake to destroy the carbons but, in fact, would keep and read them. He kept no written records, but he had had this reputation for memory since schooldays. He knew that if that tribunal ever met, if he and Amon sat in the body of the court, he would astound the commandant with the exact dating of his evidence.

Pemper saw some astonishing and classified documents. He read, for example, memoranda on the flogging of women. Camp commanders were to be reminded that it should be done to maximum effect. It was demeaning to involve SS personnel, and therefore Czech women were to be flogged by Slovak women, Slovaks by Czechs. Russians and Poles were to be bracketed for the same purposes. Commandants were to use their imagination in exploiting other national and cultural differences.

Another bulletin reminded them that they did not hold in their own persons the right to impose the death sentence. Commandants could seek authorisation by telegram or letter to the Reich Security Main Office. Amon had done this in the spring with two Jews who'd escaped from the subcamp at Wieliczka and whom he had proposed to hang. A telegram signifying permission had returned from Berlin, signed, Pemper noticed, by Dr. Ernst Kaltenbrunner, Chief of the Reich Security Main Office.

Now, in April, Pemper read a memorandum from Gerhard Maurer, the Labour Allocation Chief of General Glücks's Section D. Maurer wanted Amon to tell him how many Hungarians could be held temporarily at Plaszów. They were meant ultimately to go to the German Armament Works, DAW, which was a subsidiary of Krupp making artillery shell fuses in the enormous complex at Auschwitz. Given that Hungary had only recently been taken over as a German Protectorate, these Hungarian Jews and dissidents were in a better state of health than those who had had years of ghetto-isation and prison life. They were therefore a windfall for the factories in Auschwitz. Unfortunately, accommodation at DAW was not yet ready for them, and if the commandant of Plaszów would take up to seven thousand, pending the proper arrangements, Section D would be extremely grateful.

Goeth's answer, either seen or typed by Pemper, was that Plaszów was up to capacity and that there was no building space left inside the electric fences. However, Amon could accept up to ten thousand transit prisoners if (A) he were permitted to liquidate the unproductive element inside the camp; and (B) he were at the same time to impose double-bunking, the crowding of two sleepers into one bed space. Maurer wrote in reply that double-bunking could not be permitted in summer for fear of typhus, and that, ideally, according to the regulations, each prisoner should have a minimum three cubic metres of air per person. But he was willing to authorise Goeth to undertake the first option. Section D would advise Auschwitz-Birkenau – or at least the extermination wing of that great enterprise – to expect a shipment of reject prisoners from Plaszów. At the same time, transport would be arranged with the Ostbahn, which would run cattle wagons up the spur from the main line to the very gate of Plaszów.

Amon therefore had to conduct a sorting out process inside his camp.

With the blessing of Maurer and Section D, he would in a day abolish as many lives as Oskar Schindler was, by wit and hectic spending, harbouring in Emalia. Amon named his selection session Die Gesundheitaktion, the Health Action.

He managed it as one would manage a county fair. When it began, on the morning of Sunday, May 7th, the Appellplatz was hung with banners: *For Every Prisoner, Appropriate Work!* Loudspeakers played ballads and Strauss and love songs. Beneath them was set a table where Dr. Blancke, the SS physician, sat with Dr. Leon Gross and a number of clerks. Blancke's concept of health was as eccentric as that of any doctor in the SS. He had rid the prison clinic of the chronically ill by injecting benzine into the bloodstream. These injections could not by anyone's definition be called mercy killings. The patient was seized by convulsions which ended in a choking death after a quarter of an hour. Marek Biberstein, once president of the Judenrat and now, after his two years' imprisonment, a citizen of Plaszów, had suffered heart failure and been brought to the Krankenstube. Before Blancke could get to him with a syringe of benzine, Dr. Idek Schindel, uncle of that Genia whose distant figure had galvanised Schindler two years past, had come to Biberstein's bedside with a number of colleagues. One had injected a more merciful dose of cyanide.

Today, flanked by the filing cabinets of the entire prison population, Blancke would assess the health of the prisoners a barrack at a time, and when he finished with one battery of cards it would be taken away and replaced by the next.

As they reached the Appellplatz, prisoners were told to strip. They were lined up naked and run back and forth in front of the doctors. Blancke and Leon Gross, the collaborating Jewish physician, would make notations on the cards, point at this prisoner, call on that one to verify his name. Back the prisoners would run, the physicians looking for signs of disease or muscular weakness. It was an odd and humiliating exercise. Men with dislocated backs (Pfefferberg, for example, whose back Hujar had thrown out with the blow of a whip handle), women with chronic diarrhoea, red cabbage rubbed into their cheeks to give them colour – all of them running for their lives and understanding that it was so. Young Mrs. Kinstlinger, who'd sprinted for Poland at the Berlin Olympics, knew that all that had been just a game. This was the true contest. With your stomach turning and your breath thin, you ran – beneath the throb of the lying music – for your golden life.

No prisoner found out the results until the following Sunday when, under the same banners and band music, the mass of inmates was again assembled. As names were read out and the rejects of the Gesundheitaktion were marched to the eastern end of the square, there were cries of outrage and bewilderment. Amon had expected a riot and had sought the help of the Wehrmacht garrison of Cracow, who were on stand-by in case of a prison uprising. Nearly three hundred children had been discovered during the inspection the previous Sunday, and as they were now dragged away the protests and wailings of parents were so loud that most of the garrison, together with security police detachments called in from Cracow, had to be thrown into the cordon separating the two groups. This confrontation lasted for hours, the guards forcing back surges of demented parents and telling the usual lies to those who had relatives among the rejects. Nothing had been announced, but everyone knew that those down there had failed the test and had no future. Blurred by waltzes and comic songs from the loud-speakers, a pitiable babel of messages was shouted from one group to the other. Henry Rosner, himself in torment, his son Olek in fact hidden somewhere in the camp, had the bizarre experience of facing a young SS man who, with tears in his eyes, denounced what was happening and made a pledge to volunteer for the Eastern Front. But officers yelled that unless people showed a little discipline, they would order their men to open fire. Perhaps Amon hoped that a justifiable outbreak of shooting would further reduce over-crowding.

At the end of the process, one thousand, four hundred adults and two hundred and sixty-eight children stood, fenced by weapons, at the eastern rim of the Appellplatz, ready for speedy shipment to Auschwitz. Pemper would see and memorise the figures, which Amon would consider disappointing. Though it was not the number for which Amon had hoped, it would create immediate room for a large temporary intake of Hungarians.

In Dr. Blancke's card index system, the children of Plas-zów had not been as precisely registered as the adults. Many of them chose to spend both these Sundays in hiding, both they and their parents knowing instinctively that their age and the absence of their names and other details from the camp's documentation would make them obvious targets of the selection process.

Olek Rosner hid in the ceiling of a hut on the second Sunday. There were two other children with him all day above the rafters, and all day they kept the discipline of silence, all day held their bladders among the lice and the little packages of prisoners' belongings and the rooftop rats. For the children knew as well as any adult that the SS and the Ukrainians were wary of the spaces above the ceiling. They believed them typhus-ridden, and had been informed by Dr. Blancke that it took but a fragment of louse faeces in a crack in your skin to bring on epidemic typhus. Some of Plaszów's children had been housed for months near the men's prison in the hut marked 'Achtung Typhus'. This Sunday, for Olek Rosner, Amon's health Aktion was far more perilous than typhus-bearing lice.

Other children, some of the two hundred and sixty-eight separated out of the mass that day, had in fact begun the Aktion in hiding. Each Plaszów child, with that same toughness of mind which had kept Olek Rosner motionless and silent in the ceiling, had chosen favourite hiding places. Some favoured depressions beneath huts, some the laundry, some a shed behind a garage. Many of these hideouts had been discovered either this Sunday or last, and no longer offered refuge.

A further group had been brought without suspicion to the Appellplatz. There were parents who knew this or that NCO. It was as Himmler had once complained, for even SS Oberscharführers who did not flinch in the act of execution, had their favourites, as if the place were a school playground. If there were a question about the children, some parents thought, you could appeal to an SS man who knew you.

The previous Sunday a thirteen-year-old orphan thought he'd be safe because he had, at other rollcalls, passed for a young man. But naked, he wasn't able to argue away the childlikeness of his body. He had been told to dress and been marked down for the children's group. Now as parents at the other end of the Appellplatz keened for their rounded-up children, and while the loudspeakers brayed forth a sentimental song called *Mammi, kauf mir ein Pferdchen*

(Mummy, buy me a pony), the boy simply passed from one group to another, moved with that infallible instinct which had once characterised the movement of the red-capped child in Plac Zgody. And as with Redcap, no one had seen him. He stood, a plausible adult among the others, as the hateful music roared and his heart sought to beat its way through his rib cage. Then, faking the cramps of diarrhoea, he asked a guard to let him go to the latrine.

The long latrines lay beyond the men's camp, and arriving there the boy stepped over the plank on which men sat while defecating. An arm either side of the pit, he lowered himself, trying to find knee and toe-holds in either wall. The stench blinded him and flies invaded his mouth and ears and nostrils. As he entered the larger foulness and touched the bottom of the pit, he seemed to hear what he believed to be a hallucinatory murmur of voices behind the rage of flies. Were they behind you? said one voice. And another said, Dammit, this is our place!

There were ten children in there with him.

Amon's report, which Mietek Pemper saw over Frau Koch-mann's shoulder that Monday morning, made use of the compound word *Sonderbehandlung* – Special Treatment. It was a term that would become famous in later years, but this was the first time that Pemper had come across it. Of course, it had a sedative, even medical ring, but Mietek could tell by now that medicine was not involved.

A telegram Amon dictated that morning to be transmitted to Auschwitz gave more than a hint of its meaning. Amon explained that to make escape more difficult he had insisted that those selected for Sonderbehandlung should drop any remnants of civilian clothing they still possessed at the rail siding and should put on striped prison clothes there. Since, throughout the system, a great shortage of such garments prevailed the stripes in which the Plaszów candidates for Sonderbehandlung turned up at Auschwitz should be sent back at once to KL Plaszów for re-use.

And all the children left in Plaszów, of whom the greatest number were those who had shared the latrine with the tall orphan, hid out or impersonated adults until later searches discovered them and took them to the Ostbahn for the slow day's journey sixty kilometres to Auschwitz. The rolling stock was used that way all through high summer, taking troops and supplies east to the stalemated lines near Lwów and, on the return trip, wasting time at sidings while SS doctors watched ceaseless lines of the naked run before them.

29

Oskar, sitting in Amon's office, the windows flung open to a breathless summer's day, had the impression from the start that this meeting was a fake. Perhaps Madritsch and Bosch felt the same, for their gaze kept drifting away from Amon towards the limestone trolleys outside the window, towards any passing truck or wagon. Only Untersturmführer Leo John, who took notes, felt the need to sit up straight and keep his top button done up.

Amon had described it as a security conference. Though the front had now been stabilised, he said, the advance of the Russian centre to the suburbs of Warsaw had encouraged partisan activity all over the Government General. Jews who heard of it were encouraged to attempt escapes. Of course they did not know, Amon pointed out, that they were better off behind the wire than exposed to those Jew killers, the Polish partisans. In any case, everyone had to beware of partisan attack from outside and, worst of all, of collusion between the partisans and the prisoners.

Oskar tried to imagine the partisans invading Plaszów, letting all the Poles and Jews pour out, making of them an instant army. It was a daydream, and who could believe it? But there was Amon, straining to convince them all that *he* believed it. It had a purpose, this little act. Oskar was sure of that.

Bosch said, "If the partisans are coming out to your place, Amon, I hope it's not a night when I've been invited."

"Amen, amen," murmured Schindler.

After the meeting, whatever it meant, Oskar took Amon to his car, which was parked outside the Administration Block. He opened the boot. Inside lay a richly tooled saddle worked with designs characteristic of the Zakopane region in the mountains south of Cracow. It was necessary for Oskar to keep priming Amon with these little gifts, now that payment for the forced labour of Deutsche Email Fabrik no longer went anywhere near Haupsturmführer Goeth but, instead, was sent directly to the Cracow area representative of General Pohl's Oranienburg headquarters.

Oskar offered to drive both Amon and his saddle down to the commandant's villa.

On such a blistering day, some of the trolley-pushers were showing a little less than the required zeal. But the saddle had sweetened Amon and, in any case, it was no longer permitted for him to jump from a car and shoot people dead. The car rolled past the garrison barracks and came to the siding where stood a string of guarded cattle wagons. Oskar could tell by the haze hanging above the rolling stock and blending with and wavering in the heat rebounding from the roofs that they were full. Even above the sound of the engine, you could hear the mourning from inside, and the pleas for water.

Oskar braked his car and listened. This was permitted him, in view of the splendid multi-zloty saddle in the trunk. Amon smiled indulgently at his sentimental friend. They're partly Plaszów people, said Amon, and people from the work camp at Szebnia. And Poles and Jews from Montelupich. They're going to Mauthausen. Amon gave the name of the destination teasingly. They're complaining now? They don't know what complaint is yet. . .

The roofs of the wagons were bronzed with heat. You have no objection, said Oskar, if I call out your fire brigade?

Amon gave a What-will-you-think-of-next? sort of laugh. He implied that he wouldn't let anyone else summon the firemen, but he'd tolerate Oskar because Oskar was such a character and the whole business would make a good dinner-party anecdote.

But as Oskar sent Ukrainian guards to ring the bell for the Jewish firemen, Amon was genuinely bemused. He knew that Oskar knew what Mauthausen meant. If you hosed the wagons for people, you were making them promises about a future. And would not such promises constitute, in anyone's code, a true cruelty. So disbelief mingled with tolerant amusement in Amon as the hoses were run out and jets of water fell hissing on the scalding rooftops. Neuschel also came down from the office to shake his head and smile as the people inside the wagons moaned and roared with gratitude. Grün, Amon's bodyguard, stood chatting with Untersturmführer John and clapped his side and hooted as the water rained down. Even fully run out and at full pressure, the jets reached only halfway down the line of rolling stock. Next, Oskar was asking Amon for the loan of a truck or cart and of a few Ukrainians to drive into Zablocie and fetch the fire hoses from Deutsche Email Fabrik. They were two hundred-metre hoses, Oskar said. Amon, for some reason, found that side-splitting. Of course I'm willing to authorise a lorry, said Amon. Amon was willing to do anything for the sake of the comedy of life.

Oskar gave the Ukrainians a note for Bankier and Garde. While they were gone, Amon was so willing to enter the spirit of the event that he permitted the doors of the wagons to be opened and buckets of water to be passed in and the dead, with their pink, swollen faces, to be lifted out. And still, all around the railway siding stood amused SS officers and NCOs. "What does he think he's saving them from?"

When the large hoses from DEF arrived and all the wagons had been drenched, the joke took on new dimensions. Oskar, in his note to Bankier, had instructed that, besides providing the hoses, the manager should go into Oskar's apartment on the top floor of the office block and fill a hamper with drink and cigarettes, some good cheeses and sausages, and so on. Oskar now handed the hamper to the NCO at the rear of the train. It was an open transaction, and the man seemed a little embarrassed at the largesse, shoving the hamper quickly into the rear van in case one of the officers of KL Plaszów reported him. Yet Oskar seemed to be in such curious favour with the commandant that the NCO listened to him respectfully. When you stop near stations, said Oskar, will you open the wagon doors?

Years later, two survivors of the transport, Doctors Rubinstein and Feldstein, would let Oskar know that the

NCO had ordered the doors frequently opened and the water buckets regularly filled on the tedious journey to Mauthausen. For most of the transport, of course, that was no more than a comfort before dying.

As Oskar moves down the line, under the laughter of the SS, bringing a mercy which is in large terms futile, it can be seen that he's not so much reckless any more but possessed. Even Amon can tell that his friend has shifted into a new gear. All this frenzy about getting the hoses right to the farthest wagon, the bribing an SS man in full view of the SS personnel – it would take just a slight shift in degree of the laughter of Scheidt or John or Hujar to bring about a mass denunciation of Oskar, a piece of information the Gestapo could not ignore. And then Oskar *would* go into Montelupich and, in view of previous racial charges against him, probably on to Auschwitz. So Amon was horrified by the way Oskar insisted on treating those dead as if they were poor relations travelling third class but bound for a genuine destination.

Some time after two, a locomotive hauled the whole miserable string of cattle wagons away towards the main line, and all the hoses could again be wound up. Schindler delivered Amon and his saddle to the Goeth villa. Amon could see that Oskar was still preoccupied and, for the first time in their association, gave his friend some advice about living. You have to relax, said Amon. You can't go running after every trainload that leaves this place.

The engineer, Adam Garde, also saw symptoms of this shift in Oskar. On the night of July 20th, an SS man had come into Garde's barracks and roused him. The Herr Direktor had called the guardhouse and said it was necessary to see engineer Garde, professionally, in his office.

Garde found Oskar listening to the radio, his face flushed, a bottle and two glasses in front of him on the table. Behind the desk these days a relief map of Europe adorned the wall. It had never been there in the days of German expansion, but Oskar seemed to take a sharp interest in the shrinkage of the German fronts. Tonight he had the radio tuned to the

Deutschlandsender, not – as was usually the case – to the BBC. Inspirational music was being played, as it often was as prelude to important announcements.

Oskar seemed to be listening avidly. When Garde came in, he stood up and hustled the young engineer to a seat. He poured cognac and passed it hurriedly across the desk. There's been an attempt on Hitler's life, said Oskar. It had been announced earlier in the evening, and the story then was that Hitler had survived. They'd promised that he would soon be speaking to the German people. But it hadn't happened. Hours had passed and they hadn't been able to produce him. And they kept playing a lot of Beethoven, the way they had when Stalingrad fell.

Oskar and Garde sat together for hours. A seditious event, a Jew and a German listening together – all night if necessary – to discover if the Führer had died. Adam Garde, of course, suffered that same breathless surge of hope. He noticed that Oskar kept gesturing limply, as if the possibility that the Leader was dead had unstrung his muscles. He drank devoutly and urged Garde to drink up. If it's true, said Oskar, then Germans, ordinary Germans like himself, could begin to redeem themselves. Purely because someone close to Hitler had had the guts to remove him from the earth. It's the end of the SS, said Oskar. Himmler will be in jail by morning.

Oskar blew clouds of smoke. Oh my God, he said, the relief to see the end of this system.

The 10 p.m. news brought only the earlier statement. There had been an attempt on the Führer's life but it had failed, and the Führer would be broadcasting in a few minutes. When, as the hour passed, Hitler did not speak, Oskar turned to a fantasy which would be popular with many Germans as the war drew to a close. Our troubles are over, he said. The world's sane again. Germany can ally itself with the West against the Russians.

Garde's hopes were more modest. At worst, he hoped for a ghetto which was a ghetto in the old Franz Josef sense.

And as they drank and the music played, it seemed more and more reasonable that Europe would yield them that night the death essential for the restoration of its sanity. They were citizens of the continent again, they were not the prisoner and the Herr Direktor. The radio's promises to produce a message from the Führer recurred, and every time Oskar laughed with increasing point.

Midnight came and they paid no attention any more to the promises. Their very breath was lighter in this new post-Führer Cracow. By morning, they surmised, there would be dancing in every square, and it would go unpunished. The Wehrmacht would arrest Frank in the Wawel and encircle the SS complex in Pomorska Street.

A little before 1 a.m., Hitler was heard broadcasting from Rastenberg. Oskar had been so convinced that *that* voice was a voice he would never need to hear again that for a few seconds he did not recognise the sound, in spite of its familiarity, thinking instead that it was just another temporising Party spokesman. But engineer Garde heard the speech from its first word, and knew whose voice it was.

"My German comrades!" it began. "If I speak to you today, it is first in order that you should hear my voice and should know that I am unhurt and well, and, second, that you should know of a crime unparalleled in German history."

The speech ended four minutes later with a reference to the conspirators. "This time we shall settle accounts with them in the manner to which we National Socialists are accustomed."

Adam Garde had never quite bought the fantasy Oskar had been pushing all evening. For Hitler was more than a man: he was a system with ramifications. Even if he died, it was no guarantee the system would alter its character. Besides, it was not in the nature of a phenomenon such as Hitler to perish in the space of an evening.

But Oskar had been believing in the death with a feverish conviction for hours now, and when it turned out to be an illusion, it was young Garde who found himself cast as the comforter, while Oskar spoke with an almost operatic grief. "All our vision of deliverance is futile," he said. He poured another glass of cognac each, then pushed the bottle across the desk, opening his cigarette box. "Take the cognac and some cigarettes and get some sleep," he said. "We'll have to wait a little longer for our freedom."

In the confusion of the cognac, of the news, and of its sudden reversal in the small hours, Garde did not think it amazing that Oskar was talking about 'our freedom', as if they had an equivalent need, were both prisoners who had to wait passively to be liberated. But back in his bunk Garde thought, It's strange the Herr Direktor should talk like that, like someone easily given to fantasies and fits of depression. Usually, he was so pragmatic.

Pomorska and the camps around Cracow crawled with rumours that late summer of some imminent rearrangement of prisoners. The rumours troubled Oskar in Zablocie, and at Plaszów Amon got unofficial word that the camps would be disbanded.

In fact that meeting over security had to do not with saving Plaszów from partisans, but with the coming closure of the camp. Amon had called Madritsch and Oskar and Bosch out to Plaszów and held the meeting just to give himself protective colouring. It then became plausible for him to drive into Cracow and call on Wilhelm Koppe, the new SS police chief of the Government General. Amon sat on the far side of Koppe's desk wearing a fake frown, his long fingers opening and clenching erratically, as if from the stress of a besieged Plaszów. He told Koppe the same story he'd given Oskar and the others. That partisan organisations had sprung up inside the camp, that Zionists within the wire had had communications with radicals of the Polish People's Army and the Jewish Combat Organisation. As the Obergruppenführer could appreciate, that sort of communication was difficult to stamp out – messages could come in in a smuggled loaf of bread. But at the first sign of active rebellion, he – Amon Goeth – as commandant, would need to be able to take summary action. The question Amon wanted to ask was, if he fired first and did the paperwork for Oranienburg afterwards, would the distinguished Obergruppenführer Koppe stand by him?

No problem, said Koppe. He didn't really approve of bureaucrats either. In years past, as police chief of the Wartheland, he'd commanded the fleet of extermination lorries which carried Untermenschen out into the countryside and which then, running the engines at full throttle, pumped the exhaust back into the locked interior. That too was an off-the-cuff operation, not permitting immaculate paperwork. Of course, you have to use your judgment, he told Amon. And if you do, I'll back you.

Oskar had sensed at the meeting that Amon was not really worried about partisans. Had he known at the time that Plaszów was to be liquidated, he would have understood the deeper meaning of Amon's performance. For Amon was worried about Wilek Chilowicz, his Jewish chief of camp police, whom he had often used as an agent on the black market. Chilowicz knew Cracow. He knew where he could sell the flour, rice, butter the commandant held back from the camp supplies. He knew the dealers who would be interested in products from the custom jewellery shop staffed by interns such as Wulkan. Amon was worried about the whole Chilowicz clique, Mrs. Marysia Chilowicz, who enjoyed conjugal privileges, Mietek Finkelstein (Chilowicz's deputy), Chilowicz's sister Mrs. Ferber, and Mr. Ferber. If there had been an aristocracy inside Plaszów, it had been the Chilowiczes. They had had power over prisoners, but their knowledge was double-edged: they knew as much about Amon as they did about some miserable machinist in the Madritsch works. If, when Plaszów closed, they were shipped to another camp, Amon knew that as soon as they found themselves in the wrong line they would try to barter their inside knowledge of his rackets. Or, more likely, as soon as they were hungry.

Of course, Chilowicz was uneasy too, and Amon could sense in him the doubt that he would be allowed to leave Plaszów. Amon decided to use Chilowicz's very concern as a lever. He called Sowinski, an SS auxiliary recruited from the High Tatras of Czechoslovakia, into his office for a conference. Sowinski was to approach Chilowicz and pretend to offer him an escape deal. Amon was sure that Chilowicz would be eager to negotiate.

Sowinski went and did it well. He told Chilowicz he could get the whole clan out of the camp in one of the large fuel-burning trucks. You could sit half a dozen people in the wooden furnace if you were running on petrol.

Chilowicz was interested in the proposition. Sowinski would of course need to deliver a note to friends on the outside, who would provide a vehicle. Sowinski would deliver the clan to the rendezvous point in the truck. Chilowicz was willing to pay in diamonds. But, said Chilowicz, as a sign of mutual trust, Sowinski must provide a weapon.

Sowinski reported the meeting to the commandant, and Amon gave him a .38 mm pistol with the pin filed down. This was passed to Chilowicz, who, of course, had no opportunity to test-fire it. Yet Amon would be able to swear to both Koppe and Oranienburg that he had found a weapon on the prisoner.

It was a Sunday in mid-August when Sowinski met the Chilowiczes in the building-material shed and hid them in the truck. Then he drove down Jerozolimska to the gate. There should be routine formalities there, then the truck could roll out into the countryside. In the empty furnace, in the pulses of the five escapees, was the febrile, almost insupportable hope of leaving Amon behind.

At the gate, however, were Amon and Amthor and Hujar, and the Ukrainian Ivan Scharujew. A leisurely inspection was made. Lumbering with half smiles across the bed of the truck, the gentlemen of the SS saved the wood furnace till last. They mimed surprise when they discovered the pitiable Chilowicz clan sardine-tight in the wood hole. As soon as Chilowicz had been dragged out, Amon 'found' the illegal gun tucked into his boots. Chilowicz's pockets were laden with diamonds, bribes paid him by desperate inmates of the camp.

Prisoners at their day of rest heard that Chilowicz was under sentence down there at the gate. The news made for the same awe, the confusion of emotions, that had operated the night last year when Symche Spira and his OD had been executed. Nor could any prisoner decipher what it boded for his own chances.

The Chilowicz crowd were executed one at a time with pistols. Amon, very yellow now from liver disease and incumbent diabetes, at the height of his obesity, wheezing like an elderly uncle, put the muzzle to Chilowicz's neck. Later the corpses were displayed in the Appellplatz with placards tied to their chests. *Those who violate just laws can expect a similar death*.

That, of course, was not the moral the prisoners of KL Plaszów took from the sight.

Amon spent the afternoon drafting two long reports, one to Koppe, one to General Glücks's Section D (Concentration Camps), explaining how he had saved KL Plaszów from an insurgency in its first phase – the one in which a group of key conspirators escaped from the camp – by executing the plot's leaders. He did not finish revising either draft till 11 p.m. Frau Kochmann was too slow for such late work, and so the commandant had Mietek Pemper roused from his barracks and brought to the villa. In the front parlour, Amon stated in a level voice that he believed the young man was party to Chilowicz's escape attempt. Pemper was astounded and did not know how to answer. Looking around him for some sort of inspiration, he saw the seam of his trouser leg, which had come unsewn. How could I pass on the outside in this sort of clothing? he asked.

The balance of frank desperation in his answer satisfied Amon. He told the boy to sit down and instructed him how the typing was to be set out and the pages numbered. Amon hit the papers with his spatulate fingertips. "I want a first-class job done." And Pemper thought, That's the way of it – I can die now for being an escapee, or later in the year for having seen these justifications of Amon's.

When Pemper was leaving the villa with the drafts in his hand, Goeth followed him out on to the patio and called a last order. "When you type the list of insurgents," Amon called companionably, "I want you to leave room above my signature for another name to be inserted."

Pemper nodded, discreet as any professional typist. He stood just a half-second, trying for inspiration, some quick answer that would reverse Amon's order about the extra space. The space for his name. *Mietek Pemper*. In that hateful torrid silence of Sunday evening in Jerozolimska, nothing plausible came to him.

"Yes, Herr Commandant," said Pemper.

As Pemper stumbled up the road to the Administration Building, he remembered a letter Amon had had him type earlier that summer. It had been addressed to Amon's father, the Viennese publisher, and was full of filial concern for an allergy which had troubled the old man that spring. Amon hoped that it had lifted by now. The reason Pemper remembered that letter out of all the others was that half an hour before he'd been called into Amon's office to take it down, the commandant had dragged a girl filing clerk outside and executed her. The juxtaposition of the letter and the execution proved to Pemper that, for Amon, murder and allergies were events of equal weight. And if you told a tractable stenographer to leave a space for his name, it was a matter of course that he left it.

Pemper sat at the typewriter for more than an hour, but in the end left the space for himself. Not to do that would be even more suddenly fatal. There had been a rumour among Stern's friends that Schindler had some movement of people in mind, some rescue or other. But tonight rumours from Zablocie meant nothing. Mietek left in each report the space for his own death. And all his remembrance of the commandant's criminal carbons which he'd held up to mirrors and learned by rote, all that was made futile by the space he left.

When both typescripts were word perfect, he returned to the villa. Amon kept him waiting by the french windows while he himself sat in the parlour reading the documents. Pemper wondered if his own body would be displayed with some declamatory lettering. *So Die All Jewish Bolshevists!*

At last Amon appeared at the windows. "You may go to bed," he said.

"Herr Commandant?"

"I said, you may go to bed."

Pemper went. He walked less steadily now. After what he had seen, Amon could not let him live. But perhaps the commandant believed there would be leisure to kill him later. In the meantime, life for a day was still life.

The space, as it proved, was for a prisoner who, by unwise dealings with men such as John and Hujar, had let it be known he had a cache of diamonds somewhere outside the camp. While Pemper sank into the sleep of the reprieved, Amon had the man summoned to the villa, offered him his life for the diamonds' location, was shown the place and, of course, executed him and added his name to the reports to Koppe and Oranienburg – to his humble claim of having snuffed the spark of rebellion.

30

The orders, labelled OKH (Army High Command) already sat on Oskar's desk. Because of the war situation, the Director of Armaments told Oskar, KL Plaszów and therefore the Emalia camp were to be disbanded. Prisoners from Emalia would be sent to Plaszów, to await relocation. Oskar himself was to run down his Zablocie operation, as quickly as possible, retaining on the premises only those technicians necessary for the dismantling of plant. For further instructions, he should apply to the Evacuation Board, OKH, Berlin.

Oskar's initial reaction was cool rage. He resented the tone, the sense of a distant official trying to absolve him from further concern. There was a man in Berlin who, not knowing of the black-market bread that bound Oskar and his prisoners together, thought it was reasonable for a factory owner to open the gate and let the people be taken. But the worst arrogance was that the letter did not define 'relocation'. Governor General Frank was more honest than that and had made a notorious speech a little earlier in the year. "When we ultimately win the war, then, as far as I'm concerned, Poles, Ukrainians and all that rabble idling about here can be made into mincemeat, into anything you like." Frank had the courage to put an accurate name to the process. In Berlin, they wrote 'relocation' and believed themselves excused.

Amon knew what 'relocation' meant and, during Oskar's next visit to Plaszów, told him freely. All Plaszów men would be sent to Gröss-Rosen. The women would go to Auschwitz. Gröss-Rosen was a vast quarry camp in Lower Silesia. The German Earth & Stone Works, an SS enterprise with branches throughout Poland, Germany, and the conquered territories, consumed the prisoners of Gröss-Rosen. The processes at Auschwitz were, of course, more direct and modern.

When the news of the abolition of Emalia reached the factory floor and ran through the barracks, some Schindler people thought it was the end of all sanctuary. The Perlmans, whose daughter had come out of Aryan cover to plead for them, packed their blankets and talked philosophically to their bunk neighbours. Emalia has given us a year's rest, a year's soup, a year's sanity. Perhaps it might be enough. But they expected to die now. It was apparent from their voices.

Rabbi Levartov was resigned too. He was going back to unsettled business with Amon. Edith Liebgold, who'd been recruited by Bankier for the nightshift in the first days of the ghetto, noticed that although Oskar spent hours talking solemnly with his Jewish supervisors, he did not come up to people and make dizzying promises. Perhaps he was as baffled and diminished by these orders from Berlin as anyone else. So he wasn't quite the prophet he'd been the night she'd first come here more than three years ago.

Just the same, at the end of summer, as his prisoners packed their bundles and were marched back to Plaszów, there was a rumour among them that Oskar had spoken of buying them back. He had said it to Klein, he had said it to Bankier. You could almost hear him saying it, that level certainty, the paternal rumble of the throat. But as you went up Jerozolimska Street, past the Administration Block, staring in newcomer's disbelief at the hauling gangs from the quarry, the memory of Oskar's conviction and promises was very nearly just another burden.

The Horowitz family were back in Plaszów. Even though their father, Dolek, had last year manoeuvred them to Emalia, here they were back. The six-year-old boy Richard, the mother Regina. Niusia, eleven now, was again sewing bristles on to brush paddles and watching, from the high windows, the trucks roll up to Chujowa Górka, and the black cremation smoke rising over the hill. As Plaszów was when she had left it last year, so it continued. It was impossible for her to believe that it would ever end.

But her father believed that Oskar would make a list of people and extricate them. Oskar's list, in the mind of some, was already more than a mere tabulation. It was a *List*. It was a sweet chariot which might swing low.

Oskar raised the idea of taking Jews away from Cracow with him one night at Amon's villa. It was a still night at the end of summer. Amon seemed pleased to see him. Because of Amon's health – both Doctors Blancke and Gross, warning him that if he didn't cut his eating and drinking he would die – there had not been so many visitors to the villa of late.

They sat together, drinking at Amon's new rate of moderation. Oskar sprang the news on him. He wanted to move his factory to Czechoslovakia. He wanted to take his skilled workers with him. He might need other skills from among the Plaszów workers too. He would seek the help of the Evacuation Board in finding an appropriate site, somewhere down in Moravia, and of the Ostbahn in making the shift south-west from Cracow. He let Amon know that he'd be very grateful for any support. The mention of gratitude always excited Amon. Yes, he said, if Oskar could get all the cooperation he needed from the boards involved, Amon would then allow a list of people to be drawn up.

When that was settled, Amon wanted a game of cards. He liked blackjack, a version of the French vingt-et-un. It was a hard game for junior officers to fake losing without being obvious. It did not permit of too much sycophancy. It was therefore true sport, and Amon preferred it. Besides, Oskar wasn't interested in losing this evening. He would be paying enough to Amon for that list.

The commandant began by betting modestly, in hundred-zloty bills, as if his doctors had advised moderation in this as well. He kept busting, however, and when the beginning stake had been raised to five hundred zloty, Oskar got a 'natural', an ace and a ten, which meant that Amon had to pay him double the stake.

Amon was disconsolate about that but not too peevish.

He called for Helen Hirsch to bring coffee. She came in, a parody of a gentleman's servant, still in black, crisply dressed, but her right eye blind with swelling. She was so small that Amon would need to stoop to beat her up. The girl knew Oskar now but did not look at him. Nearly a year past, he had promised to get her out. Whenever he came to the villa he managed to slip down the corridor to the kitchen and ask her how she was. It meant something, but it had not touched the substance of her life. A few weeks back, for example, when the soup hadn't been the correct temperature – Amon was pernickety about soup, fly specks in the corridor, fleas on dogs – the commandant had called for Ivan and Petr and told them to take her to the birch tree in the garden and shoot her. He'd watched from the french windows as she walked in front of Petr's Mauser and pleaded under her breath with the young Ukrainian. "Petr, who's this you're going to shoot? It's Helen. Helen who gives you cakes. You couldn't shoot Helen, could you?" And Petr answering in the same manner, through clenched mouth, "I know, Helen. I don't want to. But if I don't, he'll kill me." She'd bent her head towards the spotted birch bark. Having often asked Amon why he wouldn't kill her, she wanted to die simply, to hurt him by her willing acceptance. But it wasn't possible. She was trembling so violently that he could have seen it. Her legs were shaking. And then she'd heard Amon call from the windows. "Bring the bitch back. There's plenty of time to shoot her. In the meantime, it might still be possible to educate her."

Insanely, in between his spates of savagery, there were brief phases in which he tried to play the benign master. He had said to her one morning, "You're really a very well trained servant. If after the war you require a reference, I shall be happy to give you one." She knew it was just talk, a daydream. She turned her deaf ear, the one whose eardrum he had perforated with a blow. Sooner or later, she knew, she would die of his customary fury.

In a life like hers, a smile from visitors was only a momentary comfort. Tonight she placed the enormous silver pot of coffee beside the Herr Commandant – he still drank it by the bucket in cups laden with sugar – made her obeisance and left.

Within an hour, when Amon was three thousand, seven hundred zloty in debt to Oskar and complaining sourly about his luck, Oskar suggested a variation on the betting. He would need a maid in Moravia, he said, when he moved to Czechoslovakia. There you couldn't get them as intelligent and well trained as Helen Hirsch. They were all country girls. Oskar suggested therefore that he and Amon play one hand, double or quits. If Amon won, Oskar would pay him seven thousand four hundred zloty. If he hit a 'natural', it would be fourteen thousand eight hundred zloty. But if I win, said Oskar, then you give me Helen Hirsch for my list.

Amon wanted to think about that. Come on, said Oskar, she's going to Auschwitz anyhow. But there was an attachment there. Amon was so used to Helen that he couldn't automatically wager her away. When he'd thought of an end for her, it had probably always been that he would finish her by his own hand, with personal passion. If he played cards for her and lost, he would be under pressure, as a Viennese sportsman, to surrender the pleasure of intimate murder.

Much earlier in Plaszów's history, Schindler had asked for Helen to be assigned to Emalia. But Amon had refused. Just a year ago it had seemed that Plaszów would exist for decades, and that the commandant and his maid would grow old together, at least until some perceived fault in Helen brought about the abrupt end of the connection. This time a year ago, no one would have believed that the relationship would be resolved because the Russians were outside Lwów. As for Oskar's part in this proposal, he had made it lightly. He did not seem to see, in his offer to Amon, any parallel with God and Satan playing cards for human souls. He did not ask himself by what right he made a bid for the girl. If he lost, his chance of extracting her some other way was slim. But all chances were slim that year. Even his own.

Oskar got up and bustled around the room, looking for

tationery with an official letterhead on it. He wrote out the tatement for Amon to sign should he lose. *I authorise that he name of prisoner Helen Hirsch should be added to any st of skilled workers relocated with Herr Oskar Schindler's DEF Works.*

Amon was dealer and gave Oskar an eight and a five. Oskar asked to be dealt more. He received a five and an ace. t would have to do. Then Amon dealt to himself. A four ame up, and then a king. God in heaven, said Amon. He was a gentleman cusser, he seemed to be too fastidious to se obscenities. I'm busted. I'm out. He laughed a little but was not really amused. My first cards, he explained, were a hree and a five. With a four I should have had a good hance. Then I got this damn king.

In the end, he signed the piece of paper. Oskar picked up ll the chits he'd won that evening from Amon and returned hem. Just look after the girl for me, he said, till it's time for s all to leave.

Out in her kitchen, Helen Hirsch did not know she'd been aved over cards.

Probably because Oskar reported his evening with Amon o Stern, rumours of Oskar's plan were heard in the Administration Block and even in the workshops. There *was* a chindler list. It was worth everything to be on it.

31

At some point in any discussion about Schindler, the surviv
ing friends of the Herr Direktor will blink and shake thei
heads and begin the almost mathematical business of find
ing the sum of his motives. For one of the most commor
sentiments of Schindler Jews is still, "I don't know why he
did it." It can be said for a start that Oskar was a gambler
was a sentimentalist who loved the transparency, the sim
plicity of doing good; that Oskar was by temperament ar
anarchist who loved to ridicule the system, and that beneath
the hearty sensuality lay a capacity to be outraged by humar
savagery, to react to it and not be overwhelmed. But none o
this, jotted down, added up, explains the doggedness with
which, in the autumn of 1944, he prepared a final haven fo
the graduates of Emalia.

And not only for them. In early September he drove to
Podgórze and visited Madritsch, who at that point em
ployed more than three thousand prisoners in his uniforn
factory. This factory would now be disbanded. Madritsch
would get his sewing machines back, and his workers woulc
vanish. If we made a combined approach, said Oskar, we
could get more than four thousand out. Yours and mine. We
could relocate them in something like safety. Down in quie
Moravia.

Madritsch would always and justly be revered by his
surviving prisoners. The bread and chickens smuggled into
his factory were paid for from his pocket and at continuous
risk. He would have been considered a more stable mar
than Oskar. Not as flamboyant and not as given to obses
sion. He had not suffered arrest. But he had been much more
humane than was safe and, without wit and energy, woulc
have ended in Auschwitz.

Now Oskar presented to him a vision of a Madritsch-Schindler camp somewhere in the High Jeseniks; some smoky, safe little industrial hamlet.

Madritsch was attracted by the idea but did not rush to say yes. He could tell that though the war was lost, the SS system had become more instead of less implacable. He was correct in believing that the prisoners of Plaszów would – in coming months – be consumed in death camps to the west. For if Oskar was stubborn and possessed, so were the SS Main Office and their prize field operatives, the commandants of the concentration camps.

He did not say no, however. He needed time to think about it. Though he couldn't say it to Oskar, it is likely he was afraid of sharing factory premises with a rash, demonic fellow like Herr Schindler.

Without any clear word from Madritsch, Oskar took to the road. He went to Berlin and bought dinner for Colonel Erich Lange. I can go completely over to the manufacture of shells, Oskar told Lange. I can transfer my heavy machinery.

Lange was crucial. He could guarantee contracts, he could write the hearty recommendations Oskar needed for the Evacuation Board and the German officials in Moravia. Later, Oskar would say of this shadowy staff officer that he had given consistent help. Lange was still in that state of exalted desperation and moral disgust characteristic of many who had worked inside the system but not always for it. We can do it, said Lange, but it will take some money. Not for me. For others.

Through Lange, Oskar talked with an officer of the Evacuation Board at OKH in the Bendlerstrasse. It was likely, said this officer, that the evacuation would be approved in principle. But there was a major obstacle. The Governor-cum-Gauleiter of Moravia, ruling from a castle at Liberec, had followed a policy of keeping Jewish labour camps out of his province. Neither the SS nor the Armaments Inspectorate had so far persuaded him to change his attitude. A good man to discuss this impasse with, said the officer, would be a middle-aged Wehrmacht engineer down

in the Troppau office of the Armaments Inspectorate, a ma
named Sussmuth. Oskar could talk to Sussmuth too abo
what relocation sites were available in Moravia. Mear
while, Herr Schindler could count on the support of th
Main Evacuation Board. But you can understand that i
view of the pressure they are under, and the inroads the wa
has made on their personal comforts, they are more likely t
give a quick answer if you could be considerate to them i
some way. We poor city fellows are short of ham, cigar
drink, cloth, coffee, that sort of thing.

The officer seemed to think that Oskar carried aroun
with him half the peacetime produce of Poland. Instead, t
get together a gift parcel for the gentlemen of the boar
Oskar had to buy luxuries at the Berlin black-market rat
An old gentleman on the desk at the Adler was able t
acquire good schnaps for Herr Schindler at a discount pric
of about eighty Reichsmarks a bottle. And you couldn
send the gentlemen of the board less than a dozen. Coffe
however, was like gold, and Havanas were an insane pric
Oskar bought them in quantity and included them in th
hamper. The gentlemen might need a head of steam if the
were to bring the Governor of Moravia round.

In the midst of Oskar's negotiations, Amon Goeth wa
arrested.

Someone must have informed on him. Some jealous junio
officer, or a concerned citizen who'd visited the villa an
been shocked by Amon's sybaritic style. A senior SS invest
gator named Eckert began to look at Amon's financia
dealings. The shots Amon had taken from the balcony wer
not germane to Eckert's enquiry. But the embezzlement
and the black-market dealings were, as were complaint
from some of his SS inferiors that he had treated ther
severely.

Amon was on leave in Vienna, staying with his fathe
Amon Franz Goeth the publisher, when the SS arrested hir
They also raided an apartment Hauptsturmführer Goet
kept in the city and discovered a cache of money, som
eighty thousand Reichsmarks, which Amon could not ex

plain to their satisfaction. They found as well, stacked to the ceiling, close to a million cigarettes. It seemed that Amon's Viennese apartment was more of a warehouse than a *pied à terre*.

It might be at first sight surprising that the SS – or rather the officers of Bureau V of the Reich Security Main Office – should want to arrest such an effective servant as Hauptsturmführer Goeth. But they had already investigated irregularities in Buchenwald and tried to pin the commandant, Koch. They had even attempted to find evidence for the arrest of the renowned Rudolf Höss, commandant of Auschwitz, and had questioned a Viennese Jewess who, they suspected, was pregnant by this star of the camp system. So Amon, raging in his apartment while they ransacked it, had no cause to hope for much immunity.

They took him to Breslau and put him in an SS prison to await investigation and trial. They showed their innocence of the way affairs were run in Plaszów by going to the villa and questioning Helen Hirsch on suspicion of her being involved in Amon's swindles. Twice in coming months she would be taken to the cells beneath the SS barracks of Plaszów for interrogation. They fired questions at her about Amon's contacts on the black market, who his agents were, how he worked the jewellery shop at Plaszów, the custom tailoring shop, the upholstery works. No one hit her or threatened her. But it was their conviction that she was a member of a gang that tormented her. If Helen had ever thought of an unlikely and glorious salvation, she would not have dared dream that Amon would be arrested by his own people. But she felt her sanity going now in the interrogation room, when under their law they tried to shackle her to Amon.

Chilowicz might have been able to help you, she told them. But Chilowicz is dead.

They were policemen by trade, and after a time would decide she could give them nothing except a little information about the sumptuous cuisine at the villa Goeth. They could have asked her about her scars, but they knew they couldn't get Amon on grounds of sadism. Investigating sadism in the camp at Sachsenhausen, they'd been forced off the premises by armed guards. In Buchenwald they had found a material witness, an NCO, to testify against the commandant, but the informer had been found dead in his cell. The head of that SS investigating team ordered samples of a poison found in the NCO's stomach to be administered to four Russian prisoners. He watched them die, and so had his proof against the commandant and camp doctor. Even though he got prosecutions for murder and sadistic practice, it was a strange justice. Above all, it made the camp personnel close ranks and dispose of living evidence. So the men of Bureau V did not question Helen about her injuries. They stuck to embezzlement, and in the end stopped troubling her.

They investigated Mietek Pemper too. He was wise enough not to tell them much about Amon, certainly not about his crimes against humans. He knew little but rumours of Amon's frauds. He played the neutral and well-mannered typist of non-classified material. "The Herr Commandant would never discuss such matters with me," he pleaded continuously. But beneath his performance, he too must have suffered the same howling disbelief as Helen Hirsch. If there was one event most likely to guarantee *him* a chance of life, it was Amon's arrest. For there had been no more certain limit to his life than this: that when the Russians reached Tarnow, Amon would dictate his last letters and then assassinate the typist. What worried Mietek, therefore, was that they would release Amon too soon.

But they were not interested solely in the question of Amon's speculations. The SS judge who questioned Pemper had been told by Oberscharführer Lorenz Landsdorfer that Hauptsturmführer Goeth had let his Jewish stenographer type up the directives and plans to be followed by the Plaszów garrison in the case of an assault on the camp by partisans. Amon, in explaining to Pemper how the typing of these plans should be set out, had even shown him copies of similar plans for other concentration camps. The judge was so alarmed by this disclosure of secret documents to a

Jewish prisoner that he ordered Pemper's arrest.

Pemper spent two miserable weeks in a cell beneath the SS barracks. He was not beaten, but was questioned regularly by a series of Bureau V investigators and by two SS judges. He thought he could read in their eyes the conclusion that the safest thing was to shoot him. One day during questioning about Plaszów's emergency plans, Pemper asked his interrogators, "Why keep me here? A prison is a prison. I have a life sentence anyhow." It was an argument calculated to bring a resolution, either release from the cells or else a bullet. After the session ended, Pemper spent some hours of anxiety until his cell door opened again. He was marched out and returned to his hut in the camp. It was not the last time however that he would be questioned on subjects relating to Commandant Goeth.

It seemed that, following his arrest, Amon's juniors did not rush to give him references. They were careful. They waited. Bosch, who'd drunk so much of the commandant's liquor, told Untersturmführer John that it was dangerous to try to bribe these fixated investigators from Bureau V. As for Amon's seniors, Scherner was gone, assigned to hunting partisans, and would in the end be killed in an ambush in the forests of Niepolomice. Amon was in the hands of men from Oranienburg who'd never dined at the Goethhaus. Or, if they had, had been either shocked or touched by envy.

After her release by the SS, Helen Hirsch, now working for the new commandant, Hauptsturmführer Büscher, received a friendly note from Amon asking her to get together a parcel of clothes, some romances and detective novels, and some alcohol to comfort him in his cell. It was, she thought, like a letter from a relative. "Would you kindly gather for me the following," it said, and ended with, "Hoping to see you again soon."

Meanwhile Oskar had been down to the market city of Troppau to see enginer Sussmuth. He'd brought along drink and diamonds, but they weren't needed in this case. Sussmuth told Oskar that he had already proposed that some small Jewish work camps be set up in the border towns of

Moravia to turn out goods for the Armaments Inspectorate. Such camps would of course be under the central control of either Auschwitz or Gröss-Rosen, for the areas of influence of the big concentration camps crossed the Polish-Czechoslovak border. But there was more safety for prisoners in little work camps than could be found in the grand necropolis of Auschwitz itself. Sussmuth had got nowhere, of course. The Castle at Liberec had trampled on the proposal. He had never had a lever. Oskar – the support Oskar had from Lange and the gentlemen of the Evacuation Board – that could be the lever.

Sussmuth had in his office a list of premises suitable to receive plant evacuated from the war zone. Near Oskar's home town of Zwittau, on the edge of a village called Brinnlitz, was a great textile plant owned by the Viennese brothers Hoffman. They'd been in butter and cheese in their home city, but had come to the Sudetenland behind the legions (just as Oskar had gone to Cracow) and become textile magnates. An entire annexe of their plant lay idle, used as a storehouse for obsolete spinning machines. A site like that was served from the rail depot at Zwittau, where Schindler's brother-in-law was in charge of the goods yard. And a loop ran close to the gates. The brothers are profiteers, said Sussmuth smiling. They have some local party backing – the County Council and the District Leader are in their pockets. But you have Colonel Lange behind you. I will write to Berlin at once, Sussmuth promised, and recommend the use of the Hoffman annexe.

Oskar knew the Germanic village of Brinnlitz from his childhood. Its racial character was in its name, since the Czechs would have called it Brnenec, just as a Czech Zwittau would have become Zvitavy. The Brinnlitz citizens would not fancy a thousand or more Jews in their neighbourhood. The Zwittau people, from whom some of Hoffman's workers were recruited, would not like it either, this contamination, so late in the war, of their rustic-industrial backwater.

In any case, Oskar drove down to take a quick look at the site. He did not approach Hoffman Brothers' front office, since that would give the tougher Hoffman brother, the one who chaired the company, too much warning. But he was able to wander into the annexe without being challenged. It was an old-fashioned two storey industrial barracks built around a courtyard. The ground floor was high-ceilinged and full of old machines and crates of wool. The upper floor must have been intended as offices and for lighter equipment. Its floor would not stand the weight of the big pressing machines. Downstairs would do for the new workshops of DEF, as offices and, in one corner, the Herr Direktor's apartment. Upstairs would be barracks for the prisoners.

He was delighted with the place. He drove back to Cracow yearning to get started, to spend the necessary money, to talk to Madritsch again. For Sussmuth could find a place for Madritsch too – perhaps even floor space in Brinnlitz.

When he got back, he found that an Allied bomber, shot down by a Luftwaffe fighter, had crashed on the two end barracks in the backyard prison. Its blackened fuselage sat crookedly across the wreckage of the flattened huts. Only a small squad of prisoners had been left behind in Emalia to wind up production and maintain the plant. They had seen it come down, flaming. There had been two men inside it and their bodies had been burned. The Luftwaffe people who came to take them away had told Adam Garde that the bomber was a Stirling and that the men were Australian. One who was holding the charred remnants of an English Bible must have crashed with it in his hand. Two others had parachuted in the suburbs. One had been found, dead of wounds, in his harness. The partisans had got to the other one first and were hiding him somewhere. What these Australians had been doing was dropping supplies to the partisans in the primaeval forest east of Cracow.

If Oskar had wanted some sort of confirmation, this was it. That men should come all this way from unimaginable little towns in Australia to hasten the end in Cracow. He put a call through at once to the official in charge of rolling stock in the office of Ostbahn president Gerteis and invited him to dinner to talk about DEF's potential need of flat wagons.

*

A week after Oskar spoke to Sussmuth, the gentlemen of the Berlin Armaments Board instructed the Governor of Moravia that Oskar's armaments company was to be allocated the annexe of Hoffman's spinning mills in Brinnlitz. The Governor's bureaucrats could do nothing more, Sussmuth told Oskar by telephone, than slow down the paperwork. But Hoffman and other Party men in the Zwittau area were already conferring and passing resolutions against Oskar's intrusion into Moravia. The Party Kreisleiter (district officer) in Zwittau wrote to Berlin complaining that Jewish prisoners from Poland would be a peril to the health of Moravian Germans. Spotted fever would very likely appear in the region for the first time in modern history, and Oskar's small armaments works, of doubtful value to the war effort, would also attract Allied bombers, with resultant damage to the important Hoffman mills. The population of Jewish criminals in the proposed Schindler camp would outweigh the small and decent population of Brinnlitz and be a cancer on the honest flank of Zwittau.

A protest of that kind didn't have a chance, since it went straight to the office of Erich Lange in Berlin. Appeals to Troppau were quashed by honest Sussmuth. Nonetheless the posters went up on walls in Oskar's home town. *Keep the Jewish Criminals Out*.

And Oskar was paying. He was paying the Evacuation Committee in Cracow to help them speed up the permits for the transfer of his machinery. The Department of the Economy in Cracow had to be encouraged to provide the clearances of bank holdings. Currency wasn't favoured these days, so he paid in goods – in kilos of tea, in pairs of leather shoes, in carpets, in coffee, in canned fish. He spent his afternoons in the little streets off the market square of Cracow haggling at staggering prices for whatever the bureaucrats desired. Otherwise, he was sure, they would keep him waiting until his last Jew had gone to Auschwitz.

It was Sussmuth who told him that people from Zwittau were writing to the Armaments Inspectorate accusing Oskar of black-marketeering. If they're writing to me, said Sussmuth, you can bet the same letters are going to the police chief of Moravia, Obersturmführer Otto Rasch. You should introduce yourself to Rasch and show him what a charming fellow you are.

Oskar had known Rasch when he was SS police chief of Katowice. Rasch was, by happy chance, a friend of the Chairman of Ferrum AG at Sosnowiec, from whom Oskar had purchased his steel. But in rushing down to Brno to head off informers, Oskar didn't rely on anything as flimsy as mutual friendships. He took a diamond cut in the *brilliant* fashion which, somehow, he introduced into the meeting. When it crossed the table and ended on Rasch's side of the desk, it secured Oskar's Brno front.

Oskar later estimated that he spent a hundred thousand Reichsmarks – nearly forty thousand dollars – to grease the transfer to Brinnlitz. Few of his survivors would ever find the figure unlikely, though there were those who shook their heads and said, "No, more! It would have had to be more than that."

Oskar had drawn up what he called a preparatory list and delivered it to the Administration Block. There were more than a thousand names on it – the names of all the prisoners of the backyard prison camp of Emalia, as well as new names. Helen Hirsch's name was freshly on the list, and Amon was not there to argue about it.

The list would expand if Madritsch agreed to go to Moravia with Oskar. So Oskar kept working on Titsch, his ally at Julius Madritsch's ear. Those Madritsch prisoners who were closest to Titsch knew the list was under compilation, that they could have access to it. Titsch told them without any ambiguity: You must get on it. In all the reams of Plaszów paperwork, Oskar's dozen pages of names were the only pages with a connection to the future.

But Madritsch still could not decide whether he wanted an alliance with Oskar, whether he would add his three thousand to the total.

There is again a haziness suitable to a legend about the precise chronology of Oskar's list. The haziness doesn't attach to the existence of the list – a copy can be seen today in the archives of the Yad Vashem. There is no uncertainty about the names thought up – as we shall see – by Oskar and Titsch at the last minute and attached to the end of the official paper. The names on the list are definite. But the circumstances encourage legends. The problem is that the list is remembered with an intensity which, by its very heat, blurs. The list is an absolute good. The list is life. All round its cramped margins lies the gulf.

Some of those whose names appeared on the list say that there was a party at Goeth's villa, a reunion of SS men and entrepreneurs to celebrate the times they'd had there. Some even believe that Goeth was there, but since the SS did not release on bail that was impossible. Others believe that the party was held at Oskar's own apartment above his factory. Oskar had for more than two years given excellent parties there. One Emalia prisoner remembers the early hours of 1944 when he was on watch duty on the factory floor and Oskar had wandered down from his apartment at one o'clock, escaping the noise upstairs and bringing with him two cakes, two hundred cigarettes and a bottle for his friend the watchman.

At the Plaszów graduation party, wherever it took place, the guests included Dr. Blancke, Bosch, and – by some reports – Oberführer Scherner, on vacation from his partisan-hunting. Madritsch was also there, and Titsch. Titsch would later say that at it Madritsch told Oskar for the first time that he would not be going to Moravia with him. "I've done everything I can for the Jews," Madritsch told him. It was a reasonable claim; he would not be persuaded, although he said Titsch had been at him for days.

Madritsch was a just man. Later he would be honoured as such. He simply did not believe that Moravia would work. If he had, the indications are that he would have attempted it.

What else is known about the party is that an urgency operated there, because the Schindler list had to be in that evening. This is an element in all the versions of the story survivors tell. The survivors could only tell and expand upon it if they had heard it in the first place from Oskar, a man with a taste for embellishing a story. But in the early 1960s, Titsch himself attested to the substantial truth of this one. Perhaps the new and temporary commandant of Plaszów, a Hauptsturmführer Büscher, had said to Oskar, Enough fooling around, Oskar! We have to finalise the paperwork and the transportation. Perhaps there was some other form of deadline imposed by the Ostbahn, by the availability of transport.

At the end of Oskar's list, therefore, Titsch now typed in above the official signatures the names of Madritsch prisoners whose faces he was able to summon up. Almost seventy names were added, written in by Titsch from his own and Oskar's memories. Among these names were those of the Feigenbaum family, the adolescent daughter who suffered from incurable bone cancer, the teenage son Lutek with his shaky expertise in repairing sewing machines. Now they were all transformed, as Titsch scribbled, into skilled armaments workers. There was singing in the apartment, loud talk and laughter, a fog of cigarette smoke and, in a corner, Oskar and Titsch quizzing each other over people's names, straining for a clue to the spelling of Polish patronyms.

In the end, Oskar had to put his hand on Titsch's wrist. We're over the limit, he said. They'll baulk at the number we have already. Titsch continued to strain for names, and tomorrow morning would wake damning himself because one had come to him too late. But now he was at the limit, wrung out by this work. He was blasphemously close to creating people anew just by thinking of them. He did not begrudge doing it. It was what it said of the world – that's what made the heavy air of Schindler's apartment so hard for Titsch to breathe.

The integrity of the list was vulnerable, however, through the personnel clerk, Marcel Goldberg. Büscher, the new commandant, himself could not have cared, within certain numerical limits, who went on the list. Therefore Goldberg had the power to tinker with its edges. It was known to prisoners already that Goldberg would take bribes. The Dresners knew it. Juda Dresner – uncle of red Genia, husband of the Mrs. Dresner who'd once been refused a hiding place in a wall, and father of Janek and of young Danka – Juda Dresner knew it. "He paid Goldberg," the family would simply say to explain how they got on the Schindler list. They never knew what was given. Wulkan the jeweller presumably got himself, his wife, his son on the list in the same manner. Poldek Pfefferberg, one-time trader in black-market rugs, poodles and diamond rings for Oskar, was told about the list by an SS NCO named Hans Schreiber. Schreiber, a young man in his mid-twenties, had as evil a name as any other SS man in Plaszów, but Pfefferberg had become something of a mild favourite of his in the way that was common to relationships – throughout the system – between individual prisoners and SS personnel. It had begun one day when Pfefferberg, as a group leader in his barracks, had had responsibility for window cleaning. Schreiber inspected the glass and found a smudge, and began browbeating Poldek in the style that was often a prelude to execution. Pfefferberg lost his temper and told Schreiber that both of them knew the windows were perfectly polished and if Schreiber wanted a reason to shoot him, he ought to do it without any more delay. The outburst had, in a contradictory way, amused Schreiber, who afterwards used occasionally to stop Pfefferberg and ask him how he and his wife were, and sometimes even gave Poldek an apple for Mila. In the summer of 1944, Poldek had appealed to him dementedly to extricate Mila from a trainload of women being sent from Plaszów to the evil camp at Stutthof on the Baltic. Mila was already in the lines boarding the cattle wagons when Schreiber came waving a piece of paper and calling her name. Another time, a Sunday, he turned up drunk at Pfefferberg's barracks and, in front of Poldek and a few other prisoners, began to weep for what he called "the dreadful things" he had done in Plaszów. He intended, he said, to expiate them on the Eastern Front. In the end, he would.

Now he told Poldek that Schindler had a list and that Poldek should do everything he could to get himself on it. Poldek went down to the Administration Block to beg

Goldberg to add his and Mila's names to the list. Schindler had in the past year and a half often visited Poldek in the camp garage and had always promised rescue. Poldek had become such an accomplished welder however that the garage supervisors, who had for their lives' sake to produce high standard work, would never let him go. Now Goldberg sat with his hand on the list – he had already added his own name to it – and this old friend of Oskar's, once a frequent guest in the apartment in Straszewskiego, expected to have himself written down for sentiment's sake. "Do you have any diamonds?" Goldberg asked Pfefferberg.

"Are you serious?" said Poldek.

"For this list," said Goldberg, pressing the pages with his index finger, a man of prodigious and accidental power, "it takes diamonds."

Now that the Viennese music lover Hauptsturmführer Goeth was in prison, the Rosner brothers, musicians to the court, were free to work their way on to the list. Dolek Horowitz also, he who had earlier got his wife and children out to Emalia, now persuaded Goldberg to include himself, his wife, his son, his young daughter. Horowitz had always worked in the central warehouse of Plaszów and had managed to put some small treasure away. Now it was paid to Marcel Goldberg.

Among those included in the list were the Bejski brothers, Uri and Moshe, officially described as machine fitter and draughtsman respectively. Uri had a knowledge of weapons, and Moshe a gift for forging documents. The circumstances of the list are so clouded that it is not possible to say whether they were included for these talents or not.

Josef Bau, the ceremonious bridegroom, would at some stage be included, but without his knowing it. It suited Goldberg to keep everyone in the dark about the list. Given his nature, it is possible to assume that if Bau made any personal approach to Goldberg it could only have been on the basis that his mother, his wife, himself should all be included. He would not find out until too late that he alone would be listed for Brinnlitz.

As for Stern, the Herr Direktor had included him from the beginning. Stern was the only father confessor Oskar had ever had and Stern's suggestions enjoyed a great authority with him. Since October 1st, no Jewish prisoner had been allowed out of Plaszów for any reason at all. At the same time the trusties in the Polish prison had begun to put guards on the barracks to stop Jewish prisoners from trading with the Poles for bread. The price of illegal bread reached a level it would be hard to express in zloty. In the past you could have bought a loaf for your second coat, two hundred and fifty grammes for a clean shirt. Now – as with Goldberg – it took diamonds.

During the first week of October, Oskar and his squat manager Bankier visited Plaszów for some reason and as usual went to see Stern in the Construction Office. Stern's desk was down the hallway from Amon's old office. It was possible to speak more freely here than ever before. Stern told Herr Schindler about the inflated price of rye bread. Oskar turned to Bankier. "Make sure Weichert gets fifty thousand zloty," murmured Oskar.

Michael Weichert was the leader of JUS, a welfare organisation permitted by the Germans for the sake of their relationship with the International Red Cross. Though many Jews found his position ambiguous, and though the underground condemned him, he worked within the narrowing limits of his post to provide bread for many prisoners and forged papers for some. He never asked for any cash reward or consideration in kind, and after the war he would be exonerated by an Israeli court on charges of having collaborated with the Germans. He was exactly the right man to contact if you wanted a quantity of food introduced into a camp.

The conversation of Stern and Oskar rapidly moved on. The fifty thousand zloty were a mere *obiter dicta* of their talk about the unsettled times and about how Amon might be enjoying his cell in Breslau.

Later in the week, black-market bread from town was smuggled into the camp hidden underneath cargoes of cloth, coal or scrap iron. Within a day, the price had fallen to its accustomed level.

It was a nice case of the connivance between Oskar and Stern, and would be followed by other instances.

32

At least one of the Emalia people crossed off by Goldberg to make room for others – for relatives, Zionists, specialists or payers – would blame Oskar.

In 1963, the Martin Buber Society would receive a pitiable letter from a New Yorker, a former Emalia prisoner. In Emalia, he said, Oskar had promised deliverance. In return the people had made him wealthy with their labour. Yet some found themselves off the edge of the list. This man saw his own omission as a very personal betrayal and – with all the fury of someone who has been made to travel through the flames to pay for another man's lie – blamed Oskar for all that had happened afterwards, for Gröss-Rosen and for the frightful cliff at Mauthausen from which prisoners were thrown, and last of all for the death march with which the war would end.

The letter, radiant with just anger, shows most graphically that life on the list was a feasible matter, while life off it was unutterable. But it seems unjust to condemn Oskar for Goldberg's fiddling with names. The camp authorities would, in the chaos of those last days, sign any list Goldberg gave them as long as it did not exceed too noticeably the eleven hundred prisoners Oskar had been granted. Oskar himself could not police Goldberg by the hour. His own day was spent speaking to bureaucrats, his evenings on buttering them up.

He had, for example, to receive shipment authorisations for his Hilo machines and metal presses from old friends in the office of General Schindler, some of whom delayed with the paperwork, finding small problems which could finish the idea of Oskar's salvage of his eleven hundred.

One of these Inspectorate men had raised the problem that Oskar's armament machines had come to him by way of the procurement section of the Berlin Inspectorate, and under approval from its licensing section, specifically for use in Poland. Neither of these sections had been notified of the proposed move to Moravia. They would need to be. It could be a month before they gave their authorisation. Oskar did not have a month. Plaszów would be empty by the end of October, everyone would be in Gröss-Rosen or Auschwitz. In the end, the problem was cleared away by the accustomed gifts.

As well as such preoccupations, Oskar was concerned about the SS investigators who had arrested Amon. He half expected to be arrested or, what was the same thing, heavily interrogated about his relationship with the former commandant. He was wise to anticipate it, for one of the explanations Amon had offered for the eighty thousand Reichsmarks the SS had found among his belongings was, "Oskar Schindler gave it to me so I'd go easy on the Jews." Oskar therefore had to keep contact with friends of his at Pomorska Street who might be able to tell him the direction Bureau V's investigation of Amon was taking.

Finally, since his camp at Brinnlitz would be under the ultimate supervision of KL Gröss-Rosen, he was already dealing with the commandant of Gröss-Rosen, Sturmbann-führer Hassebroeck. Under Hassebroeck's management, a hundred thousand would die in the Gröss-Rosen system, but when Oskar conferred with him on the telephone and drove across into Lower Silesia to meet him, he seemed the least of all Oskar's worries. Schindler was used by now to meeting charming killers and noticed that Hassebroeck even seemed grateful to him for extending the Gröss-Rosen empire into Moravia. For Hassebroeck *did* think in terms of empire. He controlled one hundred and three subcamps. (Brinnlitz would make it a hundred and four and – with its more than a thousand inmates and its sophisticated indus-try – a major addition.) Seventy-eight of Hassebroeck's camps were located in Poland, sixteen in Czechoslovakia, ten in the Reich. It was much bigger cheese than anything Amon had managed.

With so much sweetening, cajoling and form-filling to occupy him in the week Plaszów was wound down, Oskar could not have found the time to monitor Goldberg, even if he had had the power. In any case, the account the prisoners give of the camp in its last day and night is one of milling and chaos, Goldberg – Lord of the Lists – at its centre, still holding out for offers.

Dr. Idek Schindel, for example, approached Goldberg to get himself and his two young brothers into Brinnlitz. Goldberg would not give an answer, and Schindel would not find out until the evening of October 15th, when the male prisoners were marshalled for the cattle wagons, that he and his brothers were not listed for the Schindler camp. They joined the line of Schindler people anyway. It is a scene from a cautionary engraving of Judgment Day – the ones without the right mark attempting to creep on to the line of the justified and being spotted by an angel of retribution, in this case Oberscharführer Müller, who came up to the doctor with his whip and slapped him, left cheek, right cheek, left and right again with the leather butt, while asking in an amused voice, "Why would you want to get on that line?"

Schindel would be made to stay on with the small party involved in liquidating Plaszów and would then travel with a wagonload of sick women to Auschwitz. The women would be placed in a hut in some corner of Birkenau and left to die. Yet most of them, overlooked by camp officials and exempt from the usual regimen of the place, would live. Schindel himself would be sent to Flossenburg and then – with his brothers – on a death march. He would survive by a layer of skin, but the youngest Schindel boy would be shot on the march on the second last day of the war. That is an image of the way the Schindler list, without any malice on Oskar's side, with adequate malice on Goldberg's, still tantalises survivors, and tantalised them in those desperate October days.

Everyone has a story about the list. Henry Rosner lined

up with the Schindler people, but an NCO spotted his violin and, knowing that Amon would require music should he be released from prison, sent Rosner back. Rosner then hid his violin under his coat, against his side, tucking the node of the sound-post under his armpit. He lined up again and was let through to the Schindler wagons.

Rosner had been one of those to whom Oskar had made promises, and so had always been on the list. It was the same with the Jereths, old Mr. Jereth of the box factory and Mrs. Chaja Jereth, described in the list inexactly and hopefully as a Metallarbeiterin, a metal worker. The Perlmans were also included as old Emalia hands, and the Levartovs as well. In fact, in spite of Goldberg, Oskar got for the great part the people he had asked for, though there may have been some unexpected names among them. A man as worldly as Oskar could not have been amazed to find Goldberg himself among the inhabitants of Brinnlitz.

But there were more welcome additions than that. Poldek Pfefferberg, for example, accidentally overlooked and rejected by Goldberg for lack of diamonds, let it be known that he wanted to buy vodka – he could pay in clothing or bread. When he acquired the bottle, he got permission to take it down to the orderly building in Jerozolimska where Schreiber was on duty. He gave Schreiber the bottle and pleaded with him to force Goldberg to include Mila and himself. Oskar Schindler, he said, would have written us down if he'd remembered. Poldek had no doubt that he was negotiating for his life. "Yes," Schreiber agreed, "the two of you must get on it." It is a human puzzle why men like Schreiber didn't in such moments ask themselves, If this man and his wife were worth saving, why weren't the rest?

The Pfefferbergs would find themselves on the Schindler list when the time came. And so, to their surprise, would Helen Hirsch and the younger sister whose survival had always been Helen's main concern.

The men of the Schindler list entrained at the Plaszów siding on a Sunday, October 15th. It would be another full week before the women left. Though the eight hundred were kept separate during the loading of the train and were pushed into goods wagons kept exclusively for Schindler personnel, they were coupled to a train containing thirteen hundred other prisoners all bound for Gröss-Rosen. It seems that some half expected to have to pass through Gröss-Rosen on their way to Schindler's camp, but many others believed that the journey would be direct. They were prepared to endure a slow trip to Moravia – they accepted that they would be made to spend time stationary at junctions and in sidings. They might wait half a day at a time for traffic with higher priority to pass. The first snow had fallen in the last week and it would be cold. Each prisoner had been issued only three hundred grammes of bread to last the journey, and each wagon had been provided with a single water bucket. For their natural functions, the travellers would have to use a corner of the floor, or if packed too tightly, urinate and defecate where they stood. But in the end, despite all their griefs, they would tumble out at a Schindler establishment. The three hundred women of the list would enter the wagons the following Sunday in the same sanguine state of mind.

Other prisoners noticed that Goldberg travelled as lightly as any of them. He must have had contacts outside Plaszów to hold his diamonds for him. Those who still hoped to influence him on behalf of an uncle, a brother, a sister, allowed him enough space to sit in comfort. The others squatted, their knees pushed into their chins. Dolek Horo-witz held the six-year-old Richard in his arms. Henry Rosner made a nest of clothing on the floor for nine-year-old Olek.

It took three days. Sometimes, at sidings, their breath froze on the walls. Air was always scarce, but when you got a mouthful it was icy and fetid. The train halted at last on the dusk of a comfortless autumn day. The doors were unlocked and passengers were expected to alight as quickly as businessmen with appointments to keep. SS guards ran among them shouting directions and blaming them for smelling. "Take everything off," the NCOs were roaring.

"Everything for disinfection." They piled their clothing and marched naked into the camp. By six in the evening they stood in naked lines on the Appellplatz of this bitter destination. Snow stood in the surrounding woods, the surface of the Appellplatz was iced. It was not a Schindler camp. It was Gröss-Rosen. Those who had paid Goldberg glared at him, threatening murder, while SS men in overcoats walked along the lines, lashing the behinds of those who openly shivered.

They kept the men on the Appellplatz all night, for there were no huts available. It was not until mid-morning the next day that they would be put under cover. In speaking of that seventeen hours of exposure, of ineffable cold dragging down on the heart, survivors do not mention any deaths. Perhaps life under the SS, or even at Emalia, had tempered them for a night like this one. Though it was a milder evening than those earlier in the week, it was still murderous enough. Some of them of course were too distracted by the possibility of Brinnlitz to drift away with cold.

Later, Oskar would meet prisoners who had survived an even longer exposure to cold and frostbite. Certainly elderly Mr. Garde, the father of Adam, lived through this night, as did Olek Rosner and Richard Horowitz.

Towards 11 a.m. the next morning, they were taken to the showers. Poldek Pfefferberg, crowded in with the others, considered the nozzle above his head with suspicion, wondering if gas or water would rain down. It would ultimately be water, but before it was turned on, Ukrainian barbers passed among them, shaving their heads, their pubic hair, their armpits. You stood straight, eyes front, while the Ukrainian worked at you with his unhoned razor. "It's too blunt," one of the prisoners complained. "No," said the Ukrainian, and slashed the prisoner's leg to show that the blade still held a cutting edge.

After the showers, they were issued with their striped prison clothes and crowded into barracks. The SS sat them in lines, like galley slaves, one man backed up between the

legs of the man behind him, his own opened legs giving
support to the man in front. By this method, the two
thousand men were crammed into three huts. German
Kapos, armed with truncheons, sat on chairs against the
wall and watched. Men were wedged so tightly – every inch
of the floor space covered – that to leave their rows for the
latrines, even if the Kapos permitted it, meant walking on
heads and shoulders and being cursed for it.

In the middle of one hut was a kitchen where turnip soup
was being made and bread baked. Poldek Pfefferberg, coming back from an unpopular visit to the latrines, found the
kitchen was under the supervision of a Polish army NCO he
had known at the beginning of the war. The NCO gave
Poldek some bread and permitted him to sleep by the
kitchen fire. The others however spent their nights wedged
in the human chain.

Each day they were stood at attention on the Appellplatz
and remained there in silence for ten hours. In the evenings,
however, after the issue of thin soup, they were allowed to
walk around the hut, to talk to each other. The blast of a
whistle at 9 p.m. was the signal for them to take up their
curious positions for the night.

On the second day, an SS officer came to the Appellplatz
looking for the clerk who had drawn up the Schindler list. It
had not been sent off from Plaszów, it seemed. Shivering in
his coarse prison clothes, Goldberg was led off to an office
and asked to type out the list from memory. By the end of
the day he had not finished the work and, back in the
barracks, was surrounded by a spate of final pleas for
inclusion. Here, in the bitter dusk, the list still enticed and
tormented, even if all it had done so far for those on it was to
bring them to Gröss-Rosen. Pemper and others, moving in
on Goldberg, began to pressure him to type Dr. Alexander
Biberstein's name on the sheet in the morning. Biberstein
was a respected physician, brother of the Marek Biberstein
who had once been that first optimistic president of the
Cracow Judenrat. Earlier in the week Goldberg had confused Biberstein, telling him that he *was* on the list. It was
not till the trucks were loaded that the doctor found out he

was not in the Schindler group. Even in such a place as Gröss-Rosen, Mietek Pemper was sure enough of a future to threaten Goldberg with postwar reprisals if Biberstein were not added.

Then, on the third day, the eight hundred men of Schindler's revised list were separated out from the mass on the Appellplatz, taken to the delousing station for yet another wash, permitted to sit a few hours, speculating and chatting like villagers in front of their huts, and marched out once more to the siding. With a small ration of bread, they climbed up into cattle wagons. None of the guards who loaded them admitted to knowing where they were going. They squatted on the floorboards in the galley-slave fashion. They kept fixed before their minds the map of Central Europe, and made continual judgments about the passage of the sun, gauging their direction by glimpses of light through the small wire ventilators near the roofs of the wagons. Olek Rosner was lifted to the ventilator in his wagon and said that he could see forests and mountains. The navigation experts claimed the train was travelling generally south-east. It all indicated a Czech destination, but no one wanted to say.

This journey of a hundred miles took nearly two days. When the doors opened, it was early morning on the second day. They were at the Zwittau depot. They dismounted and were marched through a town not yet awake, an untouched town, a town frozen in the late 1930s. Even the graffiti on the walls – KEEP THE JEWS OUT OF BRINNLITZ – looked strangely prewar to them. They had been living in a world where their breath was begrudged. It seemed almost endearingly naïve for the people of Zwittau to begrudge them a mere location.

Three or four miles out into the hills, following a rail siding, they came to the industrial hamlet of Brinnlitz, and saw ahead in thin morning light the solid bulk of the Hoffman annexe transformed into Arbeitslager (Labour Camp) Brinnlitz, with watchtowers, a wire fence encircling it, a guard barracks inside the wire, and beyond that the gate to the factory and the prisoners' dormitories.

As they marched in through the outer gate, Oskar appeared from the factory courtyard, wearing a Tyrolean hat.

33

This camp, like Emalia, had been equipped at Oskar's expense. According to the bureaucratic theory, all factory camps were built at the owner's cost. It was thought that any industrialist got sufficient incentive from the cheap prison labour to justify a small expenditure on wire and timber. In fact, Germany's darling industrialists, such as Krupp and Farben, built their camps with materials donated from SS enterprises and with a wealth of loaned labour. Oskar was no darling and got nothing. He had been able to lever some wagonloads of SS cement out of Bosch at what Bosch would have considered a discount black-market price. From the same source he got two to three tonnes of petrol and fuel oil for use in the production and delivery of his goods. He had also brought some of the camp fencing wire from Emalia.

But around the bare premises of the Hoffman annexe, he was required to provide high-tension fences, latrines, a guard barracks for a hundred SS personnel, attached SS offices, a sickroom and kitchens. Adding to the expense, Sturmbannführer Hassebroeck had already been down from Gröss-Rosen for an inspection and gone away with a supply of cognac and porcelainware, and what Oskar described as "tea by the kilogram." Hassebroeck had also taken away inspection fees and compulsory Winter Aid contributions levied by Section D, and no receipt had been given. "His car had a considerable capacity for these things," Oskar would later declare. He had no doubt in October 1944 that Hassebroeck was already doctoring the Brinnlitz books.

Inspectors sent directly by Oranienburg had also to be satisfied. As for the goods and equipment of Deutsche Email

Fabrik, much of it still in transit, two hundred and fifty freight cars would be needed before it had all arrived. It was astounding, said Oskar, how in a crumbling state, the Ostbahn officials could, if properly encouraged, find such a number of wagons.

And the unique aspect of all this, of Oskar himself, jaunty in his mountain hat as he emerged from that frosty courtyard, is that unlike Krupp and Farben and all the other entrepreneurs who kept Jewish slaves, he had no serious industrial intention at all. He had no hopes of production, there were no sales graphs in his head. Though four years ago he had come to Cracow to get rich, he now had no manufacturing ambitions left.

It was a hectic industrial situation there in Brinnlitz. Many of the presses, drills and lathes had not yet arrived, and new cement floors would have to be poured to take their weight. The annexe was still full of Hoffman's old machinery. Even so, for these eight hundred supposed armaments workers who had just moved through the gate, Oskar was paying seven and a half Reichsmarks each day per skilled worker, six Reichsmarks per labourer. This would amount to nearly $14,000 US each week for male labour; when the women arrived the bill would top $180,000. Oskar was therefore committing a grand business folly, but celebrated it in a Tyrolean hat.

Some of Oskar's attachments had shifted too. Mrs. Emilie Schindler had come from Zwittau to live with him in his downstairs apartment. Brinnlitz, unlike Cracow, was too close to home to permit her to excuse their separation. For a Catholic like her, it was now a matter either of formalising the rift or cohabiting again. There seemed to be at least a tolerance between them, a thorough mutual respect. At first sight she might have looked like a marital cipher, an abused wife who did not know how to get out. Some of the men wondered at first what she would think when she found the sort of factory Oskar kept, the sort of camp. They did not know yet that Emilie would make her own discreet contribution, that it would be based not on conjugal obedience but on her own ideas.

Ingrid had come with Oskar to Brinnlitz to work in the new plant, but she had taken lodgings outside the camp and was at AL Brinnlitz only for office hours. There was a definite cooling in that relationship, and she would never live with Oskar again. But she would show no animosity, and throughout the coming months Oskar would frequently visit her in the apartment. The racy Klonowska, that chic Polish patriot, stayed behind in Cracow, but again there was no apparent bitterness. Oskar would have contact with her during visits to Cracow and she would again help him when the SS caused trouble. The truth was that though his attachments to Klonowska and Ingrid were winding down in the most fortunate way, without any bitterness, it would have been a mistake to believe that he was turning conjugal.

Oskar told the men, that day of their arrival, that the women could be confidently expected. He believed they would arrive after scarcely more delay than there had been with the men. The women's journey was, however, to be different. After a short trip from Plaszów, their locomotive backed them, with some hundreds of other Plaszów women, through the arched gatehouse of Auschwitz-Birkenau. When the car doors opened, they found themselves in that immense concourse bisecting the camp, and practised SS men and women, speaking in neutral tones, began to grade them. The sorting of the people went on with a terrifying detachment. When a woman was slow in moving, she was hit with a truncheon, but the blow had no personal edge to it. It was all a matter of getting the numbers through. For the SS sections at the railside of Birkenau, it was all dutiful tedium. They had already heard every plea, every story. They knew every dodge anyone was ever likely to pull.

Under the floodlights, the women numbly asked each other what it meant. But even in their daze, their shoes already filling with the mud that was Birkenau's element, they were aware of SS women pointing to them, and telling uniformed doctors who showed any interest, "Schindlergruppe!" And the spruce young physicians would turn away and leave them alone for a time.

Feet sticking in the mud, they were marched to the delousing plant and stripped by order of hefty young SS women with truncheons in their hands. Mila Pfefferberg was troubled by rumours of the type most prisoners of the Reich had by now heard – that some shower nozzles gave out a killing gas. These, she was delighted to find, merely produced icy water.

After their wash, some of them expected to be tattooed. They knew as much as that about Auschwitz. The SS tattooed your arm if they wanted to use you. If they intended to feed you into the machine, however, they did not take the trouble. The same train that had brought the women of the list had brought also some two thousand others who, not being Schindlerfrauen, were put through the normal selections. Rebecca Bau, excluded from the Schindler list, had passed and been given a number, and Josef Bau's robust mother had also won a tattoo in that preposterous Birkenau lottery. Another Plaszów girl, fifteen years old, had looked at the tattoo she'd been given and been delighted that it had two fives, a three, and two sevens, numbers enshrined in the *Tashlag*, or Jewish calendar. With a tattoo, you could leave Birkenau and go to one of the Auschwitz labour camps, where there was at least a chance.

But the Schindler women, left untattooed, were told to dress again and taken to a windowless hut in the women's camp. There, in the centre of the floor, stood a sheet-iron stove housed in bricks. It was the only comfort. There were no bunks. The Schindlerfrauen were to sleep two or three to a thin straw pallet. The clay floor was damp and water would rise from it like a tide and drench the pallets, the ragged blankets. It was a death house at the heart of Birkenau. They lay there and dozed, frozen and uneasy in that enormous acreage of mud.

It confounded their imaginings of an intimate location, a village in Moravia. This was a great if unlasting city. On a given day more than a quarter of a million Poles, Gypsies and Jews kept brief residence here. There were thousands more over in Auschwitz I, the first but smaller camp where Commandant Rudolf Höss lived. And in the great industrial area named Auschwitz III, some tens of thousands worked while they could. The Schindler women had not been exactly informed of the statistics of Birkenau or of the Auschwitz duchy in itself. They could see, though, beyond birch trees at the western end of the enormous settlement, constant smoke rising from the four crematoria and the numerous pyres. They believed they were adrift now, and that the tide would take them down there. But not with all the capacity for making and believing rumours that characterises a life in prison would they have guessed how many people could be gassed there on a day the system worked well. According to Höss himself, the number was nine thousand.

The women were equally unaware that they had arrived in Auschwitz at a time when the progress of the war and certain secret negotiations between Himmler and the Swedish Count Folke Bernadotte were imposing a new direction on it. The secret of the extermination centres had not been kept, for the Russians had excavated the Lublin camp and found the furnaces containing human bones, and over five hundred drums of Zyklon B. News of this was published throughout the world, and Himmler, who wanted to be treated seriously as the obvious postwar successor to the Führer, was willing to convey promises to the Allies that the gassing of Jews would stop. He did not, however, issue an order on the matter until some time in October – the date is not certain. One copy went to General Oswald Pohl in Oranienburg, the other to Kaltenbrunner, Chief of Reich Security. Both of them ignored the directive, and so did Adolf Eichmann. Jews from Plaszów, Theresienstadt and Italy continued to be gassed up to the middle of November. The last selection for the gas chambers is believed to have been made on October 30.

For the first eight days of their stay in Auschwitz, the Schindler women were in imminent danger of death by gassing. And even after that, as the last victims of the chambers continued throughout November to file towards the western end of Birkenau, and as the ovens and pyres worked on their backlog of corpses, they would not be aware of any change in the essential nature of the camp. All their anxieties would anyway be well founded, for most of those left after the gassing ceased would be shot – as happened to all the crematoria workers – or allowed to die of disease.

In any case, the Schindler women went through frequent mass medical inspections in both October and November. Some of them had been separated out in the first days and sent off to the huts reserved for the terminally ill. The doctors of Auschwitz – Josef Mengele, Fritz Klein, Dr. Konig and Dr. Thilo – worked not only on the Birkenau platform but roamed the camp, turning up at rollcalls, invading the showers, asking with a smile, "How old are you, mother?" Mrs. Clara Sternberg found herself put aside in a hut for older women. Mrs. Lola Krumholz (sixty years old but, until then, passing for much younger) was also cut out of the Schindlergruppe and put in a barracks for the aged where she was meant to die at no expense to the administration. Mrs. Horowitz, believing that her thin daughter of eleven years, Niusia, could not survive a 'bath-house' inspection, hustled her into an empty sauna boiler. One of the SS girls who'd been appointed to the Schindler women, the pretty one, the blonde, saw her do it but did not give her away. She was a puncher, that one, short-tempered, and later she would ask Mrs. Horowitz for a bribe and get a brooch which Regina had somehow concealed till then. Regina handed it over philosophically. There was another, heavier, gentler one who made lesbian advances and may have required a more personal pay-off.

Sometimes at rollcall, one or more of the doctors would appear in front of the barracks. Seeing the medical gentlemen, women rubbed clay into their cheeks to induce a little bogus colour. At one such inspection, Regina found stones for her daughter, Niusia, to stand on, and silver-haired young Mengele came to her and asked her a soft-voiced question concerning her daughter's age and punched her for lying. Women felled like this at inspection were meant to be picked up by the guards while still semi-conscious, dragged to the electrified fence at the edge of the women's camp, and thrown on it. They had Regina halfway there when she revived and begged them not to fry her alive, to let her return to her line. They released her, and when she crept back into the ranks, there was her bird-boned speechless daughter still, frozen to the pile of stone.

These inspections could occur at any hour. The Schindler women were called out one night to stand in the mud while their barracks were searched. Mrs. Dresner, who had once been saved by a vanished OD boy, came out with her tall teenage daughter, Danka. They stood there in that eccentric mire of Auschwitz which, like the fabled mud of Flanders, would not freeze when everything else had frozen – the roads, the rooftops, the human traveller.

Both Danka and Mrs. Dresner had left Plaszów in the summer clothing which was all they had left. Danka wore a blouse, a light jacket, a maroon skirt. Since it had begun snowing earlier in the evening, Mrs. Dresner had suggested that Danka tear a strip off her blanket and wear it beneath the skirt. Now, in the course of the barrack inspection, the SS discovered the ripped blanket.

The officer who stood before the Schindler women called out the barracks Alteste – a Dutch woman whom, until yesterday, none of them had known – and said that she was to be shot, together with any other prisoner found with a blanket strip under her dress.

Mrs. Dresner began whispering to Danka. Take it off and I'll slip it back into the barracks. It was a credible idea. The barracks stood at ground level and no step led up to them. A woman in the rear line might slip backwards through the door. As Danka had obeyed her mother once before in the matter of the wall cavity in Dabrowski Street, Cracow, she obeyed her now, slipping from beneath her dress that strip of Europe's poorest blanket. While Mrs. Dresner was in the hut, the SS officer passed by and idly extracted a woman of Mrs. Dresner's age – it was probably Mrs. Sternberg – and had her taken away to some worse part of the camp, some place where there was no Moravian illusion.

·Perhaps the other women in line did not let themselves understand what this simple act of weeding out meant. It was in fact a statement that no reserved group of so-called 'industrial prisoners' was safe in Auschwitz. No cry of *Schindlerfrauen!* would keep them immune for long. There had been other groups of 'industrial prisoners' who had vanished in Auschwitz. General Pohl's Section W had sent last year some trainloads of skilled Jewish workers from Berlin. I. G. Farben had been in need of labour and was told by Section W to select its workers from these transports. In fact, Section W had suggested to Commandant Höss that the trains should be unloaded in the I. G. Farben works, not near the crematoria in Auschwitz-Birkenau. Of seventeen hundred and fifty male prisoners in the first train, one thousand were immediately gassed. Of four thousand in the next four trainloads, two and a half thousand went at once to the 'bathhouses'. If the Auschwitz administration would not stay its hand for I. G. Farben and Department W, it was not going to be finicky about the women of some obscure German potmaker.

In barracks like those the Schindler women lived in, it was like living outdoors. The windows had no glass and served only to put an edge on the blasts of cold air from Russia. Most of the girls had dysentery. Crippled with cramp, they limped in their clogs to the steel drum out in the mud. The woman who tended it did so for an extra bowl of soup. Mila Pfefferberg staggered out one evening, seized with dysentery, and the woman on duty, not a bad woman, a woman Mila had known as a girl, insisted that she could not use the drum but had to wait for the next girl out and then empty it with her help. Mila argued but could not shake the woman. Beneath the hungry stars this tending of the drum had become something like a profession, and there were rules. With the drum as pretext, the woman had come to believe that order, hygiene, sanity were possible.

The next girl out arrived at Mila's side, gasping and bent and desperate. But she too was young and, in peaceful days in Lódź, had known the woman at the can as a respectable married woman. So the two girls were obedient and lugged the thing three hundred yards through the mud. The girl who shared the burden asked Mila, "Where's Schindler now?"

Not everyone in the barracks asked that question, or asked in that fierce, ironic way. There was twenty-two-year-old Lusia, the widow whose first experience of Schindler beneficence had been hot water from the factory floor of Emalia. She kept saying, "You'll see, it will all come out. We'll end up somewhere warm with Schindler's soup in us." She did not know herself why she kept repeating such statements. In Emalia she had never been the type to make projections. She'd done her shift, drunk her soup, and slept. She had never predicted grandiose events. Sufficient to her day had always been the survival thereof. Now she was ill and there was no reason for her to be prophetic. The cold and hunger were wasting her, and she too bore the vast obsessions of her hunger. Yet she amazed herself by repeating Oskar's promises.

Later in their stay in Auschwitz, when they had been moved to a hut closer to the crematoria and, making their lines of five outside the barracks, did not know if they were to go to the showers or the chambers, Lusia continued pushing the glad message. Even so, the tide of the camp having washed them to this geographic limit of the earth, this pole, this pit, despair wasn't quite the fashion for the Schindlerfrauen. You would still find women huddled in recipe talk and dreams of pre-war kitchens.

In Brinnlitz when the men arrived there was only the shell. There were no bunks yet, straw was strewn in the dormitories upstairs. But it was warm, with steam heat from the boilers. There were no cooks that first day. Bags of turnips lay around what would be the cookhouse, and men devoured them raw. Later, soup was brewed and bread baked, and the engineer Finder began the allocating of jobs. But from the start, unless there were SS men looking on, it was all slow. It is mysterious how a body of prisoners could sense that the Herr Direktor was no longer a party to any war effort. The pace of work grew very canny in Brinnlitz. Since Oskar was detached from the question of production, slow work became the prisoners' vengeance, their declaration.

It was a heady thing to withhold your labour. Everywhere else in Europe, the slaves worked to the limit of their six hundred calories per day, hoping to impress some foreman and delay the transfer to the death camp. But here in Brinnlitz was the intoxicating freedom to use the shovel at half pace and still survive.

None of this unconscious policy-making was evident in the first days. There were still too many prisoners fretting for their women. Dolek Horowitz, for example, with a wife and daughter in Auschwitz. The Rosner brothers with their wives. Pfefferberg knew the shock which something as vast, as appalling as Auschwitz would have on Mila. Jacob Sternberg and his teenage son were concerned about Mrs. Clara Sternberg. Pfefferberg remembers the men clustering around Schindler on the factory floor and asking him again where the women were.

"I'm getting them out," Schindler rumbled. He did not go into explanations. He did not publicly surmise that the SS in Auschwitz might need to be bribed. He did not say that he had sent the list of women to Colonel Erich Lange, or that he and Lange both intended to get them to Brinnlitz according to the list. Nothing of that. Simply, "I'm getting them out."

The SS garrison who moved into Brinnlitz in those days gave Oskar some cause to hope. They were middle-aged reservists called up to allow younger SS men a place in the front line. There were not so many lunatics as at Plaszów, and Oskar would always keep them gentle with the specialities of his kitchen – plain food, but plenty. In a visit to their barracks, he made his usual speech about the unique skills of his prisoners, the importance of his manufacturing activities. Anti-tank shells, he said, and casings for a projectile

336

still on the secret list. He asked that there be no intrusion by the garrison into the factory itself, for that would disturb the workers.

He could see it in their eyes. It suited them, this quiet town. They could imagine themselves lasting out the cataclysm there. They did not want to rampage round the workshops like a Goeth or a Hujar. They didn't want the Herr Direktor to complain about them.

Their commanding officer, however, had not yet arrived. He was on his way from the labour camp at Budzyn which had, until the recent Russian advances, manufactured Heinkel bomber parts. He would be younger, sharper, more intrusive, Oskar knew. He might not readily take to being denied access to the camp.

Among all this pouring of cement floor, the knocking of holes in the roof so that the vast Hilos would fit, the softening of NCOs, amidst the private uneasiness of settling back to married life with Emilie, Oskar was arrested a third time.

The Gestapo turned up at lunchtime. Oskar was not in his office, in fact had driven to Brno on some business earlier in the morning. A lorry had just arrived at the camp from Cracow laden with some of the Herr Direktor's portable wealth – cigarettes, cases of vodka, cognac, champagne. Some would later claim that this was Goeth's property, that Oskar had agreed to bring it into Moravia in return for Goeth's backing of his Brinnlitz plans. Since Goeth had now been a prisoner for a month and had no more authority, the luxuries on the truck could just as well be considered Oskar's.

The men doing the unloading thought so and became nervous at the sight of the Gestapo men in the courtyard. They had mechanics' privileges and so were able to drive the truck to a stream down the hill, where they threw the drink into the water by the caseful. The two hundred thousand cigarettes on the lorry were hidden more retrievably under the cover of the large transformer in the power plant.

It is significant that there were so many cigarettes and so much drink in the truck, a sign that Oskar, always keen on trade goods, intended now to make his living on the black market.

They got the truck back to the garage as the siren for midday soup was blown. In past days the Herr Direktor had eaten with the prisoners, and the mechanics hoped that today he would do so again; they could then explain what had happened to such an expensive truckload.

He did in fact return from Brno soon after, but was stopped at the inner gate by one of the Gestapo men who stood there with his hand raised. The Gestapo men ordered him to leave his car at once.

"This is my factory," a prisoner heard Oskar growl back. "If you want to talk to me, you're welcome to jump in the car. Otherwise follow me to my office."

He drove into the courtyard, the two Gestapo men walking quickly on either side of the vehicle.

In his office, they asked him about his connections with Goeth, with Goeth's loot. I do have a few suitcases here, he told them. They belong to Herr Goeth. He asked me to keep them for him until his release from prison.

The Gestapo men asked to see the cases and Oskar took them through to the apartment. He made formal and cold introductions between Frau Schindler and the men from Bureau V. Then he brought out the suitcases and opened them. They were full of Amon's civilian clothing, and old uniforms from the days when Amon had been a slim SS NCO. When they'd been through them and found nothing, they made the arrest. Emilie became aggressive now. They had no right, she said, to take her husband, unless they could say what they were taking him for. The people in Berlin will not be happy about this, she said.

Oskar advised her to be silent. But you will have to call my friend Klonowska, he told her, and cancel my appointments.

Emilie knew what it meant. Klonowska would do her trick with the telephone again, calling Martin Plathe in Breslau, the General Schindler people, all the big guns. One of the Bureau V men took out handcuffs and put them on Oskar's wrists. They took him to their car, drove him to the station in Zwittau, and escorted him by train to Cracow.

The impression is that this arrest scared him more than the previous two. There are no stories of lovelorn, handsome SS colonels who shared a cell with him and drank his vodka. Oskar did later record some details, however. As the Bureau V men escorted him from the train across the grand neo-classical loggia of Cracow central station, a man named Huth approached them. He had been a civilian engineer in Plaszów. He had always been obsequious in front of Amon, but had a reputation for many secret kindnesses. It may have been an accidental meeting, but suggests that Huth may have been working with Klonowska. Huth insisted on shaking Oskar by his shackled hand. One of the Bureau V men objected. Do you really want to go round shaking hands with prisoners? he asked Huth. The engineer at once made a speech, a testimonial to Oskar. This was the Herr Direktor Schindler, a man greatly respected throughout Cracow, an important industrialist. I can never think of him as a prisoner, said Huth.

Whatever the significance of this meeting, Oskar was put in a car and taken across the familiar city to Pomorska Street again. They put him in a room like the one he had occupied during his first arrest, a room with a bed and a chair and a washbasin, but with bars on the window. He was not easy there, even though his manner was one of bearlike tranquillity. In 1942, when they had arrested him the day after his thirty-fourth birthday, the rumour that there were torture chambers in the Pomorska cells had been terrifying but indefinite. It wasn't indefinite any more. He knew that Bureau V would torture him if they wanted Amon badly enough.

That evening Herr Huth came as a visitor, bringing with him a dinner tray and a bottle of wine. Huth had spoken to Klonowska. Oskar himself would never clarify whether or not Klonowska had pre-arranged that 'chance' encounter.

Whichever it was, Huth now told him that Klonowska was rallying all his old friends.

The next day he was interrogated by a panel of twelve SS investigators, one of them a judge of the SS Court. Oskar denied that he had given any money to ensure that the commandant would, in the words of the transcript of Amon's evidence, "Go easy on the Jews." I may have given him the money as a loan, Oskar admitted at one stage. Why would you give him a loan? they wanted to know. I run an essential war industry, said Oskar, playing the old tune. I have a body of skilled labour. If it is disturbed, there is loss to me, to the Armaments Inspectorate, to the war effort. If I found that in the mass of prisoners in Plaszów there was a skilled metalworker of a category I needed, then of course I asked the Herr Commandant for him. I wanted him fast, I wanted him without red tape. My interest was production, its value to me, to the Armaments Inspectorate. In consideration of the Herr Commandant's help in these matters, I may have given him a loan.

This defence involved some disloyalty to his old dinner host, Amon. But Oskar would not have hesitated. His eyes gleaming with transparent frankness, his tone low, his emphasis discreet, Oskar – without saying it in words – let the investigators know that the money had been extorted. It didn't impress them. They locked him away again.

The interrogation went into a second, third and fourth day. No one did him harm, but they were steely. At last he had to deny any friendship with Amon at all. It was no great task: he loathed the man profoundly anyhow. "I am not a fairy," he growled at the gentlemen of Bureau V, falling back on rumours he'd heard about Goeth and his young orderlies.

Amon himself would never understand that Oskar despised him and was willing to help the case Bureau V had against him. Amon was always deluded about friendship. In sentimental moods, he believed that Mietek Pemper and Helen Hirsch were loving servants. The investigators probably would not have let him know that Oskar was in Pomorska and would have listened mutely to Amon urging them, "Call in my old friend Schindler. He'll vouch for me."

What helped Oskar most when he faced the investigators of Bureau V was that he had had few actual business connections with the man. Though he had sometimes given Amon advice about contacts, he had never had a share in any deal, never made a zloty out of Amon's sales of prison rations, of rings from the jewellery shop, of garments from the custom tailoring works or furniture from the upholstery section. It must also have helped him that his lies were disarming even to policemen, and that when he told the truth he was positively seductive. He never gave the impression that he was grateful for being believed. For example, when the gentlemen of Bureau V looked as if they might at least give standing room to the idea that the eighty thousand Reichsmarks was a 'loan', a sum extorted, Oskar asked them whether in the end the money would be returned to him, to Herr Direktor Schindler, the impeccable industrialist.

A third factor in Oskar's favour was that his credentials checked out. Colonel Erich Lange, when telephoned by Bureau V, stressed Schindler's importance to the conduct of the war. Sussmuth, called in Troppau, said that Oskar's plant was involved in the production of 'secret weapons'. It was not, as we will see, an untrue statement. But when said bluntly, it was misleading and carried a distorted weight. For the Führer had promised 'secret weapons'. The phrase itself was charismatic and extended its protection now to Oskar. Against a phrase like 'secret weapons', any confetti of protest from the burghers of Zwittau did not count.

But even to Oskar it did not seem that the imprisonment was going well. About the fourth day, one of his interrogators visited him, not to question him but to spit at him. The spittle streaked the left breast of his suit. The man ranted at him, calling him a Jew-lover, a fucker of Jewesses. It was a departure from the strange legalism of the interrogations. But Oskar wasn't sure that it was not planned, that it did not represent the true impetus behind his imprisonment.

After a week, Oskar sent a message — by way of Huth and

Klonowska – to Oberführer Scherner. Bureau V was putting such pressure on him, the message went, that he did not believe he could protect the former police chief much longer. Scherner left his counter-insurgency work (it was soon to kill him) and arrived in Oskar's cell within a day. It was a scandal what they were doing, said Scherner. What about Amon? Oskar asked, expecting Scherner to say that that was a scandal too. He deserves all he gets, said Scherner. It seemed that everyone was deserting Amon.

Don't worry, said Scherner before leaving, we intend to get you out.

On the morning of the eighth day, they let Oskar out on the street. Oskar did not delay his going nor – for once – did he demand transport. It was enough to be deposited on the cold pavement. He travelled across Cracow by tram and walked to his old factory premises in Zablocie. A few Polish caretakers were still there, and from the upstairs office he called Brinnlitz and told Emilie that he was free.

Moshe Bejski, a Brinnlitz draughtsman, remembers the confusion while Oskar was away, the rumours, all the questions about what it meant. But Stern and Maurice Finder, Adam Garde and others had consulted Emilie about food, about work arrangements, about the provision of bunks. They were the first to discover that Emilie was no mere passenger. She was not a happy woman, and her unhappiness was compounded by Bureau V's arrest of Oskar. It must have seemed cruel that the SS should intrude on this reunion before it had got properly started. But it was clear to Stern and the others that she was not there, keeping house in that little apartment on the ground floor, purely out of wifely duty. There was what you could call an ideological commitment too. A picture of Jesus with his heart exposed and in flames hung on a wall of the apartment. Stern had seen the same design in the houses of Polish Catholics. But there had been no ornament of that kind in either of Oskar's Cracow apartments. The Jesus of the exposed heart did not always reassure when you saw it in Polish kitchens. In Emilie's apartment, however, it hung like a promise, a personal one. Emilie's.

Early in November, her husband came back by train. He was unshaven and smelly from his imprisonment. He was amazed to find that the women were still in Auschwitz-Birkenau.

In planet Auschwitz, where the Schindler women moved as warily, as full of dread as any space travellers, the commandant was still Rudolf Höss. He was its founder, its builder, its presiding genius. Readers of William Styron's novel *Sophie's Choice* encountered him as the master of Sophie, a very different sort of master than Amon was to Helen Hirsch, a more detached, mannerly and sane man, yet still the unflagging priest of that cannibal province. Though in the 1920s he had murdered a Ruhr schoolteacher for informing on a German activist and had done time for the crime, he never murdered any Auschwitz prisoner by his own hand. He saw himself instead as a technician. As the champion of Zyklon B, the hydrogen cyanide pellets which gave off fumes when exposed to air, he had engaged in a long personal and scientific conflict with his rival, Kriminalkommissar Christian Wirth, who had jurisdiction over Belzec camp and who was the head of the carbon-monoxide school. There had been an awful day at Belzec, which the SS chemical officer Kurt Gerstein had witnessed, when Kommissar Wirth's method took three hours to finish a party of Jewish males packed into the chambers. That Höss had backed the apposite technology is partially attested to by the continuous growth of Auschwitz and the decline of Belzec.

By 1943, when Rudolf Höss left Auschwitz to do a stint as Deputy Chief of Section D in Oranienburg, the place was already something more than a camp. It was even more than a wonder of organisation. It was a phenomenon. The moral universe had not so much decayed here. It had been inverted, like some black hole, under the pressure of all the earth's malice – a place where tribes and histories were sucked in and vaporised, and language flew inside out. The underground chambers were named 'disinfection cellars', the above-ground chambers 'bathhouses'. Oberscharführer

Moll, whose task it was to order the insertion of the blue crystals into the roofs of the cellars, the walls of the bath-houses, customarily cried to his assistants, "All right, let's give them something to chew on."

Höss had returned to Auschwitz in May 1944 and presided over the entire camp at the time the Schindler women occupied a barracks in Birkenau, so close to the whimsical Oberscharführer Moll. According to the Schindler mythology, it was Höss himself with whom Oskar wrestled for his three hundred women. Certainly Oskar had telephone conversations and other commerce with Höss. But he also had to deal with Sturmbannführer Fritz Hartjenstein, commandant of Auschwitz II, that is, of Auschwitz-Birkenau, and with Untersturmführer Franz Hössler, the young man in charge – in that great city – of the women's suburb.

What is certain is that Oskar now sent a young woman with a suitcase full of drink, ham and diamonds, to make a deal with these functionaries. Some say that Oskar then followed up the girl's visit in person, taking with him an associate, an influential officer in the S.A. (the Sturmabteilung, or Storm Troops), Standartenführer Peltze, who, according to what Oskar later told his friends, was a British agent. Others claimed that Oskar stayed away from Auschwitz himself as a matter of strategy and went to Oranienburg instead, and to the Armaments Inspectorate in Berlin, to try to put pressure on Höss and his associates from that end.

The story as Stern would tell it years later in a public speech in Tel Aviv is as follows. After Oskar's release from prison, Stern approached Schindler and – "under the pressure of some of my comrades" – begged Oskar to do something decisive about the women ensnared in Auschwitz. During this conference, one of Oskar's secretaries came in – Stern does not say which one. Schindler considered the girl and pointed to one of his fingers, which sported a large diamond ring. He asked the girl whether she would like this rather hefty piece of jewellery. According to Stern, the girl became very excited. Stern quotes Oskar as saying, "Take the list of the women, pack a suitcase with the best food and drink you can find in my kitchen. Then go to Auschwitz. You know the commandant has a penchant for pretty women. If you bring it off, you'll get this diamond. And more still."

It is a scene, a speech worthy of one of those events in the Old Testament when for the good of the tribe a woman is offered to the invader. It is also a Central European scene, with its gross, coruscating diamonds and its proposed transaction of the flesh.

According to Stern, the secretary went. When she did not return within two days, Schindler himself – in the company of the obscure Peltze – went to settle the matter.

According to Schindler mythology, Oskar *did* send a girlfriend of his to sleep with the commandant – be that Höss, Hartjenstein or Hössler – and leave diamonds on the pillow. While some, like Stern, say it was 'one of his secretaries', others nominate a pretty blonde SS girl, ultimately a girlfriend of Oskar and part of the Brinnlitz garrison. But the blonde may have been still at Auschwitz, together with the Schindlerfrauen.

According to Emilie Schindler herself, the emissary was a girl of twenty-two or twenty-three years. She was a native of Zwittau, and her father was an old friend of the Schindler family. She had recently returned from occupied Russia, where she'd worked as a secretary in the German administration. She was a good friend of Emilie, and volunteered for the task. It is unlikely that Oskar would demand a sexual sacrifice of a friend of the family. Even though he was a brigand in these matters, that side of the story is certainly mythical. We do not know the extent of the girl's transactions with the officers of Auschwitz. We know only that she approached the dreadful kingdom and dealt courageously.

Oskar later said that in his own dealings with the rulers of megalopolis Auschwitz, he was offered the old bait. The women have been here some weeks now. They won't be worth much as labour any more. Why don't you forget these three hundred? We'll cut out another three hundred for you, from the endless herd. In 1942, an SS NCO at Prokocim

station had pushed the same idea at Oskar. Don't get stuck
on these particular names, Herr Direktor.

Now as at Prokocim, Oskar pursued his usual line. These
are irreplaceable skilled munitions workers. I have trained
them myself over a period of years. They represent skills I
cannot quickly replace. The names I know, that is, are the
names I know.

A moment, said his tempter. I see listed here a nine year
old, daughter of one Phila Rath. I see an eleven-year-old,
daughter of one Regina Horowitz. Are you telling me that a
nine year old and an eleven year old are skilled munitions
workers?

They polish the 45mm shells, said Oskar. They were
selected for their long fingers, which can reach the interior
of the shell in a way that is beyond most adults.

Such conversation backing up the girl who was a friend of
the family took place, conducted by Oskar either in person
or by telephone. Oskar would relay news of the negotiations
to the inner circle of male prisoners, and from them the
details were passed on to the men on the workshop floor.
Oskar's claim that he needed children so that the innards of
anti-tank shells could be buffed was outrageous nonsense.
But he had already used it more than once. An orphan
named Anita Lampel had been called to the Appellplatz in
Plaszów one night in 1943 to find Oskar arguing with a
middle-aged woman, the Alteste of the women's camp. The
Alteste was saying more or less what Höss/Hössler would
say later in Auschwitz. You can't tell me you need a fourteen
year old for Emalia. You cannot tell me that Commandant
Goeth has allowed you to put a fourteen year old on your
roster for Emalia. (The Alteste was worried of course that if
the list of prisoners for Emalia had been doctored, she
would be made to pay for it.) That night in 1943, Anita
Lampel had listened flabbergasted as Oskar, a man who had
never even seen her hands, claimed that he had chosen her
for the industrial value of her long fingers and that the Herr
Commandant had given his approval.

Anita Lampel was herself in Auschwitz now, but had
grown tall and no longer needed the long-fingered ploy. So it

was transferred to the benefit of the daughters of Mrs. Horowitz and Mrs. Rath.

Schindler's contact had been correct in saying that the women had lost nearly all their industrial value. At inspections, young women like Mila Pfefferberg, Helen Hirsch and her sister, could not prevent the cramps of dysentery from bowing and ageing them. Mrs. Dresner had lost all appetite, even for the ersatz soup. Danka could not force the mean warmth of it down her mother's throat. It meant that she would soon become a 'Mussulman'. The term was camp jargon, based on people's memory of newsreels of famine in Muslim countries, for a prisoner who had crossed the borderline that separated the ravenous living from the good-as-dead.

Clara Sternberg, in her early forties, was isolated from the main Schindler group in what could be described as a 'Mussulman' hut. Here, each morning, the dying women were lined up in front of the door and a selection was made. Sometimes it was Mengele leaning towards you. Of the five hundred women in this new group of Clara Sternberg's a hundred might be detailed off on a given morning. On another, fifty. You rouged yourself with Auschwitz clay, you kept a straight back if that could be managed. You choked where you stood rather than cough.

It was after such an inspection that Clara found herself with no reserves left for the waiting, the daily risk. She had a husband and a teenage son in Brinnlitz, but now they were remoter than the canals of the planet Mars. She could not imagine Brinnlitz, or them in it. She staggered through the women's camp, looking for the electric wires. When she had first arrived, they'd seemed to be everywhere. Now that they were needed, she could not find them. Each turn took her into another quagmire street, and frustrated her with a view of identically miserable huts. When she saw an acquaintance from Plaszów, a Cracow woman like herself, Clara propped in front of her. "Where's the electric fence?" Clara asked the woman. In her disarrayed mind, it was a reasonable question to ask, and Clara had no doubt that the friend, if she had any sisterly feeling, would point the exact way to the wires. The answer the woman gave Clara was just as crazed, but it was one that had a fixed point of view, a balance, a perversely sane core.

"Don't kill yourself on the fence, Clara," the woman urged her. "If you do that, you'll never know what happened to you."

It has always been the most powerful of answers to give to the intending suicide. Kill yourself and you'll never find out how the plot ends. Clara did not have any vivid interest in the plot. But somehow the answer was adequate. She turned around. When she got back to her barracks, she felt more troubled than when she'd set out to look for the fence. But her Cracow friend had – by her reply – somehow cut her off from suicide as an option.

Something awful had happened at Brinnlitz. Oskar, the Moravian traveller, was away. He was trading in kitchenware and diamonds, liquor and cigars, all over the province. Some of it was crucial business. Biberstein speaks of the drugs and medical instruments that came into the Krankenstube at Brinnlitz. None of it was standard issue. Oskar must have traded for medicines at the depots of the Wehrmacht, or perhaps in the pharmacy of one of the big hospitals in Brno.

Whatever the cause of his absence, he was away when an inspector from Gröss-Rosen arrived and walked through the workshop with Untersturmführer Josef Liepold, the new commandant, who was always happy for a chance to intrude inside the factory. The inspector's orders, originating from Oranienburg, were that subcamps should be scoured for children to be used in Dr. Mengele's experiments at Auschwitz. Olek Rosner and his small cousin Richard Horowitz, who'd believed they had no need of a hiding place here, were spotted racing round the annexe, chasing each other upstairs, playing among the disused spinning machines. So also was the son of Dr. Leon Gross, who had detected and nursed Amon's recently developed diabetes, who had helped Dr. Blancke with the Health Aktion, and who had other crimes still to answer for. The inspector remarked to Untersturmführer Liepold that these were clearly not essential munitions workers. Liepold – short, dark, not as crazy as Amon – was still a convinced SS officer and did not bother to argue for the brats.

Further on in the inspection Roman Ginter's nine year old was discovered. Ginter had known Oskar from the time the ghetto was founded and had supplied the metalworks at Plaszów with scrap from Deutsche Email Fabrik. But Untersturmführer Liepold and the inspector did not recognise any special relationships. The Ginter boy was sent under escort to the gate with the other children. Frances Spira's boy, ten and a half years old, but tall and on the books as fourteen, was working on top of a long ladder that day, polishing the high windows. He survived the raid.

The orders required the rounding up of the children's parents as well, possibly because this step would obviate the risk of parents beginning a demented rebellion on the subcamp premises. Therefore, Rosner the violinist, Horowitz and Ginter were arrested. Leon Gross rushed down from the clinic to negotiate with the SS. He was flushed. The effort was to show this inspector from Gröss-Rosen that he was dealing with a really responsible sort of prisoner, a friend of the system. The effort counted for nothing. An SS Unterscharführer armed with an automatic weapon was given the mission of escorting them to Auschwitz.

The party of fathers and sons travelled from Zwittau as far as Katowice in Upper Silesia by ordinary passenger train. Henry Rosner expected other passengers to be hostile. Instead, one woman walked down the aisle looking defiant and gave Olek and the others a heel of bread and an apple, all the while staring the sergeant in the face, daring him to react. The Unterscharführer was polite to her, however, and nodded formally. Later, when the train stopped at Usti, he left the prisoners under the guard of his assistant and went to the station cafeteria, bringing back biscuits and coffee paid for from his own pocket. He and Rosner and Horowitz got talking. (Regina, Horowitz's wife, was Rosner's sister, so there were grounds for friendship there.) The more the Unterscharführer chatted, the less he seemed to belong to that same police force as Amon, Hujar, John, and all those others. I'm taking you to Auschwitz, he said, and then I have to collect some women and bring them back to Brinnlitz.

So, ironically, the first Brinnlitz men to discover that the women might be let out of Auschwitz were Rosner and Horowitz, themselves on their way there.

Rosner and Horowitz were ecstatic. They told their sons, This good gentlemen is bringing your mother back to Brinnlitz. Rosner asked the Unterscharführer if he would give a letter to Manci and Horowitz pleaded to be able to write to Regina. The two letters were written on pieces of paper the Unterscharführer gave them, the same stuff the man used to write to his own wife. In his letter, Rosner made arrangements with Manci to meet at an address in Podgórze if they both survived.

When Rosner and Horowitz had finished writing, the SS man put the letters in his jacket. Where have you been these past years? Rosner wondered. Did you begin as a fire-eater? Did you applaud when the gods on the rostrum screamed, "The Jews are our misfortune!"

Later in the journey, Olek turned his head in against Henry's arm and began to weep. He would not at first tell Rosner what was wrong. When he did speak at last, it was to say that he was sorry to drag his father off to Auschwitz. "To die just because of me," he said. Henry could have tried to soothe him by telling lies, but it wouldn't have worked. All the children knew about the gas. They grew petulant when you tried to deceive them.

The Unterscharführer leaned over. Surely he had not heard, but there were tears in his eyes. Olek seemed astounded by them – the way another child might be astounded by a cycling circus animal. He stared at the man. What was startling was that they looked like fraternal tears, the tears of a fellow prisoner. "I know what will happen," said the Unterscharführer. "We've lost the war. You'll get the tattoo. You'll live through."

Henry got the impression that the man was making promises not to the child but to himself, arming himself with an assurance which – in five years' time perhaps, when he remembered this train journey – he could use to soothe himself.

On the afternoon of her attempt to find the wires, Clara Sternberg heard the calling of names and the sound of women's laughter from the direction of the Schindlerfrauen barracks. She crawled from her own damp hut and saw the Schindler women lined up beyond an inner fence of the women's camp. Some of them were dressed only in blouses and long drawers. Skeleton women, without a chance. But they were chattering like girls. Even the blonde SS girl seemed delighted, for she too would be liberated from Auschwitz if they were. Schindlergruppe, she called, you're going to the sauna and then to the trains. She seemed to have a sense of the uniqueness of the event.

Doomed women from the barracks all around looked blankly out through the wire at the celebratory girls. They compelled you to watch, those list women, because they were so suddenly out of balance with the rest of the city. It meant nothing of course. It was an eccentric event, it had no bearing on the majority life, it did not reverse the process nor lighten the smoky air.

But for Clara Sternberg, the sight was intolerable. As it was also for old Mrs. Krumholz, now half dead in the hut assigned to the older women. Mrs. Krumholz began to argue with the Dutch Kapo at the door of her barracks. I'm going out to join them, she said. The Dutch Kapo put up a mist of arguments. In the end, she said, You're better off here. If you go, you'll die in the cattle wagons. Besides that, I'll have to explain why you aren't here. You can tell them, said Mrs. Krumholz, that it's because I'm on the Schindler list. It's all fixed. The books will balance. There's no question about it.

They argued for five minutes and in the process talked of their families, finding out about each other's origins, perhaps looking for a vulnerable point outside the strict logic of the dispute. It turned out the Dutch woman's name was also Krumholz. The two of them began discussing the whereabouts of their families. My husband is in Sachsenhausen, I think, said the Dutch Mrs. Krumholz. The Cracow Mrs. Krumholz said, My husband and grown son have gone somewhere. I think Mauthausen. I'm meant to be in the Schindler camp in Moravia. Those women beyond the fence, that's where they're going. They're not going anywhere, said the Dutch Mrs. Krumholz. Believe me. No one goes anywhere, except in one direction. The Cracow Mrs. Krumholz said, "They think they're going somewhere. *Please!*" For even if the Schindlerfrauen were deluded, Mrs. Krumholz from Cracow wanted to share the delusion. The Dutch Kapo understood this and at last opened the door of the barracks, for whatever it was worth.

A fence now stood between Mrs. Krumholz, Mrs. Sternberg, and the rest of the Schindler women. It was not an electrified perimeter fence. It was nonetheless built, according to the rulings of Section D, of at least eighteen strands of wire. The strands ran closest together at the top of the fence. Farther down they were stretched in twos, in parallel strands about six inches apart. But between each set of parallels, there was a gap of less than a foot. That day, according to the testimony of witnesses and of the women themselves, both Mrs. Krumholz and Mrs. Sternberg somehow tore their way through the fence to rejoin the Schindler women in whatever daydream of rescue they were enjoying. Dragging themselves through the perhaps nine inch gap, stretching the wire, ripping their clothes and tearing their flesh on the barbs, they put themselves back in the Schindler squad. No one stopped them because no one believed it possible. To the other women of Auschwitz, it was in any case an irrelevant example. For any other escapee, the breaching of that fence brought you only to another, and then another, and so to the outer voltage of the place. Whereas for Sternberg and Krumholz, this fence was the only one. The clothing they'd brought with them from the ghetto and kept in repair in muddy Plaszów hung now on the wire. Naked and streaked with blood, they ran in among the Schindler women.

Mrs. Rachela Korn, condemned to a hospital hut at the age of forty-four, had also been dragged out of the window of the place by her daughter, who now held her upright in the Schindler column. For her as for the other two, it was a birthday. Everyone in the line seemed to be congratulating them.

In the washhouse, the Schindler women were barbered. Latvian girls sheared a lice promenade down the length of their skulls and shaved their ampits and pubes. After their shower they were marched naked to a quartermaster's hut, where the clothes of the dead were issued to them. When they saw themselves shaven and in oddments of clothing, they broke into laughter – the hilarity of the very young. The sight of little Mila Pfefferberg, down to seventy pounds, occupying garments cut for the big-boned and well-fleshed had them reeling with hilarity. Half dead and dressed in their paint-coded rags, they pranced, modelled, mimed, and giggled like schoolgirls.

"What's Schindler going to do with all the old women?" Clara Sternberg heard an SS girl ask a colleague.

"It's no one's business," the colleague said. "Let him open an old people's home if he wants."

No matter what your expectations, it was always a horrifying thing to go into the trains. Even in cold weather, there was a sense of suffocation. It was compounded by blackness. On entering a wagon, the children always pushed themselves towards any sliver of light. That morning, Niusia Horowitz did that, positioning herself against the far wall at a place where a slat had come loose. When she looked out through the gap, she could see across the railway lines to the wires of the men's camp. She noticed that there were a straggle of children over there, staring at the train and waving. There seemed to be a very personal insistence to their movements. She thought it strange that one of them resembled her six-year-old brother, who was safe with Schindler. And the boy at his side was a double for their cousin Olek Rosner. Then, of course, she understood. It *was* Richard. It *was* Olek.

She turned and found her mother and pulled at her uniform. Then Regina looked, went through the same cruel cycle of identification and began to wail. The door of the car had been shut by now, they were all packed close in near darkness, and every gesture, every scent of hope or panic, was contagious. All the others took up the wailing too. Manci Rosner, standing near her sister-in-law, eased her away from the opening, looked, saw her son waving, and began keening too.

The door slid open again and a burly NCO asked in a flat voice who was making all the noise. No one else had any motive to come forward, but Manci and Regina struggled through the crush to present themselves to the man. It's my child over there, they both said. My boy, said Manci. I want to show him that I'm still alive.

He ordered them down on to the concourse. When they stood before him, they began to wonder what his purpose was. "Your name?" he asked Regina.

She told him and saw him reach behind his back and fumble under his leather belt. She expected to see his hand appear grasping a pistol. What it held however was a letter for her from her husband. He had a similar letter from Henry Rosner, too. He gave a brief summary of the journey he'd made from Brinnlitz with their husbands. Manci suggested he might be willing to let them get down under the car, between the lines, as if to urinate. It was sometimes permitted if trains were long delayed. He consented.

As soon as Manci was down there under the suspension, she let out the piercing Rosner whistle she had used on the Appellplatz of Plaszów to guide Henry and Olek to her. Olek heard it and began waving. He took Richard's head and pointed it towards their mothers, peering out between the wheels of the train.

After a spate of waving, Olek held his arm aloft and pulled back his sleeve to show a tattoo like a varicose scrawl along the flesh of his upper arm. And of course the women waved, nodded, applauded, young Richard also holding up his tattooed arm for applause. Look, the children were saying by their rolled-up sleeves. We have permanence.

But between the wheels, the women were in a frenzy. What's happened to them? they asked each other. In God's name, what are they doing here? They understood that there would be a fuller explanation in the letters. They tore them open and read them, then put them away and went on waving.

Next, Olek opened his hand and showed that he had a few pellet-like potatoes in his palm. "There," he called, and Manci could hear him distinctly. "You don't have to worry about me being hungry."

"Where's your father?" Manci shouted.

"At work," said Olek. "He'll be back from work soon. I'm saving these potatoes for him."

Oh God, Manci murmured to her sister-in-law. So much for the food in his hand. Young Richard told it straighter. "Mamushka, Mamushka, Mamushka," he yelled, "I'm so hungry."

But he too held up a few potatoes. He was keeping them for Dolek, he said. Dolek and Rosner the violinist were working at the rock quarry.

Henry Rosner arrived first. He too stood at the wire, his left arm bared and raised. "The tattoo," he called in triumph. She could see, though, that he was shivering, sweating and cold at the same time. It had not been a soft life in Plaszów, but he'd been allowed to sleep off in the paint shop the hours of work he'd put in playing Lehar at the villa. Here, in the band which sometimes accompanied the lines marching to the bathhouses, they didn't play Rosner's sort of music.

When Dolek turned up, he was led to the wire by Richard. He could see the pretty, hollow-faced women peering out from the undercarriage. What he and Henry dreaded most was that the women would offer to stay. They could not be with their sons in the male camp. They were in the most hopeful situation in Auschwitz there, hunkered under a train that was certain to move before the day was out. The idea of a clan reunion here was illusory, but the fear of the men at the Birkenau wire was that the women would opt to die for it. Therefore Dolek and Henry talked with a false cheerfulness — like peacetime fathers who'd decided to take the kids up to the Baltic that summer so that the girls could go to Carlsbad on their own. "Look after Niusia," Dolek kept calling, reminding his wife that they had another child, that she was in the car above Regina's head.

At last some merciful siren sounded in the men's camp. The men and boys now had to leave the wire. Manci and Regina climbed limply back into the train and the door was locked. They were still. Nothing could surprise them any more.

The train rolled out in the afternoon. There were the usual speculations. Mila Pfefferberg believed that if the destination was not Schindler's place, half the women crammed in the cars would not live another week. She herself considered she had only days left. The girl Lusia had scarlet fever. Mrs. Dresner, tended by Danka but leached by dysentery, seemed to be dying.

But in Niusia Horowitz's car, the women saw mountains and pine trees through the broken slat. Some of them had come to these mountains in their childhood, and to see the distinctive hills even from the floor of these putrid wagons gave them an unwarranted sense of holiday. They shook the girls who sat in the muck staring. "Nearly there," they promised. But where? Another false arrival would finish them all.

At cold dawn on the second day, they were ordered out. The locomotive could be heard hissing somewhere in the mist. Beards of dirty ice hung from the understructures of the train, and the air pierced them. But it was not the heavy, acrid air of Auschwitz. It was a rustic siding, somewhere. They marched, their feet numb in clogs, and everybody coughing. Soon they saw ahead of them a large gate and, behind it, a great bulk of masonry from which chimneys rose. In their black, two-dimensional contour, they looked like brothers to the ones left behind in Auschwitz. A party of SS men waited by the gate, clapping their hands against the cold. The group at the gate, the chimneys – it all looked part of that sickening continuum. A girl beside Mila Pfefferberg began to weep. "They've brought us all this way to send us up the chimney anyhow."

"No," said Mila, "they wouldn't waste their time. They could have done all that at Auschwitz."

Her optimism was like that of the girl Lusia – she couldn't tell where it came from.

As they got closer to the gate, they became aware that Herr Schindler was standing in the midst of the SS men. They could tell at first by his memorable height and bulk. Then they could see his features under the Tyrolean hat which he'd been wearing so much lately to celebrate his return to his home mountains. A short, dark SS officer stood beside him. It was the commandant of Brinnlitz, Untersturmführer Liepold. Oskar had already discovered – the women would discover it soon – that Liepold, unlike his middle-aged garrison, had not yet lost faith in that proposition called The Final Solution. Yet though he was the respected deputy of Sturmbannführer Hassebroeck and the supposed incarnation of authority in this place, it was Oskar who stepped forward as the lines of women stopped. They stared at him. A phenomenon in the mist. Only some of them smiled. Mila Pfefferberg, like others of the girls in the column that morning, remembers that it was an instant of the most basic and devout gratitude, and quite unutterable. Years later, one woman from those lines, remembering the morning, would face a German television crew and attempt to explain it. "He was our father, he was our mother, he was our only faith. He never let us down."

Then Oskar began to talk. It was another of his outrageous speeches, full of dazzling promises. "We knew you were coming," he said. "They called us from Zwittau. When you go inside the building, you'll find soup and bread waiting for you." And then, lightly and with pontifical assurance, he said it. "You have nothing more to worry about. You're with me now."

It was the sort of address against which the Untersturmführer was powerless. Though Liepold was angry at it, Oskar was oblivious. As the Herr Direktor moved with the prisoners into the courtyard, there was nothing Liepold could do to break into that certainty.

The men knew. They were on the balcony of their dormitory looking down. Sternberg and his son searching for Mrs. Clara Sternberg, Feigenbaum senior and young Lutek looking out for Nocha Feigenbaum and her delicate daughter. Juda Dresner and his son Janek, old Mr. Jereth, Rabbi Levartov, Ginter, Garde, even Marcel Goldberg, all strained for a sight of their women. Mundek Korn looked not only for his mother and sister but for Lusia the optimist, in whom he'd developed an interest. Bau now fell into a melancholy from which he might never fully emerge. He knew definitively, for the first time, that his mother and wife would not arrive in Brinnlitz. But Wulkan the jeweller, seeing Chaja Wulkan below him in the factory courtyard, knew with astonishment now that there *were* individuals who intervened and offered astounding rescue.

Pfefferberg waved at Mila a package he had kept for her arrival – a hank of wool stolen from one of the cases Hoffman had left behind, and a steel needle he had made in the welding department. Frances Spira's ten-year-old son also looked down from the balcony. To stop himself from calling out, he had jammed his fist into his mouth, since there were so many SS men in the yard.

The women staggered across the cobbles in their tattered Auschwitz clothes. Their heads were cropped. Some of them were too ill, too hollowed out, to be easily recognised. Yet it was an astounding assembly. It would not surprise anyone to find out later that no such reunion occurred anywhere else in stricken Europe. That there had never been, and would not be, any other Auschwitz rescue like this one.

The women were then led up into their separate dormitory. There was straw on the floor – no bunks yet. From a large DEF tureen, an SS girl served them the soup Oskar had spoken about at the gate. It was so rich. There were lumps of nutrient in it. In its fragrance, it was the outward sign of the value of the other imponderable promises. "You have nothing more to worry about."

But they could not touch their men. The women's dormitory was for the moment an isolation ward. Even Oskar, on the advice of his medical staff, was concerned about what they might have brought with them from Auschwitz.

There were however three points at which their isolation could be breached. One was the loose brick above young

Moshe Bejski's bunk. Men would spend the coming nights kneeling on Bejski's mattress, passing messages through the wall. Likewise, on the factory floor there was a small fanlight which gave into the women's latrines. Pfefferberg stacked crates there, making a cubicle where a man could sit and call messages. Finally, for early morning and late evening, there was a crowded wire barrier between the men's balcony and the women's. The Jereths met there, old Mr. Jereth from whose wood the first Emalia barracks had been built; his wife who had needed a refuge from the Aktions in the ghetto. Prisoners used to joke about the exchanges between Mr. and Mrs. Jereth. "Have your bowels moved today, dear?" Mr. Jereth would sombrely ask his wife, fresh from the dysentery-ridden huts of Birkenau.

On principle, no one wanted to be put in the clinic. In Plaszów it had been a dangerous place where you were made to take Dr. Blancke's terminal benzine treatment. Even here in Brinnlitz, there was always a risk of sudden inspections, of the type that had already taken the boy children. According to the memos of Oranienburg, a labour camp clinic should not have any patients with serious illnesses. It was not meant to be a mercy home. It was there to offer industrial first aid. But whether they wanted it or not, the clinic at Brinnlitz was full of women. The teenage Janka Feigenbaum was put in there, she who had bone cancer and would die in any case, even in the best of places. She had at least come to the best of places left to her. Mrs. Dresner was brought in, as were dozens of others who could not eat or keep food down. Two girls as well as Lusia the optimist were suffering from scarlet fever. They could not be kept in the clinic and were put in beds in the cellar, down among the warmth of the boilers. Even in the haze of her cold fever, Lusia was aware of the prodigious warmth of that cellar ward.

Emilie worked as quiet as a nun in the clinic. Those who were well in Brinnlitz, the men who were disassembling the Hoffman machines and putting them in storehouses down the road, scarcely noticed her. One of them later said that she was just a quiet and submissive wife. The healthy in Brinnlitz stayed hostage to Oskar's flamboyance, to this great Brinnlitz trick. Even the women who were still standing had their attention taken by the grand, magical, omniprovident Oskar.

Manci Rosner, for example. A little later in Brinnlitz's history, Oskar would come to the lathes where she worked the nightshift and hand her Henry's violin. Somehow, during a journey to see Hassebroeck at Gröss-Rosen, he'd got the time to go into the warehouse there and find the fiddle. It had cost him a hundred Reichsmarks to redeem it. As he handed it to her, he smiled in a way that seemed to promise her the ultimate return of the violinist to go with the violin. "Same instrument," he murmured. "But – for the moment – different tune."

It was hard for Manci, faced by hefty Oskar and the miraculous violin, to see behind the Herr Direktor to the quiet wife. But to the dying, Emilie was more visible. She fed them semolina, which she got God knows where, prepared in her own kitchen, and carried up to the Krankenstube. Dr. Alexander Biberstein believed that Mrs. Dresner was finished. Emilie spooned the semolina into her for seven days in a row, and the dysentery abated. Mrs. Dresner's case seemed to verify Mila Pfefferberg's claim that if Oskar had failed to rescue them from Birkenau, most of them would not have lived another week.

Emilie tended nineteen-year-old Janka Feigenbaum also. Lutek, Janka's brother, at work on the factory floor, sometimes noticed Emilie moving out of her ground-floor apartment with a canister of soup boiled up in her own kitchen for the dying Janka. "She was dominated by Oskar," Lutek would say. "As we all were. Yet she was her own woman."

When Lutek's glasses were broken, she arranged for them to be repaired. The prescription lay in some doctor's surgery in Cracow, had lain there since before the ghetto days. Emilie arranged for someone who was visiting Cracow to fetch the prescription and bring back the glasses made up. Young Lutek considered this more than an average kindness especially in a system that positively desired his myopia, that aimed to take the spectacles off all the Jews of Europe. There are many stories about Oskar providing new glasses for various prisoners. One wonders if some of Emilie's kindnesses in this matter may not have been absorbed into the Oskar legend, the way the deeds of minor heroes have been subsumed by the figure of Arthur or Robin Hood.

34

The doctors in the Krankenstube were Hilfstein, Handler, Lewkowicz and Biberstein. They were all concerned about the likelihood of a typhus outbreak. For typhus was not only a hazard to health. It was, by edict, a cause to close down Brinnlitz, to put the infested back in cattle wagons and ship them to die in the *Achtung Typhus!* barracks of Birkenau. On one of Oskar's morning visits to the clinic, about a week after the women arrived, Biberstein told him that there were two more possible cases among the women. Headache, fever, malaise, general pains throughout the whole body, all that had begun. Biberstein expected the characteristic typhoid rash to appear within a few days. These two would need to be isolated in a special room.

Biberstein did not have to give Oskar too much home instruction in the facts of typhus. Typhus was carried by louse bite. The prisoners were infested by uncontrollable populations of lice. The disease took perhaps two weeks to incubate. It might be incubating now in a dozen, a hundred prisoners. Even with the new bunks installed, people still lay too close. Lovers passed the virulent lice to each other when they joined, fast and secret, in some hidden corner of the factory. The typhus lice were wildly migratory. It seemed now that *their* energy would put paid to Oskar's.

So that when Oskar ordered a delousing unit – showers, a laundry to boil clothes, a disinfection plant – to be built upstairs, it was no idle administrative order. The unit was to run on hot steam piped up from the cellars. The welders were to work double shifts on the project. They did it with a will, for willingness characterised the secret industries of Brinnlitz. Official industry might be symbolised by the Hilo machines rising from the new-poured workshop floor. It was in the prisoners' interests and in Oskar's, as Moshe Bejski later observed, that these machines be properly erected, since it gave the camp a convincing front. But the uncertified industries of Brinnlitz were the ones that counted. The women knitted clothing with wool looted from Hoffman's left-behind bags. They paused and began to look industrial only when an SS officer or NCO passed through the factory on his way to the Herr Direktor's office, or when Fuchs and Schoenbrun, the inept civilian engineers ("Not up to the weight of *our* engineers," a prisoner would later say) came out of their offices.

The Brinnlitz Oskar was still the Oskar old Emalia hands remembered. A *bon vivant*, a man of wild habits. Mandel and Pfefferberg, at the end of their shift and overheated from working on the pipe fittings for the steam, visited a water tank high up near the workshop ceiling. Ladders and a catwalk took them to it. The water was warm up there, and once you climbed in, you could not be seen from the floor. Dragging themselves up, the two welders were amazed to find the tub already taken. Oskar floated, naked and enormous. A blonde SS girl, the one Regina Horowitz had bribed with a brooch, her naked breasts buoyant at the surface, shared the water with him. Oskar became aware of them, looked up at them frankly. To him sexual shame was a concept, something like existentialism, very worthy but hard to grasp. Stripped, the welders noticed, the girl was delicious.

They apologised and left, shaking their heads, expelling their breath, laughing like schoolboys. Above their heads, Oskar dallied like Zeus.

When the epidemic did not develop, Biberstein thanked the Brinnlitz delousing unit. When the dysentery faded, he thanked the food. In a testimony in the archives of Yad Vashem in Jerusalem, Biberstein declares that at the beginning of the camp, the daily ration was in excess of two thousand calories. In all the miserable winter-bound continent, only the Jews of Brinnlitz were fed this living meal.

Among the millions, only the soup of the Schindler thousand had body.

There was porridge too. Down the road from the camp, by the stream into which Oskar's mechanics had recently dumped black-market drink, stood a mill. Armed with a work pass, a prisoner could stroll down there on an errand from one or other department of Deutsche Email Fabrik. Mundek Korn remembers coming back to the camp loaded with food. At the mill you simply tied your trousers at the ankles and loosened your belt. Your friend then shovelled your trousers full of oatmeal. You belted up again and returned to the camp – a grand repository, priceless as you walked, a little bandylegged, past the sentries into the annexe. Inside, people loosened your ankles and let the oatmeal run out into pots.

In the draughting department, young Moshe Bejski and Josef Bau had already begun forging prison passes that permitted people to go down to the mill. Oskar wandered in one day and showed Bejski documents stamped with the seal of the rationing authority of the Government General. Oskar's best contracts for black-market food were still in the Cracow area. He could arrange shipments by telephone. But at the Moravian border, you had to show clearance documents from the Food and Agriculture Department of the Government General. Oskar pointed to the stamp on the papers in his hands. Could you make a stamp like that? he asked Bejski.

Bejski was a craftsman. He could work on little sleep. Now he turned out for Oskar the first of many official stamps he would craft. His tools were razorblades and various small cutting instruments. His stamps became the emblems of Brinnlitz's own outrageous bureaucracy. He cut seals of the Government General, of the Governor of Moravia, seals to adorn false travel permits so that prisoners could drive by truck to Brno or Olomouc to collect loads of bread, of black-market petrol, of flour or fabric or cigarettes. Leon Salpeter, the Cracow pharmacist, once a member of Marek Biberstein's Judenrat, kept the storehouse in Brinnlitz. Here the miserable supplies sent down from Gröss-Rosen by Hassebroeck were kept, together with the supplementary vegetables, flour, cereals bought by Oskar under Bejski's minutely careful rubber stamps, the eagle and the hooked cross of the régime painstakingly crafted on them.

"You have to remember," said an inmate of Oskar's camp, "that Brinnlitz was hard. But beside any other – paradise!" Prisoners seemed to have been aware that food was scarce everywhere; even on the outside, few were sated.

And Oskar? Did Oskar cut his rations to the same level as those of the prisoners?

The answer is indulgent laughter. "*Oskar*? Why would Oskar cut his rations? He was the Herr Direktor. Who were we to argue with his meals?" And then a frown, in case you think this attitude too serflike. "You don't understand. We were grateful to be there. There was nowhere else to be."

As in his early marriage, Oskar was still temperamentally an absentee, away from Brinnlitz for stretches of time. Sometimes Stern would wait up all night for him, for Stern was always the purveyor of the day's requests. In Oskar's apartment, Itzhak and Emilie were the keepers of vigils. The scholarly accountant would always put the most loyal interpretation on Oskar's wanderings around Moravia. In a speech years after, Stern would say, "He rode day and night, not only to purchase food for the Jews in Brinnlitz camp – by means of forged papers made by one of the prisoners – but to buy us arms and ammunition in case the SS conceived of killing us during their retreats." The picture of a restlessly provident Herr Direktor does credit to Itzhak's love and loyalty. But Emilie would have understood that not all the absences had to do with Oskar's brand of humane racketeering.

During one of Oskar's furloughs, nineteen-year-old Janek Dresner was accused of sabotage. In fact Dresner was ignorant of metalwork. He had spent his time in Plaszów in the delousing works, handing towels to the SS who came for a shower and sauna, and boiling lice-ridden clothes taken from prisoners. (From the bite of a louse he'd suffered typhus, and survived only because his cousin, Dr. Schindel, passed him off in the clinic as an angina case.)

The supposed sabotage occurred because engineer Schoenbrun, the German supervisor, transferred him from his lathe to one of the larger metal presses. It had taken a week for the engineers to set the metrics for this machine, and the first time Dresner pressed the power button and began to use it he shorted the wiring and cracked one of the plates. Schoenbrun harangued the boy and went into the office to write a report in which he defined Dresner's action as sabotage. Copies of Schoenbrun's complaint were typed up and addressed to Sections D and W in Oranienburg, to Hassebroeck at Gröss-Rosen, and to Untersturmführer Liepold in his office at the factory gate.

In the morning, Oskar had still not come home. So, rather than post the reports, Stern took them out of the office mailbag and hid them. The complaint addressed to Liepold had already been hand delivered, but Liepold was correct at least in the terms of the organisation he served and could not hang the boy until he had heard from Oranienburg and Hassebroeck. Two days later, Oskar had still not appeared. "It must be some party!" the whimsical ones on the shop floor told each other. Somehow Schoenbrun discovered that Itzhak was sitting on the letters. He raged through the office, telling Stern that his name would be added to the reports. Stern seemed to be a man of limitless calm, and when Schoenbrun finished he told the engineer that he had removed the reports from the mailbag because he thought the Herr Direktor should, as a matter of courtesy, be appraised of their contents before they were posted. The Herr Direktor, said Stern, would of course be appalled to find out that a prisoner had done ten thousand Reichsmarks' worth of damage to one of his machines. It seemed only just, said Stern, that Herr Schindler be given the chance to add his own remarks to the report.

At last Oskar drove in through the gate. Stern intercepted him and told him about the machine, about Schoenbrun's charges. Untersturmführer Liepold had been waiting to see

Schindler too and was eager to push his authority inside the factory, to use the Janek Dresner case as a pretext. I will preside over the hearing, Liepold told Oskar. You, Herr Direktor, will supply a signed statement testifying to the extent of the damage.

Oskar told him to wait a minute. It's my machine that's broken. I'm the one who will preside.

Liepold argued that the prisoner was under the jurisdiction of Section D. But the machine, replied Oskar, came under the authority of the Armaments Inspectorate. Besides, he really couldn't permit trials on the shop floor. If Brinnlitz had been a garment or chemical factory, then perhaps it wouldn't have much impact on production. But this was an armaments works, engaged in the manufacture of secret components. "I won't have my work force disturbed," said Oskar.

It was an argument that Oskar won, perhaps because Liepold gave in. The Untersturmführer was afraid of Oskar's contacts. So the court was convened at night in the machine tool section of DEF, and its members were Herr Oskar Schindler as president, Herr Schoenbrun and Herr Fuchs. A young German girl sat at the side of the judicial table to keep a record, and when young Dresner was brought in he saw in front of him a solemn and fully constituted court. According to a Section D edict of April 11th 1944, what Janek faced was the first and crucial stage of a process which should, after a report to Hassebroeck and a reply from Oranienburg, end in his hanging on the workshop floor in front of all the Brinnlitz people, his parents and sister among them.

Janek noticed that tonight there was none of that shop floor familiarity about Oskar. The Herr Direktor read aloud Schoenbrun's report of the sabotage. Janek knew about Oskar mainly from the reports of other people, particularly from his father, and couldn't tell now what Oskar's strait-laced reading of Schoenbrun's accusations meant. Was Oskar really grieving for the cracked machine? Or was it all just showmanship?

When the reading was finished, the Herr Direktor began

to ask questions. There was not much Dresner could say in answer. He pleaded that he was unfamiliar with the machine. There had been trouble setting it, he explained. He had been too anxious and had made a mistake. He assured the Herr Direktor that he had no reason to wish to sabotage the machinery. If you are not skilled at armaments work, said Schoenbrun, you shouldn't be here. The Herr Direktor has assured me that all you prisoners have had experience in the armaments industry. Yet here you are, Haftling Dresner, claiming ignorance.

With an angry gesture Schindler ordered the prisoner to detail exactly what he had done on the night of the offence. Dresner began to talk about the preparations for starting up the machine, the setting of it, the dry rehearsal at the controls, the switching on of the power, the sudden racing of the engine, the splitting of the mechanism. Herr Schindler became more and more restless as Dresner talked, and began to prowl the floor glowering at the boy. Dresner was describing some alteration he had made to one of the controls when Schindler stopped, hamfists clenched, eyes glaring.

"What did you say?" he asked the boy. Dresner repeated what he had said. I adjusted the pressure control, Herr Direktor.

Oskar raged up to him and hit him across the side of the jaw. Dresner's head sang, but in triumph, for Oskar – his back to his fellow judges – had fluttered an eyelid at Dresner in a way that could not be mistaken. Then he began waving his great arms, dismissing the boy. "The stupidity of you damned people!" he was bellowing all the while. "I can't believe it!"

He turned and appealed to Schoenbrun and Fuchs, as if they were his only allies. "I wish they were intelligent enough to sabotage a machine. Then at least I'd have their goddammed hides! But what can you do with these people? They're an utter waste of time."

Oskar's fist clenched again, and Dresner recoiled at the idea of another acquitting punch. "*Clear out!*" yelled Oskar.

As Dresner went out through the door, he heard Oskar tell the others that it was better to forget all this. "I have some good Martell upstairs," he said.

This deft subversion of the trial might not have satisfied Liepold and Schoenbrun. For the sitting had not reached a formal conclusion, it had not ended in a judgment. But they could not complain that Oskar had avoided a hearing, or treated it with levity.

Dresner's account, given later in his life, raises the supposition that Brinnlitz maintained its prisoners' lives by a series of stunts so rapid that they were nearly magical. To tell the strict truth, though, Brinnlitz, both as a prison and as a manufacturing enterprise, was itself, of its nature and in a literal sense, the one sustained, dazzling, integral confidence trick.

35

For the factory produced nothing. "Not a shell," Brinnlitz prisoners will still say, shaking their heads. Not one 45mm shell manufactured there could be used, not one rocket casing. Oskar himself contrasts the turnover of DEF in the Cracow years with the Brinnlitz record. In Zablocie, enamelware was manufactured to the value of sixteen million Reichsmarks. During the same time, the armaments section of the Zablocie plant produced shells worth half a million Reichsmarks. Oskar explains that at Brinnlitz however "as a consequence of the falling off of the enamel production" there was no output to speak of. The armaments production, he says, encountered 'starting difficulties'. But in fact he did manage to ship one truckful of 'ammunition parts', valued at thirty-five thousand Reichsmarks, during the Brinnlitz months. "These parts," said Oskar later, "had been transferred to Brinnlitz already half made. To supply still less (to the war effort) was impossible, and the excuse of 'teething troubles' became more and more dangerous for me and my Jews, because Speer (the Armaments Minister) raised his demands from month to month."

The danger of Oskar's policy of non-production was not only that it gave him a bad name at the Armaments Ministry. It made, other managements angry. For the factory system was fragmented, one workshop producing the shells, another the fuses, a third packing in the high explosives and assembling the components. In this way, it was reasoned, an air raid on any one factory could not substantially destroy the flow of armaments. Oskar's shells, despatched by freight to factories farther down the line, were inspected there by engineers Oskar did not know and could not reach. The Brinnlitz items always failed quality control. Oskar would show the complaining letters to Stern, to Finder, to Pemper or Garde. He would laugh uproariously, as if the men writing the reprimands were comic, fustian bureaucrats.

Moving forward in time and taking one such case, Itzhak Stern and Mietek Pemper were in Oskar's office on the morning of April 28th 1945, a morning when the prisoners stood at an extremity of danger, having been, as will be seen, all condemned to death by Sturmbannführer Hassebroeck. The day was Oskar's thirty-seventh birthday, and a bottle of cognac had already been opened to mark it. And on the desk lay a telegram from the armaments assembly plant near Brno. It said that Oskar's anti-tank shells were so badly produced that they failed all quality control tests. They were imprecisely calibrated, and because they had not been tempered at the right heat they split under testing.

Oskar was ecstatic at this telegram, pushing it towards Stern and Pemper, making them read it. Pemper remembers that he made another of his outrageous utterances. "It's the best birthday present I could have got. Because I know now that no poor bastard has been killed by my product."

This incident says something about two contrasting frenzies. There is some madness in a manufacturer such as Oskar, who rejoices when he does not manufacture. But there is also a cool lunacy in the German technocrat who, Vienna having fallen, Marshal Koniev's men having embraced the Americans on the Elbe, still takes it for granted that an armaments factory up in the hills has time to tidy up its performance and make a worthy offering to the grand principles of discipline and output.

But the main question that arises from the birthday telegram is how Oskar lasted those months, the seven months up to the date of his birthday.

The Brinnlitz people remember a whole series of inspections and checks. Men from Section D stalked through the factory, checklists in their hands. So did engineers from the Armaments Inspectorate. Oskar always lunched or dined these officials, softened them up with ham and cognac. In the Reich there were no longer so many good lunches and dinners to be had. The prisoners at the lathes, the furnaces, the metal presses would state that the uniformed inspectors reeked of alcohol and reeled on the factory floor. There is a story all the inmates tell of an official who boasted, on one of the final inspections of the war, that Schindler would not seduce him with camaraderie, with a lunch and drink. On the stairs leading from the dormitories down to the workshop floor, the legend has it, Oskar tripped the man, sending him to the bottom of the stairs, a journey which split the man's head and broke his leg. The Brinnlitz people are generally unable to identify this SS hardcase. One claims that it was Obersturmbannführer Rasch, SS and police chief of Moravia. Oskar himself never made any recorded claim about it. The anecdote is one of those stories that reflect people's picture of Oskar as a bounteous avatar, a provider who covers all eventualities. Whether the SS man *did* cartwheel down the steps of Deutsche Email Fabrik shattering his shin and leg-bone is not in itself important. And one has to admit, in natural justice, that the inmates had the right to spread this sort of fable. They were the ones in deepest jeopardy. If the fable let them down, they would pay for it most bitterly.

One reason Brinnlitz passed the inspections was the relentless trickery of Oskar's skilled workers. The furnace gauges were rigged by the electricians. The needle registered the correct temperature when the interior of the furnace was in fact hundreds of degrees cooler. "I've written to the manufacturers," Oskar would tell the armaments inspectors. He would play the sombre, baffled manufacturer whose profits were being eroded. He would blame the floor, the inferior German supervisors. He spoke yet again of 'teething troubles', implying future tonnages of munitions once the problems faded.

In the machine tool departments, as at the furnaces, everything looked normal. Machines seemed perfectly calibrated but were in fact a micro-millimetre off. Most of the inspectors who walked through seem to have left not only with a gift of cigarettes and cognac, but with a faint sympathy for the thorny problems this decent fellow was enduring.

Stern would always say in the end that Oskar bought boxes of shells from other Czech manufacturers and passed them off as his own during inspections. Pfefferberg makes the same claim. In any case Brinnlitz lasted, whatever sleight-of-hand Oskar used.

There were times when, to impress the hostile locals, he invited important officials in for a tour of the factory and a good dinner. But they were always men whose expertise did not run to engineering and munitions production. After the Herr Direktor's stay in Pomorska Street, Liepold, with Hoffman and the local Party Kreisleiter, wrote to every official they could think of, local, provincial, Berlin-based, complaining about him, his morals, his connections, his breaches of race and penal law. Sussmuth let him know about the barrage of letters arriving at Troppau. Oskar invited Ernst Hahn down to Brinnlitz. Hahn was second in command of the bureau of the Berlin main office devoted to services for SS families. "He was," says Oskar with a customary toper's primness, "a notorious drunkard." Hahn brought his boyhood friend, Franz Bosch, with him – the Bosch whom Oskar had known through Amon. Bosch, as Oskar has already remarked in this narrative, was 'an impenetrable drunkard', as well as the murderer of the Gutter family. However, swallowing his contempt, Oskar welcomed him for his public relations value.

When Hahn arrived in town, he was wearing exactly the splendid, untarnished uniform Oskar expected. It was festooned with ribbons and orders, for Hahn was an old-time SS man from the glorious early days of the Party. With this dazzling Standartenführer came an equally glittering adjutant.

Liepold was invited in, from his rented house outside the camp, to dine with the visitors. From the start of the evening, he was out of his depth. For Hahn loved Oskar, drunks always did. Later Oskar would describe the men and the uniforms as 'pompous'. But at least Liepold was convinced now that if he wrote complaining letters to distant authorities, they were likely to land on the desk of some old drinking friend of the Herr Direktor, and that this could well prove perilous for Untersturmführer Liepold.

In the morning, Oskar was seen driving through Zwittau, laughing with these glamorous men from Berlin. The local Nazis stood on the pavements and saluted all this Reich splendour as it passed.

Hoffman was not as easily stilled as the rest. The three hundred women of Brinnlitz had, in Oskar's own words, "no employment possibility". It has already been said that many of them spent their days knitting. In the winter of 1944, for people whose only cover was the striped uniform, knitting was no idle hobby. Hoffman, however, made a formal complaint to the SS about the wool the Schindler women had stolen from the cases in the annexe. He thought it scandalous, and that it showed up the true activities of the so-called Schindler armaments works.

When Oskar visited Hoffman, he found the old man in a triumphant mood. We've petitioned Berlin to remove you, said Hoffman. This time we've included sworn statements declaring that your factory is running in contravention of economic and race law. We've nominated an invalided Wehrmacht engineer from Brno to take over the factory and turn it into something decent.

Oskar listened to Hoffman, apologised, tried to appear penitent. Then he rang Colonel Erich Lange in Berlin and asked him to sit on the petition from the Hoffman clique in Zwittau. The out-of-court settlement still cost Oskar eight thousand Reichsmarks, and all winter the Zwittau town authorities, civil and Party, plagued him, calling him in to the town hall to acquaint him with the complaints of various citizens about his prisoners, or the state of his drains.

Lusia had a personal experience of SS inspectors which is worth recording because it typifies the Schindler method.

She was still in the cellar – would be there for the entire winter. The other girls had got better and had moved upstairs to recuperate. But it seemed to Lusia that Birkenau had filled her with a limitless poison. Her fevers recurred again and again. Her joints became inflamed and carbuncles

374

broke out in her armpits. When one burst and healed, another would form. Dr. Handler, against the advice of Dr. Biberstein, lanced one of them with a kitchen knife. She remained in the cellar, well fed, ghost-white, infectious. In all the great acreage of Europe, it was the only space in which she could have lived. She was aware of that even then, and hoped that the enormous conflict would roll by above her head.

In that warm hole under the factory camp of Brinnlitz, night and day were irrelevant. The time the door at the top of the cellar stairs burst open could have been either. She was used to quieter visits from Emilie Schindler. She heard boots on the stairs and tensed in her bed. It sounded to her like an old-fashioned Aktion.

It was in fact the Herr Direktor with two officers from Gröss-Rosen. Their boots clattered on the steps as if they would sweep over her in a wave. Oskar stood with the SS men as they looked around in the gloom at the boilers and at her. It came to Lusia that perhaps she was *it* for today, the sacrificial offering you had to give them so that they would go away satisfied. She was partially screened by a boiler, but Oskar made no attempt to hide her, actually came to the foot of her bed. Because the gentlemen of the SS seemed flushed and unsteady, Oskar had a chance to speak to her, words of wonderful banality which she would never forget. "Don't worry. Everything's all right." He stood close, as if at the same time to emphasise to the inspectors that this was not an infectious case.

"This is a Jewish girl," he said flatly. "I didn't want to put her in the Krankenstube. Inflammation of the joints. She's finished anyway. They don't give her more than thirty-six hours."

Then he rambled on about the hot water, where it came from, and the steam for the delousing. He pointed to gauges, piping, cylinders. He edged around her bed as if it too were neutral, part of the mechanism. Lusia did not know where to look, whether to open or close her eyes. She tried to appear comatose. It might seem a touch too much, but Lusia did not think so at the time, when, as he ushered the SS men back to the base of the stairs, Oskar flashed her a cautious smile.

She would stay there for six months and hobble upstairs in the spring to resume her womanhood in an altered world.

During the winter, Oskar built up an independent arsenal. Again there are the legends. Some say that the weapons were bought at the end of winter from the Czech underground. But Oskar had been an obvious National Socialist in 1938 and 1939 and may have been wary of dealing with the Czechs. Most of the weapons, in any case, came from a flawless source, from Obersturmbannführer Rasch, SS and police chief of Moravia. The small cache included carbines and automatic weapons, some pistols, some hand grenades. Oskar would later describe the transaction offhandedly. He acquired the arms, he would say, "under the pretence of protecting my factory, for the price of a brilliant ring for his (Rasch's) wife."

Oskar does not detail his performance in Rasch's office in Brno's Spilberk Castle. It is not hard to imagine though. The Herr Direktor, concerned about a possible slave uprising as the war grinds on, is willing to die expensively at his desk, automatic weapon in hand, having mercifully despatched his wife with a bullet to save her from something worse. The Herr Direktor also touches on the chance that the Russians might turn up at the gate. My civilian engineers, Fuchs and Schoenbrun, my honest technicians, my German-speaking secretary, all of them deserve to have the means of resistance. It's gloomy talk, of course. I'd rather speak of issues closer to our hearts, Herr Obersturmbannführer. I know your passion for good jewellery. May I show you this example I found last week?

And so the ring appeared on the edge of Rasch's blotter, Oskar murmuring, "As soon as I saw it, I thought of Frau Rasch."

Once Oskar took delivery of the weapons, he appointed Uri Bejski, brother of the rubber-stamp maker, as keeper of the arsenal. Uri was small, handsome, lively. People noticed that he wandered in and out of the Schindlers' apartment like a son. He was a favourite, too, with Emilie, who gave him keys to the apartment. Frau Schindler enjoyed a similar maternal relationship with the surviving Spira boy. She took him regularly into her kitchen and fed him up on slices of bread and margarine.

One at a time, Uri took the small body of prisoners selected for training into Salpeter's storehouse to teach them the mechanism of the Gewehr 41 Ws. Three commando squads of five men each had been formed. Some of Bejski's trainees were boys like Lutek Feigenbaum. Others were Polish veterans such as Poldek Pfefferberg and those other prisoners whom the Schindler prisoners called the 'Budzyn people'.

The Budzyn people were Jewish officers and men of the Polish army. They had lived through the liquidation of the Budzyn labour camp, which had been under the governance of Untersturmführer Liepold. Liepold had brought them into his new command in Brinnlitz. There were about fifty of them, and they worked in Oskar's kitchens. People remember them as very political. They had learned Marxism during their imprisonment in Budzyn, and looked forward to a Communist Poland. It was an irony that in Brinnlitz they lived in the warm kitchens of that most apolitical of capitalists, Herr Oskar Schindler.

Their rapport with the bulk of the prisoners, who, apart from the Zionists, merely followed the politics of survival, was good. A number of them took private lessons on Uri Bejski's automatics, for in the Polish army of the thirties they had never held such sophisticated weapons.

If Frau Rasch, in the last and fullest days of her husband's power in Brno, had idly – during a party say, a musical recital at the Castle – gazed into the core of the gem that had come to her from Oskar Schindler, she would have seen reflected there the worst incubus from her own dreams and her Führer's. An armed Marxist Jew.

36

Old drinking friends of Oskar's, Amon and Bosch among
them, had sometimes thought of him as the victim of a
Jewish virus. It was no metaphor. They believed it in literal
terms and attached no blame to the sufferer. They'd seen it
happen to other good men. Some area of the brain fell under
a thrall that was half bacterium, half magic. If they'd been
asked whether it was infectious, they would have said, yes,
highly. They would have seen the case of Oberleutnant
Sussmuth as an example of conspicuous contagion.

Over the winter of 1944–45, Oskar and Sussmuth connived to get a further three thousand women out of Auschwitz in groups of three hundred to five hundred at a time
and into small camps in Moravia. Oskar supplied the
influence, the sales talk, the palm-greasing for these operations. Sussmuth did the paperwork. In the textile mills of
Moravia there was a labour shorgage, and not all the
owners abhorred the Jewish presence as sharply as Hoffman. At least five German factories in Moravia – at
Freudenthal and Jagerndorf, at Liebau, Grulich and Traute-
nau – took these drafts of women and supplied a camp on
the premises. Any such camp was never paradise, and in its
management the SS were permitted to be more dominant
than Liepold could ever hope to be. Oskar would later
describe these women in the little camps as "living under
endurable treatment". But the very smallness of the textile
camps was an aid to their survival, for the garrisons were
older, slacker, less fanatical men. There was typhus to be
sidestepped, and hunger to be carried like a weight beneath
the ribs. But such tiny, almost countrified establishments
would escape, for the main part, the extermination orders
that would come to the bigger camps in the spring.

But if the Jewish sepsis had infected Sussmuth, for Oskar Schindler it galloped. Through Sussmuth, Oskar had applied for another thirty metalworkers. It is simple fact that he had lost interest in production. But he saw, with the detached side of his mind, that if his plant was ever to validate its existence in terms of Section D, he would need more qualified hands. When you look at other events of that mad winter, you can see that Oskar wanted the extra thirty not because they were used to lathes and machine tools, but simply because they were an extra thirty. It is not too fantastic to say that he desired them with some of the absolute passion that characterised the exposed and flaming heart of the Jesus that hung on Emilie's wall. Since this narrative has tried to avoid the canonisation of the Herr Direktor, the idea of the sensual Oskar as the desirer of souls has to be proved.

One of these thirty metalworkers, a man called Moshe Henigman, left a public account of their unlikely deliverance. A little after Christmas, ten thousand prisoners from the quarries of Auschwitz III – from such establishments as the Krupp Weschel-Union armaments factory and from German Earth and Stone, from the Farben synthetic petrol plant and the aeroplane dismantling enterprise – were put in a column and marched away towards Gröss-Rosen. Perhaps some planner believed that once they arrived in Lower Silesia they would be distributed among the area's factory camps. If that was the scheme, it escaped the SS officers and men who marched with the prisoners. It ignored also the devouring cold of the merciless turning of the year, and it did not enquire how the column would be fed. The limpers, the coughers, were culled at the beginning of each stage and executed. Of ten thousand, says Henigman, there were within ten days only twelve hundred left alive. To the north, Koniev's Russians had burst across the Vistula south of Warsaw and seized all the roads on the column's north-westerly route. The diminished group was therefore put in an SS compound somewhere near Opole. The commandant of the place had the prisoners interviewed, and lists made of the skilled workers. But each day the weary selections continued, and the rejects were shot. A man whose name was called out never knew what to expect, a lump of bread or a bullet. When Henigman's name was called, however, he was put in a railway wagon with thirty others and, under the care of an SS man and a Kapo, was shunted south. "We were given food for the trip," Henigman recalls. "Something unheard of."

Henigman later spoke of the exquisite unreality of arriving at Brinnlitz. "We could not believe that there was a camp left where men and women worked together, where there were no beatings, no Kapo." His reaction is marked by a little hyperbole, since there *was* segregation in Brinnlitz. Occasionally too, Oskar's blonde girlfriend let fly with an open palm, and once when a boy stole a potato from the kitchen and was reported to Liepold, the commandant made him stand on a stool all day in the courtyard, the potato clamped in his open mouth, saliva running down his chin, and the placard *I am a potato thief!* hung around his neck.

But to Henigman this sort of thing was not worthy of report. "How can one describe," he asks, "the change from hell to paradise?"

When he met Oskar, he was told to build himself up. Tell the supervisors when you're ready to work, said the Herr Direktor. And Henigman, faced with this strange reversal of policy, felt not just that he'd come to a quiet pasture, but that he had gone through the mirror.

Since thirty tinsmiths were merely a fragment of the ten thousand, it must be said again that Oskar was only a minor god of rescue. But like any tutelary spirit, he saved equally Goldberg and Helen Hirsch, and equally he tried to save Dr. Leon Gross and Olek Rosner. With this same gratuitous equality, he made a costly deal with the Gestapo in the Moravia region. We know that the bargain was struck, we do not know how expensive it was. That it cost a fortune is certain.

A prisoner called Benjamin Wrozlavski became one subject of this deal. Wrozlavski was formerly an inmate of the labour camp at Gliwice. Unlike Henigman's camp, Gliwice was not in the Auschwitz region, but was close enough to be one of the Auschwitz subsidiary camps. By January 12th – when Koniev and Zhukov launched their offensive – Höss's awesome realm and all its close satellites were in danger of instant capture. The Gliwice prisoners were put in Ostbahn wagons and shipped towards Fernwald. Somehow Wrozlavski and a friend named Roman Wilner jumped from the train. One popular form of escape was through loosened ventilators in the wagon ceilings. But prisoners who tried it were often shot by guards stationed on the roof. Wilner was hit during this escape, but he was still able to travel, and he and his friend Wrozlavski fled through the high quiet towns of the Moravian borders. They were at last arrested in one of these villages and taken to the Gestapo offices in Troppau.

As soon as they had arrived and been searched and put in a cell, one of the gentlemen of the Gestapo walked in and told them that nothing bad would happen. They had no reason to believe him. The officer said further that he would not transfer Wilner to a hospital, in spite of the wound, for he would simply be collected and fed back into the system.

Wrozlavski and Wilner were locked away for nearly two weeks. Oskar had to be contacted and a price had to be settled. During that time, the officer kept talking to them as if they were in protective custody, and the prisoners continued to find the idea absurd. When the door was opened and the two of them were taken out, they presumed they were about to be shot. Instead they were led by an SS man to the railway station, who escorted them on a train south-east toward Brno.

For both of them, the arrival at Brinnlitz had that same surreal, delightful and frightening quality it had had for Henigman. Wilner was put in the clinic, under the care of the doctors Handler, Lewkowicz, Hilfstein and Biberstein. Wrozlavski was put in a sort of convalescent area which had been set up – for extraordinary reasons soon to be explained – in a corner of the factory floor downstairs. The Herr Direktor visited them and asked how they felt. The preposterous question scared Wrozlavski; so did the surroundings. He feared, as he would put it years later, "the way from the hospital would lead to execution, as was the case in other camps." He was fed with the rich Brinnlitz porridge, and saw Schindler frequently. But, as he confesses, he was still confused, and found the phenomenon of Brinnlitz hard to grasp.

By the arrangement Oskar had with the provincial Gestapo, eleven escapees were added to the crammed-in camp population. Each one of them had wandered away from a column or jumped from a wagon. In their stinking stripes, they had tried to stay at large. By rights, they should all have been shot.

In 1963, Dr. Steinberg of Tel Aviv testifies to yet another instance of Oskar's wild, contagious and unquestioning largesse. Steinberg was the physician in a small work camp in the Sudeten hills. The Gauleiter in Liberec was less able, as Silesia fell to the Russians, to keep labour camps out of his wholesome province of Moravia. The camp in which Steinberg was imprisoned was one of the many new Lagers scattered among the mountains. It was a Luftwaffe camp devoted to the manufacture of some aircraft component which Steinberg does not specify. Four hundred prisoners lived there. The food was poor, says Steinberg, and the work loads savage.

Pursuing a rumour about the Brinnlitz camp, Steinberg managed to get a pass and the loan of a factory truck to go and see Oskar. He described the desperate conditions in the Luftwaffe camp to him. He says that Oskar quite lightly agreed to allocate him part of the Brinnlitz stores. One main question preoccupied Oskar: on what grounds could Steinberg regularly come to Brinnlitz to pick up the supplies? It was arranged that he would use some excuse to do with getting regular medical aid from the doctors in the camp clinic.

Twice a week thereafter, says Steinberg, he visited Brinnlitz and took back to his own camp quantities of bread, semolina, potatoes and cigarettes. If Schindler were around the storehouse on the day that Steinberg was loading up, he would turn his back and walk away.

Steinberg does not give any exact poundage of food, but he offers it as a medical opinion that if the Brinnlitz supplies had not been available, at least fifty of the prisoners in the Luftwaffe camp would have died by the spring.

Apart from the ransoming of the women in Auschwitz, however, the most astounding salvage of all was that of the Goleszów people. Goleszów was a quarry and cement plant inside Auschwitz III itself, home of the SS-owned German Earth and Stone Works. As has been seen with the thirty metalsmiths, throughout January 1945 the dread fiefdoms of Auschwitz were being disbanded, and in the middle of the month a hundred and twenty quarry workers from Goleszów were thrown into two cattle wagons. Their journey would be as bitter as any, but would end better than most. It is worth remembering that, like the Goleszów men, nearly everyone else in the Auschwitz area was on the move that month. Dolek Horowitz was shipped away to Mauthausen. Young Richard was however kept behind with other small children. The Russians would find him later in the month in an Auschwitz abandoned by the SS and would claim, quite correctly, that he and the others had been detained for medical experiments. Henry Rosner and the nine-year-old Olek (apparently no longer considered necessary for the laboratories) were marched away from Auschwitz in a column for thirty miles, and those who fell behind were shot. In Sosnowiec they were packed into freight cars. As a special kindness, an SS guard who was supposed to separate the children let Olek and Henry go into the same wagon. It was so crowded that everyone had to stand, but as men died of cold and thirst a gentleman whom Henry described as "a smart Jew" would suspend them in their blankets from horse hooks near the roof. In this way there was more floor space for the living. For the sake of the boy's comfort, Henry got the idea of slinging Olek in his blanket in exactly the same way from the horse hooks. This not only gave the child an easier ride: when the train stopped at stations and sidings, he would call to Germans by the rails to throw snowballs up to the wire gratings. The snow would shatter and spray the interior of the wagon with moisture, and men would struggle for a few ice crystals.

The train took seven days to get to Dachau and half the population of the Rosners' car died. When it at last arrived and the door was opened, a dead body fell out and then Olek, who picked himself up in the snow, broke an icicle off the undercarriage and began to lick it ravenously. Such was travel in Europe in January 1945.

For the Goleszów quarry prisoners it was even worse. The bill of lading for their two freight cars, preserved in the archives of the Yad Vashem, shows that they were travelling without food for more than ten days and with the doors frozen shut. R, a boy of sixteen, remembers that they scraped ice off the inside walls to quench their thirst. Even in Birkenau they weren't unloaded. The killing process was in its last furious days. It had no time for them. They were abandoned in sidings, re-attached to locomotives, dragged for fifty miles, uncoupled again. They were shunted to the gates of camps whose commandants refused them on the clear grounds that by now they lacked industrial value, and because in any case facilities – bunks and rations – were everywhere at the limit.

In the small hours of a morning at the end of January, they were uncoupled and abandoned in the railyards at Zwittau. Oskar says a friend of his telephoned from the depot to report human scratchings and cries from inside the cars. These pleadings were uttered in many tongues, for the trapped men were, according to the manifest, Slovenes, Poles, Czechs, Germans, Frenchmen, Hungarians, Netherlanders and Serbians. The friend who made the call was very likely the brother-in-law who managed the freight yards at Zwittau. Oskar told him to shunt the two cars up the siding to Brinnlitz.

It was a morning of gruesome cold – minus thirty degrees Celsius (minus twenty-two degrees Fahrenheit), says Stern. Even the exact Biberstein says that it was at least minus twenty degrees (minus four degrees Fahrenheit). Poldek Pfefferberg was summoned from his bunk, fetched his welding gear, and went out to the snowy siding to cut open the doors iced hard as iron. He too heard the unearthly complaints from within.

It is hard to describe what they saw when the doors were at last opened. In each car, a pyramid of frozen corpses, their limbs madly contorted, occupied the centre of the floor. The hundred or more still living stank awesomely, were seared black by the cold, were skeletal. Not one of them would be found to weigh more than thirty-four kilos.

Oskar was not at the siding. He was inside the factory, where a warm corner of the workshop floor was being made ready for the shipment from Goleszów. Prisoners dismantled the last of Hoffman's dumped machinery and carried it to the garages. Straw was brought in and the floor strewn with it. Already Schindler had been out to the commandant's office to speak to Liepold. The Untersturmführer didn't want to take the Goleszów men – in that he resembled all the other commandants they had met in the past few weeks. Liepold pointedly remarked that no one could pretend that *these* people were munitions workers. Oskar admitted that, but guaranteed to put them on the books, and so to pay six Reichsmarks a day for each of them. I can use them after their recuperation, said Oskar. Liepold recognised two aspects of the case. First, that Oskar was unstoppable. Second, that an increase in the size of Brinnlitz and the labour fees paid by the Herr Direktor might well please Hassebroeck. Liepold would have them quickly enrolled on the books, and the entries backdated, so that even as the Goleszów men were carried in through the factory gate Oskar was paying for them.

Inside the workshop, they were wrapped in blankets and laid down on the straw. Emilie came from her apartment, followed by two prisoners toting an enormous bucket of porridge. The doctors noted the frostbite and the need for frost ointments. Dr. Biberstein mentioned to Oskar that the Goleszów people would need vitamins, though he was sure there were none to be had in Moravia.

In the meantime the sixteen frozen corpses were placed in a shed. Rabbi Levartov, looking at them, knew that with their limbs distorted by the cold they would be hard to bury in the orthodox manner, which permitted no breaking of bones. The matter, Levartov knew, would however have to be argued with the commandant. Liepold had on file from Section D a number of directives urging SS personnel to dispose of the dead by burning. In the boiler rooms were perfect facilities, industrial furnaces capable almost of vaporising a body. Yet Schindler had so far twice refused to permit the burning of the dead.

The first time was when Janka Feigenbaum died in the Brinnlitz clinic. Liepold had at once ordered her body incinerated. Oskar heard through Stern that this was abhorrent to the Feigenbaums and to Levartov, and his resistance to the idea may have been fuelled also by the Catholic residue in his own soul. In those years the Catholic Church was firmly opposed to cremation. As well as refusing Liepold the use of the furnace, Oskar also ordered the carpenters to prepare a coffin, and himself supplied a horse and cart, allowing Levartov and the family to ride out under guard to bury the girl in the woods.

Feigenbaum father and son had walked behind the cart, counting the steps from the gate so that when the war ended they could reclaim Janka's body.

Witnesses say that Liepold was furious at this sort of pandering to the prisoners. Some Brinnlitz people even comment that Oskar could show towards Levartov and the Feigenbaums a more exacting delicacy and courtesy than he usually managed with Emilie.

The second time that Liepold wanted the furnaces used was when old Mrs. Hofstatter died. Oskar, at Stern's request, had another coffin prepared, allowing a metal plaque on which Mrs. Hofstatter's vital statistics were marked to be included in the coffin. Levartov and a *minyan*, the quorum of ten males who recite *Kaddish* over the dead, were permitted to leave camp and attend the funeral.

Stern says that it was for Mrs. Hofstatter's sake that Oskar established a Jewish cemetery in the Catholic parish of Deutsch-Bielau, a nearby village. According to him, Oskar went to the parish church on the Sunday Mrs.

Hofstatter died and put a proposition to the priest. A quickly convened parish council agreed to sell him a small parcel of land just beyond the Catholic cemetery. There is nothing surer than that some of the council resisted, for it was an era when Canon Law was interpreted narrowly in its provisions as to who could and who could not be buried in consecrated ground.

Other prisoners of some authority say, however, that the Jewish cemetery plot was bought by Oskar at the time of the arrival of the Goleszów cars with their tithe of twisted dead. In a later report, Oskar himself implies that it was the Goleszów dead who caused him to buy the land. By one account, when the parish priest pointed out the area beyond the church wall reserved for the burial of suicides and suggested that the Goleszów people be buried there, Oskar answered that these weren't suicides. These were victims of a great murder.

The Goleszów deaths and the death of Mrs. Hofstatter must, nevertheless, have come close together, and both were marked with full ritual in the unique Jewish cemetery of Deutsch-Bielau.

It is clear from the recollections of all Brinnlitz prisoners that this internment had enormous moral force within the camp. The distorted corpses unloaded from the freight cars had seemed less than human. Looking at them, you became frightened for your own precarious humanity. The inhuman thing was beyond feeding, washing, warming. The one way left to restore it – as well as yourself – to humanity was through ritual. Levartov's rites therefore, the exalted plain-chant of *Kaddish*, had a far larger gravity for the Brinnlitz prisoners than such ceremonies could ever have had in the relative tranquillity of prewar Cracow.

To keep the Jewish burial ground tidy in case of future deaths, Oskar employed a middle-aged SS Unterscharführer and paid him a retainer.

Emilie Schindler had transactions of her own to see to. Carrying a clutch of false papers supplied by Bejski, she had two prisoners load up one of the plant trucks with vodka and cigarettes, and ordered them to drive her to the large mining town of Ostrava up near the border of the Government General. At the military hospital she was able to make an arrangement with a number of Oskar's contacts and to bring back frostbite ointments, sulpha, and the vitamins Biberstein had thought impossible to procure. Such journeys now became regular events for Emilie. She was growing to be a traveller, like her husband.

After the first deaths, there were no others. The Goleszów people were Mussulmen, and it was a first principle that the condition of Mussulmen could not be reversed. But there was some intractability in Emilie which would not accept it. She harried them with her bucketfuls of farina. "Out of those rescued from Goleszów," said Dr. Biberstein, "not one would have stayed alive without her treatment." The men began to be seen, trying to look useful on the factory floor. One day a Jewish storeman asked one of them to carry a box out to a machine on the workshop floor. "The box weighs thirty-five kilos," said the boy, "and I weigh thirty-two. How the hell can I carry it?"

To this factory of ineffective machines, its floor strewn with scarecrows, Herr Amon Goeth came that winter, following his release from prison, to pay his respects to the Schindlers. The SS court had let him out of prison in Breslau because of his diabetes. He was dressed in an old suit that may have been a uniform with the markings stripped off. There are rumours about the meaning of this visit, and they persist to this day. Some thought that Goeth was looking for a hand-out, others that Oskar was holding something for him, cash or kind from one of Amon's last Cracow deals in which Oskar had perhaps acted as Amon's agent. Some who worked close to Oskar's office believed that Amon even asked for a managerial post at Brinnlitz. No one could say that he did not have the experience. In fact, all three versions of Amon's motives in coming down to Brinnlitz are possibly correct, though it is unlikely that Oskar ever acted as Amon's agent.

As Amon stepped through the gate of the camp, it could be seen that prison and tribulation had thinned him down.

The fleshiness had vanished from his face. His features were more like those of the Amon who had come to Cracow in the New Year of 1943 to liquidate the ghetto, yet they were different, too, for they were jaundice-yellow and prison-grey. And if you had the eyes for it, if you dared to look, you saw a new passivity there. Some prisoners, however, glancing up from their lathes, glimpsed that figure from the pit of their foulest dreams, there unannounced, passing by the doors and windows, through the factory yard, heading for Herr Schindler's office. Helen Hirsch sat transfixed, wanting nothing except that he should vanish again. But others hissed him as he passed, and men bent from their machines and spat. Maturer women lifted their knitting towards him like a challenge. For that was vengeance, to show that in spite of all his terror, Adam still delved and Eve span. If Amon wanted a job at Brinnlitz – and there were few other places a Hauptsturmführer under suspension could go – Oskar either talked him out of it or bought him off. In that way, this meeting was like all their others. As a courtesy the Herr Direktor took Amon on a tour of the plant, and on this circuit of the workshop floor the reaction against him was stronger still. Back in the office, Amon was overheard demanding that Oskar punish the inmates for their disrespect, and Oskar was heard rumbling away, pledging that he would do something about the pernicious Jews and expressing his own undiminished respect for Herr Goeth.

Though the SS had let him out of prison, the investigation of his affairs was still in progress. A judge of the SS court had come to Brinnlitz in the past few weeks to question Pemper again about Amon's managerial procedures. Before the interrogation began, Commandant Liepold had muttered to Pemper that he'd better be careful, that the judge would want to take him to Dachau for execution after he'd been drained of evidence. Wisely, Pemper had done all he could to convince the judge of the unimportance of his work in the main office at Plaszów.

Somehow, Amon had heard that the SS investigators had been pursuing Mietek Pemper. Soon after he arrived in Brinnlitz, he cornered his former typist in Oskar's outer office and wanted to know what questions the judge had asked. Pemper believed, reasonably enough, that he could detect in Amon's eyes resentment that his former clerk was still a breathing source of evidence for the SS court. Surely Amon was powerless here, thinned down, looking doleful in an old suit, washed up in Oskar's office? But you couldn't be sure. It was still Amon, and he had a presence, a habit of authority. Pemper said, "The judge told me I was not to talk to anyone about my interrogation." Goeth was outraged and threatened to complain to Herr Schindler. That, if you liked, was a measure of Amon's new impotence. He had never had to go to Oskar before to appeal for the chastisement of a prisoner.

By the second night of Amon's visit, the women were feeling more triumphal. He couldn't touch them. They persuaded even Helen Hirsch of this. Yet her sleep was fitful.

The last time Amon crossed the factory, it was on his way to be taken by car to the station at Zwittau. He had never in the past made three visits to any space without bringing some poor bastard's world crashing down. It was clear now that he had no power at all. Yet still not everyone could look him in the face as he left. Thirty years later, in the sleep of Plaszów veterans from Buenos Aires to Sydney, from New York to Cracow, from Los Angeles to Jerusalem, Amon would still be rampaging. "When you saw Goeth," said Poldek Pfefferberg, "you saw death."

So, in his own terms, he was never an utter failure.

37

Oskar's thirty-seventh birthday was celebrated that year by Oskar himself and all the prisoners. One of the metal-workers had crafted a small box suitable for holding cufflinks, and when the Herr Direktor appeared on the workshop floor, the twelve-year-old Niusia Horowitz was pushed towards him to make a rehearsed speech in German. "Herr Direktor," she said in a voice he had to stoop to hear. "All the prisoners wish you the very best for this your birthday."

It was a *Shabbat*, which was apt, because the Brinnlitz people would always remember it as a festival. Early in the morning, about the time Oskar had begun celebrating with Martell cognac in his office and flourishing that insulting telegram from the engineers at Brno, two truckloads of white bread rolled into the courtyard. Some went to the garrison, even to the hungover Liepold sleeping late in his house in the village. That much was necessary to stop the SS from grumbling about the way the Herr Direktor favoured prisoners. The prisoners themselves were issued with three-quarters of a kilo of the bread. They inspected it as they ate and savoured it. There was some speculation about where Oskar had got it. Perhaps it could be partially explained by the good will of the local mill manager, Daubek, the one who turned away while Brinnlitz prisoners filled their trousers with oatmeal. But it was not so much in terms of its history, of what bakery was used and the origins of the white flour, that the bread was discussed that Saturday. It was more in terms of the magic of the event, of the wonder-working.

Though the day is remembered as jubilant, there was in

fact not so much cause for festive feeling. Some time in the past week, a long telegram had been directed from Herr Commandant Hassebroeck of Gröss-Rosen to Liepold of Brinnlitz giving him instructions about the disposal of the population in the event of the Russians drawing near. There was to be a final selection, said Hassebroeck's telegram. The aged and the halt were to be shot immediately, and the healthy were to be marched out in the direction of Mauthausen.

Though the prisoners on the factory floor knew nothing of this telegram, they still had an unspecified fear of something like it. All that week there had been rumours that Poles had been brought in to dig mass graves in the woods beyond Brinnlitz. The white bread seemed to have come as an antidote to that rumour, a warranty of all their futures. Yet everyone seemed to know that an era of dangers more subtle than those of the past had begun.

If Oskar's factory hands knew nothing of the telegram, neither did Herr Commandant Liepold himself. The cable was delivered first to Mietek Pemper in Liepold's outer office. Pemper had steamed it open, resealed it and taken the news of its contents straight to Oskar. Schindler stood at his desk reading it, then turned to Mietek. "All right then," growled Oskar. "We have to say goodbye to Untersturmführer Liepold."

For it seemed both to Oskar and to Pemper that Liepold was the only SS man in the garrison capable of obeying such a telegram. The commandant's deputy was a man in his forties, an SS Oberscharführer called Motzek. While Motzek might be capable of some sort of panic slaughter, to administer the cool murder of thirteen hundred humans was beyond him.

In the days before his birthday, Oskar made a number of confidential complaints to Hassebroeck about the excessive behaviour of Herr Commandant Liepold. He called on the influential police chief, Rasch, and lodged the same sort of charges against Liepold. He showed both Hassebroeck and Rasch copies of letters he had written to the office of General Glücks in Oranienburg. Oskar was gambling that

Hassebroeck would remember Oskar's past generosities and the promise of future ones, that he would take note of the pressure for Liepold's removal now being built up by Oskar in Oranienburg and Brno, that he would transfer Liepold without bothering to investigate the Untersturmführer's behaviour towards the inmates of Brinnlitz.

It was a characteristic Schindler bid, the Amon-Oskar game of blackjack writ large. All the Brinnlitz men were in the stake, from Hirsch Krischer, Prisoner No. 68821, a forty-eight-year-old car mechanic, to Jarum Kiaf, Prisoner No. 77196, a twenty-seven-year-old unskilled worker and survivor of the Goleszów carriages. And all the Brinnlitz women were counted in as well, from 76201, twenty-nine-year-old metalworker Berta Aftergut, to 76500, thirty-six-year-old Jenta Zwetschenstiel.

Oskar got fuel for further complaints about Liepold by inviting the commandant to dinner at the apartment inside the works. It was April 27th, the eve of Schindler's birthday. About 11 p.m. that night, the prisoners at work on the floor of the plant were startled to see a drunken commandant reeling across the factory floor, assisted on his way by a steadier Herr Direktor. In the course of his passage, Liepold attempted to focus on individual workers. He raged, pointing at the great roof beams above the machinery. The Herr Direktor had always kept him off the factory floor, but here he was, the final and punishing authority. You fucking Jews, he was roaring. See that beam, see it! That's what I'll hang you from. Every one of you!

Oskar eased him along, directing him by the shoulder, murmuring at him, That's right, that's right. But not tonight, eh? Some other time.

The next day Oskar called Hassebroeck and others with predictable accusations. The man rages round the factory, drunk, making threats about *immediate* executions. They're not labourers! They're sophisticated technicians engaged on secret weapons, etc., etc. And although Hassebroeck was responsible for the deaths of thousands of quarry workers, although he believed that all Jewish labour should be liquidated when the Russians were close, he did agree that until then Herr Schindler's factory should be treated as a special case.

Liepold, said Oskar, kept stating that he'd like at last to go into combat. He's young, he's healthy, he's willing. Well, Hassebroeck told Oskar, we'll see what can be done.

Commandant Liepold himself, meanwhile, spent Oskar's birthday sleeping off the dinner of the night before.

In his absence, Oskar made an astounding birthday speech. He had been celebrating all day, yet no one remembers his delivery being unsteady. We do not have the text of what he said, but there is another speech, made ten days later, on the evening of May 8th, of which we do have a copy. According to those who listened, both speeches pursued similar lines. Both were, that is, promises of continuing life.

To call either of them speeches is to demean their effect. What Oskar was instinctively attempting was to adjust reality, to alter the self-image of both the prisoners and the SS. Long ago, with stubborn certainty, he'd told a group of shiftworkers, Edith Liebgold among them, that they would last the war. He'd flourished the same gift for prophecy when he faced the women from Auschwitz, on the morning they arrived last November, and told them, "You're safe now, you're with me." It can't be ignored that in another age and condition, the Herr Direktor could have become a demagogue of the style of Huey Long of Louisiana or John Lang of Australia, whose gift was to convince the listener that they and he were bonded together to avert by a whisker all the evil devised by other men.

Oskar's birthday speech was delivered in German at night on the workshop floor to the assembled prisoners. An SS detachment had to be brought in to guard a gathering of that size, and the German civilian personnel were present as well. As Oskar began to speak, Poldek Pfefferberg felt the short hairs growing back along his lice promenade stand up. He looked around at the mute faces of Schoenbrun and Fuchs, and at the SS men with their automatics. They will kill this man, he thought. And then everything will fall apart.

The speech pursued two main promises. First, the great

tyranny was coming to a close. He spoke of the SS men around the walls as if they too were imprisoned and yearned for liberation. Many of them, Oskar explained to the prisoners, had been conscripted from other units and without their consent into the Waffen SS. His second promise was that he would stay at Brinnlitz until the end of the hostilities was announced. "And five minutes longer," he said. For the prisoners, the speech, like past pronouncements of Oskar's, promised a future. It stated his vigorous intent that they should not go into graves in the woods. It reminded them of his investment in them, and it enlivened them.

One can only guess how it bedevilled the SS men who heard it. He had genially insulted their corps. How they protested, or whether they swallowed it, he would learn from their reaction. He had also warned them that he would stay in Brinnlitz at least as long as they would, and that therefore he was a witness.

But Oskar did not feel as blithe as he sounded. Later he confessed that at the time he was concerned about actions retreating military units in the Zwittau area might take in regard to Brinnlitz. He was to write, "We were in a panic, because we were afraid of the despairing actions of the SS guards." It must have been a quiet panic, for no prisoner, eating his white bread on Oskar's birthday, seems to have caught a whiff of it. Oskar was also concerned about some Vlasov units which had been stationed on the edges of Brinnlitz. These troops were members of the ROA, the Russian Army of Liberation, formed the year before on the authority of Himmler from the vast ranks of Russian prisoners in the Reich and commanded by General Andrei Vlasov, a former Soviet General captured in front of Moscow three years before. They were a dangerous corps for the Brinnlitz people, for they knew Stalin would want them for a special punishment and feared that the Allies would give them back to him. Vlasov units everywhere were therefore in a state of violent Slavic despair, which they stoked with vodka. When they withdrew, seeking the American lines farther west, they might do anything.

Within two days of Oskar's birthday speech, a set of

movement orders arrived on Liepold's desk. They announced that Untersturmführer Liepold had been transferred to a Waffen SS infantry battalion near Prague. Though Liepold could not have been delighted with them, he seems to have quietly packed and left. He had often said at dinners at Oskar's, particularly after the second bottle of red wine, that he would prefer to be in a combat unit. Lately there had been a number of field-rank officers, Wehrmacht and SS, from the retreating forces invited to dinner in the Herr Direktor's apartment, and their table talk had always been to stir Liepold's itch to seek combat. He had never been faced with as much evidence as the other guests that the cause was finished.

It is unlikely that he called Hassebroeck's office before packing his kit. Telephone communications were not sound, for the Russians had encircled Breslau and were within a walk of Gröss-Rosen itself. But the transfer would not have surprised anyone in Hassebroeck's office, since Liepold had often made patriotic sounds to them too. So, leaving Oberscharführer Motzek in command of Brinnlitz, Josef Liepold drove off to battle, a hardliner who had got his wish.

With Oskar, there was no mute waiting for the close. During the first days of May, he discovered somehow, perhaps even by telephone calls to Brno where lines were still operating, that one of the warehouses with which he regularly dealt had been abandoned. With half a dozen prisoners, he drove off by truck to loot it. There were a number of road blocks on the way south, but at each of them they flashed their dazzling papers, forged, as Oskar would write, with the stamps and signatures "of the highest SS police authorities in Moravia and Bohemia." When they arrived at the warehouse, they found it encircled by fire. Military storehouses in the neighbourhood had been set alight, and there had been incendiary bombing raids as well. From the direction of the inner city, where the Czechoslovak underground were fighting door to door with the garrison, they could hear firing. Herr Schindler ordered the truck to back into the loading bay of the warehouse, broke the door open and discovered that the interior was full of a brand of cigarettes called Egipski.

In spite of such light-hearted piracy, Oskar was frightened by rumours from Slovakia that the Russians were uncritically and informally executing German civilians. From listening to the BBC news each night, he was comforted to find that the war might end before any Russian reached the Zwittau area.

The prisoners also had indirect access to the BBC and knew what the realities were. Throughout the history of Brinnlitz the radio technicians, Zenon Szenwic and Artur Rabner, continuously repaired one or other radio of Oskar's. In the welding shop, Zenon listened with an earphone to the 2 p.m. news, from the Voice of London. During the nightshift, the welders plugged into the 2 a.m. broadcast. An SS man, in the factory one night to take a message to the office, discovered three of them around the radio. We've been working on it for the Herr Direktor, they told the man, and just got it going a minute ago.

Earlier in the year, prisoners had expected that Moravia would be taken by the Americans. Since Eisenhower had baulked at the Elbe, they now knew that it would be the Russians. The circle of prisoners closest to Oskar were composing a letter in Hebrew, explaining what Oskar's record was. It might do some good if presented to American forces, with their considerable Jewish component, including field rabbis. Stern, and Oskar himself, therefore considered it vital that the Herr Direktor somehow be got to the Americans. In part, Oskar's decision was influenced by the characteristic Central European idea of the Russians as barbarians, men of strange religion and uncertain humanity. But apart from that, if some of the reports from the east could be believed, he had grounds for rational fear.

But he was not debilitated by it. He was awake and in a state of hectic expectation when the news of the German surrender came to him through the BBC in the small hours of May 7th. The war in Europe was to cease at midnight on the following night, the night of Tuesday May 8th. Oskar woke Emilie, and the sleepless Stern was summoned into the office to help the Herr Direktor celebrate. Stern could tell that Oskar now felt confident about the SS garrison, but would have been alarmed if he could have guessed how Oskar's certitude would be demonstrated that day.

On the shop floor, the prisoners maintained the usual routines. If anything, they worked better than on other days. Yet, about noon, the Herr Direktor destroyed the pretence of business as usual by piping Churchill's victory speech by loudspeaker throughout the camp. Lutek Feigenbaum, who could understand English, stood by his machine flabbergasted. For others, the honking and grunting voice of Churchill was the first they'd heard in years of a language they would speak in the New World. The idiosyncratic voice, as familiar in its way as that of the dead Führer, carried to the gates and assailed the watchtowers, but the SS took it soberly. They were no longer turning inwards towards the camp. Their eyes, like Oskar's, were focused – but far more sharply – on the Russians. According to Hassebroeck's earlier telegram, they should have been busy in the rich green woods. Instead, clock-watching for midnight, they looked at the black face of the forest, speculating as to whether partisans were there. A fretful Oberscharführer Motzek kept them at their posts, and duty kept them there also. For duty, as so many of their superiors would claim in court, was the SS genius.

In those uneasy two days, between the declaration of peace and its accomplishment, one of the prisoners, a jeweller named Licht, had been crafting a present for Oskar, something more expressive than the metal stud box he'd been given on his birthday. Licht was working with a rare quantity of gold. It had been supplied by old Mr. Jereth of the box factory.

It was established – even the Budzyn men, devout Marxists, knew it – that Oskar would have to flee after midnight. The urge to mark that flight with a small ceremony was the reoccupation of the group – Stern, Finder, Garde, the ejskis, Pemper – close to Oskar. It is remarkable at a time hen they were not sure that they themselves would see the eace, that they should worry about going-away presnts.

All that was readily to hand to make a gift with, however, as base metal. It was Mr. Jereth who had suggested a ource of something better. He opened his mouth to show is gold bridgework. Without Oskar, he said, the SS would ave the damned stuff anyway. My teeth would be in a heap n some SS warehouse, along with the golden fangs of trangers from Lublin, Lódź and Lwów.

It was, of course, an appropriate offering and Jereth was nsistent. He had the bridgework dragged out by a prisoner ho had once had a dental practice in Cracow. Licht the eweller melted the gold down and by noon on May 8th was ngraving a Hebrew inscription on the inner circle of a ring. t was a Talmudic verse which Stern had quoted to Oskar in he front office of Buchheister's in October, 1939. "He who aves a single life, saves the world entire."

In one of the factory garages that afternoon, two prisonrs were engaged in removing the upholstery from the eiling and inner doors of Oskar's Mercedes, inserting small achets of the Herr Direktor's diamonds and replacing the eather work without, they hoped, leaving any bulges. For hem too it was a strange day. When they came out of the arage, the sun was setting behind the towers where the pandaus sat loaded yet weirdly ineffectual. It was as if all he world were waiting for a decisive word.

Words of that nature seem to have come in the evening. again, as on his birthday, Oskar instructed the commandant to assemble the prisoners on the factory floor. Again he German engineers and the secretaries, their escape plans lready made, were present. Among them stood Ingrid, his ld flame. She would not be leaving Brinnlitz in Schindler's ompany. She would make her escape with her brother, a oung war veteran, lame from a wound. Given that Oskar ent to so much trouble to provide his prisoners with trade oods, it is unlikely that he would let an old love like Ingrid

leave Brinnlitz without anything to barter for surviva
Surely they would meet on friendly terms later, somewher
in the West.

As at Oskar's birthday speech, armed guards stoo
around the great hall. The war had nearly six hours to ru
and the SS were sworn never to abandon it in any case
Looking at them, the prisoners tried to gauge their states o
soul.

When it was announced that the Herr Direktor woul
make another address, two women prisoners who ha
shorthand, Miss Waidmann and Mrs. Berger, had eac
fetched a pencil and prepared to take down what was sai
Because it was an *ex tempore* speech, given by a man wh
knew he would soon become a fugitive, it was more con
pelling as spoken than it is on the page in the Waidmann
Berger version. It continued the themes of his birthda
address, but it seemed to make them conclusive for both th
prisoners and the Germans. It declared the prisoners th
inheritors of the new era, it confirmed that everyone els
there – the SS, himself, Emilie, Fuchs, Schoenbrun – wer
now in need of rescue.

"The unconditional surrender of Germany," he saic
"has just been announced. After six years of the cruc
murder of human beings, victims are being mourned, an
Europe is now trying to return to peace and order. I woul
like to turn to you for unconditional order and discipline –
to all of you who together with me have worried throug
many hard years – in order that you can live through th
present and within a few days go back to your destroyed an
plundered homes, looking for survivors from your families
You will thus prevent panic, the results of which cannot b
foreseen."

He did not, of course, mean panic in the prisoners. H
meant panic among the garrison, among the men lining th
walls. He was inviting the SS to leave, and the prisoners t
let them do so. Field Marshal Montgomery, the commande
of the Allied land forces, had, he said, proclaimed that on
should act in a human way towards the conquered, an
everyone – in judging the Germans – had to distinguis

between guilt and duty. "The soldiers at the front, as well as the little man who has done his duty everywhere, shall not be responsible for what a group, calling itself German, has done."

Schindler was uttering a defence of his countrymen which every prisoner who survived the night would hear reiterated a thousand times in the era to come. Yet if anyone had earned the right to proffer that defence and have it listened to with – at least – tolerance, it was surely Herr Oskar Schindler.

"The fact that millions among you, your parents, children and brothers, have been liquidated, has been disapproved by thousands of Germans, and even today there are millions of them who do not know the extent of these horrors." The documents and records found in Dachau and Buchenwald earlier in the year, their details broadcast by the BBC, were the first, said Oskar, that many a German had heard of "this most monstrous destruction." He therefore begged them once again to act in a humane and just way, to leave justice to those authorised. "If you have to accuse a person, do it in the right place. Because in the new Europe there will be judges, incorruptible judges, who will listen to you."

Next he began to speak about his association with the prisoners in the past year. In some ways he sounded almost nostalgic, but he feared as well being judged in a lump with the Goeths and the Hassebroecks.

"Many of you know the persecutions, the chicanery and obstacles which, in order to keep my workers, I had to overcome through many years. If it was already difficult to defend the small rights of the Polish worker, to maintain work for him and to prevent him from being sent by force to the Reich, to defend the workers' apartments and their modest property, then the struggle to defend the Jewish workers has often seemed insurmountable."

He described some of the difficulties, and thanked them for their help in satisfying the demands of the armaments authorities. In view of the lack of output from Brinnlitz, the thanks may have sounded ironic. But they were not offered in an ironic way. What the Herr Direktor was saying in a quite literal sense was: Thank you for helping me make a fool of the system.

He went on to appeal for the local people. "If after a few days of staying here, the doors of freedom are opened to you, think of what many of the people in the neighbourhood of the factory have done to help you with additional food and clothing. I have done everything and spent every effort in getting you additional food, and I pledge to do the utmost in the future to protect you and safeguard your daily bread. I shall continue doing everything I can for you until five minutes past midnight.

"Don't go into the neighbouring houses to rob and plunder. Prove yourselves worthy of the millions of victims among you and refrain from any individual acts of revenge and terror."

He confessed that the prisoners had never been welcome in the area. "The Schindler Jews were taboo in Brinnlitz." But there were higher concerns than local vengeance. "I entrust your Kapos and foremen to continue keeping up order and continued understanding. Therefore tell your people of it, because this is in the interest of your safety. Thank the mill of Daubek, whose help in getting you food went beyond the realms of possibility. On behalf of you, I shall now thank the brave director Daubek, who has done everything to get food for you.

"Don't thank me for your survival. Thank your people who worked day and night to save you from extermination. Thank your fearless Stern and Pemper and a few others, who, thinking of you and worrying about you, especially in Cracow, have faced death every moment. The hour of honour makes it our duty to watch and keep order, as long as we stay here together. I beg of you, even among yourselves, to make nothing but human and just decisions. I wish to thank my personal collaborators for their complete sacrifice in connection with my work."

His speech, weaving from issue to issue, exhausting some ideas, returning tangentially to others, reached the centre of its temerity. Oskar turned to the SS garrison and thanked them for resisting the barbarity of their calling. Some prisoners on the floor thought, He's asked *us* not to provoke them? What is he doing himself? For the SS *was* the SS, the corps of Goeth and John and Hujar and Scheidt. There were things an SS man was taught, things he did and saw, which marked the limits of his humanity. Oskar, they felt, was dangerously pushing the limits.

"I would like," he said, "to thank the assembled SS guards, who without being asked were ordered from the army and navy into this service. As heads of families, they have realised for a long time the contemptibility and sense-lessness of their task. They have acted here in an extraordinarily human and correct manner."

What the prisoners did not see, aghast if a little exalted by the Herr Direktor's nerve, was that Oskar was finishing the work he'd begun on the night of his birthday. He was destroying the SS as combatants. For if they stood there and swallowed his version of what was "human and correct", then there was nothing left to them but to walk away.

"In the end," he said, "I request you all to keep a three minute silence, in memory of the countless victims among you who have died in these cruel years."

They obeyed him. Oberscharführer Motzek and Helen Hirsch, Lusia (who had come up from the cellar only in the past week) and Schoenbrun, Emilie and Goldberg. Those itching for time to pass, those itching to flee. Keeping silent among the giant Hilo machines at the limit of the noisiest of wars.

When it was over, the SS left the hall quickly. The prisoners remained. They looked around and wondered if they were at last the possessors. As Oskar and Emilie moved towards their apartment to pack, prisoners waylaid them. Licht's ring was presented. Oskar spent some time admiring it, he showed the inscription to Emilie and asked Stern for a translation. When he asked where they had got the gold from and discovered it was Jereth's bridgework, they expected him to laugh – Jereth was among the presentation committee, ready to be teased and already flashing the little points of his stripped teeth. But Oskar became very solemn and slowly placed the ring on his finger. Though nobody quite understood it, it was the instant in which they became themselves again, in which Oskar Schindler became dependent on gifts of theirs.

38

In the hours following Oskar's speech the SS garrison began to desert. Inside the factory, the commandos selected from the Budzyn people and from other elements of the prison population had already been issued with the weapons Oskar had provided. It was hoped to disarm the SS rather than wage a ritual battle with them. It was not wise, as Oskar had explained, to attract any retreating and embittered units to the gate. But unless something as outlandish as a treaty was arrived at, the towers would ultimately have to be stormed with grenades.

In truth, however, the commandos had only to formalise the disarming described in Oskar's speech. The guards at the main gate gave up their weapons almost gratefully. On the darkened steps leading up to the SS barracks, Poldek Pfefferberg and a prisoner named Jusek Horn disarmed Commandant Motzek, Pfefferberg putting his finger in the man's back and Motzek, like any sane man over forty with a home to go to, begging them to spare him. Pfefferberg took the commandant's pistol and Motzek, after a short detention during which he cried out for the Herr Direktor to save him, was released and began to walk home.

The towers, about which Uri and the other irregulars must have spent hours of speculation and scheming, were discovered abandoned. Some prisoners, newly armed with the garrison's weapons, were stationed up there to indicate to anyone who passed that the old order still held sway.

When midnight came, there were no SS men or women in the camp. Oskar called Bankier to the office and gave him the key to a particular storeroom. It was a naval supply store and had been situated, until the Russian offensive into

Silesia, somewhere in the Katowice area. It must have existed to supply the crews of river and canal patrol boats, and Oskar had found out that the Armaments Inspectorate wanted to rent storage space for it in some less threatened area. Oskar got the storage contract – "with the help of some gifts," he said later. And so eighteen trucks loaded with coat, uniform and underwear fabric, with worsted yarn and wool, as well as with half a million reels of thread and a range of shoes, had entered the Brinnlitz gate and been unloaded and stored. Stern and others would aver that Oskar knew the stores would remain with him at the end of the war and that he intended the material to provide a starting stake for his prisoners. In a later document, Oskar claims the same thing. He had sought the storage contract, he says, "with the intention of supplying my Jewish protégés at the end of the war with clothing . . . Jewish textile experts estimated the value of my clothing store at more than a hundred and fifty thousand US dollars (peace currency)."

He had in Brinnlitz men capable of making such a judgment – Juda Dresner, for example, who had owned his own textile business in Stradom Street, Cracow; Itzhak Stern, who had worked in a textile company across the road.

For the ritual passing over of this expensive key to Bankier, Oskar was already dressed in prisoner's stripes, as was his wife, Emilie. The reversal towards which he'd been working since the early days of DEF was visibly complete. When he appeared in the courtyard to say goodbye, everyone thought it a lightly put on disguise, which would be lightly taken off again once he encountered the Americans. The wearing of the coarse cloth was, however, an act that would never completely be laughed off. He would in a most thorough sense always remain a hostage to Brinnlitz and Emalia.

Eight prisoners had volunteered to travel with Oskar and Emilie. They were all very young, but they included a couple, Richard and Anka Rechen. The eldest of them was an engineer called Edek Heuberger, but he was still nearly ten years younger than the Schindlers. Later, he would supply the details of their eccentric journey.

Emilie, Oskar and a driver were meant to occupy the Mercedes. The others would follow in a truck loaded with food, and with cigarettes and drink for bartering. Oskar seemed anxious to be away. One arm of the Russian threat, the Vlasovs, was gone. They had marched out in the past few days. But the other, it was presumed, would be in Brinnlitz by the next morning, or even sooner. From the back seat of the Mercedes, where Emilie and Oskar sat up in their prison uniforms, not, it had to be admitted, much like prisoners, more like bourgeoisie off to a fancy-dress ball – Oskar still rumbled out advice for Stern, orders to Bankier and Salpeter. But you could tell he wanted to be off. Yet when the driver, Dolek Grünhaut, tried to start the Mercedes, the engine was dead. Oskar climbed out of the back seat to look under the bonnet. He was alarmed, a different man from the one who'd given the commanding speech in the factory hall a few hours earlier. What is it? he kept asking. But it was hard for Grünhaut to tell without proper light. It took him a little time to find the fault, for it was not one he expected. Someone, frightened by the idea of Oskar's departure, had cut the metal leads to the coil.

Pfefferberg, part of the crowd gathered to wave the Herr Direktor off, rushed to the welding shop, brought back his gear, and went to work. He was sweating and his hands seemed clumsy, for he was rattled by the urgency he could sense in Oskar. Schindler kept looking at the gate as if the Russians might materialise at any second. It was not an improbable fear – others in the courtyard were tormented by the same ironic possibility – if Pfefferberg worked too hard and took too long. But at last the engine caught to Grünhaut's turning of the key.

The cut and then re-welded wires ensured one thing; once the engine turned, the Mercedes left, the truck following it. Everyone was too unnerved to make formal goodbyes, but a letter signed by Dr. Hilfstein and Stern and Salpeter, attesting to Oskar's and Emilie's record, was handed to the Schindlers.

The Schindler convoy rolled out the gate and, at the road by the siding, turned left towards Havlíčkôv Brod and towards what was for Oskar the safer end of Europe. There was something nuptial about it: Oskar, who had come to Brinnlitz with so many women, was leaving with his wife. Stern and the others remained standing in the courtyard. After so many promises, they were their own people. The weight and uncertainty of that must now be borne.

The hiatus lasted three days and had its history and its dangers. Once the SS left, the only representative of the killing machine left in Brinnlitz was a German Kapo who had come from Gröss-Rosen with the Schindler men. He was a man with a murderous record in Gröss-Rosen itself, and had also made enemies in Brinnlitz. A pack of male prisoners now dragged him from his bunk down to the factory hall and enthusiastically and mercilessly hanged him from one of the same beams with which Untersturmführer Liepold had recently threatened the prison population. Some inmates tried to intervene, but the executioners were in a rage and could not be stopped.

It was an event, this first homicide of the peace, which many Brinnlitz people would forever abhor. They had seen Amon hang poor engineer Krautwirt on the Appellplatz at Plaszów, and this hanging – though for different reasons – sickened them as profoundly. For Amon was Amon and beyond altering. But these hangmen were their brothers.

When the Kapo ceased his twitching, he was left suspended above the silenced machines. He perplexed people though. He was supposed to gladden them, but he threw doubt. At last some men who had not hanged him cut him down and incinerated him. It exemplified the eccentricity of Brinnlitz that the only body fed into the furnaces which, by decree, should have been employed to burn the Jewish dead, was the corpse of an Aryan.

The distribution of the goods in the navy store went on throughout the next day. Lengths of worsted material had to be cut from the great bolts of fabric. Moshe Bejski said that each prisoner was given three yards, and a complete set of underwear and some reels of cotton. Some women began that very day to make the suits in which they would travel home. Others kept the fabric intact so that, traded, it would keep them alive in the confused days to come.

A ration of the Egipski cigarettes which Oskar had plundered from burning Brno was also issued, and each prisoner was given a bottle of vodka from Salpeter's storehouse. Few would drink it. It was, of course, simply too precious to drink.

After dark on that second night, a Panzer unit came down the road from the direction of Zwittau. Lutek Feigenbaum, behind a bush near the gate and armed with a rifle, had the urge to fire as soon as the first tank passed within sight of the camp. But he considered it rash. The vehicles rattled and edged past. A gunner in one of the rear tanks in the column, understanding that the fence and the watchtowers meant that Jewish criminals might be lying low in there, swivelled his gun and sent two shells into the camp. One exploded in the courtyard, the other on the women's balcony. It was a random exhibition of spite and, through wisdom or astonishment, none of the armed prisoners answered it.

When the last tank had vanished, the men of the commandos could hear mourning from the courtyard and from the women's dormitory upstairs. A girl had been wounded by shell fragments. She herself was in shock, but the sight of her injuries had released in the women all the barely expressed grief of the past years. While the women keened, the Brinnlitz doctors examined the girl and found that her wounds were superficial.

Oskar's party travelled for the first hours of their escape at the tail of a column of Wehrmacht trucks. At midnight feats of this nature had become feasible, and no one pestered them. Behind them they could hear German engineers dynamiting installations, and occasionally there was the clamour of a distant ambush arranged by the Czech underground. Near the town of Havlíĉkŏv Brod they must have fallen behind, being stopped by Czech partisans who stood in the middle of the road. Oskar went on impersonating a prisoner. "These good people and myself are escapees from a labour camp. The SS fled, and the Herr Direktor. This is the Herr Direktor's car."

The Czechs asked them if they had weapons. Heuberger had come from the truck and joined the discussion. He confessed that he had a rifle. All right, said the Czechs, you'd better give us what you have. If the Russians intercepted you and found that you had weapons, they might not understand why. Your defence is your prison clothes.

In this town, south-east of Prague and on the road to Austria, there was still the likelihood of meeting disgruntled units. The partisans directed Oskar and the others to the Czech Red Cross office in the town square. There they could safely bunk down for the rest of the night.

But when they reached town, the Red Cross officials suggested to them that, given the uncertainty of the peace, they would probably be safest in the town jail. The vehicles were left in the square, in sight of the Red Cross office, and Oskar, Emilie and their eight companions carried their few pieces of baggage and slept in the unlocked cells of the police station.

When they returned to the square in the morning, they found that both vehicles had been stripped. All the upholstery had been torn from the interior of the Mercedes, and the diamonds were gone; the tyres had been taken from the truck, and the engines had been plundered. The Czechs were philosophic about it. We all have to expect to lose something in times like these. Perhaps they may have even suspected Oskar, with his fair complexion and his blue eyes, of being a fugitive SS man.

The party were without their own transport, but a train ran south in the direction of Kaplice, and they caught it, dressed still in their stripes. Heuberger says that they took the train "as far as the forest, and then walked". Somewhere in that forested border region, well to the north of Linz, they could expect to encounter the Americans.

They were hiking down a wooded road when they met two young Americans sitting by a machine gun. One of Oskar's prisoners began to speak with them in English.

"Our orders are not to let anyone pass on this road," one of them said.

"Is it forbidden to circle round through the woods?" asked Oskar.

The boy chewed. This strange chewing race!

"Guess not," said the GI at last.

So they swung through the woods and, back on the road half an hour later, ran into an infantry company marching north in double column. Through the English speaker once more, they began to talk to the unit's forward scouts. The commanding officer himself drew up in a jeep, dismounted, interrogated them. They were frank with him, telling him that Oskar was the Herr Direktor, that they were Jews. They believed they were on safe ground, for they knew from the BBC that the US army included many Americans of both German and Jewish origin. "Don't move," said the captain. He drove away without explanation, leaving them in the half embarrassed command of the young infantry men, who offered them cigarettes, the Virginia kind, which had that almost glossy look – like the jeep, the uniforms, the equipment – of coming from a grand, brash, unfettered and un-ersatz manufactury.

Though Emilie and the prisoners were uneasy that Oskar might be arrested, he himself sat on the grass without seeming concerned and took in the spring scene in these high woods. He had his Hebrew letter, and New York, he knew, was ethnically a city where Hebrew was not unknown. Half an hour passed and some soldiers appeared, coming down the road in an informal bunch, not strung out in the infantry manner. They were a group of Jewish infantrymen and included a field rabbi. They were very effusive. They embraced all the party, Emilie and Oskar as well. For these, the party was told, were the first concentration camp survivors the battalion had met.

When the greetings were over, Oskar brought out his Hebrew reference, and the rabbi read it and began to weep. He relayed the details to the other Americans. There was more applause, more handshaking, more embraces. The young GIs seemed so open, so loud, so childlike. Though

411

one or two generations out of Central Europe, they had been so marked by America that the Schindlers and the prisoners looked at them with as much amazement as was returned.

The result was that the Schindler party spent two days on the Austrian frontier as guests of the regimental commander and the rabbi. They drank excellent coffee, such as the authentic prisoners in the group had not tasted since before the founding of the ghetto. They ate opulently.

After two days, the rabbi presented them with a captured ambulance in which they drove to the ruined city of Linz in Upper Austria.

On the second day of peace in Brinnlitz, the Russians still had not appeared. The commando group worried about the necessity of hanging on to the camp for longer than they had thought they'd have to. One thing they remembered was that the only time they'd seen the SS show fear – apart from the anxiety of Motzek and his colleagues in the past few days – had been when typhus broke out. So they hung typhus signs all over the wire.

Three Czech partisans turned up at the gate in the afternoon and talked through the fence to the men on sentry duty. It's all over now, they said. You're free to walk out whenever you want.

When the Russians arrive, said the prison commandos. Until then we're keeping everyone in.

Their answer exhibited some of the pathology of the prisoner, the suspicion you got after a time that the world beyond the fence was perilous and had to be re-entered by stages. It also showed their canniness. They were not convinced yet that the last German unit had gone.

The Czechs shrugged and went away.

That night, when Poldek Pfefferberg was part of the guard at the main gate, motorcycle engines were heard on the road. They did not pass by as the Panzers had done, but could be heard turning in towards the camp itself. Five cycles marked with the Death's Head corps symbol of the SS appeared out of the dark and drew up noisily by the front fence. As the SS men – very young, Poldek remembers – switched off their engines, dismounted, and approached the gate, a debate raged among the armed men inside as to whether the visitors ought to be shot out of hand.

The NCO in charge of the motorcycle party seemed to sense a threat. He stood a little way from the wire with his hands extended. They needed petrol, he said. He presumed that being a factory camp they would have some petrol.

Pfefferberg advised, during a muttered dispute, that it was better to supply them and send them packing than to create problems by opening fire. Other elements of their regiment might be in the region, and be drawn by an outburst of gunshots.

So in the end the SS were let through the gate, and some of the prisoners went to the garage for petrol. The SS NCO was careful to convey to the camp commandos – who had put on blue overalls in an attempt to look like informal guards, or at least like German Kapos – that he did not find anything peculiar in the idea of armed prisoners defending their camp from within.

"I hope you realise there's typhus here," said Pfefferberg in German, pointing to the signs.

The SS men looked at each other.

"We've already lost two dozen people," said Pfefferberg. "We have another fifty isolated in the cellar."

This claim seemed to impress the gentlemen of the Death's Head. They were tired. They were fleeing. That was enough for them. They didn't want any bacterial perils on top of the others.

When the petrol arrived in carrying cans, they expressed their thanks, bowed, and left through the gate. The prisoners watched them fill their tanks and considerately leave by the wire any cans they could not fit into their sidecars. They put on their gloves, started their engines, and left without too much revving of the motors, careful not to waste their new tankfuls on flourishes. Their clatter faded south-west through the village. For the men at the gate, this polite encounter would be their last with anyone wearing the uniform of Heinrich Himmler's strange legion.

When on the third day the camp was liberated it was by a single Russian officer. Riding a horse, he emerged through the defile through which the road and the railway siding approached the Brinnlitz gate. As he drew closer it became apparent that the horse was a mere pony, the officer's thin feet in the stirrups nearly touching the road and his legs bent in comically underneath the animal's skinny abdomen. He seemed to be bringing to Brinnlitz a personal, hard-won deliverance, for his uniform was worn, the leather strap of his rifle so withered by sweat and winter and campaigning that it had had to be replaced by rope. The reins of the pony were also of rope. The officer was fair-complexioned and, as Russians always look to Poles, immensely alien, immensely familiar.

After a short conversation in hybrid Polish-Russian, the commando at the gate let him in. Around the balconies of the second floor, the rumour of his arrival spread. As he dismounted he was kissed by Mrs. Krumholz. He smiled and called, in two languages, for a chair. One of the younger men brought it.

Standing on it to give himself a height advantage which, in relation to most of the prisoners, he did not need, he made what sounded like a standard liberation speech in Russian. Moshe Bejski could catch its gist. They had been liberated by the glorious Soviets. They were free to go to town, to move in the direction of their choosing. For under the Soviets, as in the mythical heaven, there was neither Jew nor Gentile, male nor female, bond nor free. They were not to take any cheap revenge in the town. Their allies would find their oppressors, and subject them to solemn and appropriate punishment. The fact of their freedom should, to them, outweigh any other consideration.

He got down from his chair and smiled, as if he was saying that now he had finished as a spokesman and was prepared to answer questions. Bejski and some of the others began to speak to him, and he pointed to himself and said in creaky Belorussian Yiddish, the sort you pick up from your grandparents rather than your parents, that he was Jewish.

Now the conversation took on a new intimacy.

"Have you been in Poland?" Bejski asked him.

"Yes," the officer admitted. "I've come from Poland now."

"Are there any Jews left up there?"

"I saw none."

Prisoners were crowding round, translating and relaying the conversation to each other.

"Where are you from?" the officer asked Bejski.

"Cracow."

"I was in Cracow two weeks ago."

"Auschwitz? What about Auschwitz?"

"I heard that at Auschwitz there are still a few Jews."

The prisoners grew thoughtful. The Russian made Poland sound like a vacuum now, and if they returned to Cracow they'd rattle round in it bleakly like dried peas in a jar.

"Is there anything I can do for you?" the officer asked.

There were cries for food. He thought he could get them a cartload of bread, and perhaps some horsemeat. It should arrive before dusk. "But you should see what they have in town here," the officer suggested.

It was a radical idea – that they ought to just go out of the gate and begin shopping in Brinnlitz. For some of them it was still an unimaginable option.

Young men like Pemper and Bejski pursued the officer as he left. If there were no Jews in Poland, there was nowhere to go. They didn't want him to give them instructions but felt he ought to discuss their quandary with them. The Russian paused in untying the reins of his pony from a railing.

"I don't know," he said looking them in the face. "I don't know where you ought to go. Don't go east – that much I can tell you. But don't go west either." His fingers returned to untying the knot. "They don't like us anywhere."

As the Russian officer had urged them, the Brinnlitz prisoners moved out of the gate at last to make their first tentative contact with the outer world. The young were the first to try it. Danka Dresner went out the day after the liberation and climbed the wooded hill behind the camp.

Lilies and anemones were beginning to bud, and birds were arriving from Africa. Danka sat on the hill for a while, savouring the day, then rolled down it and lay in the grass at the bottom, inhaling the fragrances and looking at the sky. She was there for so long that her parents presumed she had come to grief in the village, either at the hands of the townspeople or the Russians.

Goldberg left early too, was perhaps the first to go, on his way to pick up his riches from Cracow. He would emigrate, as quickly as he could arrange it, to Brazil.

Most of the older prisoners stayed in camp. The Russians had now moved into Brinnlitz, occupying as an officers' quarters a villa on a hill above the village. They brought to the camp a butchered horse, which the prisoners ate ravenously, some of them finding it too rich after their diet of bread and vegetables and Emilie Schindler's porridge.

Lutek Feigenbaum, Janek Dresner and young Sternberg went foraging in town. The village was patrolled by the Czech underground, and Brinnlitz folk of German descent were therefore wary of the liberated prisoners. A grocer indicated to the boys that they were welcome to a bag of sugar he'd been keeping in his storeroom. Young Sternberg found the sugar irresistible, lowering his face to it and swallowing it by the handful. It made him cruelly ill. He discovered therefore what the Schindler group were finding in Nuremberg and Ravensburg – that liberty and the day of plenty had to be approached gradually.

The main purpose of Feigenbaum's expedition to town had been to get bread. As a member of the Brinnlitz commandos, he was armed with a pistol and a rifle, and when the baker insisted there was no bread, one of the others said to him, "Threaten him with a rifle." The man, after all, was Sudetendeutsch and in theory had condoned their misery. Feigenbaum pointed the weapon at the baker and moved through the shop into the residence beyond, looking for hidden flour. He found the baker's wife and two daughters seated in the parlour and huddled in shock. In their terror, they were indistinguishable from any Cracow family during an Aktion. A great shame overwhelmed him. He nodded to the women as if he were on a social visit, and left.

The same shame overtook Mila Pfefferberg on her first visit to the village. As she entered the square, a Czech partisan stopped two Sudeten girls and made them take off their shoes so that Mila, who had only clogs, could select the pair which fitted her best. This sort of dominance made her flush, and she sat on the pavement making her embarrassed choice. The partisan gave the clogs to the Sudeten girl and passed on. Mila then turned in her tracks, ran up behind the girl and gave the shoes back. The Sudetendeutsch, Mila remembers, was not even gracious.

In the evenings, the Russians came to the camp looking for women. Pfefferberg had to put a pistol to the head of a soldier who penetrated the women's quarters and grabbed Mrs. Krumholz. (Mrs. Krumholz would for years later chide Pfefferberg, pointing at him and accusing him. "Whatever chance I had of getting off with a younger man, that scoundrel prevented it!") Three girls were taken away – more or less voluntarily – to a Russian party, and came back after three days and, they claimed, a good time.

The hold of Brinnlitz was a negative one, and within a week the prisoners began to move out. Some, whose families had been consumed, went directly to the West, never wishing to see Poland again. The Bejski boys, using their cloth and vodka to pay their way, travelled to Italy and boarded a Zionist boat to Palestine. The Dresners walked across Moravia and Bohemia and into Germany, where Janek was among the first ten students to enrol in the Bavarian University of Erlangen when it opened later in the year.

Manci Rosner returned to Podgórze, where Henry had agreed to meet her. Henry Rosner himself, liberated from Dachau with Olek, was in a pissoir in Munich one day and saw another client of the place wearing prison-camp stripes. He asked the man where he had been imprisoned. "Brinnlitz," said the man. Everyone except an old lady, the man told him (inaccurately as it turned out), had survived Brinnlitz. Manci would come to hear of Henry's survival through a cousin who turned up at the room in Podgórze where she was waiting, waving the Polish newspaper in which were listed the names of Poles liberated from Dachau. "Manci," said the cousin, "give me a kiss. Henry's alive and so is Olek."

Regina Horowitz had a similar rendezvous. It took her three weeks to travel from Brinnlitz to Cracow with her daughter Niusia. She rented a room – the handout from the navy store made that possible – and waited for Dolek. When he arrived, they made enquiries after Richard, but there was no news. One day that summer Regina saw the film of Auschwitz which the Russians had made and were showing free of charge to the Polish population. She saw the famous frames involving the camp children, who looked out from behind the wire or were escorted by nuns past the electrified fence of Auschwitz I. Being so small and so engaging, Richard figured in most of the frames. Regina got up screaming and left the theatre. The manager and a number of passing citizens tried to soothe her in the street. "It's my son, it's my son!" she kept screaming. Now that she knew he was alive, she was able to discover that Richard had been released by the Russians into the hands of one of the Jewish rescue organisations. Thinking both his parents dead, the rescue body had had him adopted by some old acquaintances of the Horowitzes, people named Liebling. Regina was given the address, and when she arrived at the Lieblings' apartment could hear Richard inside, banging on a saucepan and calling, "Today there'll be soup for everyone!" When she knocked on the door, he called to Mrs. Liebling to answer it.

So he was returned to her. But after what he had seen of the scaffolds of Plaszów and Auschwitz, she could never take him to a children's playground without his growing hysterical at the sight of the swing frames.

From Linz, where Oskar's group reported to the American authorities and were relieved of their unreliable ambulance, the party was taken by truck north to Nuremberg, to a large holding centre for wandering concentration camp prisoners. They were discovering that, as they had suspected, liberation wasn't a straightforward business.

Richard Rechen had an aunt in Constanz, by the lake on the Swiss border. When the Americans asked the group if there was anywhere they could go, they nominated this aunt. The intent of the eight young prisoners from Brinnlitz was to deliver the Schindlers, if possible, across the Swiss border, in case vengeance against Germany erupted suddenly and, even in the American zone, the Schindlers were unjustly punished. Additionally, as all eight were potential emigrants they believed that such matters would be easier to arrange from Switzerland.

Heuberger recalls that their relationship with the American commandant in Nuremberg was cordial, but the man would not spare them any transport to take them south to Constanz. They made the journey through the Black Forest as best they could, some of it on foot, some of it by train. Near Ravensburg they went to the local prison camp and spoke to the US commandant. Here again they stayed as guests for some days, resting and living high on army rations. In return for the hospitality they sat up late with the commandant, who was of Jewish descent, and told him tales of Amon and Plaszów, of Gröss-Rosen, Auschwitz, Brinnlitz. They hoped he would give them transport to Constanz. He could not spare a truck, but gave them a bus instead, as well as some provisions for the journey. Though Oskar still carried some currency and diamonds worth over a thousand Reichsmarks, the bus does not appear to have been bought but was given freely. After his dealings with the German bureaucrats, it must have been difficult for Oskar to adjust to that sort of transaction.

West of Constanz, on the Swiss border and in the French-occupied zone, they parked the bus in the village of Kreuzlingen. Rechen went to the town hardware store and bought a pair of wire cutters. It seems that the party was still wearing their prison clothes when the wire cutters were frankly purchased by Rechen. Perhaps the man behind the counter was influenced by one of two considerations: (a) this was a prisoner, and if thwarted might call his French protectors; (b) this was in fact a German officer escaping in disguise and perhaps should be helped.

The border fence ran through the middle of Kreuzlingen and was guarded on the German side by French sentries of the Sûreté Militaire. The group approached this barrier on the edge of the village and, snipping the wires, waited for the sentry to near the end of his beat before scurrying through to Switzerland. Unhappily, a woman from the village observed them from a bend of the road and rushed to the border to alert the French and Swiss. In a quiet Swiss village square, a mirror image of one on the German side, the Swiss police surrounded the party, but Richard and Anka Rechen broke away and had to be chased and apprehended by a patrol car. The party was, within half an hour, passed back to the French, who at once searched their possessions and, discovering jewels and currency, drove them to the former German prison and locked them in separate cells.

It was clear to Heuberger that they were under suspicion of having been concentration camp guards. In that sense the weight they had put on as guests of the Americans rebounded on them, for they did not look as deprived as when they'd first left Brinnlitz. They were interrogated separately about their journey, about the valuables they were carrying. Each of them could tell a plausible story, but did not know if the others were telling the same one. They seem to have been afraid, in a way that had not applied with the Americans, that if the French discovered Oskar's identity and his function in Brinnlitz, they would arraign him as a matter of course.

Prevaricating for Oskar's sake and Emilie's, they remained a week there. The Schindlers themselves now knew enough about Judaism to pass the obvious cultural tests. But Oskar's manner and physical condition didn't make his posture of recent-prisoner-of-the-SS very credible. Unhappily his Hebrew letter was over in Linz, on the files of the Americans.

Edek Heuberger, as the doyen of the eight, was interrogated most regularly, and on the seventh day of his imprisonment was brought into the interrogation room to find a second person there, a man in civilian clothes, a speaker of Polish, brought in to test Heuberger's claim that he came from Cracow. For some reason, because the Pole played the compassionate rôle in the questioning that followed, or because of the familiarity of the language, Heuberger broke down, began to weep, and told the full story in fluent Polish. The rest were called one by one, were shown Heuberger, were told he had confessed, and then ordered to recite their version of the truth in Polish. When at the end of the morning the versions matched, the whole group, the Schindlers included, were gathered in the interrogation room and embraced by both interrogators. The Frenchman, says Heuberger, was weeping. Everyone was delighted at the phenomenon – a weeping interrogator. When he managed to compose himself, he called for lunch to be brought in for himself, his colleagues, the Schindlers, the eight.

That afternoon he had them transferred to a lakeside hotel in Constanz, where they stayed for some days at the expense of the French military government.

By the time he sat down to dinner that evening at the hotel with Emilie, Heuberger, the Rechens and the others, Oskar's property had passed to the Soviets, and his last few jewels and currency were lost in the interstices of the liberating bureaucracy. He was as good as penniless, but was eating as well as could be managed in a good hotel with a number of his 'family'. All of which would be the pattern of his future.

Epilogue

Oskar's high season ended now. The peace would never exalt him as had the war. Oskar and Emilie came to Munich. For a time they shared lodgings with the Rosners, for Henry and his brother had been engaged to play at a Munich restaurant and had achieved a modest prosperity. One of his former prisoners, meeting him at the Rosners' cramped apartment, was shocked by his torn coat. His property in Cracow and Moravia had of course been confiscated by the Russians, and his remaining jewellery had been traded for food and drink.

When the Feigenbaums arrived in Munich, they met his latest mistress, a Jewish girl, a survivor not of Brinnlitz but of worse camps than that. Many of the visitors to Oskar's rented rooms, indulgent as they were towards Oskar's heroic weaknesses, felt ashamed for Emilie's sake.

He was still a wildly generous friend and a great discoverer of unprocurables. Henry Rosner remembers that he unearthed a source of chickens in the midst of chickenless Munich. He clung to the company of those of his Jews who had come to Germany – the Rosners, the Pfefferbergs, the Dresners, the Feigenbaums, the Sternbergs. Some cynics would later say that at the time it was wise of anyone involved in concentration camps to stay close to Jewish friends as protective colouring. But his dependence went beyond that sort of instinctive cunning. The Schindlerjuden had become his family.

In common with them, he heard that Amon Goeth had been captured by Patton's Americans the previous February, while a patient in an SS sanatorium at Bad Tolz, imprisoned in Dachau, and at the close of the war handed over to the new Polish government. Amon was in fact one of the first Germans despatched to Poland for judgment. A number of former prisoners were invited to attend the trial as witnesses; a deluded Amon even considered calling Helen Hirsch and Oskar Schindler for the defence. Oskar himself did not go to Cracow for the trials. Those who did, found that Goeth, lean from his diabetes, offered a subdued but unrepentant defence. All the orders for each of his acts of execution and transportation had been signed by superiors, he claimed, and were therefore *their* crimes, not his. Witnesses who told of murders committed by the commandant's own hand were, said Amon, maliciously exaggerating. There had been some prisoners executed as saboteurs, but there were always saboteurs in war.

Mietek Pemper, waiting in the body of the court to be called to give evidence, sat beside another Plaszów graduate who stared at Amon in the dock and whispered, "That man still terrifies me." But Pemper himself, as first witness for the prosecution, delivered an exact catalogue of Amon's crimes. He was followed by others, among them Dr. Biberstein and Helen Hirsch, who had precise and painful memories. Amon was condemned to death and hanged in Cracow on September 13th 1946. It was two years to the day since his arrest by the SS in Vienna on black-marketeering charges. According to the Cracow press, he went to the gallows without compunction and gave the National Socialist salute before dying.

In Munich, Oskar himself identified Liepold, who had been detained by the Americans. A Brinnlitz prisoner accompanied Oskar at the line-up, and says that Oskar asked the protesting Liepold, "Do you want *me* to do it, or would you rather leave it to the fifty angry Jews who are waiting downstairs in the street?" Liepold would also be hanged – not for his crimes in Brinnlitz, but for earlier murders in Budzyn.

Oskar had probably already conceived the scheme of becoming a farmer in Argentina, a breeder of nutria, the large South American aquatic rodents considered precious for their skins. Oskar presumed that the same excellent commercial instincts which had brought him to Cracow in

1939 were now urging him to cross the Atlantic. He was penniless, but the Joint Distribution Committee, the international Jewish relief organisation to whom Oskar had made reports during the war and to whom his record was known, were willing to help him. In 1949 they made him an *ex gratia* payment of fifteen thousand dollars and gave a reference (*To whom it may concern*) signed by M. W. Beckelman, the Vice Chairman of the 'Joint's' Executive Council. It said,

> The American Joint Distribution Committee has thoroughly investigated the wartime and occupation activities of Mr. Schindler. . . We recommend wholeheartedly that all organisations and individuals contacted by Mr. Schindler do their utmost to help him, in recognition of his outstanding service. . . Under the guise of operating a Nazi labour factory first in Poland and then in the Sudetenland, Mr. Schindler managed to take in as employees and protect Jewish men and women destined for death in Auschwitz or other infamous concentration camps. . . "Schindler's camp in Brinnlitz," witnesses have told the Joint Distribution Committee, "was the only camp in the Nazi-occupied territories where a Jew was never killed, or even beaten, but was always treated as a human being." Now that he is about to begin his life anew, let us help him as once he helped our brethren.

When he sailed for Argentina, he took with him half a dozen families of Schindlerjuden, paying the passage for many of them. With Emilie, he settled on a farm in Buenos Aires province and worked it for nearly ten years. Those of Oskar's survivors who did not see him in those years find it hard now to imagine him as a farmer, since he was never a man of steady routine. It is said, and there is some truth in it, that Emalia and Brinnlitz succeeded in their eccentric way because of the acumen of men like Stern and Bankier. In Argentina, Oskar had no such support, apart, of course, from the good sense and rural industriousness of his wife.

The decade in which Oskar farmed nutria, however, was the period in which it was demonstrated that breeding, as distinct from trapping, did not produce pelts of adequate quality. Many other nutria enterprises failed in that time, and in 1957 the Schindlers' farm went bankrupt. Emilie and Oskar moved into a house provided by B'nai B'rith in San Vicente, a southern suburb of Buenos Aires, and for a time Oskar looked for work as a sales representative. Within a year, however, he left for Germany. He would never live with Emilie again.

From a small apartment in Frankfurt, he sought capital to buy a cement works, and pursued the possibility of major compensation from the West German Ministry of Finance for the loss of his Polish and Czechoslovakian properties. Little came of this effort. Some of Oskar's survivors considered that the failure of the German government to pay him his due arose from lingering Hitlerism in the middle reaches of the civil service. But Oskar's claim probably failed for technical reasons, and it is not possible to detect bureaucratic malice in the correspondence addressed to Oskar from the ministry.

The Schindler cement enterprise was launched on capital from the Joint Distribution Committee and 'loans' from a number of Schindler Jews who had done well in postwar Germany. It had a brief history. By 1961, Oskar was insolvent again. His factory had been crippled by a series of harsh winters in which the construction industry had closed down, but some of the Schindler survivors believe the company's failure was abetted by Oskar's restlessness and low tolerance for routine.

That year, hearing that he was in trouble, the Schindler-juden in Israel invited him to visit them at their expense. An advertisement appeared in Israel's Polish language press asking all former inmates of Concentration Camp Brinnlitz who had known "Oskar Schindler the German" to contact the newspaper. In Tel Aviv, Oskar was welcomed ecstatically. The postwar children of his survivors mobbed him. He had grown heavier and his features had thickened. But at the parties and receptions, those who had known him saw that he was the same indomitable Oskar. The growling deft wit, the outrageous Charles Boyer charm, the voracious thirst had all survived his two bankruptcies.

It was the year of the Adolf Eichmann trial, and Oskar's visit to Israel aroused some interest from the international press. On the eve of the opening of Eichmann's trial, the correspondent of the London *Daily Mail* wrote a feature on the contrast between the records of the two men, and quoted the preamble of an appeal the Schindlerjuden had opened to assist Oskar. "We do not forget the sorrows of Egypt, we do not forget Haman, we do not forget Hitler. Thus, among the unjust, we do not forget the just. Remember Oskar Schindler."

There was some incredulity among Holocaust survivors about the idea of a beneficent labour camp such as Oskar's, and this disbelief found its voice through a journalist at a press conference with Schindler in Jerusalem. "How do you explain," he asked, "that you knew all the senior SS men in the Cracow region and had regular dealings with them?" "At that stage in history," Oskar answered, "it was rather difficult to discuss the fate of Jews with the Chief Rabbi of Jerusalem."

The Department of Testimonies of the Yad Vashem had, near the end of Oskar's Argentine residence, asked for and been given by him a general statement of his activities in Cracow and Brinnlitz. Now, on their own initiative and under the influence of Itzhak Stern, Jakob Sternberg and Moshe Bejski (once Oskar's forger of official stamps, now a respected and scholarly lawyer), the Board of Trustees of Yad Vashem began to consider the question of an official tribute to Oskar. The chairman of the board was Justice Landau, the presiding judge at the Eichmann trial. Yad Vashem sought and received a mass of testimonies concerning Oskar. Of this large body of statements, four are critical of him. Though these four all state that without Oskar they would have perished, they criticise his business methods in the early months of the war. Two of the four disparaging testimonies are written by a father and son, called, earlier in this account, the Cs. In their enamelware outlet in Cracow, Oskar had installed his mistress Ingrid as Treuhänder. A third statement is by the Cs' secretary and repeats the allegations of punching and bullying, rumours of which Stern had reported back to Oskar in 1940. The fourth comes from a man who claims to have had a pre-war interest in Oskar's enamel factory under its former name Rekord, an interest, he claimed, that Oskar had ignored.

Justice Landau and his Board must have considered these four statements insignificant against the massed testimony of other Schindlerjuden, and they made no comment on them. Since all four stated that Oskar was their saviour in any case, it is said to have occurred to the board to ask why, if Oskar had committed crimes against these people, he went to such extravagant pains to save them?

The municipality of Tel Aviv was the first body to honour Oskar. On his fifty-third birthday he unveiled a plaque in the Park of Heroes. The inscription describes him as saviour of twelve hundred prisoners of KL Brinnlitz, and though it understates numerically the extent of his rescue, it declares that it had been erected in love and gratitude. Ten days later in Jerusalem, he was declared a Righteous Person, this title being a peculiarly Israeli honour based on an ancient tribal assumption that in the mass of Gentiles, the God of Israel would always provide a leavening of just men. Oskar was invited also to plant a carob tree in the Avenue of the Righteous leading to the Yad Vashem Museum. The tree is still there, marked by a plaque, in a grove which contains trees planted in the name of all the other Righteous. A tree for Julius Madritsch, who had illicitly fed and protected his workers in a manner quite unheard of among the Krupps and the Farbens, stands there also, and a tree for Raimund Titsch, the Madritsch supervisor in Plaszów. On that stony ridge, few of the memorial trees have grown to more than ten feet.

The German press carried stories of Oskar's wartime rescues and of the Yad Vashem ceremonies. These reports, always laudatory, did not make his life easier. He was hissed on the streets of Frankfurt, stones were thrown, a group of workmen jeered him and called out that he ought to have been burned with the Jews. In 1963 he punched a factory worker who'd called him a Jew-kisser, and the man lodged a charge of assault. In the local court, the lowest level of the German judiciary, Oskar received a lecture from the judge and was ordered to pay damages. "I would kill myself," he wrote to Henry Rosner in New York, "if it wouldn't give them so much satisfaction."

These humiliations increased his dependence on the survivors. They were his only emotional and financial surety. For the rest of his life he would spend some months of every year with them, living honoured and well in Tel Aviv and Jerusalem, eating free of charge at a Rumanian restaurant in Ben Yehudah Street, Tel Aviv, though subject sometimes to Moshe Bejski's filial efforts to limit his drinking to three double cognacs a night. In the end, he would always return to the other half of his soul, the disinherited self, the mean, cramped apartment a few hundred yards from Frankfurt central railway station. Writing from Los Angeles to other Schindlerjuden in the United States that year, Poldek Pfefferberg urged all survivors to donate at least a day's pay a year to Oskar Schindler, whose state he described as "discouragement, loneliness, disillusion." Oskar's contacts with the Schindlerjuden continued on a yearly basis. It was a seasonal matter – half the year as the Israeli butterfly, half the year as the Frankfurt grub. He was continually short of money.

A Tel Aviv committee of which Itzhak Stern, Jakob Sternberg and Moshe Bejski were again members, continued to lobby the West German government for an adequate pension for Oskar. The grounds for their appeal were his wartime heroism, the property he had lost, and the by-now fragile state of his health. The first official reaction from the German government was however the award of the Cross of Merit in 1966, in a ceremony at which Konrad Adenauer presided. It was not till July 1st 1968 that the Ministry of Finance was happy to report that from that date it would pay him a pension of two hundred Marks per month. Three months later, pensioner Schindler received the Papal Knighthood of St. Sylvester from the hands of the Archbishop of Limburg.

Oskar was still willing to cooperate with the Federal

Justice Department in the pursuit of war criminals. In this matter he seems to have been implacable. On his birthday in 1967, he gave confidential information concerning many of the personnel of KL Plaszów. The transcript of his evidence of that date shows that he does not hesitate to testify, but also that he is a scrupulous witness. If he knows nothing or little of a particular SS man, he says so. He says it of Amthor, of the SS man Zugsburger, of Fraülein Ohnesorge, one of the quick-tempered women survivors. He does not hesitate, however, to call Bosch a murderer and an exploiter, and says that he recognised Bosch at a railway station in Munich in 1946 and approached him and asked him if – after Plaszów – he could manage to sleep. Bosch, says Oskar, was at that stage living under an East German passport. A supervisor called Mohwinkel, representative in Plaszów of the German Armaments Works, is also roundly condemned – "Intelligent but brutal," says Oskar of him. Of Goeth's bodyguard, Grün, he tells the story of the attempted execution of the Emalia prisoner, Lamus, which he himself prevented by a gift of vodka. (It is a story to which a great number of prisoners also testify in their statements in Yad Vashem.) Of the NCO Ritchek, Oskar says that he has a bad reputation but that he himself knows nothing of his crimes. He is also uncertain whether the photograph the Justice Department showed him is in fact Ritchek. There is only one person on the Justice Department list for whom Oskar is willing to give an unqualified commendation. That is the engineer Huth, who had helped him during his last arrest. Huth, he says, was highly respected and highly spoken of by the prisoners themselves.

As he entered his sixties, he began working for the German Friends of the Hebrew University, raising funds. This involvement resulted from the urgings of those Schindler-juden who were concerned with restoring some new purpose to Oskar's life. His old capacity to inveigle and charm officials and businessmen was exercised once again. He also helped set up a scheme of exchanges between German and Israeli children.

Despite the state of his health, he still lived and drank like a young man. He was in love with a German woman called Annemarie, whom he had met at the King David Hotel in Jerusalem. She would become the emotional linchpin of his later life.

His wife Emilie still lived, without any financial help from him, in her little house in San Vicente south of Buenos Aires. She lives there at the time of the writing of this book. As in Brinnlitz, she is a figure of quiet dignity. In a documentary made by German television in 1973, she spoke – without any of the abandoned wife's bitterness or sense of grievance – about Oskar and Brinnlitz, about her own behaviour in Brinnlitz. Perceptively, she remarked that Oskar had done nothing astounding before the war and had been unexceptional since. He was fortunate therefore that in that short fierce era between 1939 and 1945 he had met people who had summoned forth his deeper talents.

In 1972, during a visit by Oskar to the New York executive office of the American Friends of the Hebrew University, three Schindlerjuden, partners in a large New Jersey construction company, led a group of seventy-five other Schindler prisoners in raising a hundred and twenty thousand dollars to dedicate to Oskar a floor of the Truman Research Center at the Hebrew University. The floor would house a Book of Life, containing an account of Oskar's rescues and a list of the rescued. Two of these partners, Murray Pantirer and Isak Levenstein, had been sixteen years old when Oskar had brought them to Brinnlitz. Now Oskar's children had become his parents, his best recourse, his source of honour.

He was very ill. The men who had been physicians in Brinnlitz – Alexander Biberstein, for example – knew it. One of them warned Oskar's close friends, "The man should not be alive. His heart is working through pure stubbornness."

In October 1974, he collapsed at his small apartment near the railway station in Frankfurt and died in hospital on October 9th. His death certificate says that advanced hardening of the arteries of the brain and heart had caused the final seizure. His will declared a wish he had already expressed to a number of Schindlerjuden – that he be buried in Jerusalem. Within two weeks the Franciscan parish priest of Jerusalem had given his permission for Herr Oskar Schindler, one of the Church's least observant sons, to be buried in the Latin Cemetery of Jerusalem.

Another month passed before Oskar's body was carried in a lead coffin through the crammed streets of the old city of Jerusalem to the Catholic Cemetery, which looks south over the Valley of Hinnom, called Gehenna in the New Testament. In the press photograph of the procession can be seen – amidst a stream of other Schindler Jews – Itzhak Stern, Moshe Bejski, Helen Hirsch, Jakob Sternberg, Juda Dresner.

He was mourned in every continent.